Child Influences on Marital and Family Interaction

A LIFE-SPAN PERSPECTIVE

CONTRIBUTORS

William Aquilino

Vern L. Bengtson

Stella Chess

Candice Feiring

Paulina Fernandez

Richard Galligan

Willard W. Hartup

Beth B. Hess

Lois Wladis Hoffman

Judy Howard

Stephen R. Jorgensen

David M. Klein

Sam J. Korn

Michael E. Lamb

Richard M. Lerner

Michael Lewis

Jean Denby Manis

Brent C. Miller

Boyd C. Rollins

Graham B. Spanier

Lillian Troll

Joan M. Waring

Child Influences on Marital and Family Interaction

A LIFE-SPAN PERSPECTIVE

Edited by

Richard M. Lerner
Graham B. Spanier

Division of Individual and Family Studies
College of Human Development
The Pennsylvania State University
University Park, Pennsylvania

ACADEMIC PRESS

New York   San Francisco   London   1978

A Subsidiary of Harcourt Brace Jovanovich, Publishers

ACADEMIC PRESS, INC.
111 Fifth Avenue, New York, New York 10003

United Kingdom Edition published by
ACADEMIC PRESS, INC. (LONDON) LTD.
24/28 Oval Road, London NW1 7DX

Library of Congress Cataloging in Publication Data
Main entry under title:

Child influences on marital and family interaction.

Includes bibliographies.
1. Family--Addresses, essays, lectures. 2. Parent
and child--Addresses, essays, lectures. 3. Social
interaction--Addresses, essays, lectures. I. Lerner,
Richard M. II. Spanier, Graham B.
HQ728.C473   301.42'7   78-12987
ISBN 0-12-444450-4

To our grandmothers
Leah Turkewitz Goldfarb
and
Annie Lurie

Contents

The Child's Social World

Michael Lewis and Candice Feiring

3

The Developing Child and Marital Satisfaction of Parents

Boyd C. Rollins and Richard Galligan

4

Research Methods and Developmental Reciprocity in Families

David M. Klein, Stephen R. Jorgensen, and Brent C. Miller

5

Parent and Child in Later Life: Rethinking the Relationship

9

Beth B. Hess and Joan M. Waring

The Influence of Children's Developmental Dysfunctions on Marital Quality and Family Interaction

10

Judy Howard

The Impact of Children's Physical Handicaps on Marital Quality and Family Interaction

11

Sam J. Korn, Stella Chess, and Paulina Fernandez

The Study of Child–Family Interactions: A Perspective for the Future

12

Graham B. Spanier, Richard M. Lerner, and William Aquilino

List of Contributors

Numbers in parentheses indicate the pages on which the authors' contributions begin.

William Aquilino (327), Division of Individual and Family Studies, College of Human Development, The Pennsylvania State University, University Park, Pennsylvania 16802

Vern L. Bengtson (215), Andrus Gerontology Center, University of Southern California, Los Angeles, California, 90007

Stella Chess (299), Department of Psychiatry, New York University Medical Center, New York, New York 10016

Candice Feiring (47), The Infant Laboratory, Institute for Research in Human Development, Educational Testing Service, Princeton, New Jersey 08540

Paulina Fernandez (299), Department of Psychiatry, New York University Medical Center, New York, New York 10016

Richard Galligan (71), Family Studies Program, Brigham Young University, Provo, Utah 84602

Willard W. Hartup (23), Institute of Child Development, University of Minnesota, Minneapolis, Minnesota 55455

Beth B. Hess (241), Department of Sociology, County College of Morris, Dover, New Jersey 07801

Lois Wladis Hoffman (165), Department of Psychology, Rutgers University, The State University of New Jersey, Douglas College, New Brunswick, New Jersey 08902

Judy Howard (275), University of California, Los Angeles, Department of Pediatrics, Child Development Division, Los Angeles, California 90024

Stephen R. Jorgensen (107), Division of Child Development and Family Relations, School of Home Economics, University of Arizona, Tucson, Arizona 85717

David M. Klein (107), Department of Sociology and Anthropology, University of Notre Dame, Notre Dame, Indiana 46635

Sam J. Korn (299), Department of Psychology, Hunter College, New York, New York 10021

Michael E. Lamb (137), Department of Psychology and Center for Human Growth and Development, University of Michigan, Ann Arbor, Michigan 48109

Richard M. Lerner (1, 327), Division of Individual and Family Studies, College of Human Development, The Pennsylvania State University, University Park, Pennsylvania 16802

Michael Lewis (47), The Infant Laboratory, Institute for Research in Human Development, Educational Testing Service, Princeton, New Jersey 08540

Jean Denby Manis (165),Institute of Social Research, University of Michigan, Ann Arbor, Michigan 48109

Brent C. Miller (107), Department of Child and Family Studies, University of Tennessee, Knoxville, Tennessee 37916

Boyd C. Rollins (71), Department of Child Development and Family Relationships, Brigham Young University, Provo, Utah 84602

Graham B. Spanier (1, 327), Division of Individual and Family Studies, College of Human Development, The Pennsylvania State University, University Park, Pennsylvania 16802

Lillian Troll (215), Department of Psychology, Rutgers University, The State University of New Jersey, New Brunswick, New Jersey 08902

Joan M. Waring (241), Russell Sage Foundation, Program on Age and Aging, New York, New York 10017

Preface

There is an emerging synthesis in social science of sociologists, psychologists, and physicians. The family is the central social institution in society and has been the focus of much research and scholarship among, in particular, family sociologists. Additionally, perhaps no topic in the social sciences has received as much attention, particularly from developmental psychologists, as has the behavioral development of the individual. Yet, these two closely related and obviously interdependent topics have not adequately been studied jointly.

This book is part of this merger, endeavoring to integrate knowledge from these disciplines through the exploration of the conceptual, methodological, and empirical issues in the study of the child and his or her family. And it is an earnest attempt to suggest why such a synthesis of disciplines and of units of analysis is necessary. Furthermore, the volume is an effort to enhance our understanding of the relationship between child development and marital and family interaction.

Specifically, the book details how the age-normative and atypical development of the child contributes to the parents' marital quality and to the entire family's interaction patterns across the life-span of both the child and parents. Consequently, the child is seen as capable of contributing to marriage and family relationships not only when he or she is in utero, a neonate, or an infant, but also when the child reaches middle and late childhood, adolescence, and the adulthood and aged years as well.

Moreover, the nature of the parent–child relationship across the life-span is viewed as a dynamic one. That is, we are not only interested in the effect of the child's mere presence in the family network. Rather—and more important—we are concerned with the child's development, his or her social relations with other family members, and how these processes affect the parents' marital interaction, the parents' interaction with their other children, and ultimately with the child in question. Thus, we see that the child influences the functioning and development of his or her parents and family, and consequently, through the feedback received, we view the child as an active shaper of his or her own development. In addition, this book explores how variations in the child's physical and physiological development (e.g., handicapping conditions, disease contraction, and health problems) influence such marital and family interaction.

While one purpose of this book is to detail existing knowledge about reciprocal, dynamic interactions among the child, the parents, and the entire family network, it is recognized that the extent of this knowledge varies across the life-span. There is an inverse relationship between age of the child and amount of empirical evidence pertaining to the nature of his or her contribution to marital quality and family interaction. More problematic is the fact that there have been few conceptual attempts to understand the simultaneous, reciprocal influences involved in child–family interactions across the life-span, and few methodologies developed to assess the processes involved in these complex, reciprocal interchanges.

These issues led us to specify three rather ambitious goals for this volume: (1) to propose conceptual approaches useful for understanding the reciprocal, dynamic interactions among the child, parents, and other family members across the life-span; (2) to identify the methodological problems previously encountered in such research and to propose new strategies for adequately assessing child–family interaction; and (3) to review the data available, and propose data still needed, in order to generate a knowledge base which will lead to social policy programs and human intervention strategies designed to enhance marital quality, facilitate successful family interaction, and foster psychologically healthy development of the child.

This book grew out of a conference sponsored by the Division of Individual and Family Studies in the College of Human Development at the Pennsylvania State University in April, 1977. Scientists from several disciplines were brought together to discuss the issues presented above. The chapters for this volume are revised versions of the papers originally presented at the conference.

We are grateful to our colleagues in the Division of Individual and

Family Studies for providing a superb context for the conference. Paul Baltes, our colleague and Division Director, was especially helpful. Several of our graduate students, Robert Casto, Carole Hatch, John Woroby, and Marion Palmero, helped us prepare intellectually and socially for the conference. Theodore Blau, Past President of the American Psychological Association, provided encouragement for this project, and gave the keynote address at the conference. Mary Kay Falck performed flawlessly in her role as administrative coordinator for the conference. Diane Bernd, Anita Helton, and Joy Lose cheerfully provided invaluable secretarial support. Frances Hoffman and Gwendolyn T. Sorell assisted in the preparation of the final version of the manuscript; their help is gratefully acknowledged.

We have learned something important in preparing this volume. Our lesson has been that multidisciplinary collaboration and cooperation in the social sciences is intellectually fruitful and professionally rewarding. Our speculation is that the future success of areas of study such as life-span human development and family relations depends on such collaboration and cooperation.

A Dynamic Interactional View of Child and Family Development

Richard M. Lerner and Graham B. Spanier

1

I. Introduction: The Need to Consider Individual–Social Interfaces

Children are invariantly born into a social network, typically a family. The family, too, is embedded in a social system. The family, the primary institution responsible for transforming societal maintenance and perpetuation goals into directives for the new individual, is thus at the core of socialization. Hence the family is society's adaptational unit. In turn, of course, societies are adaptive social units that change through history.

Such embeddedness of a child in a family, of a family in society, and of all social systems in history is obvious, at first glance. However, the dynamics of the interaction between these levels of analysis is not readily apparent nor adequately explored. Traditional, disciplinary approaches have been the predominate work done by social scientists concerned with any of these levels of analysis. Processes of individual development have rarely been used to explicate those of family development, and family change similarly has been ignored by those interested in understanding intraindividual change. Furthermore, the *reciprocal* dependency of familial change on intraindividual ontogeny has, until relatively recently, been largely unrecognized. In turn, the causal reciprocities among individuals, their families, and history have been similarly disregarded.

Fortunately, this era of disciplinary isolationism and intellectual egocentrism is passing in the social sciences. Social scientists increas-

1

Child Influences on Marital and Family Interaction: A Life-Span Perspective

ingly recognize that what happens on any one level of analysis depends largely on what happens on all others. Both theoretical and empirical developments are buttressing this idea. Attempts to account for large proportions of the variance in either intraindividual or interindividual change through the examination of unidisciplinarily derived constructs have failed. Accordingly, and seemingly with some reluctance, social scientists have had to go beyond their disciplinary training. They have found the joint utilization of constructs and variables selected from different disciplines more useful in accounting for such variance. For example, notions about both social change and affective and cognitive development have recently been seen as necessary for understanding the development of attachment across the life-span—a process that had previously been conceptualized exclusively from the perspective of psychology (Lerner & Ryff, 1978). Similarly, Elder (1974) has drawn jointly on ideas derived from historical as well as from sociological and psychological analysis in order to explain the development of children during and after the Great Depression.

Thus, the apparent utility of simultaneously integrating ideas from numerous disciplines has fostered a need for general, multidisciplinary theories. It is clear that what happens at the sociological level of analysis, for example, influences what happens at the psychological level, and vice versa. Accordingly, the constructs favored in any one discipline should have no precedence over those of others, and changes at any level of analysis should be understood as occurring relative to changes at the other levels within which it is reciprocally embedded.

Such conceptual relativism necessitates a pluralistic approach to social science endeavors. This pluralism involves not only description and theory but also methodology and analysis. From this perspective it is inappropriate to evaluate a given discipline's conceptual or methodological approach to a phenomenon along continua such as right–wrong or true–false. Rather, criteria of usefulness need to be advanced. In other words, ideas from two or more disciplines may be combined on the basis of the fact that together they are more useful in accounting for variance in behavior change processes or social interaction than either is independently.

Whereas psychologists have been most active in the study of the individual and social development of individuals across the life-span, sociologists have been concerned with a number of closely related topics, such as the sociohistorical context of the individual's development (Neugarten & Datan, 1973), family history and the life course (Elder, 1977), the sociology of age stratification (Riley, Johnson, & Foner, 1972), the social analysis of cohorts (Ryder, 1965), the transmission of social attributes across generations (Bengtson & Black, 1973), the continuing process of socialization after childhood (Brim, 1966), and the development of families across their life cycle (Hill & Mattessich, 1977). These various treatments have resulted in important contributions to the theoretical and methodological literatures of human development and social interaction. Accordingly, conceptualizations that integrate constructs from the literatures of traditionally disparate disciplines are likely to be most useful in this era of transition in social science (Baltes, 1977; Lerner & Ryff, 1978; Riegel, 1975, 1976a).

For example, neither psychological, sociological, nor historical constructs alone may best integrate data about the development of relationships. Instead it recently has been stated (Burgess & Huston, in press) that variables associated with all of these disciplines, as well as with that of evolutionary biology (Alexander, in press), need to be integrated into one broad theoretical scheme in order to best account for the nature of relationships.

Accordingly, the emergence of a multidisciplinary orientation among social scientists has resulted in the recognition of the need for a superordinate view of behavior change and social interaction processes. Such processes can be seen in a multicausal, reciprocal framework, which promotes the notions of plasticity, multilinearity, and multidirectionality. Moreover, due to the embeddedness of biological, psychological, and sociocultural changes within a constantly changing historical context, those descriptive and explanatory accounts that are best able to integrate these interdependent change dimensions are likely to be advanced. That is, a dialectical (Riegel, 1975, 1976a), relational (Looft, 1973), transactional (Sameroff, 1975), or dynamic-interactional (Lerner, 1976, 1978, in press) view of change is promoted. This approach is in contrast with metatheoretical views, which consider the universe as uniform and permanent (Kaufmann, 1968) and hence consider change a to-be-explained phenomenon, a perturbation of a stable system.

A dynamic interactional view, the one to which we subscribe, assumes change to be given (see Overton, 1977) and views all levels of analysis as components of a constantly evolving, historical, semiopen system. In short, the current transition in social science to a multidisciplinary, multicausal, multidirectional, and plastic conception of behavioral and social change has led to the advancement of the life-span view of human development (Baltes, 1977; Baltes & Schaie, 1973). Moreover, the metatheoretical conceptualization of such change as involving reciprocal dependencies between changing individuals and their changing social milieu has led to the formulation of dialectic (Overton, 1977; Riegel, 1975, 1976a) or dynamic-interactional (Lerner, 1976, 1978, in press) theoretical depictions of change. Such a view sees development as arising from the confluence of constantly changing inner-biological, individual-psychological, physical-environmental, and sociocultural-historical processes that are reciprocally embedded one in the other (Riegel, 1976a).

A. Child–Family Reciprocities and the Life-Span View

Our appraisal of current developments within social science is that the basic units of analysis in traditional disciplinary discussions of behavioral and social change need to be reconceptualized. Those scholars concerned with individual ontogeny may not usefully hold that the individual is an appropriate unit for study *unless* the reciprocal relationship between the individual and his or her social and historical context is considered. In turn, scholars interested primarily in family or small group functioning must move beyond the dyad, triad, or network as a static unit of analysis and begin to concern themselves with the contributions of ontogenetic changes to social structure and function. Accordingly, at the core of any concern for either individual ontogeny or family development is a "new" unit of analysis: the individual within a family system. This unit of analysis must be thought of as a constantly evolving unit.

Although the question of what constitutes a family is of interest, we do not feel that any particular definition of *family* ought to detract from our central point. We shall choose to define the family as the social unit that accepts the primary responsibility for socialization and nurturance of a child. Typically, families consist of persons occupying three differentiated social positions: husband–father, wife–mother, and child–sibling. Some families, of course, may be missing one of these categories for all or part of the time during which the family is in existence.

As stated earlier, the family is but one of the many social systems within which each individual must function. It is, however, the most basic of all social institutions and thus is the social unit with which we are most concerned. The new unit of analysis we propose can perhaps best be examined by focusing on the child–family interface. It is this unit—involving individuals across the life-span interacting reciprocally with their families—that best allows for the convergence of the psychological, sociological, biological, cultural, and historical modes of analysis. The dynamics of this focus involves the contributions of the individual—from his or her conception, through gestation, birth, childhood, adolescence, adulthood, and death—to the familial world in which he or she lives. Simultaneously, this view focuses on the contribution of the familial context—as it is embedded in a continually evolving social and historical context—to the individual's life-span development. Such an approach requires a sensitivity to the complexity of this child and family interface and to the many forms of the relationship that may emerge over the course of the life cycle. Thus, the life-span view of human development seems particularly appropriate as a framework for exploring such relationships.

To summarize, the current transition toward a multidisciplinary approach to social science leads to a consideration of the dynamic reciprocities in child–family interaction. To describe and explain the dynamics of this relationship, the life-span view of human development is advanced. We furthermore propose that a dynamic-interactional model of development is appropriate. As such, in order to consider some of the relevant issues for studying child–family interfaces and the implications for social science theory and method, we will first detail the attributes of the life-span view of human development. We shall then provide the rationale for the dynamic-interactional position. This position will, in turn, allow us to specify the theoretical and methodological importance of understanding the reciprocal influences of the child and the family across the life-span.

II. A Life-Span View of Human Development and Social Interaction

Much has been written about the characteristics and implications of a life-span view of human development (Baltes & Schaie, 1973). Furthermore, a life-span view of socialization has received increasing attention (Brim, 1966; Clausen, 1968; Riley, *et al.* 1972). Accordingly, we need only summarize here some of the salient features of previous discussions. We shall focus specifically on the elaboration of a dynamic-interactional theoretical perspective and on reciprocal child–family influences. We have chosen to elaborate a life-span view with regard to the description and explanation of behavior change.

A. Description of Developmental Change

Description in human development research focuses on the systematic representation of intraindividual change and of interindividual differences in intraindividual change as such change may occur across the life-span. The presence of such change across the life-span has been demonstrated empirically in several ways. In developmental psychology, for example, such change has been shown in data derived from studies of intellectual abilities (Baltes, Baltes, & Reinert, 1970; Baltes & Reinert, 1969; Schaie, Labouvie, & Buech, 1973; Schaie & Strother, 1968). These data serve to (a) counteract child developmental views of developmental change as being finalized in early life (Flavell, 1970); (b) counteract depictions of later life as inevitably involving decrement and deterioration (Baltes & Labouvie, 1973; Birren, 1964); and (c) clarify issues about the continuities and discontinuities involved in developmental change (Baltes & Schaie, 1973).

Data indicate that individuals continue to change throughout the life-span, even during the adult and aged years. These changes characteristically involve increasingly greater interindividual differences. The data furthermore indicate that multilinearity and multidirectionality characterize life-span development. For example, the data indicate stabilities, increases, and decreases in ability scores, that are dependent on processes apparently related to birth cohort. Thus, since such multidirectional, multilinear change occurs across the life span, both progressive and regressive models are necessary to account fully for the directionality of developmental change. Both continuity and discontinuity models can thus be useful.

Because of the relativism of descriptive accounts of the continuity or discontinuity of developmental change, there is a recognition that change can only be described through a pluralistic approach. In other words, on both an empirical and a theoretical level behavior change processes should be seen as interdependent. It has been empirically demonstrated that differences in psychological attributes at different ages can be explained by birth-cohort related processes (Baltes, Cornelius, & Nesselroade, in press). Moreover, the role of sociocultural and historical factors has accounted for both intraindividual change and interindividual differences in such change in personality research done with adolescents (Nesselroade & Baltes, 1974). Developmental psychologists have examined three descriptive components of developmental change functions: age, cohort, and time. These components have been theoretically linked by Riegel (1975, 1976a, b), who asserts that behavior change phenomena are simultaneously related to a multiplicity of variables—derived from all levels of biocultural through historical analysis—and can therefore be adequately evaluated only when pluralistically approached.

Thus, to explain life-span development, a pluralism involving a wide array of theories and empirical strategies pertinent to both the developing individual and his or her evolving social milieu must be followed. Descriptive research, then, is recognized as being a probabilistic representation of change. Change should be studied relative to personological, setting, and epochal contexts.

B. Explanation of Developmental Change

The explanation of developmental change involves the clarification of behavior change processes by showing their relationship to antecedent and/or concurrent conditions. The emphasis here is on which variables account for intraindividual and interindividual change and how they do so. The emphasis in life-span explanation on change processes may be highlighted by depicting the explanatory status of the age variable when considered in a life-span framework.

Prior to the elaboration of the life-span perspective, the age variable almost exclusively had been used as an explanatory principle of developmental change. In other words, age per se was given a causal character. For instance, deviations from age norms (interindividual differences within the same age group) were often seen as retardation or precociousness (Oerter, 1973) and were frequently reified through the postulation of a maturational ground plan (Erikson, 1959).

However, from the life-span perspective, the age variable is seen as noncausal, inevitably in need of further explanation, and as little more than a marker variable correlated with underlying processes (Baer, 1970; Wohlwill, 1973). Thus, age, perhaps unlike some demographic variables (e.g., socioeconomic status), but like others (e.g., sex, race) is a static, nonexplanatory variable that must inevitably be related to processes of behavior change in order to explicate the variance in ontogenetic progression.

This focus on process leads, however, to a reconsideration of the continuity–discontinuity issue in regard to explanation. This issue pertains to whether the same or different explanations may be used to account for change processes at different stages of the life-span. Since it has been noted that explanations reflect the paradigm of the theorist (Reese & Overton, 1970), they may not be considered true or false. Moreover, the findings noted above regarding the description of developmental change argue against any attempt to define a single cause of development.

Thus, one is obligated to advance many theoretical explanations of change processes on multiple levels of analysis. Explanation must also be conducted through theoretical pluralism in order to deal with the dynamic interdependencies among the many variables that can account for behavior change. A dynamic-interactional approach to the study of developmental change has begun to be elaborated (Lerner, 1976, 1978, in press), and in the next section we shall evaluate the usefulness of such an approach for the life-span view of human development, including the study of the reciprocal impact of the child on the family.

III. Dynamic Interactions of Development

The life-span view of the explanation of human development leads to an emphasis on process. This emphasis in turn results in a need for dynamic accounts of individual–environment interactions. As noted earlier, such accounts have begun to be elaborated and fall within a dialectical–metatheoretical model (Riegel, 1975, 1976a, b). Although such attempts do emphasize the constantly changing biocultural and historical contexts as affecting and being affected by the changing individual and his or her social environment, not all dialectical-theoretical attempts successfully explain the nature of the behavior change process. Although all dialectically oriented theorists call for attention to the interrelatedness of variables derived from different levels of analysis in order to understand human development, they are not necessarily precise about how such reciprocities provide a basis of intraindividual change and of interindividual differences in such change.

Accordingly, we will offer a theoretical view of development that, although consistent with a dialectical metamodel, offers an account of processes of intraindividual change and their relation to interindividual differences in such change. As detailed elsewhere (Lerner, 1976, 1978, in press), this theory conceives of development as involving systematic changes in the organization of individuals, organisms seen as functional, adaptive, and open to change throughout the life cycle. Although development is thus seen as biological, it is appropriate, we believe, to focus at the same time on social and environmental influences. That is, adaptation involves, in part, adjustment of the individual's characteristics in order to meet the demands of his or her ecological milieu. The study of human development considers how individuals adjust to a continually changing environment and, in turn, how such an environment is continually and progressively dealt with by an individual also undergoing constant alterations. In short, the study of development is the study of processes of individual–environment relations. But we may refine this statement further. It is the sociocultural setting that shapes and textures the environment. The study of development becomes an assessment of how such an environment affects and is affected by a continually changing individual—for example, a developing child. Moreover, since the family unit is the major mediator between the child and his or her environment, the study of human development becomes most fundamentally the study of reciprocal child–family relationships.

In essence, then, the concept of development on which we base our discussion involves the continuous interdependency of individual and social change processes and as such suggests that the bases of the changes that characterize development lie in components of this dynamic interaction. In order to understand the principles of dynamic interaction and how they provide a basis of behavior change processes it will be useful to consider in greater detail this model of human development. This model depicts the dynamic interactions among the components of development, and we may begin to understand the contributions of these components by viewing the model from the level of the individual.

A. Components of Development

The dynamic-interactional model of development (Lerner, 1976, 1978, in press; Schneirla, 1957; Tobach & Schneirla, 1968) views ontogeny as involving the probabilistically timed confluence of intraorganismic and extraorganismic processes. Many of the labels used to represent the components of these processes (e.g., *maturation*, *experience*) are selected on the basis of their traditional use in the literature of comparative and developmental psychology. However, the choice of any particular label is unimportant in depicting the dynamic interactions of development, since terms such as *genotype* or *heredity* may be substituted for *maturation*, and *environment* or *learning* may be substituted for *experience* with no change whatsoever in the central conception (Anastasi, 1958; Lerner, 1976; Schneirla, 1957; White, 1968). The processes linking the components of development are the critical contributions of the model.

1. Maturation

Maturation refers to processes of growth and differentiation (Schneirla, 1957). Although these processes have often been considered as independent of experiential influence (Gesell, 1929; Hamburger, 1957), our conception of development indicates that such processes are in fact interdependent. Stated differently, the qualities of maturational changes are shaped by the quality and timing of the experiential context in which they occur. To consider this interdependency, let us turn to the role of experience.

2. Experience

Experience is a broad term denoting all influences acting on the individual over the course of the life-span (Schneirla, 1957). *Experience* is relevant from conception until death and hence may be applied to the intrauterine period. In addition, of course, experiences may occur endogenously and exogenously. In other words, experiences may occur at both an intraorganismic and an extraorganismic level. In any case, experiential contributions to development take the form of *trace effects*, that is, changes that result from experience and that limit the effects of future experience (Schneirla, 1957).

However, all these effects of experience are limited by the maturational status of the organism. The same experience may lead to a different developmental outcome depending on the maturational level of the organism. Excessive maternal stress during pregnancy may lead either to a cleft palate or a normal palate depending on whether growth and differentiation are at an early embryonic stage or at the late fetal stage, respectively. Thus, just as experience provides a basis of growth and differentiation (e.g., maturation proceeds at different rates and with different outcomes depending on the nutritional and health status of the mother), the effects of experience are limited by the individual's maturational level. Thus, although maturation and experience are conceptually distinct, they both exist in an inseparable synthesis. Finally, we must note that since the various dimensions of these interdependent sources of influence vary over time across individuals, lawful individual differences will emerge. A consideration of this individuality is important.

3. Organism Individuality and Its Role in Development

As each person's maturation–experience interactions intermesh to provide a singular individual, this individual consequently interacts differently with his or her environment. In turn, these new interactions are a component of the individual's further experience and thus serve to promote further his or her individuality. Maturation–experience relations provide a basis of individuality, and as a consequence, differential individual–environment relations develop.

The endogenous maturation–experience interactions are *not* discontinuous with the exogenous organism–environment interactions; yet, it is convenient to distinguish between these two sets of interactions in order to indicate how they are interdependent. To do this, we identify two levels of interaction. The person's developmental history of maturation–experience interactions—termed Level 1 development—provides a basis of differential individual–environment interactions; in turn, differential experiences accruing from the developmental history of person–environment interactions—or Level 2 development—provide a further basis of Level 1 development.

The target person is unique because of the quality and timing of endogenous, Level 1 maturation–experience interactions. Yet, the experiences that provide a basis of Level 1 development are not discontinuous with other, extraindividual experiences influencing the target. The target interacts with environmental influences composed of other people (themselves having intraindividual, Level 1 developmental distinctiveness) and of physical effects. These Level 2 interchanges also will show interindividual differences because of Level 1 intraindividual distinctiveness. Thus, the feedback received as a consequence of these differential interactions will also differ from person to person and will promote further Level 1 and Level 2 individuality. This process provides the basis of a circular function (Schneirla, 1957), between an individual and his or her environment—a function that has important implications for the understanding of social relations.

4. Circular Functions and Social Interactions

Other individuals are part of a person's experiential context, and these others will interact differently with different people. These interactions constitute the feedback for the individual, providing further differential bases of development.

As noted earlier, development is basically a phenomenon tied to social relations, and the person-person interaction—the social relation—is the exemplar of a circular function. Other individuals are an obvious component of the typical experiential world of any person, and on this basis alone relations with these others are inextricable dimensions of ecologically valid developmental milieus. Moreover, human social relations are special individual–environment relations. These Level 2 interchanges invariably involve processes of reciprocal stimulation and hence interdependent influences. Not only do social interactions appear, then, to be a special, as well as an invariant, component of human development but results of social isolation experiments (Harlow & Harlow, 1962; Tobach & Schneirla, 1968) indicate that individuals deprived of social relations develop aberrant social and nonsocial behaviors.

Moreover, until the transitions between organic and inorganic matter are better understood, one may assume that any living cell comes into existence on the basis of a relation to another living cell (Tobach & Schneirla, 1968). Thus, the dependency for existence of one organism on another appears basic to all life matter and suggests that individuals exist basically in relation to one another. In other words, "no existing form of life is truly solitary and no organism is completely independent of others at all times in its history" (Tobach & Schneirla, 1968, p. 505). In sum then, the dynamic interaction between individuals and their social world is the prime arena of concern for those involved in appraising and understanding human existence.

B. Sociocultural–Historical Dimensions of the Individual–Social Interface

Our dynamic-interactional model views individual development as invariably embedded in social relations and vice versa. As such, our position leads to the view that development is basically a social, as well as a biological, phenomenon. However, in addition to stressing individual–social reciprocities, our model has other components. All individuals involved in social reciprocities are constantly changing. Thus, not only is the effect of the person on others moderated by his or her developmental level but these effects and the feedback received are influenced by the developmental levels of the other people in the social relation. For example, the effect of a toddler having a temper tantrum differs from that of an adolescent having one, an experienced parent will probably be affected differently by his or her child's tantrum than will an inexperienced one, and the feedback the child gets from the parent will in part be determined by such developmental differences.

However, the probability of occurrence of a particular child behavior, the concomitant evaluation of the behavior by others (e.g., parents), and the modes (e.g., child-rearing practices) of dealing with the behavior by these others are dependent on the sociocultural milieu of the relation. People are always embedded in a sociocultural setting. Parents in one sociocultural milieu may be more or less permissive than parents of another. In addition, the sociocultural arena also influences the physical setting of any social interaction, and it may be expected that in relation to changes in physical environmental variables such as noise level, pollution level, housing conditions, crowding, and recreational facilities the quality and timing of person–person exchanges will vary and provide differential feedback to all individuals involved.

Moreover, it must be recognized that all sociocultural milieus are embedded in history. A middle-class sociocultural milieu of the 1930s did not include some variables relevant today, such as the pervasive influence of television. Hence, the profound effect of such variables (Stein & Friedrich, 1975) on the nature of current social relations and on individuals embedded in these relations could not even have existed in the earlier historical era.

Moreover, with each of the levels we have discussed there exist reciprocal effects on all of the other levels. Thus, just as we must consider the dynamic interactions between the individual and the social unit, we must consider how such change processes contribute to changing the cultural norms and historical epochs within which they exist.

C. The Dynamic Child–Family Relationship

We may summarize our model of the dynamic interactions involved in developmental change by reiterating and expanding our view of the role of the child–family relationship. Our dynamic-interactional model has proposed the view that individual development may only be adequately understood in the context of the constant reciprocal interaction between a changing person and his or her changing environment. This environment is necessarily composed of other people, themselves developing within a dynamic environmental setting. The setting, too, is shaped and textured by the evolving cultural and historical contexts within which all of the actors are embedded.

Such continuous circularity may be studied at any of these levels of analysis. Yet, since it is the historical epoch that shapes the cultural and social contexts and since these in turn influence the nature of the adaptational demands necessary for both maintenance and perpetuation of individuals and their social world, the core focus of the study of human development may be expanded beyond the individual–social unit.

Since it is the family unit that typically provides the immediate social context for any new member of society, the child–family interface is of primary concern in any attempt to understand the reciprocal relationships among the various levels of analysis described. In short, the family is the major mediator between social and historical change, on the one hand, and biocultural and ontogenetic change, on the other. Thus, the dynamic interactions between a developing child and his or her changing family becomes, as we have argued, the core concern of social scientists in this era of intellectual transition.

IV. Methodological and Research Implications of Child–Family Interactions

The interdisciplinary, life-span transition in the social sciences involves more than a conceptual reorientation. Additionally, methodological and research issues are being raised. The human development literature has always emphasized that conceptual issues determine not only the form of research questions but also suggest which methods and data analytic techniques are needed to study these questions (Baltes & Nesselroade, 1973; Lerner, 1976, 1978; Looft, 1973; Werner, 1957). Accordingly, one thrust of the life-span view of human development is to lead researchers to new, pluralistic descriptive and explanatory approaches to developmental research. The dynamic-interactional theoretical view of life-span development is consistent with this emphasis in the field.

New questions need to be addressed, and, as we shall note, the invention of new methodological and data analytic techniques may be required to provide the data necessary to address these questions. We shall treat the related implications of the life-span and the dynamic-interactional approaches successively.

A. Implications of the Life-Span View

The complexity of studying human development requires that many methodological and interpretative tools available to science be employed. Only through collaborative, interdisciplinary work will the nature, direction, and extent of social and behavioral change be explained. In addition, such a multifaceted approach will reduce the extent to which accurate descriptive work is limited by a particular methodological strategy.

Moreover, research in human development must go beyond merely detailing patterns of covariation among behaviors and age and, instead, consider how the confluence of all potential contributions to change functions influences development. Accordingly, it is necessary to have descriptive designs that are capable of simultaneously determining the contribution to developmental change functions of birth- and/or event-cohort variables, of time of measurement variables, and of age-related processes. Thus, whereas all research designs may contribute to an understanding of life-span development if used appropriately, the sequential research strategies, discussed by Schaie (1965) and by Baltes (1968), remain the exemplars of life-span research designs.

Whereas accurate descriptions of the roles of age, cohort, and time of measurement in developmental changes in a changing historical context may best be achieved by application of sequential designs, explanations of life-span development will ultimately depend on the findings of independent research endeavors (Schaie & Baltes, 1973, 1975). As such, in addition to manipulative, experimental research, involving the study of concurrent effects, simulation strategies have been suggested. Such studies involve experimentally produced short-term change patterns as simulations of naturalistic long-term (historical) change phenomena (Baltes & Goulet, 1971). Thus, both current and historical determinants of developmental change may be studied in a common effort. In addition, the methodological repertoire of the life-span researcher may be expanded through use of causal modeling procedures (Baltes, Cornelius, & Nesselroade, in press). These may test causal representations of phenomena not available for experimental manipulation. These procedures permit the use of multiple indices of constructs and the representation of reciprocal causation. Thus, they highlight the more general utility of multivariate techniques. Additionally, they provide tools capable of dealing with the reciprocally acting multiple bases of developmental change (Lerner & Ryff, 1978).

Such strategies must be compatible with theories of behavior change linked to a single level of analysis and, simultaneously, to theories of behavior change linked to multiple levels of analysis (e.g., biocultural, ontogenetic, and historical). As discussed earlier, such a pluralistic theoretical account of life-span behavior change processes may be found in the dynamic-interactional model. Let us now discuss the methodological and research implications of this position.

B. Implications of Dynamic Interactionism

The methodological and research problems of the dynamic-interactionist position are not seen as issues in organismic or mechanistic frameworks. Dialectical positions such as dynamic interactionism state that all the components of development do more than continuously interact with each other. Rather, each component is a source of each of the other components with which it interacts. Thus, part of component A (maturation, individual, or society, for example) is component not-A (experience, environment, or history, respectively, for example); that is, parts of each source of development are the very things with which that source interacts.

We have conceptualized this dynamic interaction as involving a circular function, a notion that implies the need for new statistical models and new conceptualizations of the variables analyzed within these models. That is, if development is conceptualized in a circular manner, then the utility of linear statistical models seems limited. In turn, the variables involved in this circularity may not be appropriately seen as antecedent to or consequences of each other. Rather, since the point of entry into a circle is arbitrary (Lewis & Lee-Painter, 1974), traditional notions pertaining to independent and dependent variables seem anachronistic.

Moreover, the continuity of a circle, having no starting or ending point, implies constant movement, continual change. Thus, the components of this circle—the components of development—constantly change; as such, since each component is a source of every other, as each constantly changes, so do all others. Accordingly, rather than the social universe being seen as constant and permanent—and change being the to-be-explained phenomenon—this model assumes that change is the rule (Overton, 1977). The problem for developmental research, then, is to derive an index of developmental change within constantly changing contexts.

As indicated by several authors (e.g., Lerner, 1978; Overton & Reese, 1973; Reese & Overton, 1970; Sameroff, 1975), this problem of circularity is generally not applicable to research questions derived from mechanistic- and organismic-based theories. Although interactions among components of development are discussed among theories derived from each respective world view, the meaning of interaction is quite different. In the mechanistically derived position of Bijou (1976), interactions involve qualitatively identical elements that are additive, cumulative, and thus can be appropriately studied with assumptions of linearity. Seen in an analysis of variance analogy, only main effects (i.e., one source) can ever be handled by this conception. Stated differently, although it is possible to look at two sources of variation—A (an organism variable such as age) and B (some stimulus condition)—and presumably an $A \times B$ interaction, such an analysis would be misleading. Since A is functionally defined in terms of past reinforcement history whereas B is seen as the current reinforcement situation, all that is really being considered is a linear combination of current and historical elements that are not qualitatively distinct.

In turn, the "moderate" interactions of some organismically derived views are not significantly more powerful than some "weak" mechanistic ones. Although two qualitatively distinct sources of variation are seen to exist, it is either the case that (a) one source (e.g., maturation) is primary, whereas the other is viewed as an inhibitor or a facilitator of these primarily intrinsic trends (Emmerich, 1968); or (b) both sources are given equal status in the interaction, and thus although neither one is primary, neither changes the status of the other as a consequence of their interaction. Although sources of variation A and B may be involved in a significant $A \times B$ interaction, the status or quality of neither source is altered by virtue of their interactions. For instance, although a particular component of the physical environment may interact with an organism, the physical environmental source is in no way transformed by virtue of this interaction. Although the organism is active, the environment is not (see Riegel, 1976b). These two types of "moderate" views of interaction may be seen in the accounts of Freud (1949) and of Piaget (1970), respectively.

With either instance of moderate interaction, however, the appropriateness of a linear statistical model and the use of such notions as *independent* and *dependent variable* are apparent. However, the dynamic interactions involved in our model lead to a rejection of the appropriateness of a linear statistical model and an antecedent–consequent, independent–dependent conception of variables involved in behavioral or social change.

Accordingly, although our dynamic-interactional model requires a circular statistical model, a conception of variables as constantly interrelated, and an assumption of constant change, it is recognized that satisfactory tools to meet these needs presently do not exist. This does not mean that the model is a nonscientific one. Indeed, these issues can be addressed by empirical scientific methods. Let us indicate why.

Our model leads to a conception of development that is interdisciplinary, dynamic, and involves multiple sources of change. For example, we have raised the issue of the continual reciprocities between components of development, and we have formulated the research problem of what are the reciprocal contributions of a child and a family over the life-span. These tasks would not be as likely to be adequately subjected to social scientific inquiry with other conceptions of development. Moreover, since the issues raised and problems asked are often different, empirical strategies useful for addressing them may have to be different. Thus, although currently available methodological and data analytic strategies are of some use in addressing these issues, they are not totally adequate.

Our conception of development thus implies that further advancement in scientific methodology is needed. It does *not* imply that the methods to be devised will need to be exotic or nonscientific. An analogous argument has been made by Baltes and Cornelius (1977), who view dialectics as leading potentially to the formulation of novel research questions. Dialectics does not, they believe, necessitate that the answer to those questions be found through the application of anything other than empirical, scientific methods.

To summarize, in order to address the issues raised by our model, we have to relinquish notions of universal, permanent laws and instead conceptualize development as a probabilistic phenomenon. That is, the nature, direction, and extent of developmental change are relative to the changing boundaries imposed by the ever-changing context within which it exists.

C. From the Future to the Present

To begin to understand this dynamic interaction requires collaborative scientific action, both now and in the future. To enter the future with an adequate conception of precisely where elaboration and refinement are needed, it is necessary to adequately appraise the present. Although we have discussed in this chapter some substantive, methodological, and research implications of the current transition in the social sciences, it is still necessary to determine the current status of this transition, especially as it pertains to the core, focal child–family unit. What, for example, do we know of the reciprocal impact of the child on the family? Do currently available data fit the proposed model of development? Is change across the life span and across different types of person–family characteristics taken into account? Are data currently being collected sufficient to address the unique problems raised by the model? What methodological revisions are thus seen as necessary to provide data to evaluate and/or advance the use of the model and the life-span view surrounding it?

Only by answering these questions can we determine the precise location of social science in this historical period of transition and, in turn, project ourselves into the future. The goal of this volume is to begin to answer these questions. The concluding section of this chapter details how the succeeding chapters of this book are intended to fulfill this purpose.

V. The Plan of This Book

The goal of this book is to summarize some existing information about reciprocal child–family interactions and to provide a basis for extending this knowledge. Yet, although all chapters have this common aim, each chapter is intended to make a differential contribution. The overall intent is to provide an accurate depiction of what social scientists know about these reciprocities and what we still need to know.

The present chapter has outlined some substantive and methodological implications for the interdisciplinary study of child–family interactions. The next chapter, by Hartup, will provide the historical bases of this current conceptual refocusing in social science. Consequently, with an understanding of the precursors of current interdisciplinary endeavors, an evaluation of the current utility of such an approach will be undertaken. In Chapter 3, Lewis and Feiring indicate how the notion of social networks may better elucidate child development, and in Chapter 4, Rollins and Galligan detail the contribution of a child's development to family life cycle changes. Moreover, as several contributors to this volume note, there are important and potentially unique methodological problems associated with exploring the reciprocal child–family interface. Klein, Jorgensen, and Miller discuss and evaluate these issues in Chapter 5.

Chapters 6 through 9 are devoted to discussion of the reciprocities involved in child–family interaction within specific portions of the life-span. Lamb (Chapter 6) discusses these reciprocities during the prenatal, perinatal, and infancy portions of the life-span and, as a consequence of his review, derives an explanation of child abuse that stresses reciprocal influences. Hoffman and Manis (Chapter 7) explore the child–family interface during childhood; to evaluate this impact, they provide data from an extensive cross-sectional study of child effects on parents. In turn, Bengtson and Troll (Chapter 8) consider the reciprocal relationships between adolescents and their parents and, in so doing, focus on social change and intergenerational conflict as sources of these reciprocities. Finally, the bidirectional contributions of the child-as-adult to aged parents are explored (Chapter 9) by Hess and Waring. A social exchange framework is advanced as useful for understanding child–family interaction during the child's adulthood.

Not only may the child alter the family network as a consequence of the development of long-term behavior change processes but within any developmental period the child also is developing along physiological, anatomical, and health-related dimensions. Variations in such development may provide a basis for the child's impact on the family and the family's impact on the child through, for example, the emergence of handicapping conditions, contraction of disease, and other health problems. Accordingly, in Chapter 10, Howard reviews literature pertinent to the effect of physical handicaps and disease as they pertain to reciprocal child–family interactions across the life-span. In Chapter 11, Korn, Chess, and Fernandez report data from a longitudinal study of such effects among children who have multiple handicaps as a consequence of contraction of rubella by their mothers during pregnancy.

Finally, Chapter 12, by Spanier, Lerner, and Aquilino is devoted to a synthesis of the ideas and directives gleaned from preceding chapters. It is through the synthesis in this last chapter that the overall requirements will be specified for using the knowledge base developed in Chapters 1 through 11 as a stepping stone into the future.

References

Alexander, R. D. Natural selection and social exchange. In R. L. Burgess & T. L. Huston (Eds.), *Social exchange in developing relationships*. New York: Academic Press, in press.

Anastasi, A. Heredity, environment, and the question "how?" *Psychological Review*, 1958, 65, 197–208.

Baer, D. M. An age-irrelevant concept of development. *Merrill Palmer Quarterly of Behavior and Development*, 1970, 16, 238–245.

Baltes, P. B. Longitudinal and cross-sectional sequences in the study of age and generation effects. *Human Development*, 1968, 11, 145–171.

Baltes, P. B. Life-span developmental psychology: Some observations on history and theory. Presidential address, Division 20, Eighty-Fifth Convention of the American Psychological Association, San Francisco, California, August, 1977.

Baltes, P. B., Baltes, M. M., & Reinert, G. The relationship between time of measurement and age in cognitive development of children: An application of cross-sectional sequences. *Human Development*, 1970, 13, 258–268.

Baltes, P. B., & Cornelius, S. W. Some critical observations on the theoretical and methodological status of dialectics in developmental psychology. In N. Datan & H. W. Reese (Eds.), *Life-span developmental psychology: Dialectical perspectives*. New York: Academic Press, 1977.

Baltes, P. B., Cornelius, S. W., & Nesselroade, J. R. Cohort effects in developmental psychology: Theoretical and methodological perspectives. In W. A. Collins (Ed.), *Minnesota Symposium on Child Psychology*. (Vol. II). Minneapolis: University of Minnesota, in press.

Baltes, P. B., & Goulet, L. R. Exploration of developmental variables by manipulation and simulation of age differences in behavior. *Human Development*, 1971, 14, 149–170.

Baltes, P. B., & Labouvie, G. V. Adult development of intellectual performance: Description, explanation, and modification. In C. Eisdorfer & M. P. Lawton (Eds.), *The psychology of adult development and aging*. Washington, D.C.: American Psychological Association, 1973.

Baltes, P. B., & Nesselroade, J. R. The developmental analysis of individual differences on multiple measures. In J. R. Nesselroade and H. W. Reese (Eds.), *Life-span developmental psychology: Methodological issues*. New York: Academic Press, 1973.

Baltes, P. B., & Reinert, G. Cohort effects in cognitive development of children as revealed by cross-sectional sequences. *Developmental Psychology*, 1969, 1, 169–177.

Baltes, P. B., & Schaie, K. W. On life-span developmental research paradigms: Retrospects and prospects. In P. B. Baltes and K. W. Schaie (Eds.), *Life-span developmental psychology: Personality and socialization*. New York: Academic Press, 1973.

Bengtson, V. L., & Black, K. D. Intergenerational relations and continuities in socialization. In P. B. Baltes and K. W. Schaie (Eds.), *Life-span developmental psychology: Personality and socialization*. New York: Academic Press, 1973.

Bijou, S. W. *Child development: The basic stage of early childhood*. Englewood Cliffs, New Jersey: Prentice-Hall, 1976.

Birren, J. E. (Ed.). *Relations of development and aging*. Springfield, Illinois: Thomas, 1964.
Brim, Orville G. Socialization through the life cycle. In Orville G. Brim, Jr., & Stanton Wheeler, *Socialization after childhood*. New York: Wiley, 1966.
Burgess, R. L., & Huston, T. L. (Eds.), *Social exchange in developing relationships*. New York: Academic Press, in press.
Clausen, John A. (Ed.). *Socialization and society*. Boston: Little, Brown, and Company, 1968.
Elder, G. H. *Children of the Great Depression*. Chicago: University of Chicago, 1974.
Elder, G. H. Family history and the life course. *Journal of Family History*, 1977, *2*, in press.
Emmerich, W. Personality development and concepts of structure. *Child Development*, 1968, *39*, 671–690.
Erikson, E. H. Identity and the life cycle. *Psychological Issues*, 1959, *1*, 18–164.
Flavell, J. H. Cognitive changes in adulthood. In L. R. Goulet & P. B. Baltes (Eds.), *Life-span developmental psychology: Research and theory*. New York: Academic Press, 1970.
Freud, S. *Outline of psychoanalysis*. New York: Norton, 1949.
Gesell, A. L. Maturation and infant behavior pattern. *Psychological Review*, 1929, *36*, 307–319.
Hamburger, V. The concept of development in biology. In D. B. Harris (Ed.), *The concept of development*. Minneapolis: University of Minnesota Press, 1957.
Harlow, H. F., & Harlow, M. K. Social deprivation in monkeys. *Scientific American*, 1962, *207*, 137–146.
Hill, R. & Mattessich, P. Reconstruction of family development theories: A progress report. Paper presented in the Theory Development and Methodology Workshop of the National Council on Family Relations, San Diego, California, 1977.
Kaufmann, H. *Introduction to the study of human behavior*. Philadelphia: Saunders, 1968.
Lerner, R. *Concepts and theories of human development*. Reading, Mass.: Addison-Wesley Publishing Co., 1976.
Lerner, R. M. Nature, nurture, and dynamic interactionism. *Human Development*, 1978, *21*, 1–20.
Lerner, R. M. A dialectical concept of individual and social relationship development. In R. L. Burgess & T. L. Huston (Eds.), *Social exchange in developing relationships*. New York: Academic Press, in press.
Lerner, R. M., & Ryff, C. D. Implementation of the life-span view of human development: The sample case of attachment. In P. B. Baltes (Ed.), *Life-span development and behavior*. *Volume 1*. New York: Academic Press, 1978.
Lewis, M., & Lee-Painter, S. An interactional approach to the mother-infant dyad. In M. Lewis & L. A. Rosenblum (Eds.), *The effect of the infant on its caregiver*. New York: Wiley, 1974.
Looft, W. R. Socialization and personality throughout the life span: An examination of contemporary psychological approaches. In P. B. Baltes & K. W. Schaie (Eds.), *Life-span developmental psychology: Personality and socialization*. New York: Academic Press, 1973.
Nesselroade, J. R., & Baltes, P. B. Adolescent personality development and historical change: 1970–1972. *Monographs of the Society for Research in Child Development*, 1974, *39*, (1, Serial No. 154).
Neugarten, B. L. & Datan, N. Sociological perspectives on the life cycle. In P. B. Baltes and K. W. Schaie (Eds.), *Life-span developmental psychology: Personality and socialization*. New York: Academic Press, 1973.
Oerter, R. Moderne Entwicklungspsychologie. Donauworth: Ludwig Auer, 1973.

Overton, W. F. Klaus Riegel's theoretical contributions: Some thoughts on stability and change. Paper presented at the Eighty-Fifth Annual Convention of the American Psychological Association, San Francisco, California, August, 1977.

Overton, W. F., & Reese, H. W. Models of development: Methodological implications. In J. R. Nesselroade & H. W. Reese (Eds.), *Life-span developmental psychology: Methodological issues*. New York: Academic Press, 1973.

Piaget, J. Piaget's theory. In P. H. Mussen (Ed.), *Carmichael's manual of child psychology. Volume 1*. New York: Wiley, 1970.

Reese, H. W., & Overton, W. F. Models of development and theories of development. In L. R. Goulet & P. B. Baltes (Eds.), *Life-span developmental psychology: Research and theory*. New York: Academic Press, 1970.

Riegel, K. F. Toward a dialectical theory of development. *Human Development*, 1975, *18*, 50–64.

Riegel, K. F. The dialectics of human development. *American Psychologist*, 1976, *31*, 689–700. (a)

Riegel, K. F. From traits and equilibrium toward developmental dialectics. In W. Arnold (Ed.), *Nebraska symposium on motivation*. Lincoln: University of Nebraska Press, 1976. (b)

Riley, M. W., Johnson, W., & Foner, A. (Eds.). *Aging and society, Volume 3, A sociology of age stratification*. New York: Russell Sage Foundation, 1972.

Ryder, N. B. The cohort as a concept in the study of social change. *American Sociological Review*, 1965, *30*, 843–61.

Sameroff, A. Transactional models in early social relations. *Human Development*, 1975, *18*, 65–79.

Schaie, K. W. A general model for the study of developmental problems. *Psychological Bulletin*, 1965, *64*, 92–107.

Schaie, K. W., & Baltes, P. B. On sequential strategies in developmental research: Description or explanation? *Human Development*, 1973, *9*, 191–166.

Schaie, K. W., & Baltes, P. B. On sequential strategies in developmental research and the Schaie-Baltes controversy: Description or explanation. *Human Development*, 1975, *18*, 384–390.

Schaie, K. W., Labouvie, G. V., & Buech, B. V. Generational and cohort-specific differences in adult cognitive functioning: A fourteen-year study of independent samples. *Developmental Psychology*, 1973, *9*, 151–166.

Schaie, K. W., & Strother, C. R. A cross-sequential study of age-changes in cognitive behavior. *Psychological Bulletin*, 1968, *70*, 671–680.

Schneirla, T. C. The concept of development in comparative psychology. In D. B. Harris (Ed.), *The concept of development*. Minneapolis: University of Minnesota Press, 1957.

Stein, A. H., & Friedrich, L. K. Impact of television on children and youth. In E. M. Hetherington (Ed.), *Review of child development research. Volume 5*. Chicago: University of Chicago Press, 1975.

Tobach, E., & Schneirla, T. C. The biopsychology of social behavior of animals. In R. E. Cooke and S. Levin (Eds.), *Biologic basis of pediatric practice*. New York: McGraw-Hill, 1968.

Werner, H. The concept of development from a comparative and organismic point of view. In D. B. Harris (Ed.), *The concept of development*. Minneapolis: University of Minnesota Press, 1957.

White, S. H. The learning-maturation controversy: Hall to Hull. *Merrill-Palmer Quarterly*, 1968, *14*, 187–196.

Wohlwill, J. F. *The study of behavioral development*. New York: Academic Press, 1973.

Perspectives on Child and Family Interaction: Past, Present, and Future[1]

Willard W. Hartup

2

I. Introduction

Perspectives on child and family interaction have changed greatly over the past 75 years. Pragmatic concerns, which gave birth to the child study movement at the turn of the century, were responsible for most of the early studies. Within a few years, however, sufficient systemization was achieved within the social sciences to permit a more theoretically sound analysis of socialization. The purpose of this chapter is to review modern trends in family interaction research, that is, the theories and methodologies that have been in ascendance since World War II. The earlier research traditions will be contrasted with those of the present, and the future will be discussed briefly.

II. The Past

A. Theoretical Traditions

Interest in the processes of socialization (i.e., the processes by which children are reared to become competent members of the society to which they belong) reached a high-water mark in the 1950s. That decade was devoted to the creation of "miniature theories of social ac-

[1]Preparation of this manuscript was assisted by funds from Grant No. 5-P01-05027, National Institute of Child Health and Human Development.

23

Child Influences on Marital and Family Interaction:
A Life-Span Perspective

tion" to account for the development of behavior systems such as dependency, aggression, achievement, and conscience (Sears, 1959). "Social mold" theories were in their heyday, with the greatest weight being carried by psychoanalysis (including the variations that were elaborated within both clinical psychiatry and social anthropology) and stimulus–response theory.

Within psychoanalysis, socialization was seen as an elaborative process involving interactions between biogenetic and social forces. The child's experiences within the family were given a major role as determinants of personality and social behavior, and a significant feature of this theoretical system was the concern with these functions over time—that is, with *development*. Mechanisms were postulated to account for constancy as well as change in human behavior, and certain experiences (e.g., those involved in the Oedipus complex) were identified as universal crises in individual adaptation. But these linkages between biological and social processes in epigenesis have been difficult to render into statements that are amenable to test. Consequently, the developmental implications of this theory have made a thinner impact on child development research than some of the implications contained in the theory about short-term behavior maintenance and change (e.g., primary drive reduction).

Stimulus–response theory was also a "social mold" accounting for individual differences in social behavior. Sometimes called social learning theory (Bandura, 1977), this theoretical system was not the work of a single individual nor was it a unified set of theoretical propositions (Sears, 1959). Actually, three major variants of stimulus–response theory account for most of the social learning research dealing with child and family interaction.

First, there were the works on aggression, imitation, and dependency based on theories of classical conditioning and produced under the direction of Clark L. Hull (e.g., Dollard, Doob, Miller, Mowrer, & Sears, 1939; Miller & Dollard, 1941; Whiting, 1941). Modern students have forgotten the enormous range of social phenomena to which these formulations were applied and the richness of the ideas that were derived from Thorndike, Watson, Hull, Mowrer, Miller, and others.

A second variant, important to the study of personality dynamics as well as the processes of socialization, is traceable to Julian B. Rotter (1954) and his students. In their hands, cognitive variables were incorporated into the stimulus–response analysis, and an extremely viable personality theory has been the result (see Mischel, 1973). This effort, however, yielded a social learning model with more potential for indirect application to child and family interaction than to direct analysis of constancy and change in this social context.

A third variation on stimulus–response theory emerged in the 1950s, derived from Skinner's (1938) work on instrumental learning. It is difficult to overestimate the impact that this most mechanistic of the stimulus–response theories has had upon contemporary views of the socialization process. On the one hand, there is a large literature that demonstrates the malleability of the young infant's affective and social repertoire (e.g., Rheingold, Gewirtz, & Ross, 1959; Etzel & Gewirtz, 1967) and, on the other hand, literatures that trace the linkages between accelerations and decelerations in family interaction as these are related to aggressive and coercive behaviors (e.g., Patterson, in press). The results of the experimentation are convincing: The child's social repertoire (at least after the first several weeks of life) is subject to change. It is dependent both on the behavior of the caretaker and on the nature of the family context.

Throughout the heyday of the "social mold" theories biogenetic factors received relatively little attention among students of socialization. Only in the work of (Gesell, 1929; Werner, 1948; Piaget, 1951) was much attention paid to the role of maturational processes in social development. This seems to have been less a conscious exclusion on the part of the major "social mold" investigators than it was a pragmatic choice; during the 1940s and 1950s, the biogenetic and cognitive sciences were in an unproductive period. Statements by the social learning theorists themselves (e.g., Sears, 1959) reveal that they eschewed any argument to the effect that development is the same thing as learning or that the child plays no role in his own socialization. But, in toto, the research literature gave the impression that the most interesting phenomena to be explained by any theory of socialization are the processes by which the actions of an asocial infant are assimilated to the complex demands of society. "Built-in" features of the behavioral repertoire and the child's effects on the other members of his family received little attention.

The "social mold" traditions came under attack within a variety of disciplines. In psychiatry, for example, interactionist notions of child and family relations emerged in the form of strong statements about mutual regulation in early mother–infant interaction by Erikson (1950) and in conceptions of human development as "interacting dynamisms" by Sullivan (1953). These statements about the socialization process were more child centered than systems centered, but the role of social systems was central to each.

Pressure on "social mold" conceptualizations also came from ethology, particularly primate anthropology. In these disciplines scientists found themselves unable to understand the nature of social adaptation in "social mold" terms. A comprehensive treatment of social adaptation seemed to demand the recognition of innate releasing mechanisms regardless of the degree to which an animal's behavior is known to be plastic. And it was discovered that the functions of animal behavior cannot be understood without the use of interactional and social-structural concepts (Hinde, 1976). Certain evolutionary continuities might be evident in the analysis of simple motor patterns (e.g., "beating" movements or eyebrow flashes) without consideration of their interactional implications. But dominance, affiliation, and many other behavior patterns cannot be understood—in either laboratory or feral situations—unless a transactional analysis is conducted. So, then, dominance came to be conceived as an interaction in which one individual defeats another rather than the persona that an individual animal carries around with him.

Similarly, attachment has come to be conceived as mutually regulated proximity maintenance rather than separation-induced activity in the child or some psychic pseudopod focused on the maternal breast (Freud, 1963). Bowlby (1958), in his famous paper "The Nature of the Child's Tie to His Mother," conceptualized attachment as a social system in which innate releaser mechanisms initially govern both species specific maternal behaviors and species specific child behaviors. This analysis was unclear about the manner in which cognitive development serves to "integrate" these action patterns, but attachment was conceived as mutually regulated. Proximity maintenance between the mother and child was believed to be governed by (a) the mother's attachment to the child; (b) the mother's antiattachment (i.e., activities that are incompatible or interfering with proximity maintenance); (c) the child's attachment to the mother; and (d) the child's antiattachment (i.e., activities, such as exploratory behavior, that are incompatible with the maintenance of proximity to the mother). Later, Ainsworth (1972) postulated that the integration of this behavior system derives from advances in cognitive and motor development, especially the child's understanding of means–ends relations and object permanence.

Other "closet" activities in child development research served to underscore the thesis that socialization must be more than social molding. Roger Barker (1969) and his associates insisted over many years that the study of behavior requires a view of the environment that is more than an instrument for unraveling the behavior-relevant programming within persons. "It is not a passive probabilistic arena of objects and events," he said, and used evidence of situational variance in social activity to support his arguments

> We made long records of children's behavior throughout whole, ordinary days by means of traditional person-centered approaches, and we were surprised to find that some attributes of behavior varied less across children within settings than within the days of children across settings. . . .Many aspects of children's behavior [were] more adequately [predicted] from knowledge of the behavior characteristics of drugstores, arithmetic classes, and basketball games than from knowledge of the behavior tendencies of the particular children [p. 35].

Finally, the pressure of social activism coincided with ivory tower arguments in criticism of "social mold" conceptions of family interaction. Child-centered theories of socialization may work well in circumscribed laboratory or field settings, but in most everyday situations it is difficult to ignore the obvious condition that the ebb and flow of the behavioral stream is polyadic. Essential questions relating to behavior management, child and family education, and policy formulation in the human services fields all require bidirectional or multidirectional models of social development (Lamb, 1977b).

Acknowledgment of these criticisms can be found in many places in the "social mold" literature. Frequently, however, these acknowledgments are understated and their impact negligible. Bijou (1968) issued one statement concerning the role of biogenetic factors in human development, in which he described psychological development as "stimulus and response functions which evolve from the genetic endowment of the individual, the current situation, and the interactional history." [p. 420] In this essay, he described human development as that specialized branch of science concerned with the historical aspects of psychological events—the interactions between a biologically changing organism and sequential change in environmental events through time. Note that two kinds of interaction received attention: (a) the well-known and infinitely complex interactions between biological and social forces in ontogeny; and (b) the child's interactional history, that is, his history of "inter-acts" with both the social and the nonsocial environment. Not specified were the ways in which the child elicits specific behaviors in the individuals he lives with and the manner in which the child changes the self-perceptions and social attitudes of others. To a considerable extent, then, this essay centers on individual ontogeny rather than the development of social systems. Interaction is accorded a place in this scheme (along with biological forces), but that "place" is not well-described.

The most famous demur to traditional, child-centered views of socialization was the presidential address that Robert R. Sears contributed to the 1951 meetings of the American Psychological Association (Sears, 1951). Widely reprinted, that essay was based on the argument that the behavior of the child serves stimulus functions for the parent by eliciting, motivating, and rewarding parental action and vice versa. Even short sequences of interaction must be conceived as tightly woven double strands of behavioral events involving two individuals rather than one. An important supplemental hypothesis was contributed to account for stability in human relations—namely, that individuals acquire "expectancies" about one another that alter the nature of their interaction with the passage of time. This formulation had relatively little impact on child development research, either as a scheme for reinterpreting earlier data or as a scheme for generating new studies: The existing studies mostly could not be reworked within the dyadic model, and before new ones could be generated, the field took a 180-degree shift. Whereas the decade 1950–1959 had been devoted largely to the study of the processes of socialization, the decade 1960–1969 was devoted considerably to studies dealing with the organization and maturation of intellective functioning. Unfortunately, this shift to organismic concerns in child development was accompanied by a diminution in interest in the entire problem to which Sears' dyadic model had been directed.

A bit later, Gewirtz (1961) contributed a conditioning analysis to account for the simultaneous attachment of mother-to-infant and infant-to-mother and succeeded in providing an excellent model to explain the manner in which mother and child come to respond differentially to one another. This analysis was compatible with notions stressing the biological bases of social behavior (e.g., that innate releasing mechanisms are the basis for attachment formation). The main thrust of the analysis, though, was devoted to the "social molding" of such interaction. And Gewirtz's most important contribution was his elaboration of the assumption that early social learning is a dyadic, interactive process rather than a series of monadic events.

Students of family sociology also voiced concern about "social mold" theories and, in turn, stressed the need for interaction analysis. Studies based on systems concepts were conducted on normative functions, conflict and conflict resolution, marital interaction and satisfaction, and many other topics. Indeed, the later eurekas of Bell (1968), Rheingold (1969), and other developmental psychologists (cf. Hartup & Lempers, 1973) when they discovered the necessities of interaction analysis in the study of socialization must be amusing to many family social scientists. Family sociology, however, has neglected one central concern in the analysis of socialization, that is, its ontogenetic character. In a few instances, notions about human development and family process were intermixed—for example, in Parsons' writings (cf. Parsons & Bales, 1955). But in recent years family social science has not dealt very effectively with the interaction between ontogeny and the family context. Most of the family sociological literature is not a developmental literature. Even when developmental analogues are applied to family variables such as marriage (e.g., Aldous, 1974; Hill & Rodgers, 1964), the concept of development is used in a sense that pertains to changes in family relations rather than to changing individuals within these changing contexts. Marriage development needs to be analyzed in a manner that gives as much emphasis to ontogenesis as to group structures.

Such comments may also be applied to the literature on marital satisfaction. Most of the early empirical work was devoted to exploring the impact of childbearing, the presence of children, their number, and their spacing on marital satisfaction—generally without the sort of longitudinal analysis that would make it possible to explore the complex interactions between ontogenetic factors (involving both the parents and the child) and marital satisfaction (see Miller, 1976; Spanier, Lewis & Cole, 1975). However, clear conceptions about cognitive and social development are essential to the analysis of marital satisfaction and its developmental course: What, for example, is known about the impact on marital relations of the semantic and syntactical adjustments that a mother of two preschool children must make in her interactions with her children and husband as compared with the cognitive adjustments that must be made by a mother of two adolescents? The operative variables that connect family structure and marital satisfaction simply cannot be elucidated, over time, without considering these correlations from a developmental perspective. The lack of such a perspective has been the most serious deficiency in the family social science of the past 25 years.

B. Methodological Contributions

Social interaction must be studied with a variety of research methods. Historically, the interview and the questionnaire have been the most commonly used techniques for studying family interaction. Dominant in the years prior to World War II, they remained in ascendance during the immediate postwar period (Hoffman & Lippitt, 1960). Although many early studies can be subsumed under the rubric of "parent–child relations," most of them did not deal with parent–child interaction. The early data actually told us more about "parenting" than parent–child interaction and reflected the unidirectional bias of "social mold" theories. *Patterns of Child Rearing* (Sears, Maccoby, & Levin, 1957) was the culmination of this sort of research on socialization. This study was based on an elegantly constructed maternal interview, from which a great deal was learned about parental activity in both middle- and lower-class families. But it was flawed as a device for independent assessment of the variables involved in dyadic exchange within the family and, like most interview methods, had limited success as a predictor of *anything* (Yarrow, Campbell, & Burton, 1968).

Observational procedures for assessing parent–child interaction in natural settings fared somewhat better, although the record of accomplishment was extremely variable. The early work (e.g., the Fels Parent Behavior Rating Scales [Baldwin, Kalhorn, & Breese, 1945]) was based on conglomerate strategies in which observation was combined with direct behavior ratings and with verbal material supplied by the parents. The predictive validity of these instruments was weak, too, although the factorial structure obtained by Roff (1949) in his analysis of the Fels Scales has held up rather well.

Observational methods (again combined with verbal reports) formed the basis for the classic cross-cultural studies (Minturn & Lambert, 1964; Whiting, 1963), work on patterns of parental authority (Baumrind, 1971), and more recent studies of coercive family environments (Patterson, in press). In many instances, ratings and observations were combined and supplemented with interview materials in order to increase the predictive validity of the parental measures. Baumrind's (1971) findings, showing a linkage between authoritative patterns in parent behavior and social competence in young children, attest to this increased validity. But these conglomerate methodologies were directed, in most instances, at "social mold" hypotheses. Few investigators denied the significance of interactive processes in child development, but their work was not focused on the prediction of interaction as much as it was focused on the prediction of individual differences in interactive situations. A few field-based observational studies were focused on social interaction (Barker & Wright, 1949), but these investigators emphasized setting dynamics rather than interaction dynamics, and the studies have not elucidated long-term effects of children on their parents or the long-term effects of children on family interaction.

As a supplement to interviews and home observations, laboratory settings began to be employed in the study of parent–child interaction over four decades ago. As a context for both intervention and nonintervention research, the social relations laboratory is one of the great creations of modern social science. Three strategies should be mentioned: (a) the situational test, (b) the intervention experiment, and (c) the analogue experiment.

As a situational test, the laboratory is selected as a research locus in order to reduce unwanted variance. Behaviors studied in standard laboratory environments have included both verbal and nonverbal "conversations" between mothers and infants (e.g., Bakeman & Brown, 1977; Lewis & Freedle, 1973); differential attentiveness by mothers to their infant sons and daughters (Moss & Robson, 1968); mother–child interaction in problem-solving tasks (Hess & Shipman, 1967; Van Lieshout *et al.*, 1975), and the relation between authoritative patterns of adult behavior and social competencies in preschool children (Baumrind & Black, 1967). Laboratory environments are ecologically constrained sources of normative information about family interaction, of course, but it is difficult to imagine the study of socialization processes without them.

Most intervention studies in family interaction have been directed at the manner in which parent behavior affects child behavior rather than the reverse. Nevertheless, a great deal has been learned about parent–child interaction with them. For example, the mother's role as a "secure base" has been elucidated by investigating the child's reactions to experimentally programmed separations and the experimentally programmed approaches of strangers (e.g., Ainsworth & Bell, 1970); the role of novel stimulation as an elicitor of antiattachment activity has been established by experimental methods (e.g., Rheingold & Eckerman, 1969); other experiments have established the relation between children's behavior in a cooperative situation and the mother's behavior (Cohen, 1962) as well as the effects of negative evaluations of the child on the mother's involvement in the child's play (Bishop, 1951). In a few instances, the child's effects on the parent's behavior have been examined. Gewirtz and Boyd (1976) exposed the mother to simulated infant vocalizations and head turns, finding these events to function as stimuli that conditioned the mother's behavior as she talked to her baby through a one-way window (i.e., her speech and various expressive actions such as smiling and nodding). Such studies suggest that the mother's caretaking repertoire is changeworthy in the same sense that the infant's behavior is changeworthy and that the infant is an active participant in his own (and his mother's) socialization. Similarly, Moss (1974) explored the role of crying and fussing by the infant in eliciting parent responsiveness. But, by and large, experimental strategies in which the child's behavior is the independent variable and the parent's behavior is the dependent variable have not been widely used.

Experimental methods can be used in combination with differential research strategies in the laboratory analysis of family interaction. Thus,

Hetherington (1967) identified certain fathers and mothers as dominant and others as submissive by means of the decision-making test designed by Farina (1960). The effectiveness of these parents as models was then studied in a persuasibility test with their children. The children were exposed to either their mothers or their fathers, with dominance scores varied across the sex of the model. Dominance facilitated imitation regardless of the relation between the sex of the child and the sex of the parent. In later studies, Hetherington and her colleagues (Hetherington, 1967) used a similar paradigm to show that warmth and dominance interact in the development of identification and sex typing. Stevenson, Keen, and Knights (1963) trained preschool children's mothers and fathers to participate as experimenters in an investigation of the effects of verbal approval on marble-dropping activity of preschool children. Both boys and girls showed marked decrements in performance when the experimenter was the father, but the effects of the mother's praise was different according to the sex of the child. Girls increased their performance levels under such conditions, whereas boys did not. The dynamics of these differences were never clarified, so we do not know whether fathers in this role struck awe into their children or whether the mother's praise was an embarrassment to little boys. But the methodology is a promising one.

Such strategies have also been used with the parent's behavior as the dependent variable rather than the independent variable. Rosen and D'Andrade (1959) assessed parent behavior in test situations with sons who had been rated as either extremely high or extremely low in *need achievement* (*n* achievement) according to the Thematic Apperception Test. As compared with parents of low *n* achievement boys, the parents of high *n* achievement boys held higher aspirations and expectations for their sons' performances, setting higher standards for them. Again, though, investigations in which children have been differentiated by some standard assessment device and then cast in programmed roles in a laboratory experiment are relatively rare.

The so-called analogue experiment was devised to simulate in the laboratory the conditions of childhood socialization using individuals who are not related to one another. The "social mold" literature has been enormously enriched through analogue experiments dealing with modeling and reinforcement effects (Bandura, 1969), affective relations as determinants of social influence (Ross, 1966), the effects of withdrawal of love and/or nurturance (Gewirtz, 1954; Hartup, 1958) and the consequences of punishment (Parke, 1972). This material has buttressed the cluttered and relatively weak correlational data emerging from field studies, and it is difficult to imagine the state of the art in socialization research had we not brought the power of this sort of experiment to bear on certain issues. Doubts still linger about the ecological validity of some of these designs, but the role of the analogue experiment in socialization research seems secure.

Relatively few analogue experiments have been conducted in which child effects on adult behavior have been examined. Rothbart and Maccoby (1966), in one happy exception, studied the effects of information about a child's sex on the reactions of parents to the child's voice in situations simulating dependency, aggression, and independence. Fathers tended to be more permissive in their reactions toward girls than toward boys with respect to both aggression and dependency. A similar pattern prevailed for the mothers—they were more permissive toward boys than toward girls. And, in addition, those parents who favored high sex role differentiation were more permissive with respect to opposite sex children, a tendency that was less obvious for parents who did not espouse such sex-typed views.

In another analogue experiment, research assistants (the actual subjects in the investigation) were trained to play either nurturant or nonnurturant roles while interacting with small groups of preschool children (Yarrow, Waxler, & Scott, 1971). The training produced tremendous differences in the behavior of the experimenters toward the children, but in spite of the intervention, individual differences in the behavior of the children produced large variations in the behavior of the adults toward them. Dependent children, for example, were more successful than other children in claiming attention from the nurturant adults, but they were also more likely to bear the brunt of rebuff from the nonnurturant adults. These concordances occurred within inter-acts (i.e., within sequences), within days, and across days. Such relations (i.e., between the child's dependency and the adult's nurturance) undoubtedly exist in family interaction, although no one has ever examined family interaction to find out. So, even though examples of analogue experiments dealing with child effects on adult behavior are relatively few, the extant studies attest to the power of this strategy.

C. Summary

Within the child development sciences, the earlier theories of socialization did not assign a central role to the child in his own socialization and did not conceptualize the socialization process in interactional terms. Within family social science, socialization was not well-elucidated in relation to the development of the individuals who constitute the family social system.

Tremendous advances in the methodological armamentarium occurred in socialization research in the post World War II period. Field studies based on interviews and home observations were dominant earlier, but laboratory studies gained preeminence more recently. Experimental studies, involving either family members or nonrelated individuals in situations simulating family interaction, have enjoyed an increased vogue. Most often, these strategies have been employed to study parent effects on child behavior rather than the reverse.

III. The Present

A. Theoretical Reconsiderations

About 1970, after a long decline, interest in socialization research reawakened. At the moment, we are in a transitional stage, not knowing exactly how to formulate the right questions and not knowing exactly how to solve the methodological problems that have plagued us. But younger scientists are electing to specialize in the study of socialization in increasing numbers, and theoretical perspectives have changed. The new era in socialization research is strikingly different from the social science of 25 and 30 years ago.

Current thinking about the processes of socialization is centered on *social adaptation*. To consider socialization within this conceptual framework moves the so-called "social mold" theories to a much less central position in our thinking. The individual's integration into society can no longer be conceived as social learning but involves a complex series of events, all aimed at maintaining those traits that enhance genetic survival and eliminating those associated with reduced fitness. Any analysis of these selection processes must account for the phenomena we call learning, since vast capacity for behavior change is in our nature. But to view socialization as social adaptation requires more than a learning analysis.

The study of social adaptation requires consideration of the individual's relation to the environment: Adaptation refers explicitly to the fitness of behavior *within a particular environmental context*. Adaptational views of the socialization process thus require a consideration of the individual in relation to the environment in which he lives. But the individual is not a constant entity over time: It is thus necessary to consider socialization as involving changing individuals within those environmental contexts. Such views necessitate a developmental perspective on the processes of socialization (see Lerner, 1978). Furthermore, the human environment is not constant from place to place. Social adaptation must be conceived in terms of changing individuals in multiple environments. Such views necessitate ecological (situational) perspectives on socialization, including a consideration of both microcosmic elements (i.e., within-situation elements) and macrocosmic elements (i.e., cross-cultural elements). Finally, adaptational analysis necessitates an historical perspective—a consideration of changing individuals in changing environments. Environments change concurrently with the individual's own development and, of course, across generations.

These perspectives on socialization are bringing vast changes to the social sciences. Although many psychologists retain their interest in the processes underlying short-term behavior maintenance and change, others are now concerned with the *functions* of social activity. *Why* questions are being asked, for example, *Why* do specific attachments occur in normal development during the second half-year of life? *Why* are peer relations necessary to the child's development? *Why* does play differ in early and middle childhood?

Answers to such questions are exquisitely complex, owing to the vast number of different environments to which human beings are adapted. Man's social repertoire seems actually to be *polyadaptive*, in that some traits (e.g., aggression) are associated with fitness in one environment but lack of fitness in others. Fine-grained analyses are needed of both social development (i.e., social ontogeny) and the evolution of social behavior (i.e., social phylogeny). The student of socialization must consider seriously such diverse and nontraditional problems as (a) the biological as well as social elements in perception and cognition; (b) social, contextual, and biological issues in language development; (c) the selection value of various social relationships; and (d) the biological regulators of social activity.

Increasingly, socialization is studied within evolutionary as well as developmental and historical perspectives. No longer is socialization conceived as a set of monadic events. Social scientists have learned, as their ethological colleagues learned long ago, that the adaptive significance of social activity can only be appreciated in systemic (polyadic) terms and with reference to survival in a particular social and cultural context.

1. The Developmental Perspective

The so-called developmental perspective in socialization and family interaction has been carried furtherest in research on mothers and infants. A convergent series of events made this possible: First, better documentation was provided concerning preprogrammed regulators in early social behavior, ranging from controlling mechanisms in infant vision to the maturational constraints on sensorimotor intelligence. The fundamentals of smiling, vocalizing, crying, visual preferences, auditory discrimination, fear reactions, and imitation have been explored extensively within an ontogenetic framework, with research from the past decade outstripping everything from earlier decades a hundred times over. This research reveals that the neonate, as well as the older infant, has an outstanding capacity to socialize the caretaker and to control interaction with that individual (Rheingold, 1969). There is still controversy concerning the extent to which early social interaction produces social learning—at least social learning of any permanence. And there are controversies concerning the relative contribution of the child and his caretaker to the emergence of certain social skills, for example, imitation. Does imitation manifest itself first in spontaneous replication by the infant of mouth and hand movements he observes in others (Maratos, 1973), being shaped only later by contingencies of reinforcement? Or does generalized imitation become established in the child's repertoire by parental prompting, coupled with social reinforcement and elaborated by mental representations when these finally occur (cf. Gewirtz & Stingle, 1968; Hartup & Coates, 1970)? Answers to these questions lie in the future. But consider the nature of the questions currently being asked about attachment, imitation, and affective development: What significance do these mechanisms have in the child's development? How are they regulated? What are their polydirectional parameters? What are their developmental courses? Indeed, this treatment of social behavior is not the same as the theoretical treatment given to social behavior 25 years ago.

Unfortunately, a developmental perspective is less visible in current research on social adaptation involving older children and their parents. Some signs are promising. There is a growing literature on developmental aspects of perspective taking; on cognitive–mediational factors in social comparison, moral judgment, person perception, impression formation; and on the utilization of implicit personality theories. The National Children's Survey, conducted in 1976 under the aegis of the Foundation for Child Development, is a promising attempt to gain a better understanding of what children think about their social world. And, in a few places, most notably in the study of peer relations, new insights are being gained about the adaptive significance of experience with other children (Hartup, 1976). But there has been little in the literature of family relations to parallel these trends beyond the explosion in mother–infant studies that has already been mentioned. Here lies a challenge of great magnitude.

2. The Ecological Perspective

Ecological perspectives are much in the news. Scarcely anyone in the social sciences has escaped the flood of "white papers" that has threatened to drown us all in this topic. Actually, there are several types of "setting conditions" that enter into a perspective that stresses context in social adaptation. The first is the microenvironment, (i.e., the immediate situation), which can be regarded as consisting of three elements, one of which is the physical setting, including physical space, number and placement of objects, lighting, noise levels in both foreground and background, and many others. The significance of the physical setting on family interaction is sketchily described in certain studies by Barker and Wright (1955) and in research by Wohlwill (1973), but setting conditions have been better elucidated in infancy research than elsewhere in the literature on parent–child interaction. Much of this new work has an important bearing on the dynamics of early attachment: For example, differences in mother–infant interaction between home and laboratory show the close relation between familiarity with the environment and the operation of proximal set goals (Waters, Matas, & Sroufe, 1975). It would be useful if there were more extensive studies, however, of the physical setting in relation to family interaction, particularly the manner in which such effects change with age (of both child and parent). In some instances, parameters of the setting have been studied concurrently with developmental parameters. Thus, both mothers and babies have been found to tolerate greater and greater physical separation in public parks with advances in the age of the babies (Rheingold & Eckerman, 1970). But what else like this do we know, particularly with respect to older children?

Another element in the "immediate situation" is the task, that is, the salient or central stimulus. Again, excellent examples of ecological research can be found in the literature on mother–infant interaction: Children will leave their mothers more readily when an attractive toy is in the room than when no toy is available; these results show the interaction between exploratory motivation and attachment motivation (Rheingold & Eckerman, 1969). Other studies show that babies are more frightened of an approaching stranger when placed in an infant seat 3 feet from the mother than when seated on her lap, showing the interaction between affective reactions and proximity-to-mother (Morgan & Ricciuti, 1969). Once again, ecological analysis elucidates the dynamics of attachment through describing setting differences in social interaction. These variations in the stimulus field can also be studied concurrently with chronological age. A number of investigators (e.g., Bronson, 1972; Morgan & Ricciuti, 1969) have reported that proximity-to-mother exerts greater control over the infant's wariness as baby (and mother) get older.

The third major element in the "immediate situation" is the actors—the individuals with whom the child interacts. Research shows interaction with fathers to be different from interaction with mothers in the neonatal period (Lamb, 1977a; Parke & Sawin, 1975); interaction with strangers to be different from interaction with caretakers; and, among 2-year-olds, interaction with other children to be both similar and different from interaction with mothers (Eckerman, Whatley & Kutz, 1975). Such studies have considerable explanatory value, as well as descriptive value, although one must always make certain assumptions about why the actor and actor-related cues have acquired differential stimulus efficacy. With older children and their families, the actor-related literature thins out. Observational data on mother–child interaction and teacher–child interaction are relatively plentiful, being actually abundant with respect to various kinds of child–child interaction. Most of this literature, however, has a "social mold" orientation, and not much carries a developmental perspective.

Macrocosmic analysis of socialization is also in transition. Cross-cultural studies, of course, have been a fixture of the social science literature for many years. Most of the traditional cross-cultural studies adhered to the various "social mold" theories. Recently, however, indications are emerging to show that cross-cultural researchers are mounting an effort to differentiate the contributions to social development that emanate from different social experiences in adaptational terms. Interactional analysis is being used in these efforts. Changes can be noted, for example, in the final volume of the "Six Cultures" series, *Children of Six Cultures* (Whiting & Whiting, 1975). There it is established that: (a) child–child relations actually make a more important contribution to the socialization of aggression, to the development of sociable behavior, and to the emergence of prosocial activity than parent–child relations; (b) parent-child interaction, on the other hand, contributes most to the child's acquisition of dependent and intimate behaviors; and (c) the child's interaction with infants is the social context in which nurturant behavior occurs most frequently. These differences within family interaction are pancultural, lending credence to the hypothesis that adaptive mechanisms in social development require, from an early age, experience with a variety of social agents.

3. The Historical Perspective

The study of child and family development in historical context scarcely exists. A small literature, more familiar to historians than to psychologists, consists of descriptive data on children's environments at various points in historical time, with an emphasis on the more dramatic changes in Western culture as these affected children. Thus, there are important studies of child labor, child welfare, and family life in various epochs, and histories of institutions and institutional practices as these have involved children—the history of education, the history of social welfare, and the history of residential treatment (Bremner, 1974). Disagreement concerning the implications of the historical findings is commonplace. Some investigators conclude that the psychological support systems inherent in family interaction were more effective in earlier epochs, whereas others argue that such support systems were no more extensive in former days than at present (Bane, 1976). Many of these accounts, of course, are based on bits and pieces of data, and it has only been recently that intensive study of cohort differences in social behavior has begun (Baltes, Cornelius, & Nesselroade, 1978). All indications are that the historical context is an extremely important factor in social adaptation and one that has been virtually ignored in the socialization literature.

It is difficult to know just how to correct this state of affairs. One can contrast family interaction data across epochs, in the manner of Miller and Swanson (1958), or one can examine antecedent–consequent relations across historical epochs in the global, indirect manner that Whiting and Child (1953) used to test such relations across cultures. In this manner, the correlation between economic conditions and changes in school and work roles can be examined; the relation between family structure and sex role development can be studied; and the relation between child care regimes and affectional relations can be investigated. Critical problems such as "cross-pressures," those normative conflicts between parent–child interaction and peer interaction, need study within such a perspective. We could correct this state of affairs by increasing the number of replication studies that are carried out—and published. But historical replications carry different implications from the ordinary replication study that is performed to establish the "reliability" of one's results.

B. Methodological Advances

The current era in socialization research is characterized by a resurgence of interest in field methods. The overall trend, however, is toward a balanced range of methodologies in which the analysis of social behavior occurs across numerous environments and across numerous settings. The field experiment, particularly with developmental considerations taken into account, is a method of choice. Longitudinal studies of family interaction remain scarce (except, once again, for short-term longitudinal studies of mother–infant interaction), but more and more investigators are choosing field techniques to elucidate the dynamics of socialization.

Three types of field experimentation are in use at the current time: (a) studies in which the natural environment (e.g., the home) is the locus of the outcome measurement although not the locus of the experimental intervention; (b) investigations in which the field serves as the locus for the experimental treatment but not as the basis for the measurement of the dependent variable; and (c) experiments in which a natural environment is employed as the locus for both treatments and outcome measurement. Each of these paradigms has considerable potential for the study of parent–child interaction.

With respect to technology, the greatest problem faced by the current student of family interaction is "tyranny of the data" (Bakeman & Cairns, in press). The invention of closed-circuit television systems and the high-speed computer have generated a whole series of new problems in family interaction research. Essentially, the problem consists of the volume of data that automatic recording and computer storage can produce. Thirty minutes of observation yield 360 discrete 5-second intervals on each participant in a dyadic situation. If 36 dyads are observed, 25,920 intervals are involved. Scores may be generated on any number of different variables in each of these intervals. The reduction of such amounts of data is a task of staggering magnitude and, in many respects, beyond the capacities of current statistical models.

Several writers (Bakeman & Cairns, in press; Rheingold, in press) point out that there will be no technological or mathematical solutions for this kind of tyranny. Future solutions will be the same solutions as those of former days—logical and theoretical solutions rather than mathematical ones. The most essential caution, needing clear reiteration in this transitional era, is to exhort investigators *to ask the right question*. Videotaped records are too frequently obtained to provide answers to questions that have never been formulated. Or if a question has been articulated, no prior guidelines are established for selecting, categorizing, counting, and combining the inter-acts accumulated en masse on videotape. Unfortunately, there is no substitute for rational selectivity in avoiding the tyranny of one's own data.

Some technological areas show signs of progress. Until now, good methods for interaction analysis have been lacking. It has been possible to chart simple sequential dependencies and short linkages in social interaction through conventional Markovian techniques. But longer term dependencies have been more elusive. Repeated measures using data in which the actions of each individual are not independent of the actions of the other individual present nightmarish problems. Reexaminations of these issues, however, are now occurring (e.g., Cairns, in press), and it is not unreasonable to hope for modest mathematical and logical breakthroughs in the years ahead.

C. Summary

The present decade is a transitional period in research on the child and the child's impact on family interaction—both theoretically and methodologically. Contemporary views emphasize adaptation, in which socialization is studied in polydirectional terms from developmental, ecological, and historical perspectives. The laboratory has been successfully utilized in the study of family interaction, but, once again, field settings are increasingly used. The fruits of these transitions are most clearly visible in research on parent–child interaction involving infants. Important technological problems—particularly the problem of sequential analysis—must be solved in order for investigators to avoid being tyrannized by their data. Traditional modes of "good science," however, must continue to be used in order to avoid such tyranny.

IV. The Future

The shortest section of this chapter is devoted to the future. Not a cop-out, the decision to keep this section short was motivated by a sincere wish to avoid the responsibilities of the seer. Besides, the future has already been sketched in the preceding analyses of the past and the present.

One prediction can be made with confidence: Unless the social sciences misuse the opportunity, the next 10 to 15 years could be a new golden age in research on socialization. Our theoretical arguments are coming together; our methodologies are improving; our scientific manpower resources are at an all-time high. There are pitfalls, of course: (a) excommunication of our scientific heritage—not only a horrendous waste, but a fruitless denial; (b) failure to engage the "tough" issues—for example, historical analysis or the study of sequential dependencies or the role of ontogenetic issues in family development; (c) failure to become engaged in the "tougher" large-scale studies, particularly of the same individuals over time; (d) failure to wed the perspectives associated with one discipline to perspectives associated with others (e.g., the developmental, evolutionary, and social systems perspectives). And, it goes without saying, we must successfully walk tightropes that stretch between national science priorities, economic vagaries, and community-shared ethical standards.

But the future looks good. It looks particularly good to someone who has always been more interested in the nature of children's inter-acts than the contents of their minds. The future looks good, too, be-cause we are on the threshold of a pluralistic period—in theoretical analysis and in research technology. Actually, the new era in socializa-tion research is already here, as evidenced by a marked increase in the number of empirical studies of child and family interaction appearing in the journals and on convention programs. It is fortunate that there is to be a second chance.

References

Ainsworth, M. D. S. Attachment and dependency: A comparison. In J. L. Gewirtz (Ed.), *Attachment and dependency*. Washington: Winston, 1972.

Ainsworth, M. D. S., & Bell, S. M. Attachment, exploration, and separation: Illustrated by the behavior of one-year-olds in a strange situation. *Child Development*, 1970, *41*, 49–67.

Aldous, J. *The developmental approach to family analysis*. Athens, Ga.: University of Georgia, 1974.

Bakeman, R., & Brown, J. V. Behavioral dialogues: An approach to the assessment of mother–infant interaction. *Child Development*, 1977, *48*, 195–203.

Bakeman, R., & Cairns, R. B. Describing and analyzing interactional data: Some first steps. In R. B. Cairns (Ed.), *Social interaction: Methods, analysis, and illustrations*. Hillsdale, N.J.: Erlbaum, in press.

Baldwin, A. L., Kalhorn, J., & Breese, F. H. Patterns of parent behavior. *Psychological Monographs*, 1945, *58*, Whole No. 268.

Baltes, P. B., Cornelius, S. W., & Nesselroade, J. R. Cohort effects in behavioral develop-ment: Theoretical and methodological perspectives. In W. A. Collins (Ed.), *Minnesota symposia on child psychology. Vol. 11*. Hillsdale, N.J. Erlbaum, 1978.

Bandura, A. Social learning theory of identificatory processes. In D. A. Goslin (Ed.), *Handbook of socialization theory and research*. Chicago: Rand McNally, 1969.

Bandura, A. *Social learning theory*. Englewood Cliffs, New Jersey: Prentice-Hall, 1977.

Bane, M. J. *Here to stay: American families in the twentieth century*. New York: Basic Books, 1976.

Barker, R. G. Wanted: An eco-behavioral science. In E. P. Willems & H. L. Raush (Eds.), *Naturalistic viewpoints in psychological research*. New York: Holt, Rinehart and Winston, 1969.

Barker, R. G., & Wright, H. F. Psychological ecology and the problem of psychosocial development. *Child Development*, 1949, *20*, 131–143.

Barker, R. G., & Wright, H. F. *Midwest and its children*. New York: Harper & Row, 1955.

Baumrind, D. Current patterns of parental authority. *Developmental Psychology Monograph*, 1971, *4*, (No. 1, Part 2).

Baumrind, D., & Black, A. E. Socialization practices associated with dimensions of compe-tence in preschool boys and girls. *Child Development*, 1967, *38*, 291–327.

Bell, R. Q. A reinterpretation of the direction of effects in studies of socialization. *Psychological Review*, 1968, *75*, 81–95.

Bijou, S. W. Ages, stages, and the naturalization of human development. *American Psychologist*, 1968, *23*, 419–427.

Bishop, B. M. Mother-child interaction and the social behavior of children. *Psychological Monographs*, 1951, *65*, Whole No. 328.

Bowlby, J. The nature of the child's tie to his mother. *International Journal of Psychoanalysis*, 1958, *39*, 1–34.

Bremner, R. H. (Ed.). *Children and youth in America*. Cambridge, Mass.: Harvard University Press, 1974.

Bronson, G. W. Infants' reactions to unfamiliar persons and novel objects. *Monographs of the Society for Research in Child Development*, 1972, *37*, (3, Serial No. 148).

Cairns, R. B. Towards guidelines for interactional research. In *Social interaction: Methods, analysis, and illustrations*. Hillsdale, N.J.: Erlbaum, in press.

Cohen, D. J. Justin and his peers: an experimental analysis of a child's social world. *Child Development*, 1962, *33*, 697–717.

Dollard, J., Doob, L. W., Miller, N. E., Mowrer, O. H., & Sears, R. R. *Frustration and aggression*. New Haven: Yale University Press, 1939.

Eckerman, C. O., Whatley, J. L., & Kutz, S. L. The growth of social play with peers during the second year of life. *Developmental Psychology*, 1975, *11*, 42–49.

Erickson, E. H. *Childhood and society*, New York: Norton, 1950.

Etzel, B. C., & Gewirtz, J. L. Experimental modification of caretaker-maintained high-rate operant crying in a 6- and a 20-week-old infant (*Infans tyrannotearus*): Extinction of crying with reinforcement of eye contact and smiling. *Journal of Experimental Child Psychology*, 1967, *5*, 303–317.

Farina, A. Patterns of role dominance and conflict in parents of schizophrenic patients. *Journal of Abnormal and Social Psychology*, 1960, *61*, 31–38.

Freud, S. *Introductory lectures on psychoanalysis. The standard edition of the complete psychological works of Sigmund Freud*, Vol. XVI. London: Hogarth Press, 1963.

Gesell, A. Maturation and infant behavior pattern. *Psychological Review*, 1929, *36*, 307–319.

Gewirtz, J. L. Three determinants of attention-seeking in young children. *Monographs of the Society for Research in Child Development*, 1954, *19*, (2, Serial No. 59).

Gewirtz, J. L. A learning analysis of the effects of normal stimulation, privation, and deprivation on the acquisition of social motivation and attachment. In B. M. Foss (Ed.), *Determinants of infant behaviour*. Vol. 1. London: Methuen, 1961.

Gewirtz, J. L., & Boyd, E. F. Mother–infant interaction and its study. In H. W. Reese (Ed.), *Advances in child development and behavior*. Vol. 11. New York: Academic Press, 1976.

Gewirtz, J. L., & Stingle, K. G. Learning of generalized imitation as the basis for identification. *Psychological Review*, 1968, *15*, 374–397.

Hartup, W. W. Nurturance and nurturance-withdrawal in relation to the dependency behavior of preschool children. *Child Development*, 1958, *29*, 191–201.

Hartup, W. W. Peer interaction and the behavioral development of the individual child. In E. Schopler & R. J. Reichler (Eds.), *Psychopathology and child development: Research and treatment*. New York: Plenum Press, 1976.

Hartup, W. W., & Coates, B. The role of imitation in childhood socialization. In Hoppe, R. A., Simmel, E. C., & Milton, G. A. (Eds.), *Early experiences and the processes of socialization*. New York: Academic Press, 1970.

Hartup, W. W., & Lempers, J. A problem in life-span development: The interactional analysis of family attachments. In P. B. Baltes & K. W. Schaie (Eds.), *Life-span developmental psychology*. Vol. 3. New York: Academic Press, 1973.

Hess, R. D., & Shipman, V. C. Cognitive elements in maternal behavior. In J. P. Hill (Ed.), *Minnesota symposia on child psychology*, Vol. I. Minneapolis: University of Minnesota Press, 1967.

Hetherington, E. M. The effects of familial variables on sex-typing, on parent–child similarity, and on imitation in children. In J. P. Hill (Ed.), *Minnesota symposia on child psychology, Vol. 1.* Minneapolis: University of Minnesota Press, 1967.

Hill, R., & Rodgers, R. H. The developmental approach. In H. T. Christensen (Ed.), *Handbook of marriage and the family.* Chicago: Rand McNally, 1964.

Hinde, R. A. On describing relationships. *Journal of Child Psychology and Psychiatry*, 1976, *17*, 1–19.

Hoffman, L. W., & Lippitt, R. The measurement of family life variables. In P. H. Mussen (Ed.), *Handbook of research methods in child development.* New York: Wiley, 1960.

Lamb, M. E. Father–infant and mother–infant interaction in the first year of life. *Child Development*, 1977, *48*, 167–181. (a)

Lamb, M. E. A reexamination of the infant social world. *Human Development*, 1977, *20*, 65–85. (b)

Lerner, R. M. Nature, nurture, and dynamic interactionism. *Human Development*, 1978, *21*, 1–20.

Lewis, M., & Freedle, R. Mother–infant dyad: The cradle of meaning. In P. Pliner, L. Krames, & T. Alloway (Eds.), *Communication and affect: Language and thought.* New York: Academic Press, 1973.

Maratos, O. The origin and development of imitation in the first six months of life. Paper presented at the Annual Meetings of the British Psychological Society, Liverpool, April, 1973.

Miller, B. C. A multivariate developmental model of marital satisfaction. *Journal of Marriage and the Family*, 1976, *38*, 643–657.

Miller, D. R., & Swanson, G. E. *The changing American parent: A study in the Detroit area.* New York: Wiley, 1958.

Miller, N. E., & Dollard, J. *Social learning and imitation.* New Haven: Yale University Press, 1941.

Minturn, L., & Lambert, W. W. *Mothers of six cultures: Antecedents of child rearing.* New York: Wiley, 1964.

Mischel, W. Toward a cognitive social learning reconceptualization of personality. *Psychological Review*, 1973, *80*, 252–283.

Morgan, G. A., & Ricciuti, H. N. Infants' responses to strangers during the first year. In B. M. Foss (Ed.), *Determinants of infant behaviour.* Vol. 4. London: Methuen, 1969.

Moss, H. A. Communication in mother–infant interaction. In L. Kramer, P. Pliner, & T. Alloway (Eds.), *Advances in the study of communication and affect. Nonverbal communication.* New York: Plenum Press, 1974.

Moss, H. A., & Robson, K. S. Maternal influences in early social visual behavior. *Child Development*, 1968, *39*, 401–408.

Parke, R. D. Some effects of punishment on children's behavior. In W. W. Hartup (Ed.), *The young child.* Vol. 2. Washington: National Association for the Education of Young Children, 1972.

Parke, R. D., & Sawin, D. B. Infant characteristics and behavior as elicitors of maternal and paternal responsivity. Paper presented at the Biennial Meeting of the Society for Research in Child Development, Denver, April, 1975.

Parsons, T., & Bales, R. F. *Family, socialization and interaction process.* Glencoe, Ill.: Fress Press, 1955.

Patterson, G. R. A performance theory for coersive family interaction. In R. B. Cairns (Ed.), *Social interaction: Methods, analysis, and illustrations*. Hillsdale, N.J.: Erlbaum, in press.

Piaget, J. *Play, dreams, and imitation in childhood*. New York: Norton, 1951.

Rheingold, H. L. The social and socializing infant. In D. A. Goslin (Ed.), *Handbook of socialization theory and research*. Chicago: Rand McNally, 1969.

Rheingold, H. L. A guide to non-intervention studies. In R. B. Cairns (Ed.), *Social interaction: Methods, analysis, and illustrations*. Hillsdale, N.J.: Erlbaum, in press.

Rheingold, H. L., & Eckerman, C. O. The infant's free entry into a new environment. *Journal of Experimental Child Psychology*, 1969, *8*, 271–283.

Rheingold, H. L., & Eckerman, C. O. The infant separates himself from the mother. *Science*, 1970, *168*, 78–83.

Rheingold, H. L., Gewirtz, J. L., & Ross, H. W. Social conditioning of vocalizations in the infant. *Journal of Comparative and Physiological Psychology*, 1959, *52*, 68–73.

Roff, M. A. A factorial study of the Fels Parent Behavior Rating Scales. *Child Development*, 1949, *20*, 29–44.

Rosen, B., & D'Andrade, R. The psychosocial origins of achievement motivation. *Sociometry*, 1959, *22*, 185–218.

Ross, D. Relationship between dependency, intentional learning, and incidental learning in preschool children. *Journal of Personality and Social Psychology*, 1966, *4*, 374–381.

Rothbart, M. K., & Maccoby, E. E. Parents' differential reactions to sons and daughters. *Journal of Personality and Social Psychology*, 1966, *4*, 237–243.

Rotter, J. B. *Social learning and clinical psychology*. New York: Prentice-Hall, 1954.

Sears, R. R. A theoretical framework for personality and social behavior. *American Psychologist*, 1951, *6*, 476–483.

Sears, R. R. Personality theory: The next forty years. In B. R. McCandless (Ed.), Iowa Child Welfare Research Station, State University of Iowa: The fortieth anniversary. *Monographs of the Society for Research in Child Development*, 1959, *24*, (3, Serial No. 74).

Sears, R. R., Maccoby, E. E., & Levin, H. *Patterns of child rearing*. Evanston, Illinois: Row & Peterson, 1957.

Skinner, B. F. *The behavior of organisms*. New York: Appleton-Century-Crofts, 1938.

Spanier, G. B., Lewis, R. A., & Cole, C. L. Marital adjustment over the family life cycle: The issue of curvilinearity. *Journal of Marriage and the Family*, 1975, *37*, 263–275.

Stevenson, H. W., Keen, R., & Knights, R. M. Parents and strangers as reinforcing agents for children's performance. *Journal of Abnormal and Social Psychology*, 1963, *67*, 183–186.

Sullivan, H. S. *The interpersonal theory of psychiatry*. New York: Norton, 1953.

Van Lieshout, C. F. M. Young children's reactions to barriers placed by their mothers. *Child Development*, 1975, *46*, 879–886.

Waters, E., Matas, L., & Sroufe, L. A. Infants' reactions to an approaching stranger: Description, validation, and functional significance of wariness. *Child Development*, 1975, *46*, 348–356.

Werner, H. *Comparative psychology of mental development*. New York: International Universities Press, 1948.

Whiting, B. B. (Ed.) *Six cultures: Studies of child rearing*. New York: Wiley, 1963.

Whiting, B. B., & Whiting, J. W. M. *Children of six cultures: A psychocultural analysis*. Cambridge, Mass.: Harvard University Press, 1975.

Whiting, J. W. M. *Becoming a Kwoma*. New Haven: Yale University Press, 1941.

Whiting, J. W. M., and Child, I. *Child training and personality*. New Haven: Yale University Press, 1953.

Wohlwill, J. F. The concept of experience: S or R? *Human Development*, 1973, *16*, 90–107.
Yarrow, M. R., Campbell, J. D., & Burton, R. V. *Child rearing: An inquiry into research and methods*. San Francisco: Jossey-Bass Inc., 1968.
Yarrow, M. R., Waxler, C. Z., & Scott, P. M. Child effects on adult behavior. *Developmental Psychology*, 1971, *5*, 300–311.

The Child's Social World[1]

Michael Lewis and Candice Feiring

3

I. Introduction

The infant enters into the world with the potential to influence and be influenced by a wide variety of persons and events. It is a social world full of conspecifics, a small segment of which share the child's gene pool; a larger segment of which will influence the child; and finally the largest segment, which forms the background in which these other interactions will take place. The smallest segment we call family; the larger, friends, acquaintances, and peers; and the largest segment, the culture.

Contemporary psychological theory and thought places the most stress on the smallest segment—the family—seeking to explain the child's growth and development by understanding the interaction of this family—the mother, father, siblings, and infant. In common language we talk of the parents' role in raising the infant, by which we make reference to the parental role in helping the child to grow. The phrase *to raise* conveys the function of helping something to grow as the gardener helps the flowers to grow or the parents their child. Thus, *to raise* has come to mean 'to help develop.'

The raising of children by parents does involve helping them develop. The phrase has this private meaning; however, it also has a very public meaning, one related to the child's entrance into the social world. Nicole Belmont (1976) in an essay entitled, *Levana: or, How to Raise Up Children*, refers to this public role by pointing out that *to raise up* has an

[1]Preparation of this chapter was made possible through support from the Foundation for Child Development and a postdoctoral fellowship, Grant No. MH05542.

47

older meaning, one that is similar across cultures and historical time. Briefly, *to raise* has a literal meaning, that of taking the newborn infant up from the ground, where it is placed soon after birth, and lifting it up in the air. This raising up was a public act, declaring paternity, in some cases, that is, entrance into the family, and declaring as well that the newborn is a member of the social group. In the case of a deformed infant, it would not be raised up but left to die on the ground. Thus, to raise up in a literal sense meant to be accepted into the social group. This social group included a wide range of individuals: kin, for example, parents, siblings, grandparents; and nonkin, for example, friends and teachers. In order to explore the child as a member of its social group or network, it will be necessary to explore a number of propositions concerning the nature and functioning of social objects and the process of effect (Weinraub, Brooks, & Lewis, 1977).

II. Nature and Function of Social Objects

Although there are considerable exceptions, it would nonetheless not be unfair to characterize the study of psychological socialization in the last 50 years and certainly in the last 2 decades as the study of the role of the parents, but specifically the mother, in the infant's development. In order, therefore, to understand the socialization processes whereby the infant becomes the child and the child the adult, it has been thought necessary primarily to study the role of the mother. In a word, and with the exception of maturational theories, however phrased, the child was viewed as the product of the mother's behavior. To understand the relationship was to understand the processes of development.

The role of the mother as the primary socializer has a long history, yet it was for psychoanalysis in particular to give it a strong theoretical perspective (Freud, 1905). This position was strengthened by such theorists as Erikson (1950), Mahler (1968), and Spitz (1945), who believed that development was dependent upon the mother's capabilities in fulfilling her infant's needs, the fulfillment leading to trust. This trust was the basis for the next step, that of establishing a secure attachment, one that could lead to identification and the socialization of the child through the incorporation of the beliefs, goals, and values of the parent.

It was Bowlby (1951), in his earliest efforts, who stressed both the biological function of the social relationship, on the one hand, and the unique role of the mother, on the other. The biological function of the attachment relationship was used by Bowlby to argue for the primacy of early social experience. By turning to survival and failure to thrive as the criteria of biological as opposed to learned needs, Bowlby and others (for example, Spitz, 1965) were able to show that the lack of love and attention of an adult was sufficient for the organism to fail to thrive and even die.

Bowlby (1969), in his theory of attachment, went one step further than the original demonstration of the primary importance of love for the development of the human infant. By wishing to make love a biological necessity and imperative of development and growth, Bowlby argued for the biological unit of mother and infant. For him, the mother–infant dyad was a biological entity endowed with unique features. It was distinguished from all other relationships and derived from biological and evolutionary pressures. Thus, the theory and the research derived from it centered the most important socialization task in the hands of a single member of the child's social world.

The battle was too hard fought to deny the role of the mother in the socialization of the child. Without question the mother's role is vital. However, what do we mean by mother? Is it restricted to the biological mother? Can the father play an equal role? Might there be multiple mothers? All these questions and more have been raised, none of which deny the importance of an adult figure or figures as necessary, or essential, for the well-being and successful socialization of the child. Although the role of the mother cannot be questioned, the role of others in the child's life and the role they play in socialization need both some theoretical attention and some empirical research. Thus, although the infant interacts with the mother, he or she must also interact with others. Indeed, from the moment of birth the infant is embedded in a large social network, the fabric of which is made up of many people, functions, and situations. This network includes fathers, but also can include grandparents, friends, animals, and a large kinship group.

A. Social Objects

By referring to social objects as opposed to other objects we intend to make some sort of differentiation between *social* and *nonsocial*. The basis of this differentiation is unclear; nevertheless, our aim is to construct a taxonomy based on the differences between these two classes of objects. Whether infants use this taxonomy is not known; however, work on the acquisition of self-recognition (Brooks & Lewis, 1975; Lewis & Brooks, 1974; Lewis & Brooks, 1975) strongly suggests that *social objects are different from other objects in as much as the social object shares something in common with—is like—the perceiver*. Thus, *social* and *nonsocial* are not some static, unchanging dichotomy but rather change as a function of ontogeny as well as history. The knowing of an object is, as Hamlyn (1974) has pointed out, dependent on the infant's knowledge of its relationship to that object. This position, not unlike that of G. H. Mead (1934), finds further support in the interactional theory of Piaget (1954).

The potential array of social objects that influence the infant and are influenced by the infant is exceedingly large. How to make sense of this varied and large array is one of the more important goals of the child, since it is to this array that the child must learn to adapt. For some theorists adaptation is sequential; the infant first adapts to the mother, then perhaps the father, and still later other social objects such as siblings, peers, and grandparents. Moreover, these same theorists would argue quite convincingly that the nature of the adaptation to the earlier objects determines the nature of the adaptation to others that follow. Psychoanalytic theory certainly seems to support the notion that poor adjustment with parents has profound implications for subsequent social behavior. Yet, alternative views exist (Harlow & Harlow, 1969; Lewis, Young, Brooks, & Michalson, 1975) that express the idea that the child's relationships to social objects other than the mother, although mutually interdependent, do not have to (a) follow sequentially; or (b) be completely determined by the nature of the mother-child relationship. Harlow and Harlow (1969), Lewis et al. (1975), and Mueller and Vandell (in press) have argued for functional independence of at least the mother-infant and infant-peer systems. Mother-infant and infant-peer relationships may occur at the same time, and both may appear very early, within the first 12 weeks of life. Although not all the evidence is gathered, still that which does exist would lend support for separate systems.

Given that the infant must learn to make its way through a large and complex social array, how might it go around constructing its social knowledge? The use of the schematic representation of space presented in Figure 3.1 may offer one possibility. The construction of the child's social world is possible if we allow for the use of only several dimensions. One basis for the selection of dimensions, alluded to earlier, is the self. Lewis and Brooks (in press), in a series of studies, have demonstrated the presence of some concept similar to self in infants in the last quarter of the first year. Using this notion, the infant has the potential to differentiate not only self from other but to use this "like me" comparison in order to dichotomize its world. It can be argued that for the infant social objects are therefore objects "like me." The self-comparison is open to change as the concept of self is altered, as a function of both the growing cognitive capacity and the infant's experiences. Three dimensions—age, familiarity, and gender—are attributes of the self and of the social world that the child acquires early, and they can be used as

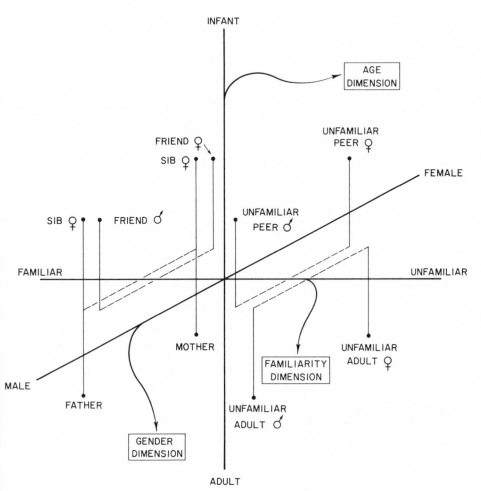

FIGURE 3.1 *A taxonomy of the child's social world. Note that the dimensions of familiarity–unfamiliarity and adult–infant are continuous, whereas the dimension of male–female is dichotomous (although it is possible that, psychologically speaking, from the young child's point of view, sex is more or less a continuous variable, e.g., mothers are more female than 5-year-old girls). Also note that siblings and parents have been represented as equally familiar, whereas adult strangers are represented as less familiar than peer strangers. The points given in the figure are merely illustrative of possible location of persons in a child's social world and may vary depending on the child's perception.*

dimensions within the social array that helps order them into a workable taxonomy.

Figure 3.1 presents this three-dimensional space along with the placement of some of the more common social objects in the child's life. As these dimensions become more differentiated, the social objects within the space become differentiated as well. Thus, as age becomes differentiated (larger than a two-category system), one can add grand-parents and adolescents, or within the familiar dimension different degrees of familiar-unfamiliar allow for strangers, friends, and family to be placed.

Whether the infant uses these dimensions to help create the social array is indeterminate; however, the ability to construct such an array from just three dimensions indicates that it may be possible. From a structural point of view, it appears to be an interesting possibility that should be further explored.

Over the last decade data have been gathered that could be used to support the development of gender, age, and familiarity concepts. Bronson (1972), as well as others (Lewis, Goldberg, & Campbell, 1969), has shown that familiarity in the social as well as nonsocial world is a salient dimension of the child's cognitive structures. Moreover, Bronson has demonstrated stranger fear in infants as young as 3 months, a finding compatible with our own observations of some infants. Money and Ehr-hardt's (1972) data on hermaphroditic females supports the notion of early gender identity and other work (Lewis & Brooks, 1975; Lewis & Weinraub, 1974) have shown infants to be responsive to gender. Responses to age have been shown repeatedly, both to live subjects (Brooks & Lewis, 1976a; Lewis & Brooks, 1974; Greenberg, Hillman, & Grice, 1973) and to pictures (Brooks & Lewis, 1976b). The data are not wanting to argue that these dimensions, a necessary condition for the construction of the social array, at least from the structural position we have presented, exist early in the child's life.

B. Social Functions

In the study of the infant's early social relationships, besides restricting the nature of those relationships by focusing more or less exclusively on the mother (or father), a careful analysis of the types of situations or activities between the social objects has not been undertaken. Although it is true that the mother and child have been observed in free-play situations, in separation and reunion, and in the presence or absence of a stranger, these situations, for the most part, have not been analyzed into activities or functions. This limitation has had important consequences on the theoretical models that have been considered, leading to a restricted view of what infants and children do and with whom they do them. The restricted view of function has also affected the study of the number of social objects that the infant interacts with. If only nurturant and protective functions are considered, then the mother as the most important (and only) social object to be studied makes some sense. However, other functions exist as needs in the infant's life, including, for example, play and exploration. This being the case, other social objects more appropriate to the function should be considered. The realization that this is the case, especially for play, has led to a renewal of interest in peer relationships and should result in a continuing study of the origins of friendship and the nature of siblings' interactions (Lewis & Rosenblum, 1975).

In any analysis of the social network, it is necessary not only to consider the range of social objects involved but also the range of functions and situations. Although different social objects may be characterized by particular social functions, it is often the case that social objects, functions, and situations are only partially related (proposition 4, Lewis & Weinraub, 1976). Consequently, the identity of the social object does not necessarily define the type or range of its social functions. For example, "mothering" (a function) and mother (an object) have been considered to be highly related. Some recent work with other social objects would seem to indicate that fathers (Parke & O'Leary, 1975) are more than adequate in performing this function. On the other hand, it could be the case that for some specific functions only a specific social object could fulfill that need. The feeding function, prior to technological advances, required the mother—but even then the use of a wet nurse suggests that a one-to-one relationship between object and function may be difficult to demonstrate.

Whereas the discussion of social objects was based upon a set of theoretical notions and empirical data, social functions or activities are without such support. Although social objects are difficult to define, social functions are considerably harder. The following comments are directed toward such an endeavor, with the realization that these are halting first attempts.

To start, we would define social functions as those activities that take place within the social network that involve other social objects. Functions that do not need the involvement of other social objects are not social functions. Although social functions involve other social objects, it remains to be determined whether the presence of another social object is necessary for this distinction. For example, imitation in the absence of the other social object might still be considered a social function. A set of specific social activities would include sexual activity, talking, communication, and play. These are just some of the functions or activities, and they involve, first of all, other social objects, such as in sexual behavior, talking, or playing.

Social activities or functions have been thought of as having some specific use for the organism's survival or well-being. Talking or communication, for example, or even play, are activities that are usually thought of as facilitating some aspect of development or growth. More specifically, we talk or ask questions in order to obtain information. Recently, Garvey (1977), Lewis and Cherry (1977), and Lewis (1977) have suggested that talking and communication have as a function the act of maintaining social contact. That is, rather than as an information exchange, the more significant function of question asking may be in its social facilitation rather than in its information-producing capacity. This seems clear when we consider questions asked at conferences and meetings; more often than not they have more to do with gaining the floor, seeking recognition, or embarrassing the other.

Play behavior can also be argued to have as a primary goal the establishment and maintenance of social relations (Mueller & Vandell, in press) rather than what has commonly been thought, the acquisition of skills. It would seem, then, that one aspect of a function is its social or nonsocial nature. Social functions take place with social objects and may be important because they facilitate and maintain the relationship between these objects. In some sense any activity or function may be considered social. Symbols and words are for Levi-Strauss (1962) social contracts, the social agreement that words have a common meaning. Even so, it may be profitable to make the distinction between social and nonsocial functions or activities.

One of the most important features of social functions is their subjective nature. That is, although it is possible to define a set of functions structurally—some of which we would be more willing to consider social than others—these functions or activities really have a subjective and phenomenological basis. This is less so for social objects.

Consider the function called play. It is clear that this activity is a construct that can subsume a large set of diverse activities—fantasy, games, and symbolic representation being just three examples. Moreover, the play of children is work, whereas work, when enjoyed, has for some adults the quality of play. This being the case, a phenomenological approach (Harré & Secord, 1972) may be necessary. Pervin (1975) has made some interesting attempts toward this problem by looking at the multiple dimension of subjects' consideration of situations. The activity, asking questions, as we have pointed out, can have a multitude of functions.

In order to specify a set of functions, we could borrow from sets created around adaptive functions (Wilson, 1975), need functions (Murray, 1938), or some similar set. That task is beyond the scope of these comments, since they themselves required considerable analysis. In any event, several large differences in function make themselves felt even from the beginning of life and must include at least play, protection, nurturance, caregiving, and exploration.

Although we do not feel that a complete list of functions can be adequately realized, the following is an attempt to delineate some of the more important ones:

1. *Protection.* This function would include protection from potential sources of danger, including inanimate sources—falling off trees or being burnt in fires—and animate, as in being eaten by a predator or taken by a nonkin.
2. *Caregiving.* This function includes feeding and cleaning (at the least) and refers to a set of activities that center around biological needs relating to bodily activities.
3. *Nurturance.* This is the function of love, or attachment, as specified by Bowlby (1969) and Ainsworth (1969).
4. *Play.* This function refers to activities with no immediately obvious goal that are engaged in for their own sake.
5. *Exploration–learning.* This social activity involves the activity of finding out about the environment through either watching others, asking for information, or engaging in information acquisition with others.

Although functions as they relate to different objects have not been extensively studied, mothers' behavior toward their children as a function of situation, in which social function has been captured in part, has been examined (Lewis & Freedle, 1973, 1977). In one study the conversational relationship between dyads, 12-week-old infants and their mothers, was examined when the infant was on the mother's lap (presumably when the mother wished to interact, e.g., play function) and when the infant was in an infant seat (presumably when the mother wished to do housework and keep her eye on her child, e.g., protective function). Under the former, initiation and responsivity was many times greater than under the latter function, even though the amount of vocalization the mother produced was not different.

C. The Relationship between Social Objects and Social Functions

In a pilot study, Edwards and Lewis have tried to direct attention more specifically to the problem of function and object. Thirty-two children between 3 and 4 years of age were asked to pick the picture of three strangers—a peer (3 years old), an older child (7 years old), and an adult (20 years old), all the same sex as the subject, who the child would go to if (a) the child needed help; (b) the child wanted to play; or (c) the child wished to get information on how an object worked. Both girls and boys chose help more from the adult than from either child and chose to get information from an older child more than from an adult, but chose to play with a peer more than with an adult (or older child). The second finding was of some surprise, since one might expect the child to choose to get information from an adult. That this was not the case suggests that even for information seeking, children may choose other children over adults. It is suspected that this may be true for certain tasks but not others, a result supported by some of the work on imitation. These findings once again point up the role of friends, peers, and older children and the significant part they play in the infant's life (Lewis, et al., 1975).

If we are to understand the child's social behavior and social knowledge, a consideration of the array of social objects and functions needs to be undertaken. Although much has been learned about the mother–infant relationship, it is limited to a few functions and needs to be broadened. Our interest in fathers must receive, again from a broad perspective, further attention (Lamb, 1976). Exploration of peer and friendship relationships has just started (Lewis & Rosenblum, 1975) and has already contributed to our appreciation of both the complexity of the social network and the limitation of our theories. There are, however, large gaps in our conceptualization and data. Little is known of sibling relationships, and the infant's relationship to grandparents, uncles, aunts, and cousins (the larger kinship group) have all but been ignored. Much work is necessary in light of the common observations that children at very young ages can form and conceptualize aspects of the kinship system and that related members appear to have significant and emotional ties with the young child. In this regard, Nathan Fox (personal communication) reports that children raised on a very strict kibbutz (one that takes the child soon after birth and keeps it in the child's house all week, allowing it only 1 night a week at home and minimum contact during the week with its parents) do not appear to have any delay or disruption of kinship relationships. Given the little time spent with the parents, let alone grandparents or uncles and aunts, such a finding would suggest both (a) the importance and therefore effect of these kin; and (b) the cognitive underpinning and the process of effect involved in forming these relationships.

The data are too scant and no psychological theory broad enough to encompass the total social array of objects and functions that influence the infant's development. Our efforts should be directed toward such theory building.

III. Process of Effect

Because the exploration of social relationships has been studied in the context of a behaviorist viewpoint, most theory and empirical findings have centered on the direct effect of one object upon another. How much and in what way one person does something to another has been measured in both the laboratory and the home. This general approach we have called "the direct effects of experience" approach. It is equally plausible to believe that social objects affect one another indirectly. This measurement of indirect effects is, of course, harder than the measurement of direct effects; nonetheless, it may be the case that a substantial portion of social knowledge and influence is established through indirect means.

A. Direct Effects

Direct effects always involve the target person—for us the child—as one of the participants in an interaction and occur when all of the participants are present. Direct effects, therefore, represent the effect or influence of one person on the behavior of another in the presence of each other. Historically, direct effects in their simplest form, using the mother–infant interaction data, were represented by the effect of the mother's behavior on the infant. This we represent as

$$M \rightarrow I$$

Thus, the question usually asked was, What is the effect, for example, of the mother's vocalization on the infant's vocalization, either concurrently or at some future time? Since the interactional view has become more popular (Lewis & Rosenblum, 1974), it is now recognized that the mother and infant both influence and affect each other. This has now been characterized as

$$M \rightleftarrows I$$

A direct effect is still possible to observe. In this case the direct effect is interactional in nature and takes the form, for example, of the effect of the vocalization behavior of the mother and infant on each other. In both the interactional and the unidirectional models the majority of the variance of the behavior of each is assumed, although usually not stated explicitly, to be accounted for by the interaction. The discussion of where to observe this mother–infant interaction arises out of the concern that the proper situation need be found so that an accurate estimate of the relationship can be obtained. The problem here is not only that situations influence behavior (Lewis, 1977) but that the direct effect of each on the other cannot hope to account for all of the variance of the particular observation, that is, cannot account for all the behavior emitted.

Interest in other social objects and their influence on the infant do little to alter our study of direct effects. In addition to the mother, the direct effects of the father, sibling, or peer have been studied. Yarrow (1975) has warned of the danger of taking our methodologies and concepts from the study of mother–infant relationships into the study of other relationships, that is, peer–peer relationships. This warning has particular meaning within the framework of our comments. Although a few studies have come to recognize the limitation of the range of social objects currently thought of as comprising the infant's social network, little effort has been made in the conceptualization of more than a dyadic relationship. It appears that regardless of the nature of the social object, most investigations proceed with a dyadic inquiry. Dyadic relationships, though important, are insufficient, since by definition *all* studies of dyadic relationships are studies of direct effects. In fact, it is a logical necessity to study indirect effects as we go to any interactive system larger than a dyadic one. Consider a triad—for example, the mother, father, and infant. In this case we have at least the dyadic relationships: the M $\rightleftarrows$ I, the F $\rightleftarrows$ I, and the M $\rightleftarrows$ F; the relationships between an individual and a dyad, I $\rightleftarrows$ M/F, I $\rightleftarrows$ F/M, M $\rightleftarrows$ F/I; and the triad itself M/F/I. Note that a good way of conceptualizing an increase in size from dyads to larger systems is in terms of the number of possible relationships in the social network by dyads and larger subsystems rather than by the number of participants in the interaction. As we have seen in the particular shift from a dyad to a triad, as the number of individuals increases, the number of possible relationships increase more rapidly than size. Not only do the number of relationships increase, from a dyad to a triad, but the nature of the dyadic relationships changes as they are embedded in a larger system.

Although the mother–infant and father–infant relationships have usually been considered from a dyadic perspective, that is, observing the direct effects, evidence already exists to indicate that the mother–infant or father–infant dyad is affected by the presence of the other. Lamb (1976) reports that infants interact more with either parent in isolated dyads than when these parent–child dyads are embedded in a three-element system. Furthermore, parents interact much less with the child when their spouse is present. One must also consider the effect on the mother–father interaction of the child. For example, Rosenblatt (1974) found that when one or more children were present, there was less adult–adult touching, talking, and smiling in selected public places such as zoos, parks, and shopping centers. In some real sense, then, the consideration of a more than two-member interaction forces us to consider indirect effects. Thus, the study of the family, assuming an $N + 2$ system, requires the study of indirect as well as direct influences.

B. Indirect Effects

Indirect effects refer to a set of influences on the target person that occur in the absence of one member of a system and in addition to direct effects. "In the absence of" refers to interactions among members of the social network when all the members themselves are not present—for example, the effect of the mother $\rightleftarrows$ father relationship on the mother's behavior toward the infant when she and the infant are alone. *Indirect effects may also occur in addition to direct effects when the interaction among members of the social network occurs in the presence of the other even though the interaction is not directed toward the other.* An example is when the child observes the mother and father having an argument.

The consideration of the indirect effects among members of the social network may take on several different forms. In the following discussion we shall explore four quite different ways indirect effects are manifested, that is, in support, representations, transitivity, and modeling.

1. Support

In general, support system views suggest that A's effect on B will have an effect on C even in the absence of A. The particular case studied within the social network is the father's support of the mother as it affects the mother–infant dyad. It seems evident that the father's emotional as well as economic support for the mother (and vice versa, of course) can affect even the very young child in a variety of ways. For example, by allaying the mother's doubts, anxiety, and frustrations and by making her feel more self-confident and secure, the father can enable the mother to be more responsive to the child. Feiring (1975) studied the relationship between maternal involvement and responsivity to the infant and the mother's perception of how much support she received from the secondary parent. The results of this study indicated that a strong positive association existed between maternal involvement and responsivity to the infant and maternal perception of support from the secondary parent.

Many of the effects of father absence may be explained by the differences in the mother's behavior toward her children as a result of lack of support, not necessarily the father's absence per se (Pedersen, 1976). In many cases, mothers whose husbands are absent must provide economic support for the family. Whether or not they want to work, they must. They must also do all the household tasks by themselves with little help from people outside the family. Lynn (1974) reports several studies (e.g., Kriesberg, 1967; Parker & Kleiner, 1966; Tiller, 1958) in which mothers without husbands on a regular or temporary basis described some of the difficulties they experience. Mothers without husbands felt worse off psychologically and were not so goal oriented. They were more concerned about the children's educational achievements than other mothers, they made more inappropriate efforts to help their children, they were more likely to be dissatisfied with the child's level of work and less likely to be involved with the schools or to aspire to a college education for their children. Finally, mothers whose husbands were temporarily absent on a regular basis led less active social lives, worked less outside the home, were more overprotective of children, and were more likely to be concerned with their child's obedience and manners rather than happiness and self-realization. Hoffman (1971) suggests that not having a husband might make a woman feel "busier and more harassed and hence impatient with the child and oriented toward immediate compliance rather than long-range character goals [p. 405]."

Indirect effects in support systems may also operate when all the members are present. Pedersen (1975), studying the ways in which each person in a three-element system influences and is influenced by other members of that system, suggests that the father's warmth and affection may help to support the mother and help her to be a more effective mother. Pedersen and his associates (1977) have also reported that the expression of criticism in the husband–wife dyad (perhaps a reflection of the lack of mutual support) is associated with maternal and paternal expression of negative affect to the infant. A study by Parke and O'Leary (1975) suggests that the father's interest in the infant is likely to accelerate the mother's interest. When mothers were with their husbands, they were more likely to explore the infant and smile at the infant than when they were alone. Also, the father's attitudes toward the infant may be contagious. When mothers were with fathers, they tended to touch their male infants more than their female infants. However, there were no sex of child differences in touching when the mother and child were alone.

2. Representations

Representations of absent social objects can occur (a) when one member tells another about a third; and (b) when one member, in the absence of another, thinks about that other. In both cases the absent social object has an effect on the other member.

The first case can be characterized by the mother telling the child about the father in the absence of the father. For example, the mother might say, "Daddy is away on a trip, but he misses you," or "You behave just like your father." Lewis and Weinraub (1976) suggest that children's ability to remember or think about their fathers even in their absence may account for the lack of consistent findings in father absence studies. Consider the father absent in two cases; in the first the mother represents the father as "he is working to obtain money for your education," whereas in the second "he is out with his friends." The child's feelings about the missing father might be quite different under these two conditions.

The second representational activity involves the child's representing of an absent object. Most of our notions support the view that relationships and their representations are built up and maintained by contact, that which we have called direct effects. Representations may best be constructed by the child experiencing periods of both direct effects and the absence of these effects in some as yet unknown ratio.

This distancing (Sigel, 1970) requires the child to construct, elaborate, and label the absent one and promotes abstraction. Social objects in the child's network have different ratios of direct effect–indirect effect. Lewis and Weinraub (1976) point out that the father may be more distanced than the mother and may therefore facilitate more abstraction around himself than the mother does around herself. Data to support this view come from a study by Brooks and Lewis (1975), in which infants label pictures of their fathers prior to those of their mothers, a finding similar to Jakobson's (1962) finding that *daddy* precedes *mommy* in children's first speech.

This view is quite similar to that held by ego psychologists, who view the construction of the ego as a consequence of the mother's (or others') inability to continuously affect the child. That is, in the absence of direct effects, the construction of reality in general, and of social objects in particular, occurs. There is some further support of this in a study by Rosenblum (personal communication), in which he reports that macaque monkeys reared alone with their mothers have difficulty in recognizing and therefore finding them when placed in a situation where their mother and other female monkeys are present.

The importance of this type of indirect effect on the members of the social network is broad. First, different social objects may be more or less distant (or absent) from the child. This may have an effect on the influence of these members on the child's development. Second, different social functions require differential degrees of distancing (or absence). The social object who traditionally provides for the other members is away more of the time than the object who cares for the child.

3. Transitivity

The principle of transitivity takes the following form: A has a relationship to B, B has a relationship to C, therefore A has a relationship to C. The relation between elements (A, B, C) may be positive or negative and may vary in intensity; however, A's relationship to C is based in part on $A \rightleftarrows B$ and $B \rightleftarrows C$. Thus, even in the absence of a direct $A \rightleftarrows C$ relationship, A/C form a relationship through $A \rightleftarrows B$, $B \rightleftarrows C$. For example, the child's relationship to the mother and the mother's relationship to the father should influence the child's relationship to the father in addition to or regardless of the amount of direct interaction between father and child.

Transitivity relationships are determined by the intensity and sign of the direct relationships. In other words, a very positive child–mother relationship and a very positive mother–father relationship, even in the absence of a direct father–child relationship, should result in a positive father–child relationship. Given the sign of a relationship, the various other outcomes can be worked out where the $A \rightleftarrows B$ is weak, but the $B \rightleftarrows C$ is strong, and alternatively, the $A \rightleftarrows B$ is strong, but the $B \rightleftarrows C$ is weak. Each should have a different outcome on the $A \rightleftarrows C$ relationship. The conceptualization is further complicated when there are direct $A \rightleftarrows C$ effects, since these effects now interact with the already described indirect effects.

Some informal observations at a day care center lend support for the operation of transitivity effects in interactions. At the appearance of a stranger some young children show stranger fear—they refuse to move toward the stranger to play or to take an object from his or her hand. We have found that in a group setting, if another child approaches the stranger, plays, and takes the toy, the first child's fear seems to dissipate. We propose that in this case the stranger's relationship with the child's peer facilitates, through the child–peer relationship, the child–stranger interaction.

Transitivity may help in establishing and maintaining all extended social networks. Not only may it explain the child's relationship to his or her immediate family but to the kinship group in general. Transitivity, in the absence of direct effects, may be the mechanism whereby children establish relationships with aunts and uncles (the sisters and brothers of their parents) and grandparents (the parents of their parents). Transitivity may operate when others are or are not present. Transitivity may help explain Fox's report that even in the absence of direct effect in the Israeli kubbutz, child-house-raised children still have significant relationships with kin other than their parents.

4. Modeling

Modeling behavior is also indirect and usually takes place in the presence of other social objects. Simple modeling behavior is characterized by A doing what B does even though B does not do it to A. Examples of this abound. That more learned behavior is not credited to imitation rests on the difficulty to demonstrate modeling. Most tests of modeling impose a time and behavior constraint, so that in order for A to be said to model B, it is necessary for A to act like B in X time. The problem is that X time is usually too short and *act like* difficult to define. For example, A sees B playing with blocks by banging them together. If A does not play with the blocks and bang them together, for example, in 3 minutes, then A is said not to have imitated B. Unfortunately, A may not immediately play with the blocks. Therefore, A may not model; however, A may play with the blocks in 2 hours. At that time A may bang them. Even more to the point, a child may not be able to model a parental caregiving behavior until the child becomes a parent—a time span of perhaps 20 years!

The more complex modeling behavior involves A modeling from the interaction of B and C. For example, A is a girl watching her mother and father interact with each other. A learns about her mother by watching her interaction with the father as well as learning about her mother by watching the father's behavior toward the mother. Hetherington (1967) also has made this point when she states that femininity in girls is related to the father's approval of the mother as a model as well as the father's own masculinity.

C. Social Complexity within the Family

The number of potential relationships as well as the possibilities of indirect as well as direct effects in more than two-element interactions present a complex picture of the child's social world. Taking things further, in the spirit of R. D. Laing's *Knots*, consider what happens when we move from a three-element to a four-element system, such as a system composed of mother, father, and two children. Indeed, the average American family has 2.23 children, and recognition of this fact alone necessitates examining the implications of a four-element interaction. Inclusion of another element in the interaction system increases complexity considerably. For example, in an $N + 2$ system, the number of possible reciprocal *dyads* is three, whereas in an $N + 3$ system, this number is doubled. Addition of a sibling into the family creates a new dyad, namely a child–child dyad. Thus, in addition to influence within and between adult–adult and adult–child dyads, an $N + 3$ system includes direct and indirect influences within and between the child–child dyad and the former mentioned dyads. $N + 3$ systems also include more possibilities for triadic relationships than $N + 2$ systems. Whereas an $N + 2$ system only has one triadic relationship, an $N + 3$ system has four triadic relationships (i.e., MFC_1, MFC_2, MC_1C_2, FC_1C_2). Given the possibilities for unidirectional, bidirectional, direct, and indirect effects of individuals, and for dyads, triads, and quadrads, it becomes rather an understatement to say that a four-element system is quite complex. Of course, it may not make sense to study all the possible effects inherent in an $N + 3$ system, but at least recognition of the wide range of possibilities may keep us from overlooking some sources of important influence.

Considering the potential complexity of an $N + 3$ over an $N + 2$ element interaction, it is tempting to ignore the existence of two-parent, two-child systems. However, the literature on birth order and family size indicates that this would be a mistake. Both parents and children appear to behave differently depending on how many siblings are present in the family. Zajonc and Markus's work (1975) has examined the relationship between family configuration and intelligence and indicates that the influence of siblings' and parents' intellectual levels on the child's growth is mediated by diverse processes of social interaction in the family. Two constraints that operate on this social interaction are family size and the spacing of siblings. Zajonc and Markus's formulation stresses the importance of both parental as well as sibling effects on the development of the child's IQ.

Within the domain of infancy, cognitive development has been shown to be related to birth order. Gallas and Lewis (1976) have found that birth order affects performance on the Bayley MDI, with firstborns scoring the highest and fourthborns the lowest. Other studies of the effects of birth order (i.e., of the presence of more than one child) in infancy have focused on how the parents' behavior toward the child is different depending on whether the child is a member of an $N + 2$ or an $N + 3$ system. For example, in a series of studies that compared feeding situations of firstborn with latterborn infants, primiparous mothers were found to talk more, to use a great number of feeding intervals, to spend more time in nonfeeding activities, and to provide more stimulation to their infants (Thoman, Barnett, & Leiderman, 1971; Thoman, Leiderman, & Olson, 1972; Thoman, Turner, Leiderman, & Barnett, 1970).

A study by Jacobs and Moss (1976) is of interest because it examined how the mother's behavior alters in the shift from an $N + 2$ to an $N + 3$ system. Jacobs and Moss found that mothers spent significantly less time in social, affectionate, and caretaking interaction (with the exception of feeding) with their secondborn as compared with their firstborn children. The data also indicated that certain maternal behaviors toward the secondborns seem to elicit demands for attention from the mother by the firstborns. Note that this result illustrates the direct effect of one mother–child dyad on another $(M \rightleftarrows C_2) \rightarrow (C_1 \rightleftarrows M)$. A study reported by Judd and Lewis (1976) explored the effects of birth order on the vocalization behavior of mothers, fathers, and siblings in the family system. The data for mother and father indicated that parental vocalization decreased as the birth order position of the infant increased. The infant itself behaved in what appeared to be a complementary fashion with the parents' behavior, with decreasing infant vocalization being associated with an increase in ordinal position. Siblings, on the other hand, showed an opposite pattern compared with that of parents; that is, their vocalization frequency increased with increasing infant birth order. The results of this study highlight how parent–child and child–child dyads may operate differently. Lamb (1977) examined how an $N + 2$ system differed from an $N + 3$ system. The results of this study indicated that preschoolers and infants interacted less with each parent and with one another when both parents were present than when only one parent was present.

IV. Conclusions

A child's social network forms a social environment through which pressure is extended to influence the child's behavior and is also a vehicle through which the child exerts influence on others. Within the social network, one can differentiate between the people that directly or indirectly affect the infant. Thus, a social network can be viewed as a flexibly bounded grouping of persons consisting of a focal person, here the child, everyone whom the child knows or interacts with, the set of relationships between those persons and the child, and the set of relationships that exist independently of the child. Social networks extend over time and space, and the nature of the persons, roles, activities, values, etc., that characterize the network will influence, through both direct and indirect ways, the child who is a member of this network.

References

Ainsworth, M. D. S. Object relations, dependency, and attachment: A theoretical review of the infant–mother relationship. *Child Development*, 1969, 40, 969–1025.

Belmont, N. Levana or how to raise up children. In R. Forester & O. Ranum (Eds.), *Family and Society*. Baltimore: The Johns Hopkins University Press, 1976. Pp. 1–15.

Bowlby, J. *Maternal care and mental health*. Geneva: World Health Organization, 1951.

Bowlby, J. *Attachment and loss*. In *Attachment*. Volume 1. New York: Basic Books, 1969.

Brooks, J., & Lewis, M. Mirror-image stimulation and self recognition in infancy. Paper presented at the Society for Research in Child Development meetings, Denver, April 1975.

Brooks, J., & Lewis, M. Visual self recognition in infancy: Contingency and the self-other distinction. Paper presented at the Southeastern Conference on Human Development meetings, Nashville, Tennessee, April 1976. (a)

Brooks, J., & Lewis, M. Visual self recognition in different representational forms. Paper presented at the Twenty-First International Congress, Paris, July 1976. (b)

Bronson, G. W. Infants' reactions to unfamiliar persons and novel objects. *Monographs of the Society for Research in Child Development*, 1972, 47 (148).

Erikson, E. H. Growth and crises of the healthy personality. In M. J. E. Senn (Ed.), *Problems of infancy and childhood*, Transactions of the sixth conference. New York: Josiah Macy, Jr. Foundation, 1950, 91–146.

Feiring, C. The influence of the child and secondary parent on maternal behavior: Toward a social systems view of early infant-mother attachment. Doctoral dissertation, University of Pittsburgh, 1975.

Freud, S. *Three essays on the theory of sexuality*. Standard edition, VII., 1905. London: Hogarth, 1953, pp. 125–245.

Gallas, H., & Lewis, M. Cognitive performance in the 12-week-old infant: The effects of birth order, birth spacing, sex and social class. Paper presented at the Eastern Psychological Association meetings, New York, N.Y., April 1976.

Garvey, C. The contingent query: A dependent act in conversation. In M. Lewis & L. Rosenblum (Eds.), *Interaction, conversation and the development of language: The origins of behavior, Vol. V*. New York: Wiley, 1977.

Greenberg, D. J., Hillman, D., & Grice, D. Infant and stranger variables related to stranger anxiety in the first year of life. *Developmental Psychology*, 1973, 9, 207–212.

Hamlyn, D. W. Person-perception and our understanding of others. In T. Mischel (Ed.), *Understanding other persons*. Totowa, New Jersey: Rowman & Littlefield, 1974. Pp. 1–36.

Harlow, H. F., & Harlow, M. K. Age mate or peer affectional system. In P. S. Lehrman, R. A. Hinde, & E. Shaw (Eds.), *Advances in the study of behavior. Volume 2*. New York: Academic Press, 1969.

Harré, R. & Secord, P. F. *The explanation of social behavior.* Oxford: Basil Blackwell & Mott, 1972.

Hetherington, E. M. The effects of familiar variables on sex typing, on parent-child similarity and on imitation in children. In J. P. Hill (Ed.), *Minnesota symposia on child psychology, Vol. 1.* Minneapolis: The University of Minnesota Press, 1967. Pp. 82–107.

Hoffman, M. L. Father absence and conscience development. *Developmental Psychology,* 1971, *4,* 400–406.

Jacobs, B. S., & Moss, H. A. Birth order and sex of sibling as determinants of mother-infant interaction. *Child Development, 47,* 1976, 315–322.

Jakobson, R. Why "Mama" and "Papa"? In *Selected writings of Roman Jakobson.* The Hague: Mouton, 1962.

Judd, E., & Lewis, M. The effects of birth order and spacing on mother-infant relationships. Paper presented at the Eastern Psychological Association meetings, New York, N.Y., April 1976.

Kriesberg, L. Rearing children for educational achievement in fatherless families. *Journal of Marriage and the Family,* 1967, *29,* 288–301.

Lamb, M. E. The effects of ecological variables on parent-infant interaction. Paper presented at the biennial meeting of the Society for Research in Child Development, New Orleans, March 1977.

Lamb, M. E. Effects of stress and cohort on mother- and father-infant interaction. *Developmental Psychology,* 1976, *12,* 435–443.

Lamb, M. (Ed.) *The role of the father in child development.* New York: Wiley, 1976.

Levi-Strauss, C. *The savage mind.* Chicago, Ill.: University of Chicago Press, 1962.

Lewis, M. Early socioemotional development and its relevance for curriculum. Invited address for the American Educational Research Association meetings, San Francisco, April 1976. In *Merrill-Palmer Quarterly,* 1977, *23,* 279–286.

Lewis, M. What is natural? Paper presented at the New York Academy of Sciences, New York, N.Y., October 1976. *The Sciences,* 1977.

Lewis, M., & Brooks, J. Self, other and fear: Infants' reactions to people. In M. Lewis & L. Rosenblum (Eds.), *The origin of fear: The origins of behavior. Volume II.* New York: Wiley, 1974, pp. 195–227.

Lewis, M., & Brooks, J. Infants' social perception: A constructivist view. In L. Cohen & P. Salapatek (Eds.), *Infant perception: From sensation to cognition, Vol. II.* New York: Academic Press, 1975.

Lewis, M., & Brooks, J. *The origins of the concept of self.* New York: Plenum, in press.

Lewis, M., & Cherry, L. Social behavior and language acquisition. In M. Lewis & L. Rosenblum (Eds.), *Interaction, conversation, and the development of language: The origins of behavior. Volume V.* New York: Wiley, 1977.

Lewis, M., & Freedle, R. Mother-infant dyad: The cradle of meaning. In P. Pliner, L. Krames, & T. Alloway (Eds.), *Communication and affect: Language and thought.* New York: Academic Press, 1973.

Lewis, M., & Freedle, R. The mother and infant communication system: The effects of poverty. In H. McGurk (Ed.), *Ecological factors in human development.* Amsterdam, The Netherlands: North-Holland Publishing Company, 1977, pp. 205–215.

Lewis, M., Goldberg, S., & Campbell, H. A developmental study of learning within the first three years of life: Response decrement to a redundant signal. *Monographs of the Society for Research in Child Development,* 1969, *34*(9, Serial No. 133).

Lewis, M., & Rosenblum, L. (Eds.) *The effect of the infant on its caregiver: The origins of behavior. Volume 1.* New York: Wiley, 1974.

Lewis, M., & Rosenblum, L. (Eds.), *Friendship and peer relations: The origins of behavior. Volume IV.* New York: Wiley, 1975.

Lewis, M., & Weinraub, M. Sex of parent x sex of child: Socioemotional development. In R. C. Friedman, R. M. Richart, & R. L. Vande Wiele (Eds.), *Sex differences in behavior.* Huntington, New York: Krieger, 1974.

Lewis, M., & Weinraub, M. The father's role in the child's social network. In M. Lamb (Ed.), *The role of the father in child development,* New York: Wiley, 1976.

Lewis, M., Young, G., Brooks, J., & Michalson, L. The beginning of friendship. In M. Lewis & L. Rosenblum (Eds.), *Friendship and peer relations: The origins of behavior. Volume IV.* New York: Wiley, 1975.

Lynn, D. B. *The father: His role in child development.* Monterey, California: Brooks/Cole Publishing Company, 1974.

Mahler, M. S. *On human symbiosis and the vicissitudes of individuation.* Volume I. New York: International Universities Press, Inc., 1968.

Mead, G. H. *Mind, self, and society.* Chicago: University of Chicago Press, 1934.

Money, J., & Ehrhardt, A. A. *Man and woman, boy and girl.* Baltimore, Maryland: The Johns Hopkins University Press, 1972.

Mueller, E., & Vandell, D. Infant-infant interaction. In J. Osofsky (Ed.), *Handbook of infant development.* New York: Wiley, in press.

Murray, H. A. *Explorations in personality.* New York: Oxford University Press, 1938.

Parke, R. D., & O'Leary, S. Father-mother-infant interaction in the newborn period: Some findings, some observations, and some unresolved issues. In K. Riegel & J. Meacham (Eds.), *The developing individual in a changing world. Vol. II. Social and environmental issues.* The Hague: Mouton, 1975.

Parker, S., & Kleiner, R. J. Characteristics of Negro mothers in single-headed households. *Journal of Marriage and the Family,* 1966, *28,* 507–513.

Pedersen, F. A. Mother, father and infant as an interactive system. Paper presented in the Symposium, Fathers and Infants, at the meetings of the American Psychological Association, Chicago, August 1975.

Pedersen, F. A. Does research in children reared in father-absent families yield information on father influences? *The Family Coordinator,* October 1976, 459–464.

Pedersen, F. A., Anderson, B. J., & Cain, R. L. An approach to understanding link ups between the parent-infant and spouse relationship. Paper presented at the Society for Research in Child Development Convention, New Orleans, Louisiana, 1977.

Pervin, L. Definitions, measurements, and classifications of stimuli, situations, and environments. Research Bulletin 75–23. Princeton, New Jersey: Educational Testing Service, 1975.

Piaget, J. *The construction of reality in the child.* (1937). New York: Basic Books (English translation by M. Cook), 1954.

Rosenblatt, P. C. Behavior in public places: Comparison of couples accompanied and unaccompanied by children. *Journal of Marriage and the Family,* 1974, *36,* 750–755.

Sigel, I. The distancing hypothesis: A causal hypothesis for the acquisition of representational thought. In M. R. Jones (Ed.), *Miami Symposium on the Prediction of Behavior, 1968: Effect of early experiences.* Coral Gables, Florida: University of Miami Press, 1970. Pp. 99–118.

Spitz, R. A. Hospitalism: An inquiry into the genesis of psychiatric conditions in early childhood. In A. Freud *et al.* (Eds.), *The psychoanalytic study of the child.* New York: International Universities Press, 1945.

Spitz, R. A. *The first year of life*. New York: International Universities Press, 1965.

Thoman, E. B., Barnett, C. R., & Leiderman, P. H. Feeding behavior of newborn infants as a function of parity of the mother. *Child Development*, 1971, *42*, 1471–1483.

Thoman, E. B., Leiderman, P. H., & Olson, J. P. Neonate-mother interaction during breast feeding. *Developmental Psychology*, 1972, *6*, 110–118.

Thoman, E. B., Turner, A. M., Leiderman, P. H., & Barnett, C. R. Neonate-mother interaction and effects of parity in feeding behavior. *Child Development*, 1970, *41*, 1103–1111.

Tiller, P. O. Father absence and personality development of children in sailor families. Nordisk Psykolgis Monographs, 1958, Ser. No. 9.

Weinraub, M., Brooks, J., & Lewis, M. The social network: A reconsideration of the concept of attachment. *Human Development*, 1977, *20*, 31–47.

Wilson, E. O. *Sociobiology*. Cambridge: The Belknap Press of Harvard University Press, 1975.

Yarrow, M. Some perspectives on research in peer relations. In M. Lewis & L. Rosenblum (Eds.), *Friendship and peer relations: The origins of behavior. Volume IV*. New York: Wiley, 1975.

Zajonc, R. B., & Markus, G. B. Birth order and intellectual development. *Psychological Review*, 1975, *82*, 74–88.

The Developing Child and Marital Satisfaction of Parents

Boyd C. Rollins and Richard Galligan

4

We have two major purposes in this chapter. They are: (*a*) to review literature on the presence, density, and age of children in a family in relation to evaluations of the quality of the marital relationship of their parents; and (*b*) to develop a theory of marital satisfaction in parents as a function of the presence, density, and age of their children. We view this as a difficult task because of the lack of an empirical base of information that directly focuses on developmental issues. Nevertheless, recent events have given us the courage to try. They include theoretical advances concerning antecedents of marital satisfaction (Burr, 1973; Miller, 1976), the emerging emphasis in several disciplines on the development and systemic (polyadic) significance of social activity in socialization research (see Hartup, Chapter 2, this volume), and conceptualizations of polyadic interaction in families in terms of systems of social roles in transition (Nye & Berardo, 1973; Rodgers, 1964).

I. Introduction

The myth of the passive child, who is socialized by responding to environmental stimuli, especially the very young child responding to the behavior of parents, has been fairly well refuted (Bell, 1968; Gewirtz & Boyd, 1976; Lewis & Rosenblum, 1974). The effect of the child on parent–child interaction has been documented and has been observed to vary with sex of child (Lewis, 1972; Parke & Sawin, 1976), sex of parent (Osofsky & O'Connell, 1972), and age of child (Harper, 1975). In addi-

Child Influences on Marital and Family Interaction:
A Life-Span Perspective

tion, interaction effects of age of child, sex of child, and sex of parent on parent–child interaction have been observed (Parke & Sawin, 1977). Emde, Gaensbauer, and Harmon (1976) found that infants elicit different responses from caregivers as different levels of emotional development emerge. Parents have also been observed to impose more restrictions on children coincident with new developmental stages where parents are expected by cultural norms to release children into new spheres of freedom. This was found by Baldwin (1946) to occur when children start school and by Steinberg and Hill (1977) to occur with the emergence of adolescense.

The evidence for a child effect in the parent–child relationship seems well-established. However, the demonstration that infants or children can influence parent–infant or parent–child interaction has not taken us down the road very far. Knowledge can be advanced by recognizing that both children and parents can act as stimuli for parent–child interaction. However, we still must address questions about the adaptive significance of interaction itself, whether patterns and sequences of interaction are instigated by the child, the parent, or both.

A. The Adaptive Significance of Family Interaction

The adaptive significance of family interaction for quality outcomes in parent–child relationships is of primary importance. This argument suggests some very complex questions. For example, what is the contribution of the child or the parent to quality outcomes for either of them? To answer such a question, we must consider the stimulus of parent or child, social interaction, and the response of the parent or child. Social interaction is an intervening variable in such a model.

In the model just described, either a feedback loop of child stimulus/parent–child interaction/child response or a feedback loop of parent stimulus/parent–child interaction/parent response could exist. Baumrind (1967) seemed to have had this idea in mind when she operationalized mothers' control attempts in terms of mothers' reactions to childrens' noncompliance with previous directives. On the other hand, the parent stimulus/parent–child interaction/child response, or the child stimulus/parent–child interaction/parent response in the more traditional manner is still a logical part of the model. It is the latter issue, the impact of the developing child on the parents' marriage, through parent–child interaction that is our primary concern in the literature review and theoretical development to follow.

The simplicity of child stimulus/parent–child interaction/parent response in family relationships is quickly complicated when we realize that dyadic interaction does not take place in a vacuum. This has been amply demonstrated by Lamb (1976). Mother–infant interaction was different when the father was present than when he was absent. We interpret this to mean that research and theory on socialization in the family must consider polyadic interaction of at least a triad. A moment's reflection will surely suggest that the presence or absence of siblings will also have an influence.

However, instead of an almost endless addition of participants in a monolithic polyadic interaction system, we propose to conceptualize the family in terms of four basic social positions, namely; (a) husband–father; (b) wife–mother; (c) daughter–sister; and (d) son–brother. With these four positions, questions about dyadic interaction as subsystems of the family system and interchanges between these subsystems can be addressed.

With such conceptualization, the four social positions result in three basic dyads, namely, marital, parent–child, and sibling. Of course the marital dyad is nonexistant in a one-parent family, but it has several replications in a polygamous family. Also, the parent–child and sibling dyads depend on the presence of children in a family. The parent–child and sibling dyads can be subdivided into subtypes based upon sex of parent or sex of child and number of children (Rodgers, 1964).

Whatever the pattern of parent–child interaction that is a function of the presence, density, and age of children, the quality of that interaction, at least from the viewpoint of the parent, should be reflected in the parent's satisfaction with the parent–child dyadic relationship or satisfaction with the marital dyadic relationship. Such a subjective state is one type of response to the interaction. This is congruent with the experience of Parke and Sawin (1977) when they found that mother–infant interaction made more sense to them when they obtained attitudinal information from the mothers concerning the meaning of the interaction.

We are primarily concerned in this work with marital satisfaction as a reflection of the quality of family relationships. However, within our general framework, parent–child satisfaction or sibling satisfaction could also be studied. The quality of the marital relationship, reflective of interaction in the marital dyad, has been used as an index of successful families in over 300 studies (Spanier, 1976).

But how is marital satisfaction related to the presence, density, and age of children? We suggest that systematic exchanges take place between the parent–child dyad and the marital dyad. In other words, the child influences parent–child interaction, which influences behaviors and attitudes of the parent. The parent, also being a spouse, influences

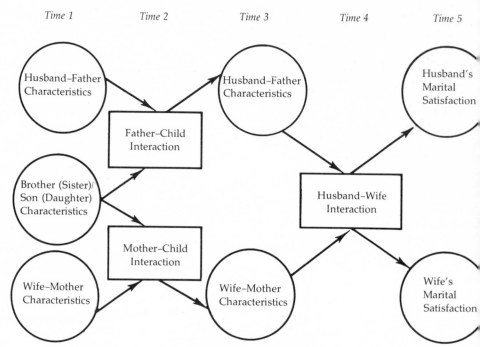

FIGURE 4.1. *A model of the indirect effects of children on marital quality.*

marital interaction, which influences the spouse's evaluations of the quality of the marital relationship (see Figure 4.1). Therefore, the child indirectly influences the marital dyad by influencing parent–child interactions, which also indirectly influence marital interaction. Marital interaction is reflected in the marital satisfaction of one or both spouses. Thus, we assume that marital satisfaction is indirectly influenced by the presence, density, and age of children.

B. Marital Satisfaction as an Evaluation of Marital Quality

The quality of marital relationships has been a primary aspect of family research for several decades (Burr, 1967, 1973; Spanier, 1976; Spanier & Cole, 1976). The most popular labels used in recent years have been adjustment, stability, and satisfaction. Of the above three labels for marital quality, stability is the easiest to define as a construct, and the operational indicators are fairly objective. Indicators of instability are annulment, divorce, desertion, and separation. However, since many marriages that were not low on adjustment or satisfaction have been observed to have low stability, we consider stability the least useful of the three labels for marital quality. Social pressures, laws, and the attractiveness of alternatives logically account for some unstable marriages of "high quality" and some stable marriages of "low quality." Of the remaining two labels, we prefer satisfaction over adjustment.

What rationale justifies our choice? Of those who have made serious and consistent attempts to use these labels to conceptualize and measure quality in the marital relationship in recent years, Burr (1967, 1973), Miller (1975a, 1976), and Rollins and colleagues (Rollins & Feldman, 1970; Rollins & Cannon, 1974) have chosen the label of satisfaction, whereas Spanier and colleagues (Spanier, 1976; Spanier, Lewis and Cole, 1974) have chosen adjustment. One reason for our preference for satisfaction is that Burr (1973) and Miller (1976) have presented fairly formal theories of the antecedents of marital satisfaction, which we find useful in pursuing the goals of this chapter. Perhaps more important, however, is what appears to us to be ambiguity in the conceptualization of adjustment and a lack of fit between the conceptual and operational definitions of this construct.

Spanier and Cole (1976) defined marital adjustment as "a process, the outcome of which is determined by the degree of: (1) troublesome marital differences; (2) interspousal tensions and personal anxiety; (3) marital satisfaction; (4) dyadic cohesion; (5) and consensus on matters of importance to marital functioning [pp. 127–128]." In their efforts to include both the dynamics of process and the quality of outcome in their definition, confusion seems to be introduced. It seems reasonable to us that marital adjustment at a given point in time is the consequence of preceding interaction processes over time. However, Spanier's definition seems to imply that the qualitative outcome of the adjustment process is the consequence of several other states, for example, cohesion, consensus, satisfaction. This seems to us to be more a theory of antecedent "states," which influence an adjustment process as an intervening variable, which in turn influences a final "state" of the marriage.

Spanier and Cole (1976) note that when viewed as a process, it is possible to conceptualize "marital adjustment as a theory rather than a variable [p. 128]." It seems preferable to us to use a variable that reflects the quality of the marital relationship rather than infer the quality from how well a theory is supported. The measurement of an individual variable can be used to assess the quality of a single marriage, but a test of a theory requires many observations of multiple variables and many subjects.

Instead of the five states mentioned by Spanier and Cole (1976) as antecedents of some marital quality undefined, we think that four empirically verified states (Spanier, 1976) more likely antecede marital satisfaction at any one point in time. We think this is especially so for two states, operationalized by Spanier (1976), cohesion and consensus.

While emphasizing a process of dyadic interaction in the conceptual definition, Spanier (1976) operationalized consensus as "perceived consensus" and cohesion as "perceived cohesion." Perceived consensus and cohesion, like satisfaction, are subjective states of an individual. Rather than operationalizing structural elements of interacting participants, such data reflect the thinking of a single individual, and relationships between such variables as perceived consensus and satisfaction would most likely be accounted for by cognitive consistency theory rather than by social interaction. In support of our judgment, Rollins (1961) found that perceived values agreement of spouses (perceived consensus) predicted marital satisfaction of either spouse, whereas actual values agreement ("objective" consensus) predicted marital satisfaction for neither. Most attempts to operationalize marital adjustment have measured "perceived consensus" (i.e., Locke & Wallace, 1959). Therefore, we think the attempts to measure social interaction processes with such operationalized concepts as perceived consensus and perceived cohesion have a problem of fit between constitutive and operational definitions.

It seems preferable to us to use marital satisfaction as a conceptualization of level of quality in a marital relationship rather than a multidimensional construct such as marital adjustment, with its associated conceptual and operational problems identified in the preceding discussion. In so doing, we consciously and clearly relegate evaluation of the quality of marriage both conceptually and operationally to the realm of subjective evaluation. At the conceptual level we accept Hawkins' (1968) definition of marital satisfaction, that is,

> the subjective feelings of happiness, satisfaction, and pleasure experienced by a spouse when considering all current aspects of his marriage. This variable is conceived of as a continuum running from much satisfaction to much dissatisfaction. Marital satisfaction is clearly an attitudinal variable and, thus, is a property of individual spouses [p. 648].

We acknowledge this variable as a one-sided summary variable, the type criticized by Gewirtz (1969) in socialization research. However, we think such variables are necessary, at present, to answer questions about the adaptive significance of social interaction.

In as much as we conceptualize the family as a system of social positions and dyads, allowing for social interaction within dyads and interchanges between dyads, marital satisfaction is a relevant variable for assessing the quality of role performances in the marital dyad.

Likewise, sibling satisfaction or parent–child satisfaction is relevant to the role performances of siblings in the sibling dyad or the role performances of parents or children in the parent–child dyad. Therefore, one approach to the evaluation of quality in families is to measure marital satisfaction. This is the approach we take in the remainder of this chapter.

II. Empirical Evidence of the Impact of Children on Marital Satisfaction

The primary focus of this chapter is to seek an answer to the question, Does the presence and the developmental level of children in a family influence the marital quality of the parents? The empirical bases for answering this question provide conclusions that are at best only suggestive. Most of the studies have used cross-sectional post hoc research designs. Typically they have compared unrandomized groups of subjects with known differences on such variables as presence or absence of children, number and spacing of children, and age of oldest child. Such studies lack control over a host of variables that might bias the results. As a consequence, a child effect might be suggested from the research when in fact some other unrecognized variable accounts for the observed variation in marital quality. Since the arrival, aging, and departure of children from the home is a family developmental phenomenon, cross-sectional research designs provide a poor basis for detecting developmental trends (Baltes, 1968; Rollins, 1975; Spanier et al., 1975). Nevertheless, in most cases these are the best data we have at this time in attempting to answer the question.

A. Transition to Parenthood

The arrival of children, especially the first child, as a stimulus for change in the marital relationship not only makes sense intuitively but has received empirical support (Christensen, 1968; Dyer, 1963; Feldman, 1971; Feldman & Rogoff, 1968; Hobbs, 1965; LeMasters, 1957; Luckey & Bain, 1970; Meyerowitz & Feldman, 1966; Rossi, 1968; Russell, 1974; Ryder, 1973). At least for many couples, the arrival of children seems to have a negative impact upon the marriage, especially for wives. However, the question still remains as to the conditions under which impact is most likely to be felt and the magnitude of the impact.

Analysis of a small number of individual cases by LeMasters (1957), using open-ended questions to gauge the felt impact of the arrival of the first child, led to the conclusion that the adjustments required were of "crisis" proportions for about 80% of the parents. Dyer (1963), in a small sample of middle-class families, found a smaller number (about 50%) of parents going through a "crisis" transition after the first child was born. However, extensive crisis was most common for those who had not planned their pregnancy. Hobbs (1965) and Hobbs & Cole (1976), using objective questions requiring a short recall time, came to the conclusion that although some disruption to the ongoing state of the marriage occurred, it was certainly not a crisis for most couples. They also found the transition more difficult for mothers than for fathers.

To avoid the methodological weakness of using recall data, Feldman and colleagues (1968, 1971) presented data from a short-term longitudinal study where data were obtained early in pregnancy and after the first child was born. Two conclusions emerged from this work. First, there was evidence of postpartum decrements in general marital satisfaction, and second, decrements were greatest among those who were highest in marital satisfaction before the child arrived. This latter conclusion seemed contrary to much of the prevailing opinion that having children might be detrimental to the marriage of couples with low marital adjustment by adding fuel to the fires of existing frustration in the marriage. Couples with high marital adjustment might be assumed to be mature enough to take the added responsibility of parenthood in stride.

A possible explanation of the Feldman and Rogoff (1968) findings is based on measurement artifacts. Only couples who were initially high had very far to drop on marital satisfaction scores (i.e., the "basement effect"). Regression toward the mean could account for the decrease, when retested, of those with initially high scores. Ryder (1973) presented longitudinal data covering the period before pregnancy through 6 to 18 months after the first child was born, suggesting such an artifact. He had a control group of childless couples who had no children during the time interval studied. The control group was used as a comparison group for those to whom an infant was born. Furthermore, after the initial testing, he identified high and low marital satisfaction couples in each group.

From his data analysis, Ryder (1973) found no difference in general marital satisfaction between those having a child and those not having a child. However, in terms of satisfaction with companionship experiences with their husbands, there was a greater decrease for wives who had an infant than for those who did not. This was true whether the wives who had an infant were initially high or low on general marital satisfaction. Ryder concluded from these data that the intrusion of the first infant into a marriage at least changes the wife's definition of satisfaction with the companionship aspect of her marriage. She apparently either perceives less companionship than before or wants even more.

Before concluding that the intrusion of parenthood is invariantly disruptive of the marital relationship, some qualifications seem appropriate. Luckey and Bain (1970) followed up two groups of married couples several years after children had arrived. One group consisted of couples where both spouses were high on marital satisfaction early in the marriage. In the other group both spouses were initially low in marital satisfaction. After several years of marriage both groups were requested to indicate sources of mutual satisfaction in their marriage. For couples in the low satisfaction group their children were the only source of mutual satisfaction indicated. Perhaps in this case children strengthened the marriage. Russell (1974) has also found that children provide a source of gratification and satisfaction as well as frustration in marriage.

After reviewing research on the effect of the presence and number of children in a family on the marital satisfaction of parents, Christensen (1968) invoked his value discrepancy hypothesis to account for the results. He concluded that the impact of children on the marriage relationship of their parents depends on whether or not the spouses planned for children and desired to have them arrive when they did. According to his hypothesis, desired children would strengthen a marriage, and undesired children would weaken it.

B. Child Density and Marital Satisfaction

If transition to parenthood has a negative impact on the marital quality of some categories of married couples, as suggested in the foregoing, does the number and spacing of children also have an impact? For several decades, attempts to find a relationship between family size and marital satisfaction have produced inconsistent results (Udry, 1966). Thus, to account for such results, Christensen (1968) formulated the value behavior discrepancy hypothesis, arguing that it is not the number of children in a family but the number of children relative to the number desired "which leaves married couples in varying states of harmony or dissonance [p. 285]."

In a study of married college students, Christensen and Philbrick (1952) found a positive relationship between the number of children ultimately desired and marital satisfaction, but a negative relationship, especially for wives, between the present number and marital satisfaction. Christensen (1968) interpreted these apparent contradictions to mean that when the ultimately desired children arrived before the couple was ready for them (i.e., pressure of school), values were violated, and dissatisfaction occurred. They also found a disproportionate number of persons with low marital satisfaction scores who (a) had unplanned children; (b) would have fewer children if starting over, or would wait until after college to have children if they could have another chance; and (c) regarded college and parenthood as producing conflicting demands.

Relative to the spacing of children, only a few studies have investigated the relationship between child density (defined as number of children in the home divided by the number of years married) and marital satisfaction. Hurley & Palonen (1967) found a negative relationship between child density and marital satisfaction. Their sample consisted of married university students. This seemed especially significant when they failed to find a significant relationship in the same sample between number of children and marital satisfaction. However, in subsequent studies with samples more representative of the population at large, Figley (1973) and Miller (1975) failed to find a relationship between child density and marital satisfaction. These results were consistent even when they considered only couples in the early stages of the family life cycle.

The impact on the marital relationship of number and spacing of children as well as the initial arrival of a child seems to depend upon specific circumstances within the family. In terms of the impact of the arrival of the first child, the number of children, and the spacing of children on the marital relationship, it is probably the desire for children in relation to present life circumstances (value behavior discrepancy hypothesis) that is the determining factor in whether or not marital satisfaction is negatively or positively affected.

C. Family Career Transitions and Marital Satisfaction

There seems to be no literature that directly focuses on the influence of developmental changes in the child on the marriage. The literature on marital satisfaction over the family career might provide some insights along this line. The family career categories are typically defined by the presence of children in the home and the age of the oldest child at transition points such as emergence from infancy, beginning school, and reaching adolescence (Duvall, 1962; Rollins & Feldman, 1970). However, such classification is not an unambiguous indicator of developmental changes in the child (even the oldest child) because it confounds age of oldest child with age of parents, length of time the parents have been married and number of children in the home. This limitation should be remembered as we discuss differences in marital satisfaction for couples in different categories of the family career.

Twelve of the earlier studies using both cross-sectional and longitudinal designs and covering either the first few or all stages of the family career were summarized by Rollins and Feldman (1970). Especially for females, the studies collectively indicated a decrease in marital satisfaction over the early stages from the "newly married couple" category through infancy and preschool years to the "oldest child in school" category. Most of the studies indicate that the most dramatic decrease is between newly married couples and couples with an infant.

This is congruent with the transition-to-parenthood literature. Beyond this initial change, the subsequent decreases might be associated with developmental changes in the oldest child. However, they might also be associated with the arrival of additional infants. There might be a cumulative effect of parents repeatedly going through adjustments to the demands of infant caregiving.

Of the 12 studies published before 1970, there were only 4 that covered the later stages of the family career. Of these 3 suggested that marital satisfaction increases over the later stages as children mature and leave home. The fourth study (Blood & Wolfe, 1960) indicated a continual decline through the later stages. However, Rollins and Cannon (1974) have demonstrated that the data in this discrepant study were obtained from a faulty measuring instrument and that corrections in the instrument as used on a new sample indicated an increase over the later stages also.

Later studies have continued to support, in most instances, the idea that marital satisfaction follows a U-shaped pattern over the family career. Rollins and Feldman (1970) found general marital satisfaction to follow such a pattern in a probability sample of middle-class families in upstate New York, as did Rollins and Cannon (1974) in a nonprobability sample of middle-class Mormons. Spanier, Lewis, and Cole (1975) found such a pattern for working-class families in Ohio. They found only a decline over the early stages in a middle-class Georgia sample and no relationship between family career categories and general marital satisfaction for middle-class families in an Iowa sample. Axelson (1960, Deutscher (1964), and Miller (1976) found an increase in satisfaction in the later stages of marriage. Other studies (Burr, 1970; Bradburn and Caplovitz, 1965; Figley, 1973, Orthner, 1975; and Smart & Smart, 1975) also lend support to the U-shaped curvilinear interpretation.

In general, the research seems to support the idea that general marital satisfaction decreases during marriage simultaneously with the arrival and development of the oldest child in the family until about adolescence, and then as children mature and leave home, it increases. The study by Spanier et al. (1975) is an exception that challenges this generalization, especially for middle-class families. Though the apparent trend mentioned above has been found fairly consistently, the implications should be tempered by the evidence from Rollins and Cannon (1974) that the U-shaped curve must be very flat in as much as only 4–8% of the variation in marital satisfaction is associated with stages of the family career. This caution seems important inasmuch as textbook writers imply that the effect is very dramatic and couples should prepare for the storm. In one study (Smart & Smart, 1975), after reviewing the literature, the authors concluded: "thus a deep U-shaped curve seems to be typical [p. 408]." This is a gross overstatement of the data.

Another qualification of the picture derived from the fairly consistent evidence of a U-shaped curvilinear relationship between marital satisfaction and transitions over the family career centers on methodological issues. Most of the empirical studies and all of the ones covering all the transition stages used cross-sectional research designs. The few longitudinal studies are consistent with cross-sectional studies pertaining to decreases in marital satisfaction over the transitions from "newly married" through the "oldest child is school age" stages.

However, neither cross-sectional nor longitudinal research designs provide a strong basis for evidence of developmental trends of marital satisfaction in terms of transitions over the career of the family (Baltes, 1968; Riley, 1973). Developmental trend interpretations from cross-sectional data might result in a "generational fallacy" in which life course differences are ignored; observed differences might be due to generation differences in self-reports of marital satisfaction (Rollins, 1975; Spanier et al., 1975). In addition, with the elimination at later transition points of those who divorce, we can assume that at each successive transition stage of the family career the reported marital satisfaction scores are an inflation for life trend interpretations (Spanier et al., 1975). Of course, this would work to depress the observed decline over the earlier transitions as well as inflating the observed increases over the later transitions.

Longitudinal data have their limitations for describing developmental trends also. In this case a "life course fallacy" of interpretation confronts us; the results ignore cohort differences (Rollins, 1975). For example, if a longitudinal study extended over a time period in which some unusual event occurred, such as the Great Depression or World War II, observed changes would likely differ greatly from cohorts studied at other points in time.

Spanier et al. (1975) raised another methodological issue concerning the basis for statistical inference for curvilinearity. Their implication is that comparisons of transition stage mean scores by analysis of variance techniques are inappropriate. They suggested two basic approaches to test for nonlinear relationships and requested that other researchers "reanalyze their data with similar appropriate methods to assess whether their data truly reflect a curvilinear, linear, or no relationship [p. 274]." We did this with the Rollins and Feldman data and the Rollins and Cannon data, using orthogonal polynominals of linear and quadratic magnitudes. In both sets of data a significant curvilinear relationship was found after controlling for any linear relationship. Therefore, at least some of the data from which the fairly consistent U-shaped curvilinear relationship have come can be used to discount the speculation by Spanier *et al.* (1975) "that the significant F tests in previous studies may be accounted for primarily by declines in marital adjustment (or satisfaction) from stages 1 to 3 [p. 271]" rather than a decline followed by a leveling off and then an increase over the later transitions.

We consider that the number of empirical studies of various populations, using different measurement instruments and different types of research designs, that obtained similar results, warrants the generalization that of those couples who remain married there is a U-shaped relationship between transition stages of the family career and reported marital satisfaction. Nevertheless, the data do not warrant a generalization that it is the presence or absence or developmental level of children that affects the marital satisfaction. Too many other uncontrolled variables such as ages of husband and wife, number of years married, and stage in the occupational career of the husband (and wife) are highly correlated with child-referenced transitions over the family career. The data are, however, congruent with the notion that the presence of dependent children in the home put a "crunch" on the time, energy, and economic resources of parents and result in a decrease in the marital satisfaction of the parents.

Satisfaction with companionship with spouse might provide the best insight into the possible impact of the developing child on the marital quality. At least in the United States, companionship with spouse, especially from the standpoint of the wife, has been observed to decrease with the arrival of the infant (Feldman & Rogoff, 1968; Ryder, 1973). Companionship with spouse is highly valued in the United States as a goal of marriage (Blood and Wolfe, 1960). Rollins and Feldman (1970) found a decline in the frequency of positive companionship experiences from marriage through the preschool stage, then a leveling off over the remainder of the family career. The difference was most dramatic between the newly married and those with an infant. This finding supports the transition-to-parenthood literature. Rollins and Cannon (1974) found a similar pattern for satisfaction with companionship, except that they found an increase over the later stages similar to that found for general marital satisfaction. Additional analysis of the Rollins and Cannon data indicated that frequency of companionship, followed the U-shaped curve over the career of marriage. Similar results have been found by Miller (1976) and Orthner (1975).

Orthner (1975) specifically investigated the relationship between the amount of "joint leisure time activities" of husband and wife and their marital satisfactions across transition stages of the family career. It was only for "newly married" couples and those married 18 to 23 years (oldest child would probably be a teen-ager or would have left home) that a relationship was found between the amount of joint leisure activities and marital satisfaction. However, it should be noted that all marital companionship would be "joint" activity for those without children, whereas for those with children in the home, companionship needs might be met during common family activity and not just when husband and wife are isolated from the family in joint activity.

Miller's (1976) data analysis also provided some important additional insights relevant to companionship in marriage and marital satisfaction. In a path analysis he found that companionship is an intervening variable between family social status, length of time married, family size, and marital satisfaction. He also found an interaction effect between number of children and companionship as they relate to marital satisfaction. When companionship was high, there was a positive correlation between number of children and marital satisfaction. However, when companionship was low, the relationship was negative. Miller (1976) concluded from his data analysis that "for couples who share many companionate activities, having children and marital satisfaction went together [p. 651]." Perhaps it is marital companionship embedded in family companionship rather than joint leisure activity that correlates with marital satisfaction during periods of the family career when dependent children are in the home.

What conclusions can we draw about the presence and developmental level of a child on the marital quality of the child's parents? The data suggest that in general there is a decrease in both companionship and marital satisfaction as families make transitions into career stages where dependent children are present in the home. Both variables increase as children mature and leave home.

Two further questions seem important to ask at this point. First, are the phenomena just described fairly common, or are they unique to only a small percentage of families? Second, can the observed changes be attributed to children, or might length of marriage or other uncontrolled variables account for them?

First, since most of the research has used a cross-sectional research design, we don't know if many couples follow the pattern suggested in the preceding. Since only a small percentage of variation in marital satisfaction is systematically associated with transition through the family career, we suspect that only a small percentage of married couples actually follow this pattern. If there is no systematic pattern for the majority of couples, averaging scores of all couples in a stage, in a cross-sectional design, might suggest a systematic pattern for all when it applies to only a few.

The second question also does not have an unequivocal answer. Again from cross-sectional research designs and with lack of control over other possible independent variables, this question cannot be answered with much confidence. The transition-to-parenthood literature suggests that it is the child's presence rather than duration of marriage that is the stimulus for the observed pattern of change. Also, research by Feldman (1965), involving a control group of childless couples who had been married as long as the child-bearing couples, indicated that in terms of communication, companionship, methods of handling conflict, and marital satisfaction, the control group was much more like newly married couples than like those with an infant or a preschool-age child. These data suggest that it is the child rather than length of marriage that instigates changes in marital quality.

Theoretical reasons, more than the evidence provided by the empirical data reviewed earlier, have the most influence on our judgment that children do have an impact on their parents' marriage. We propose a family career transitions (developmental) theory of marital roles strain and marital satisfaction that will account for the correlations observed in our literature review. The theory suggests the circumstances under which children do or do not have an impact on the quality of their parents' marriage.

III. A Theory of Family Career Transitions and Marital Satisfaction

Two theoretical developments provide a basis for the specification of a theory of family career transitions and marital satisfaction. One of these is a theoretical framework conceptualizing the family as a transitional system of family roles (in the Fredrick Bates tradition) by Rodgers (1964) and Nye and Berardo (1973). The other attempts to formulate a theory of the antecedents of marital satisfaction by Burr (1973) and Miller (1976) according to the symbolic interaction tradition. We rely upon both of these theoretical developments along with our review of the empirical literature on the impact of children on marital satisfaction to formulate our theory of family career transitions and marital satisfaction.

A. The Family as a Transitional System of Social Positions and Roles

Our conceptualization of the family as a system of roles comes primarily from Rodgers (1964) and Nye and Berardo (1973). We define the family as a semiclosed system of interacting persons varying in age and sex, whose interaction is organized in terms of interrelated social positions (dyads) with norms and roles defined by both the society and the interacting persons as unique to that system.

1. Social Position

A social position is the defining location of an actor in the structure of a family system. It includes clusters of more or less integrated sets of roles, with at least one cluster for each dyadic relationship in the family. The full complement of social positions in the contemporary American nuclear family includes husband–father, wife–mother, son–brother, and sister–daughter. For example, in the husband–father position, the classes of dyadic relationships implied are husband–wife, father–son, and father–daughter. One or more sets of roles exists for a husband–father for each of these dyadic relationships.

2. Social Role

A social role is a more or less integrated set of social norms. Each role in a family is paired with a reciprocal role of another social position in the family. For example, the sexual role of husband is paired with the sexual role of the wife in the husband–wife dyad such that the norms about the wife's rights and privileges are reciprocally linked to the norms about the husband's obligations and responsibilities, and vice versa. Furthermore, at least one of the social roles of each social position in a family is linked reciprocally to at least one role in each of the other social positions in that family. These reciprocally linked roles provide the structural basis for dyadic relationships in families.

3. Social Norms

Social norms are commonly shared behavioral expectations. In terms of dyadic relationships in families they are reciprocally linked rights, obligations, privileges, and responsibilities to which sanctions are expected in response to approved or disapproved role behavior. Therefore, norms constitute role expectations.

4. Role Enactment

As a behavioral counterpart to social role, role enactment is a social response in a dyadic relationship in a family that can be evaluated in terms of the normative expectations of and for the role participants.

5. Roles Accumulation

Roles accumulation refers to the total number of roles in a person's social position in a family and their associated norms. Thus, it includes the total number of prescribed activities that an actor in a social position is expected to perform.

6. Role Transition

The social roles attached to the social positions in a family change frequently. Either the norms within a role change so that role expectations are adjusted from time to time or roles are added or deleted from a family social position. For example, until the first child arrives in the family, a wife–mother does not have a child caregiver role. After these roles emerge, they are continually modified by the age, sex, and number of children. When children have grown up and left home, the child caregiver role or roles become practically eliminated.

7. Family Career Transition

Inasmuch as roles in one social position in a family are reciprocally linked with roles in other social positions, role transitions within the family operate in a tandum manner so that some of the norms in two or more social positions are simultaneously changing. Major changes in social positions in the family seem to be associated with the presence·or absence and developmental level of children. The plotting of changes over time in the life history of an individual family identifies a profile of family career transitions. Major transitions, common to most families, based primarily on the age of the oldest child, have been identified by Duvall (1962) and Rodgers (1962). Eight transition stages of the family career typically used in empirical studies (Duvall, 1962; Rollins & Feldman, 1970) include (I) newly married; (II) oldest child an infant; (III) oldest child of preschool age; (IV) oldest child of school age; (V) oldest child a teenager; (VI) one or more children gone from home; (VII) all children gone from home; (VIII) husband retired.

8. Roles Strain

Roles strain is an intrapersonal phenomenon. In terms of the family, it refers to the degree of felt difficulty experienced by the occupant of a social position (i.e., husband–father) in measuring up to the obligations and demands in the role expectations for the roles in that position. It refers to stress within a person who perceives that he or she either cannot measure up or has difficulty measuring up to their expectations for their roles.

9. Perceived Quality of Role Enactment of Salient Roles

Whereas roles strain refers to intrapersonal stress from felt difficulty in performing one's own roles, the enactment or behavior performance of important roles by either self or other in an interacting dyad are evaluated by the participants in terms of each participant's norms (role expectations). For example, the husband evaluates the quality of his own behavior in marital roles in terms of his own norms for role behaviors he thinks are important. In a like manner, he evaluates the quality of his wife's behavior in her marital roles.

Families will vary considerably in terms of structural complexity. This is so primarily because of cultural differences, age and sex composition, and quantity of family members (see Rodgers, 1964, for detailed conceptualization of this idea). The reciprocal roles in a single family dyad can vary from being few and homogeneous (simple) to many and highly differentiated (complex). When variability associated with accumulation of roles in a single dyadic relationship is added to the variability in reciprocal roles introduced by the number of types of social positions in a family and the number of family members in each type, extensive variation in structural and evaluative dimensions of families is possible.

Our conceptualization of the family as a system of roles provides a basis for comparisons between families at particular points in their family careers in terms of structural and/or behavioral differences. Such comparisons would include differences associated with family size, presence of both versus one parent, and sex and age of children. It also provides a basis for comparisons within a family in terms of developmental changes over the life career of given families.

B. A Symbolic-Interaction Theory of Marital Satisfaction

From a general theory of satisfaction in a social situation, Burr, Leigh, Day & Constantine (in press) derived a specific theory of marital satisfaction. They identified as antecedents to marital satisfaction four variables that function in an additive manner to influence the level of marital satisfaction of a marriage partner. They are (a) perceived quality of role enactment of salient marital roles by self; (b) perceived quality of role enactment of salient marital roles by spouse; (c) perceived consensus with spouse about role expectations for salient marital roles; (d) perceived relative deprivation in the enactment of marital roles by self.

The first three variables in the preceding list were defined earlier. Perceived relative deprivation in the performance of marital roles refers to an individual's evaluation of the social profit (social rewards minus social costs) obtained in the performance of his or her marital roles compared to the social profit obtained by reference group friends who occupy a similar social position.

1. Perceived Quality of Role Enactments

From a symbolic-interaction theoretical framework many empirical studies have supported the theoretical proposition that *the perceived quality of role enactment of salient marital roles influences the marital satisfaction of the perceiving spouse, and this is a positive, linear relationship*. Some of the studies investigated the relationship between perceived quality of roles enactments of spouse and marital satisfaction (Burr, 1971; Brinley, 1975; Hawkins & Johnson, 1959; Hurvitz, 1960, 1965; Nye & McLaughlin, 1974; Ort, 1950). Others studied the relationship in terms of roles enactments of self (Brinley, 1975; Kotlar, 1965; Luckey, 1960; Nye and McLaughlin, 1974). These studies were consistent in finding positive, zero order correlations ranging from .50 to .85. Ort (1950) and Burr (1971) obtained supporting evidence that the relationship was linear. Nye and McLaughlin (1974) and Brinley (1975) found that perceived quality of roles enactments of spouse were more highly correlated with marital satisfaction of self than was perceived quality of roles enactments of self. Therefore, we will keep perceived quality of roles enactment of spouse and self as separate variables in our theoretical model.

2. Perceived Consensus with Spouse about Role Expectations

Consensus among interacting participants about objects and meanings of objects relevant to their interaction has been attributed to the status of an independent variable in much sociological and sociopsychological research. Rollins (1961) found that perceived consensus with spouse on salient marital values had a positive correlation with own marital satisfaction. However, there was no correlation between "objective" consensus of the spouses and marital satisfaction of either, nor was perceived consensus by one spouse correlated with the marital satisfaction of the other. This is what one would expect from a symbolic-interaction theoretical position. The positive, linear relationship proposed by Burr, *et al.* (in press) between perceived consensus with spouse about role expectations for salient marital roles and marital satisfaction also seems to be a special case of a theoretical proposition in balance theory, that is, that we like or feel positive about our relationship with those we think are in agreement with us on important and relevant issues (Heider, 1958; Newcomb, 1961).

A specific test of the preceding theoretical proposition of Burr was made by Hawkins and Johnsen (1969). They found a high, bivariate zero order correlation of .73. This empirical support, along with the congruence of the hypothesis and several social psychological theories, lends credence to the proposition. However, we think the general theoretical proposition just stated concerning perceived quality of role enactments and marital satisfaction makes the consensus–satisfaction proposition unnecessary. Our decision is influenced mainly by the idea that it is through the symbolic-interaction process of "taking the role of the other" that a perception of similarities or differences in the role expectations of self and others emerges. Through interaction, the perception gets modified by the behavior of the other. If the role enactments of the other are repeatedly discrepant with the role expectations imputed to them, then over time the expectations imputed to the other will change. The changes will be in the direction of congruence with the observed behavior of other. Thus, the degree of perceived consensus with other and the degree of conformity–discrepancy between role expectations and perceived role enactments would be highly correlated.

We have defined the perceived quality of role enactments of spouse as the degree of conformity–discrepancy between role expectations for spouse and perceived role enactments by spouse. If perceived consensus with spouse on salient marital roles is a function, over time, of the perceived quality of the role enactments of the spouse, and if both variables correlate with marital satisfaction for self, then the consensus–satisfaction relationship is a spurious one. This was so argued by Hawkins and Johnsen (1969).

Hawkins and Johnsen (1969) found perceived roles consensus highly correlated ($r = .73$) with marital satisfaction as did perceived quality of roles enactments ($r = .85$). Also, the relationship between perceived consensus and perceived quality was reported as "high, but not perfect [p. 510]." They obtained a partial correlation of only .06 between perceived consensus and marital satisfaction when controlling for perceived quality of role enactments. Compared to the initial bivariate zero order correlation of .72, this is a substantial drop. We agree with Hawkins and Johnsen (1969) that the consensus–satisfaction relationship is most likely spurious. Thus, we think perceived consensus is a redundant variable to include in our theoretical model of antecedents of marital satisfaction, and we do not include it.

3. Perceived Relative Deprivation

Symbolic-interaction theory suggests that the definition of a situation is in part a function of reference group comparisons. The idea is that evaluation of satisfaction with a situation is partly a function of how well-off one defines his or her own situation relative to significant others in the reference group. Though we are unaware of any explicit tests in the family literature to support the theoretical proposition, we include in our theoretical model Burr's proposition that *the greater the relative deprivation in a marriage relationship, the less one's satisfaction with the marriage*.

In summary, we have proposed so far that three variables—perceived quality of role enactments of salient marital roles by self, perceived quality of role enactments of salient marital roles by spouse, and perceived relative deprivation for self in the performance of salient marital roles—have a functional relationship with marital satisfaction (see Figure 4.2). We postulate that the presence, number, and ages of children in a home indirectly influence marital satisfaction by the impact of parent–child interaction on these three variables.

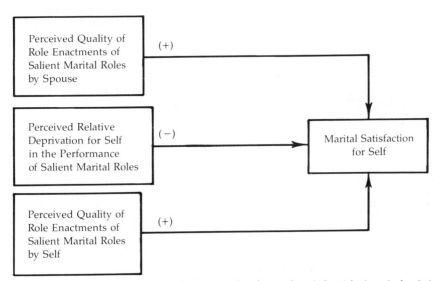

FIGURE 4.2. *A model of a symbolic-interaction theory of marital satisfaction. A plus (+) refers to a positive linear relationship, and a minus (-) refers to a negative linear relationship.*

C. Roles Strain and Marital Satisfaction

Building on the theoretical work of Burr (1973), Rollins and Cannon (1974) suggested that the accumulation of family roles varies with transitional stages of the family career, being greatest when dependent children are in the home. They used this idea to account for the relationship between family career transitions and marital satisfaction. The chain of logic was that as family roles for adults in the family increased, each spouse was more likely to experience roles strain. As roles strain increased for one spouse, his or her enactment of roles would be hampered, and the other spouse would experience a more negative evaluation of the partner's role enactments, thus becoming more dissatisfied with the marriage. Miller's (1976) interpretation of his data supported the Rollins and Cannon model. However, the most explicit theoretical statement of the connecting links between roles accumulation and roles strain, between role strain and evaluation of quality of role enactments, and between evaluation of quality of role enactments and marital satisfaction, is in the recent work of Burr et al. (in press).

1. Roles Strain and Perceived Quality of Role Enactments

Burr et al. (in press) hypothesize that as people's roles strains increase, they engage in activities to eliminate the strain. However, if the strain persists, it eventually influences a person's role enactments and thus one's perception of the quality of his or her own role enactments. This suggests a time lag between the buildup of roles strain and decreases in the perceived quality of role enactments. As applied to the marital dyad, the theoretical proposition from Burr et al. is the greater the family roles strain of a married person, the lower the perceived quality of their salient marital role enactments, and this is probably a curvilinear relationship that has a time lag.

Inasmuch as one's perception of the quality of both one's own and his or her spouse's salient marital roles are hypothesized to influence one's marital satisfaction, the roles strain of both spouses must be considered in studying the marital satisfaction of either one (see Figure 4.3). We assume, as did Rollins and Cannon (1974) that one spouse's roles strain will influence his or her role enactments, and changes in role enactments will influence both one's own and one's spouse's perceptions of the quality of such role enactments.

Also, roles strain will most likely have a positive, linear relationship, with one's perception of the quality of his or her spouse's role enactments of salient marital roles independent of the spouse's roles strain. Though family roles strain will be related to the perceived quality

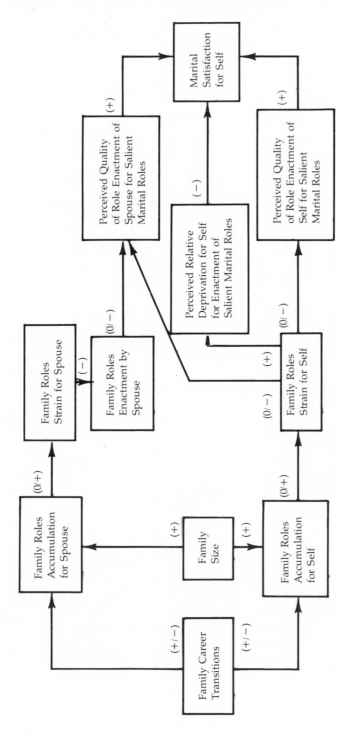

FIGURE 4.3. A symbolic-interaction theoretical model of family career transitions and marital satisfaction. A plus (+) refers to a positive relationship, a minus (−) refers to a negative relationship, and a zero (0) refers to no relationship. A slash mark (/) refers to a change in the slope of a curvilinear relationship.

of the role enactments of all salient family roles, it is only the salient marital roles that we expect to influence marital satisfaction. In addition to the explanation of Burr *et al.* (in press) for the curvilinear relationship between roles strain and perceived quality of role enactments, we think that when roles strain exists, the most salient roles will receive priority attention, and this should also result in a time lag before roles strain affects the salient roles.

2. *Roles Strain and Relative Deprivation*

We suggest another connection between one's own family roles strain and one's marital satisfaction. As roles strain increases, a person is likely to experience many negative attitudes, one of which might be relative self-deprivation in the enactment of marital roles. We propose that *the greater the family roles strain of a married person, the greater the relative deprivation for enactment of marital roles, and this is a positive, linear relationship*.

In summary, our symbolic-interaction theory of family roles strain and quality of family relationships has focused on marital satisfaction as an index of family quality. This was so because we linked family roles strain for the husband–father and the wife–mother to marital satisfaction through perceived quality of role enactments of salient marital roles for self and spouse and through perceived relative deprivation for self in the performance of marital roles. If our interest had been on parental satisfaction as an index of the quality of family relations rather than marital satisfaction, we would have substituted salient parent and child roles for marital roles in the theoretical model.

D. Roles Accumulation and Marital Satisfaction

The construct labeled roles strain is the central concept in our symbolic-interaction theory of marital satisfaction. It comes primarily from the conceptualization of social interaction processes by Goode (1960). We limit roles strain in our theory to the felt difficulty in fulfilling family role obligations irrespective of nonfamily roles. This is because we are interested in marital satisfaction as an outcome of dyadic interactions within the family. If we were interested in the impact of social interactions from social relationships outside the family on marital satisfaction, we would still use roles strain as a central concept and would look for sources of roles strain in nonfamily roles as well.

Since we have already indicated the consequences of roles strain for marital satisfaction in the previous section, we will now attempt to link roles strain to children as an antecedent condition. Family roles accumulation refers to the total rights and obligations of roles in a social position in the family. Obligations especially imply prescribed activities. In conceptualizing the family as a set of contingent roles, we emphasized that in each dyadic relationship in a family some of the norms for a role were reciprocal to norms for a role in another social position. Inasmuch as there might be only one child in a family or several children of different ages, including both sexes, the norms for the socialization role of a father can vary extensively in terms of the amount of activity prescribed. Therefore, not only do roles vary in number but they also vary in amount of activity that is prescribed within a role. Thus, role accumulation includes the total number of prescribed activities an actor is expected to perform.

As the magnitude of prescribed activity of a social actor increases, ultimately a roles overload is likely to occur. It is in this area of possible role overload that Goode (1960) indicated role strain is likely to emerge. Burr *et al.* (in press) has made Goode's theoretical proposition explicit as follows: "The more activity that individuals believe is prescribed for them, the greater is their role strain, and this is a curvilinear relationship [p. 100]."

Sieber (1974) argued that since roles have norms about rights as well as obligations, role accumulation would not lead to strain as long as the rights accumulate as fast as or faster than the obligations. However, time is a finite entity, and an overload in obligations with time demands is likely to reach a point where time conflicts force an actor to honor some role demands at the expense of neglecting others. It is doubtful that many of the rights received in a role enactment will buy off time demands. Therefore, we agree with Goode (1960) and Burr *et al.* (in press) that role strain tends to increase with increasing roles accumulation. However, Sieber (1974) has sensitized us to look for mechanisms that might hold role strain in check. We will suggest several contingent variables that mediate the effects of accumulation.

Our basic proposition is that *the greater the perceived roles accumulation of family roles by a married person, the greater their family roles strain, and this is a curvilinear relationship with a time lag*. The reason we suggest a time lag before roles accumulation results in roles strain is because of the suggestion by Burr *et al.* (in press), Goode (1960), and Sieber (1974) that many mechanisms are used to try to avoid role strain. Also, we expect that less salient roles would be the first to be ignored in a time crunch, and we also expect that ignoring them would less likely produce role strain.

A catalog of family roles for adult members of the nuclear family has been established by Nye and Berardo (1973). They include (*a*) the provider role; (b) the socialization of children role; (c) the child care giver role; (d) the housekeeper role; (e) the sexual role; (f) the therapeutic role; and (g) the recreational role.

The last two roles focus on companionship, which is highly valued in contemporary American society (Blood & Wolfe, 1960). All of the roles except socialization of children and child care giving have normative expectations for the marital dyad, and all except the sexual role have normative expectations for the parent–child dyad.

For either the wife–mother or the husband–father, we think that roles accumulation for families in general is greatest at the school age and teenage stages of the family career. The peak might be earlier for families with only one or two children. However, with increased numbers of children, there is a greater chance of variation in ages and sex of children. This probably brings role demands to a peak just before older children start leaving home. Wilensky (1961) refers to the preschool stage of the family career as a "life cycle bind," in which mothers, especially with large families, are too burdened with housekeeper, child care giving, and child socialization roles to be able to share with the father in the provider role. At the same time the father is described as under tremendous pressure to supply the necessary family income. In order to meet the demands of the provider role, he resorts to "moonlighting." These particular roles for both parents demand extensive amounts of time and compete for this limited resource with the companionship oriented roles in either the parent–child or the marital dyads.

Whereas Wilensky (1961) identifies the preschool stage as a "financial crunch," Harry (1976) suggests that it is the school-age stage when the "time crunch" occurs in the family career. Supporting data were found by Rollins (1967). At the school-age stage not only were husband–fathers spending more time in the provider role than at other stages but they were also more likely to express feelings of inability to meet the demands of their other family roles. The time commitments of parents to school-age children are so demanding that Harry (1976) found fathers with young children and school-age children seeking very little personal happiness in nonroutine, extrafamilial events. Because of the constraint of school-age children on the parents' time, Harry (1976) contends that "the time-commitments of school-age children require that parents adapt their own schedules to them. For instance, parents must avoid commitments which conflict with those occasions on which preteen children must be portaged to various places [p. 293]."

Almost by definition, but with the preceding supporting evidence, we conclude that family roles accumulation is greatest at stages of the family career when dependent children are in the home. We propose that *family career transitions influence the roles accumulation of adult family members, and the relationship is in the form of an inverted U-shaped curve.* Such a relationship would probably be magnified in large families or when children have special needs because of some physical or mental handicap. It would probably also be magnified in a single-parent family, even though spouse-oriented roles are absent.

In summary, our theory proposes that the roles accumulation of husband-fathers and wife-mothers varies with transitions over the family career and influences role strain, which indirectly influences the marital satisfaction of these adults. This theory is congruent, with the empirical generalization that marital satisfaction for couples who remain married over the transitions of the family career follows the shape of an inverted U-shaped curve. However, the findings of Spanier *et al.* (1975) and the small amount of variance accounted for by Rollins and Cannon (1974) suggest that we identify contingencies in which such a relationship will not exist. In the next section we suggest some possible conditions that might act as depressors on roles strain generated by roles accumulation.

E. Contingencies for the Roles Accumulation–Roles Strain Hypothesis

Burr *et al.* (in press) suggested a contingency for the relationship between roles accumulation and roles strain. The contingency condition was the amount of rewards received for enactment of roles. In terms of family roles, it is primarily parental roles of child caregiving, child socialization, provider, and housekeeper that produce the overburden from dependent children in the family. If children are highly valued as a reason for marriage in the first place, then parents are more likely to get reward from the enactment of these parental roles. These rewards, we propose, would insulate the parents from at least some of the role strain generated. This idea seems congruent with Christensen's (1968) value behavior discrepancy hypothesis. It would partially explain why the arrival of unwanted children increases marital dissatisfaction more than the arrival of wanted children. It would also partially account for the inconsistent findings regarding family size and marital satisfaction. If parents valued a large family and received reward for enactment of parental roles, then the family roles strain generating effects of roles accumulation would be weakened.

Another possible contingent variable is family roles delegation. If some of the prescribed activities in parental roles can be delegated to others, then it seems logical to us that the effects of roles accumulation would be weakened. Especially with the economic resources of higher social status families, domestic help could be acquired for housekeeper and child care giver activities, thus weakening the demands of family roles accumulation. Also, in high social status families it would be less necessary for the father to "moonlight" to meet basic financial needs of the family. In essence, roles delegation provides a broader basis for sharing the prescribed activities and would likely reduce to some extent the time crunch experienced at the school-age child stage of the family career.

Related to family roles delegation is the ability of the parents to manage the enactment of family roles. Such personal resources, along with financial resources, should help to prevent strain through the management of time, energy, and money. In general, we would expect that fathers and mothers with higher family social status would, through education and the use of consultants, have greater personal resources.

A final contingent variable that we suggest is family roles integration. At the abstract level, family roles integration refers to the ability to combine the prescribed role activity of two or more roles into a behavior performance at one time and place. This is primarily a management technique to reduce overburden of roles accumulation. However, we specifically highlight it with regard to the companionship aspects of the therapeutic and recreational roles. The recreational roles especially provide a possibility for roles integration in the marital and parent–child dyads.

Several studies of marital companionship and the family career transitions provide us with information that helps to convince us that roles integration weakens the strain-inducing effects of roles accumulation. As indicated earlier, some studies have found a curvilinear relationship between marital companionship and family career transition. Miller (1976) also found positive linear relationships between marital companionship and marital satisfaction and between family social status and marital companionship. This would suggest that some families might avoid a decline in marital satisfaction at the dependent child stages if marital companionship is maintained at a high level, and this is more likely for those with higher family social status.

The foregoing idea, however, appears not to be supported by the research of Orthner (1975). In family career stages in which dependent children were in the home, he found no relationship between "joint" leisure activity of husband and wife and marital satisfaction, though such a relationship existed where dependent children were absent.

Perhaps much joint leisure is too costly in terms of overburdening role obligations when dependent children are in the home and add to family roles strain. However, if the marital couple combined at least part of their joint leisure with other family recreational activity, then the overburden might be reduced. In terms of the leisure activities of the husband–father, Harry (1976) concluded from his data on sources of happiness that during the dependent child stages of the family career "the family so dominates the husband's activities and interest that it becomes the central institution around which other activities are planned. Friends are friends of the family and leisure activities are family leisure activities [p. 294]." He argues that at this stage of the family career the husband–father is likely to experience unhappiness unless he can integrate family activities with the activities of other institutions.

The integration of family companionship roles would seem to be enhanced if parents were to have positive values about having and rearing children. Perhaps the reason Miller (1976) found a positive relationship between family size and marital satisfaction when marital companionship was high is that the high marital companionship was embedded in family companionship, and the strain-inducing effects of the overload of prescribed role activity was weakened by family roles integration. Miller (1976) suggested such an interpretation as follows: "Possibly those who had high companionship, more children than average, and high marital satisfaction were primarily oriented to the roles of spouse *and* parent, and found meaning and satisfaction in these joint activities [p. 651]." Those couples with higher family social status would have more financial resources to use to support family recreation in such role integration.

In summary, we have identified four possible contingent variables that would weaken the proposed relationship between family roles accumulation and family roles strain for the husband–father or the wife–mother (see Figure 4.4). Since three of these variables seem to be influenced by family social status, our theoretical model not only accounts for the often found U-shaped relationship between marital satisfaction and family career transition but the deviant finding by Spanier *et al.* (1975) as well. They found the typical relationship for a working-class sample but not for a middle-class sample. Such findings are congruent with our theory.

Perhaps the reason that such a small percentage of the variation in marital satisfaction over the family career was found by Rollins and Cannon (1974) is because they used primarily middle-class subjects. Our theory would suggest that substantial roles accumulation overload

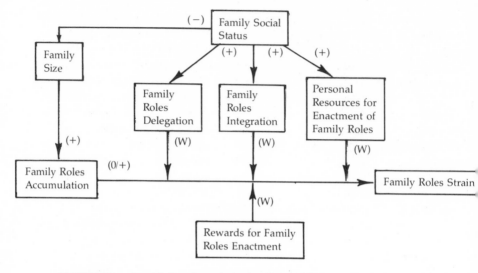

FIGURE 4.4. *A model of contingencies for the relationship between roles accumulation and roles strain. A plus (+) refers to a positive relationship, a minus (-) to a negative relationship, and a zero (0) to no relationship. A slash mark (/) refers to a change in the slope of a curvilinear relationship. A (W) refers to a weakening of a relationship.*

without depressor contingent conditions are necessary before increases in roles accumulation results in roles strain and thus affects the level of marital satisfaction.

F. Conclusions and Recommendations

The theory of family career transitions and marital satisfaction just presented was developed from other middle-range theories and scattered bits of empirical data that were not directly focused on the theoretical propositions that emerged. Therefore, much empirical work is necessary to validate and refine the theory. We suggest two basic approaches to accomplish this. One is the use of sequential, short, longitudinal designs, as suggested in other chapters in this volume, to describe and evaluate developmental phenomena. Designs appropriate for such research have been detailed by Baltes (1968). The other approach we suggest is to use computer simulation to test and refine the model.

With a sequential, short, longitudinal design, different cohorts could be studied over two or more overlapping family career role transitions. With such a design, within-cohort trends could be compared with between-cohort trends for evidence of congruence in the descriptive interpretation of a systematic pattern of change over stages of the family career. At the same time, a within-cohort comparison of those in a stage at a normative length of marriage with those in the stage later in the duration of their marriage would provide evidence as to whether or not the developmental level of the oldest child rather than length of marriage accounts for observed trends. Also, we think future research should proceed out of a developmental model such as the one we present in this chapter, rather than out of the mere exploration of whether any life career trends are visible. The work of Miller (1976), operating out of such a model, provided us with clues as to when and under what conditions roles accumulation associated with family career transitions will or will not result in increased roles strain.

We propose that in addition to sequential, short, longitudinal research, simulation be employed as a method for testing and refining the model. Simulation is the mirroring or modeling of reality. It can be very useful in the middle stage of theory development. The method allows a way to translate a set of ideas into a system of action. The concepts can be embedded in the rules and equations of the simulation and the proposed relationships studied (Boocock & Schild, 1968). The results from the simulation are compared to reality, forming a check on the adequacy of the theoretical model to explain the relationships studied. The comparison of simulation outcome with reality is then utilized in revision of the theoretical model.

Our theoretical model proposes that the impacts of relative deprivation or perceived quality of enactments of salient marital roles on marital satisfaction are immediate. However, there are two distinct time effects in the dynamic antecedents to the perceptions of quality of role enactments.

One time effect is the variation in the number of prescribed role activities over the course of the family career. The impact of both roles accumulation and the depressor effects on the roles accumulation relationship to roles strain change as a function of this variation. Computer simulation allows us to conceptualize this variation as either a continuous or a discontinuous function of time in the family career.

The second time effect is the proposed time lag between heightened roles strain and a perception of a decrease in the quality of roles enactment. Time refers here to the elapsed time since roles strain was greater than zero. By simulating variations in both the magnitude of roles strain and the elapsed time, we can develop an understanding of the possible boundary values for these parameters of the indirect effects of roles strain on marital satisfaction.

The computer simulation cannot be accepted as proof of the existence or functioning of the relationships in our proposed model. However, the results of the simulation in comparison with self-reports from individual families provide a basis for changing the proposed relationships in the model as well as research hypotheses for testing in experiments or survey studies.

References

Axelson, F. J. Personal adjustment in the postparental period. *Marriage and Family Living*, 1960, *22*, 66–68.

Baldwin, A. P. Differences in parent behavior toward three- and nine-year-old children. *Journal of Personality*, 1946, *15*, 143–165.

Baltes, P. B. Longitudinal and cross-sectional sequences in the study of age and generational effects. *Human Development*, 1968, *11*, 145–171.

Baumrind, D. Child care practices anteceding three patterns of preschool behavior. *Genetic Psychology Monographs*, 1967, *75*, 43–88.

Bell, R. Q. A reinterpretation of the direction of effects in studies of socialization. *Psychological Review*, 1968, *75*, 81–95.

Blood, R. O. & Wolfe, D. M. *Husbands and wives: The dynamics of married living*. Glencol, Illinois: Free Press, 1960.

Boocock, S. S. & Schild, E. O. *Simulation games in learning*. Beverly Hills, California: Sage Publications, Inc., 1968.

Bradburn, N. M. & Caplovitz, D. *Reports on happiness*. Chicago: Oldine, 1965.

Brinley, D. Role competence and marital satisfaction. Unpublished Ph.D. dissertation, Brigham Young University, 1975.

Burr, W. R. Marital satisfaction: A conceptual reformulation, theory and partial test of the theory. Unpublished Ph.D. dissertation, University of Minnesota, 1967.

Burr, W. R. Satisfaction with various aspects of marriage over the life cycle: A random middle class sample. *Journal of Marriage and the Family*, 1970, *32*, 29–37.

Burr, W. R. An expansion and test of a role theory of marital satisfaction. *Journal of Marriage and the Family*, 1971, *33*, 368–372.

Burr, W. R. *Theory construction and the sociology of the family*. New York: Wiley, 1973.

Burr, W. R., Leigh, G., Day, R., & Constantine, J. Symbolic interaction and the family. In W. R. Burr, R. Hill, F. I. Nye, & I. Reiss (Eds.), *Theories about the family*. (Vol. II) New York: Free Press, in press.

Christensen, H. T. Children in the family: Relationship of number and spacing to marital success. *Journal of Marriage and the Family*, 1968, *30*, 283–289.

Christensen, H. T. & Philbrick, R. E. Family size as a factor in the marital adjustments of college couples. *American Sociological Review*, 1952, *17*, 306–312.

Deutscher, I. The quality of postparental life. *Journal of Marriage and the Family*, 1964, *26*, 52–60.

Duvall, E. M. *Family development*. 2nd edition. New York: Lippincott, 1962.

Dyer, E. D. Parenthood as crisis: A re-study. *Marriage and Family Living*, 1963, *25*, 196–201.

Emde, R. N., Gaensbauer, T. J., & Harmon, R. J. Emotional expression in infancy: A biobehavioral study. New York: International Universities Press, 1976.

Feldman, H. Development of the husband-wife relationship. Report of research to National Institute of Mental Health, 1965.

Feldman, H. The effects of children on the family. In A. Michell (Ed.), *Family issues of employed women in Europe and America*. Leiden: Brill, 1971.

Feldman, H., & Rogoff, M. Correlates of changes in marital satisfaction with the birth of the first child. Paper presented at the American Psychological Association Annual Meeting, San Francisco, 1968.

Figley, C. R. Child density and the marital relationship. *Journal of Marriage and the Family*, 1973, *35*, 272–282.

Gewirtz, J. L. Mechanisms of social learning. In D. A. Goslin (Ed.), *Handbook of socialization theory and research*. Chicago: Rand McNally, 1969.

Gewirtz, J. L., & Boyd, E. F. Experiments on mother–infant interaction underlying mutual attachment acquisition: The infant conditions the mother. In T. Alloway, L. Kranes and P. Pliner (Eds.), *Attachment behavior: Advances in the study of communication and affect*. Vol. 3. New York: Plenum Press, 1976.

Goode, W. J. A theory of role strain. *American Sociological Review*, 1960, *25*, 488–496.

Harper, L. V. The scope of offspring effects: From care giver to culture. *Psychological Bulletin*, 1975, *82*, 784–801.

Harry, J. Evolving sources of happiness for men over the life cycle: A structural analysis. *Journal of Marriage and the Family*, 1976, *38*, 289–296.

Hawkins, J. L. Associations between, companionship, hostility, and marital satisfaction. *Journal of Marriage and the Family*, 1968, *30*, 647–650.

Hawkins, J. L., & Johnsen, K. Perceptions of behavioral conformity, imputation of consensus, and marital satisfaction. *Journal of Marriage and the Family*, 1969, *31*, 507–511.

Heider, F. The psychology of interpersonal relations. New York: Wiley, 1958.

Hobbs, D. F. Parenthood as crisis: A third study. *Journal of Marriage and the Family*, 1965, *27*, 367–372.

Hobbs, D. F., & Cole, S. P. Transition to parenthood: A decade replication. *Journal of Marriage and the Family*, 1976, *38*, 723–732.

Hurley, J. R. & Palonen, D. Marital satisfaction and child density among university student parents. *Journal of Marriage and the Family*, 1967, *29*, 483–484.

Hurvitz, N. The meausrement of marital strain. *American Journal of Sociology*, 1960, *65*, 610–615.

Hurvitz, N. Control roles, marital strain, role deviation, and marital adjustment. *Journal of Marriage and the Family*, 1965, *27*, 29–31.

Kotlar, S. L. Middle-class marital role perceptions and marital adjustment. *Sociology and Social Research*, 1965, *49*, 281–294.

Lamb, M. E. Interactions between eight-month-old children and their fathers and mothers. In M. E. Lamb (Ed.), *The role of the father in child development*. New York: Wiley, 1976.

LeMasters, E. E. Parenthood as crisis. *Marriage and Family Living*, 1957, *19*, 352–355.

Lewis, M. State as an infant-environment interaction: An analysis of mother–infant interaction as a function of sex. *Merrill-Palmer Quarterly*, 1972, *18*, 95–121.

Lewis, M., & Rosenblum, L. A. (Eds.), *The effect of the infant on its caregiver*. New York: Wiley, 1974.

Locke, H. J., & Wallace, K. M. Short marital adjustment tests: Their reliability and validity. *Marriage and Family Living*, 1959, *21*, 251–255.

Luckey, E. B. Marital satisfaction and its association with congruence of perception. *Marriage and Family Living*, 1960, *22*, 49–54.

Luckey, E. B., & Bain, J. K. Children: A factor in marital satisfaction. *Journal of Marriage and the Family*, 1970, 32, 43–44.

Meyerowitz, J. H., & Feldman, H. Transition to parenthood. *Psychiatric Research Reports*, 1966, 20, 78–84.

Miller, B. C. Child density, marital satisfaction, and conventionalization: A research note. *Journal of Marriage and the Family*, 1975, 37, 345–347.

Miller, B. C. A multivariate developmental model of marital satisfaction. *Journal of Marriage and the Family*, 1976, 38, 643–658.

Newcomb, T. M. *The acquaintance process*. New York: Holt, Rinehart, and Winston, 1961.

Nye, F. I. & Berardo, F. M. *The family: Its structure and interaction*. New York: Macmillan, 1973.

Nye, F. I., & McLaughlin, S. D. Social exchange, role competence and marital satisfaction. Paper presented at the Pacific Sociological Association annual meeting, San Jose, California, April 1974.

Ort, R. S. A study of role conflicts as related to happiness in marriage. *Journal of Abnormal and Social Psychology*, 1950, 45, 691–699.

Orthner, D. K. Leisure activity patterns and marital satisfaction over the marital career. *Journal of Marriage and the Family*, 1975, 37, 91–104.

Osofsky, J. D., & O'Connell, E. J. Parent–child interaction: Daughters' effect upon mothers' and fathers' behaviors. *Developmental Psychology*, 1972, 7, 157–168.

Parke, R. D., & Sawin, D. B. The father's role in infancy: A re-evaluation. *The Family Coordinator*, 1976, 25, 365–371.

Parke, R. D., & Sawin, D. B. The family in early infancy: Social interactional and attitudinal analyses. Paper presented to the Society for Research in Child Development, New Orleans, La., March 1977.

Riley, M. W. Aging and cohort succession: interpretations and misinterpretations. *Public Opinion Quarterly*, 1973, 37, 35–49.

Rodgers, R. H. *Improvements in the construction and analysis of family life cycle categories*. Kalamazoo, Michigan: Western Michigan University, 1962.

Rodgers, R. H. Toward a theory of family development. *Journal of Marriage and the Family*, 1964, 26, 262–270.

Rollins, B. C. Values consensus and cohesion in the marital dyad. Unpublished Ph.D. dissertation, Cornell University, 1961.

Rollins, B. C. The Latter-day Saint husband–father's use of time. *Family Perspective*, 1967, 2 (No. 1), 17–21.

Rollins, B. C. Response to Miller about cross-sectional family life cycle research. *Journal of Marriage and the Family*, 1975, 37, 259–260.

Rollins, B. C., & Cannon, K. F. Marital satisfaction over the family life cycle: A re-evaluation. *Journal of Marriage and the Family*, 1974, 36, 271–282.

Rollins, B. C., & Feldman, H. Marital satisfaction over the family life cycle. *Journal of Marriage and the Family*, 1970, 32, 20–27.

Rossi, A. Transition to parenthood. *Journal of Marriage and the Family*, 1968, 30, 26–39.

Russell, C. S. Transition to parenthood: Problems and gratifications. *Journal of Marriage and the Family*, 1974, 36, 294–302.

Ryder, R. G. Longitudinal data relating marital satisfaction and having a child. *Journal of Marriage and the Family*, 1973, 35, 604–607.

Sieber, S. D. Toward a theory of role accumulation. *American Sociological Review*, 1974, 39, 567–578.

Smart, M. S., & Smart, R. C. Recalled, present and predicted satisfaction in stages of the family life cycle in New Zealand. *Journal of Marriage and the Family*, 1975, 37, 408–415.

Spanier, G. B. Measuring dyadic adjustment: New scales for assessing the quality of marriage and similar dyads. *Journal of Marriage and the Family*, 1976, *38*, 15–30.
Spanier, G. B., & Cole, C. L. Toward clarification and investigation of marital adjustment. *International Journal of Sociology of the Family*, 1976, *6*, 121–146.
Spanier, G. B., Lewis, R. A., & Cole, C. L. Marital adjustment over the family life cycle: The issue of curvilinearity. *Journal of Marriage and the Family*, 1975, *37*, 263–276.
Steinberg, L. D., & Hill, J. P. Family interaction in early adolescence. Paper presented to the Society for Research in Child Development, New Orleans, La., March 1977.
Udry, J. R. *The social context of marriage*. Philadephia: Lippincott, 1966, p. 489.
Wilensky, H. L. Life cycle, work situation, and participation in formal associations. In R. Kleemeier (Ed.), *Aging and leisure*, New York: Oxford, 1961.

Research Methods and Developmental Reciprocity in Families[1]

5

David M. Klein, Stephen R. Jorgensen, and Brent C. Miller

I. Introduction

Our mission in this chapter is to sort out the methodological issues and strategies involved in the developmental study of the relationship between the child and the other members of the child's family. We have divided this mission into three tasks.

First, we will discuss fundamental conceptual issues associated with the notions of reciprocity and development. Such issues will be seen to have important methodological implications. Second, we will explore the range of available data collection strategies. A profile analysis of these strategies will be used to argue for a pluralistic methodological framework. Finally, we will review the research designs most often used to study development in families. We will critically examine the utility of these designs for answering developmental and reciprocity questions and suggest needed refinements and extensions in their application.

Most of the topics we will cover have been treated in a variety of other contexts. We have experienced some frustration in a discovery that it is easier to raise interesting issues than it is to resolve them. Hence, we view this chapter as one contribution to a continuing dialogue rather than as a novel framework with well-founded prescriptions.

[1]Support to work on this chapter was provided by a Faculty Research Grant and the College of Home Economics at the University of Tennessee, Knoxville.

II. Reciprocity and Developmental Analysis

The primary methodological issue set by the theme of this volume is how to study the reciprocity of effects between developing individuals and developing families. But before methodological issues are raised, it is important to consider ways in which reciprocity and developmental analysis can be conceptualized.

A. Conceptualizing Reciprocity in Families

Other writers increasingly have recognized that "social mold" theories of socialization are inadequate (see, for example, Hartup, Chapter 2, this volume, and Lamb, Chapter 6, this volume). The child is presumably as much an active force in his or her own development as a passive receptacle of social forces. But where do we go from here? It is certainly not satisfactory to turn these theories on their head and assert that the child is the major determinant of his or her own personality and developing social relationships (Bell, 1968).

Contemporary models of individual and family development are beginning to emphasize reciprocal causality in their descriptions and explanations (see, for example, Aldous, 1978; Lerner, 1978). *Reciprocity* may be viewed as a generic term that characterizes all social interaction. It is therefore a feature of social relationships, involving mutual influence of one kind or another. Useful as a starting point, this conceptualization of reciprocity can be further specified in a number of distinct ways.

One way to treat reciprocal interaction is in *linear* terms. Thus, the behavior of person A is viewed as affecting the behavior of person B, which in turn affects the behavior of person A, and so on in a potentially infinite chain. This linear view of reciprocal interaction has heuristic appeal, and experience tells us that it is realistic. However, researchers are obliged to place boundaries on chains of events, and these boundaries often seem arbitrary.

Nevertheless, several forms of sequence analysis have been successfully applied to the study of behavior chains in families (Hertel, 1968; Lewis & Lee-Painter, 1974; Miller, Wackman, & Jorgensen, 1974; Rausch, Barry, Hertel, & Swain, 1974). Since the analysis of interaction sequences must have a microscopic focus for practical reasons, it is not especially useful for longer term developmental studies unless a series of interaction sequences are studied at fairly widely separated intervals. Therefore, the primary methods of developmental analysis for this model of reciprocity have been familiar multivariate statistical techniques based on linear correlation and regression.

Reciprocal interaction may also be treated as simultaneous mutual influence. Thus, the effects of person A on person B are viewed as occurring at the same time that the effects of person B on person A are occurring. This *synchronous* view is also intuitively appealing, but it must cope with the problem of indeterminacy. Since it is practically infeasible to distinguish cause from effect when interpersonal influences are treated as simultaneous, someone who adopts this model would probably deny that causality is important or would claim that it cannot be empirically untangled. Methodologically, a synchronous perspective implies that family relationships can only be studied using qualitative and descriptive methods.

A third option is to adopt the language of general systems theory and treat reciprocity as *cyclical* causation. Thus, the behavior of person A influences the subsequent behavior of person B, and person B's behavior completes a feedback loop by influencing the subsequent behavior of person A. These loops then become the units of analysis, and we can explore whether they are positive (deviation amplifying) or negative (deviation reducing). The research techniques for studying cyclical causation are beginning to be worked out (see, for example, Blalock, 1971; Kohn & Schooler, 1973), but the family interaction literature has not yet gone beyond discussing the interpretive utility of cyclical models (Black & Broderick, 1972).

A final approach, and perhaps the one most often adopted, is to view reciprocity as the content of relatively stable patterns of social interaction. Thus, when person A repeatedly emits a particular kind of behavior toward person B and person B repeatedly emits a particular kind of behavior toward person A, their relationship is said to be reciprocal. This *relational* view elevates the unit of analysis to a relatively stable pattern of interaction, and the research task is to identify these patterns. Although not necessarily so, the focus here may be on the proportionate distribution of acts of the same type between actors. In this restricted application the concern might be, for example, to determine whether person A smiles at person B at the same rate that person B smiles at person A. Equal rates of exchange of the same behavior would be taken as evidence of reciprocity (Burgess and Conger, 1977). Another application employs social exchange theory, which defines reciprocity in relational terms as a fair, just, or equitable exchange of reward–cost ratios or profit–investment ratios (see, for example, Hess and Waring, Chapter 9, this volume).

Recognizing the merits of the linear, synchronous, and cyclical models of reciprocity, we will focus here on the relational model. The next step is to go beyond a dyadic conception of social interaction and place reciprocity in a family context.

Consider the following questions that might be asked about families. For each question we have attached symbolic notation to represent the nature of the social relationships involved. Here, HF corresponds to the husband–father, and WM corresponds to the wife–mother; C_i, C_j, and C_k correspond to different children, and C_n corresponds to all the children taken one at a time. The bidirectional arrows indicate reciprocal relationships, and the parentheses indicate that a relationship (not an individual family member) is itself reciprocally related to something else.

1. How do spouses affect each other?

$$HF \rightleftarrows WM$$

2. How do parents affect their children, and vice versa?

$$HF \rightleftarrows C_n, \quad WM \rightleftarrows C_n$$

3. How do siblings affect each other?

$$C_i \rightleftarrows C_j$$

4. How does the relationship between spouses affect their children, and vice versa?

$$(HF \rightleftarrows WM) \rightleftarrows C_n$$

5. How does the relationship between parent and child affect the other parent, and vice versa?

$$(HF \rightleftarrows C_n) \rightleftarrows WM, \quad (WM \rightleftarrows C_n) \rightleftarrows HF$$

6. How does the relationship between parent and child affect the other children, and vice versa?

$$(HF \rightleftarrows C_i) \rightleftarrows C_j, \quad (WM \rightleftarrows C_i) \rightleftarrows C_j$$

7. How do the relationships between siblings affect the parent, and vice versa?

$$(C_i \rightleftarrows C_j) \rightleftarrows HF, \quad (C_i \rightleftarrows C_j) \rightleftarrows WM$$

8. How do the relationships between siblings affect the other children, and vice versa?

$$(C_i \rightleftarrows C_j) \rightleftarrows C_k$$

9. How does the relationship between spouses affect the relationship between siblings, and vice versa?

$$(HF \rightleftarrows WM) \rightleftarrows (C_i \rightleftarrows C_j)$$

10. How does the relationship between spouses affect the relationship between parent and child, and vice versa?

$$(HF \rightleftarrows WM) \rightleftarrows (HF \rightleftarrows C_n), \qquad (HF \rightleftarrows WM) \rightleftarrows (WM \rightleftarrows C_n)$$

11. How does the relationship between parent and child affect the relationship between siblings, and vice versa?

$$(HF \rightleftarrows C_n) \rightleftarrows (C_i \rightleftarrows C_j), \qquad (WM \rightleftarrows C_n) \rightleftarrows (C_i \rightleftarrows C_j)$$

12. How does the relationship between one parent and the children affect the relationship between the other parent and the children?

$$(HF \rightleftarrows C_n) \rightleftarrows (WM \rightleftarrows C_n)$$

It is clear that when we move to the level of family interaction, the possible relational networks become very complex. Not only must we attend to reciprocity between individual members (Questions 1–3) but also reciprocity between members and relationships (Questions 4–8), as well as reciprocity between sets of relationships (Questions 9–12).

The complexity of family interaction is partly a function of family size. It can be shown, for example, that in a childless family only Question 1 is relevant, and therefore only one relational network need be investigated. With the addition of the first child, Questions 2, 4, 5, 10, and 12 also become relevant, and 9 relational networks are implied. With two children in a family, all of the questions except Question 8 are relevant, and 31 relational networks are implied. With three children, 76 relational networks are implied; with four children, 147 networks; and so on.

If this set of questions is viewed as a minimum requirement for a complete investigation of reciprocity in families, it is not difficult to see why researchers have been selective in their focus on certain aspects of family structure. Probably because of the inordinate complexity of such structures, we know little about reciprocity in larger families and not much more about the "higher order" reciprocities involving relationships as units of analysis. Instead, the tendency is to slur over the differences among children and among parents, treating them as aggregates, or to concentrate on particular sectors such as the mother–child and husband–wife dyads.

The picture is further clouded because there is every reason to believe that the 12 questions we have posed are not sufficient to capture the full richness of family interaction. All of the following "facts" are ignored by this scheme.

1. Due to cultural, social structural, and situational factors, some families have either more or fewer than two functioning parents.
2. A family member may affect and be affected by his or her relationship with other family members, as is depicted by HF ⇄ (HF ⇄ WM), among other possibilities.
3. Family members also have relationships with individuals, groups, and other social systems that lie outside the members' nuclear family. We may ask, for example, how a boy's relationship with peers at school affects his relationship with his parents, and vice versa.
4. The effects between relational networks may be indirect, suggesting that several of the networks could be linked together, as in (HF ⇄ WM) ⇄ (WM ⇄ C_i) ⇄ (C_i ⇄ C_j).
5. Family members may act "in concert" with one another or be jointly affected by the actions of other family members. Thus, at least some of the important reciprocal relationships in families may involve coalitions and other collective units.

It might also be argued that analytical distinctions among relational units in families ignore the holistic character of family interaction and that the various relationships do not add up to a complete picture of the family for this reason. Whatever the merits of such an argument, most of the salient themes and undercurrents in family interaction ought to be detectable so long as a comparative analysis of the answers to our 12 questions is undertaken, supplemented by investigations of the kinds of ignored "facts" we have indicated.

Once a set of reciprocal networks is selected for analysis, attention must turn to the "how" part of the questions raised. Essentially, this involves a specification of the crucial characteristics of individual family members as well as the content of the relationships among those members.

In the case of children, we may want to know how their physical presence, appearance, personality, health, temperament, overt behavior, attitudes, and values, among a host of other variable properties, are involved in reciprocal relationships with other family members and relationships. The same can be said for the characteristics of adult family members. It should be obvious, however, that the nature of the characteristics chosen for attention will likely influence the research strategy that is used. For example, some of the characteristics can be directly observed, whereas others must be inferred from observation or elicited through verbal reports.

As for the content of relationships, another wide variety of alternatives is possible. Frequencies and styles of communication, power, affect, decision making, conflict management, role allocation, as well as a qualitative evaluation of these in terms of their meaning and adequacy, are among the aspects of relationships usually thought to be worthy of investigation. Here, too, the selection of relationship parameters is likely to affect research strategies in obvious ways.

This preliminary discussion of the nature of reciprocity in family life is intended to suggest that conceptualizing the issue leads to an appreciation of its complexity and, furthermore, that the way in which this complexity is organized is likely to affect research decisions.

B. Conceptualizing Development in Families

Once reciprocity is conceptualized in relational terms, we might seek comfort in our ability to identify stable patterns of family interaction. We know, however, that these patterns have a dynamic quality to them, that they change and develop over time. Hence, we need to place reciprocity in a developmental context.

The first and fundamental question to ask is, What is developing? It is precisely at this point that the behavioral sciences have traditionally split. Developmental psychologists are prone to be concerned with the development of individuals, whereas developmental sociologists are prone to be concerned with the development of family groups, if not the institution of the family in a broader sociohistorical sense. To be sure, social factors loom large in psychological explanations of individual development, and the characteristics of individual family members are normally acknowledged in sociological explanations of family development. Nevertheless, this difference in dependent variable and unit of analysis raises serious questions about the isomorphism between theories, models, assumptions, and methods of research used by psychologists and sociologists.

One potential value of a reciprocal orientation to development is that it may help bridge this gap between disciplines. Thus, we can view the development of each family member as contributing to the development of the various relational networks in the family that we have identified, and at the same time we can view the development of these networks as contributing to the development of each family member.

Models of the development of individuals have had a long history of articulation, debate, and clarification (Lerner, 1976). Models of the development of families have been somewhat less well developed (Aldous,

1978; Duvall, 1977; Hill & Rodgers, 1964; Rodgers, 1973). Models of the reciprocal development of families and their members are implied in the family development literature but seldom given explicit attention. Whatever approach to development is adopted, it is likely to have certain key features.

First, development implies change over time. In terms of our 12 questions about reciprocity, the problem then becomes one of identifying shifts between one set of relatively stable relational networks and subsequent sets of such networks. This is no easy task because (a) stability and change are themselves relative matters; and (b) different networks are liable to change at different rates. Thus, any short-term picture of development in families (where members and/or interaction patterns are changing) is likely to be characterized by change in some of its sectors and stability in the rest of its sectors. Methodologically, this suggests that a longitudinal approach to data collection is essential, even if this means synthetically reconstructing changes from retrospective history taking when the direct observation of changes is not practical.

Beyond change itself is the question of the orderliness of change. We might expect development in families to be patterned and not random and to involve some sort of stage or phase progression. Developmental psychologists differ greatly among themselves in terms of the way they conceptualize the orderliness of change, and stage theories are by no means universally accepted (Lerner, 1976).

There is much less disagreement among sociologists about the regularity of family development. Some version of the family life cycle stages articulated by Duvall (1977) appears widely accepted and has been almost universally employed in family development research. From time to time the Duvall scheme has been challenged on the grounds of its oversimplicity and lack of generalizability (Rodgers, 1962) or its lack of predictive utility (Spanier, Sauer, & Larzelere, 1977). However, no satisfactory alternative has been offered in its place.

The underlying rationale for family stage designations has been that they signal significant transitions in roles by way of accretion, loss, or modifications of content. Unfortunately, we have little research evidence to confirm the tacit assumption by Duvall and others that the transitions that these stages entail constitute the most critical developmental events or periods as they are experienced by family members (Aldous, 1978). Just as we can expect a great amount of interindividual variation in development, we can expect a great amount of interfamily variation in development. Thus, until a more satisfactory view of the family life cycle is forthcoming, it may be a wise methodological strategy to inquire from each family studied about the critical role changes it has experienced. This strategy at least avoids the questionable assumption that all families go through the same critical role transitions. Eventually, this may lead us to a more probabilistic "game tree" model of family development, wherein the nature and timing of previous changes affect the current stable patterns of interaction and the likelihood of future developmental changes (Magrabi & Marshall, 1965).

The final conceptual issue with regard to development that we will consider concerns its directionality and time span. Both psychologists and sociologists have traditionally held a broadly organismic image of development. For psychologists this is a natural image because individuals are born, mature, age, and die. Family sociologists tend to retain this organismic image by treating families as forming, growing in complexity as members and roles are added, diminishing in complexity as young adult members are launched, and eventually dissolving through death, divorce, or other means.

The organismic image tends to break down, however, when we consider the regenerative capacities of families. In some sense at least, the life of a family transcends the boundaries of family membership. Sensitivity to this weakness in an organismic analogy has led some family sociologists to study multigenerational patterns of development among living adult members (see, for example, Hill, 1970).

This emphasis may be carried even further by exploring the continuity and discontinuity of family patterns that are tied to more genealogically distant myths, rituals, beliefs, and practices (Bossard & Boll, 1950). Within a reciprocal developmental framework, this concern with "roots" surely can be maintained, and it has direct implications for the methodological strategies used to study families and family members. We can observe symbolic evidence of ancestry by the accumulation of photographs and other artifacts in the home. We can observe the way that elder family members verbally communicate and interpret family histories to younger members and to each other. We can also ask family members to construct genealogies and biographical accounts and to interpret them for us.

In this section we have tried to tantalize the reader by exploring some of the conceptual issues surrounding the notions of reciprocity and development. The issues vary in complexion depending on whether they are considered from the perspective of individuals or families as the primary units of analysis. We suggest that a commitment to development as a reciprocal phenomenon is necessary in order to bring together the insights of developmental psychology and developmental sociology. It seems likely that this multidisciplinary perspective will require much greater exploration and discussion before it will yield significant methodological advances. Therefore, we turn now to consider some of the conventional ways of differentiating data collection options.

III. Data Collection Parameters and Profiles

For some time we have thought that the typical textbook discussions of social science research designs or data collection alternatives are inadequate. Such presentations frequently tend to overdifferentiate, reify, and even set into competition alternatives that are more nearly compatible or complementary. Experiments, for example, are not appropriate solely in the sterile confines of the campus laboratory. Experiments cannot even be conducted without resort to direct observation or to the kind of interview or questionnaire commonly associated with surveys. Asking questions and eliciting oral or written answers is certainly not antithetical to watching for behavior or taking note of the research environment. Indeed, there is some sense in which all research methodologies combine to form a reservoir of possibilities with subtle distinctions and overlapping utility. The question then becomes one of determining the most useful way to make these distinctions clear along some meaningful dimensions.

The following parameters seem to encompass most of the ways in which data collection techniques can vary:

1. *Manipulation* refers to the degree to which the independent variable is controlled by the researcher. Manipulation varies from the active presentation or withholding of the treatment commonly associated with true experiments to the very passive role characteristic of naturalistic observation.

2. *Setting* refers to the ecological location in which the data are collected. The setting varies from highly artificial or contrived, characteristic of some laboratory and simulation research, to naturalistic, characteristic of field research.

3. *Obtrusiveness* refers to the potential for reactivity due to the awareness of being investigated on the part of research subjects. Again, we should expect this dimension to be a matter of degree, varying from highly obtrusive to totally unobtrusive.

4. *Experiential involvement* refers to the degree of phenomenological proximity between the researcher and the object of investigation. Firsthand involvement refers to personal, experiential collection of data via participant observation. Secondhand involvement refers to the gathering of information from participant–informants. Thirdhand in-

volvement refers to the gathering of information from bystanders and witnesses. Fourthhand involvement refers to information collected from confidants, people who didn't see things for themselves but were told about them before or after the fact. A fifthhand level of involvement might be associated with rumor or other speculative information sources.

5. *Contemporaneousness* refers to the length of time between the occurrence of the phenomenon under study and its entry into the scientific community. Ignoring for the moment that all research takes time to conduct, assess, and publish, we still can observe great variability in the time perspectives involved. At one extreme are researches into past events that reach back a century or more with the aid of documentary and archival records. Focused on the nearer past are retrospective reports about events within the memory of an individual or family history. At the other extreme are researches in the present that probe contemporaneously occurring events, as is characterized by direct observation.

6. *Duration* refers to the amount of time coverage in a research study. At one end of this continuum are synchronic studies dealing with a single point in time, characteristic of cross-sectional research. At the other end of this continuum are polychronic studies, involving repeated measures, panel designs, time series, historical comparisons, and the like.

7. *Contact media* refer to the communication channel(s) used to gather data. This continuum varies from exclusive use of verbal reportage (oral in the case of interviews and written in the case of questionnaires) to exclusive use of direct observation by visual or other sensory means.

8. *Sequence standardization* refers to the degree to which data are gathered in a predefined and fixed order for all subjects. The prototype of an instrument whose sequence is fully standardized is the self-administered questionnaire. The prototype of an instrument whose sequence is random is the totally unstructured interview.

9. *Stimulus standardization* refers to the degree to which conceptually equivalent types of data are gathered from all subjects. When stimuli are standardized, all subjects are given the same experimental treatment or variety of treatments or are asked the same questions and given the same items. In observational settings employing standardized stimuli, the researcher has a uniform set of categories of information that are to be recorded. When stimuli are unstandardized, the subject defines the types of information that he or she will provide.

10. *Response standardization* refers to the degree to which the range of responses is specified and limited before the data are collected. This

continuum varies between high standardization, characteristic of closed-ended survey questions and interaction coding protocols, and low standardization, characteristic of open-ended survey questions and inductively coded interaction sequences.

11. *Depth of content coverage* refers to the degree to which the rich detail of a phenomenon is investigated. This continuum varies from deep to shallow coverage. Great depth is characterized, for example, by asking many questions about a topic from a number of different perspectives. Shallow coverage is characterized, for example, by a single global question about the phenomenon of interest.

12. *Breadth of content coverage* refers to the number of conceptually distinct phenomena investigated. This continuum varies from broad to narrow coverage. Broad coverage is characterized by multivariate research, whereas narrow coverage is characterized by univariate, descriptive research.

If we were to array the profiles of commonly discussed research strategies on these 12 dimensions, they would look something like the patterns in Figure 5.1. For demonstration purposes, profiles for the survey, the experiment, the research study based on archival records, and the qualitative study have been arrived at impressionistically in terms of the stereotypic image of each technique and the average potential performance of that technique. More precise and empirically valid scores presumably could be calculated.

There are several things worth noting about the profiles presented. First, a good deal of variability on the 12 dimensions is observed. Second, each strategy has a unique profile, similar to other strategies at some points, although different at other points. Third, and most important, only a few of the possible configurations are represented. It looks as though there ought to be ample opportunity to create hybrid and otherwise exotic designs, as well as to take advantage of some of the assets of each design in a single research project or program. Hence, we ought to expect more use of research designs that employ multiple methods (Campbell & Fiske, 1959) or methodological triangulation (Denzin, 1970).

A pluralistic methodological framework has far-reaching implications for the way we conduct research on reciprocal development in families. A few of these implications will be explored here.

One implication is that we can make greater use of designs that we normally do not consider. For example, naturalistic settings, unobtrusive measures, and archival or other historical documents are infrequently used in research on individual or family development. More-

Dimension	Range	

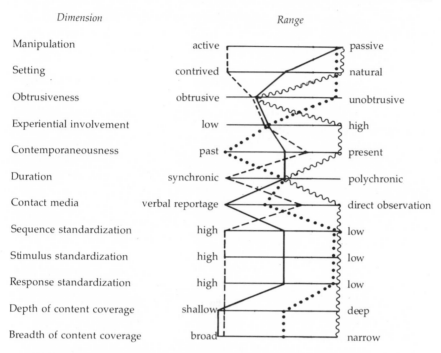

Manipulation	active	passive
Setting	contrived	natural
Obtrusiveness	obtrusive	unobtrusive
Experiential involvement	low	high
Contemporaneousness	past	present
Duration	synchronic	polychronic
Contact media	verbal reportage	direct observation
Sequence standardization	high	low
Stimulus standardization	high	low
Response standardization	high	low
Depth of content coverage	shallow	deep
Breadth of content coverage	broad	narrow

FIGURE 5.1 *Research design parameters and the profiles of conventional strategies. (Survey = ———, Experiment = - - - -, Archival = ooooo, Qualitative = ∿∿∿.)*

over, although experimental designs are often used by developmental psychologists to study short-term effects, developmental sociologists have seldom employed these techniques, and the longer term trends in individual and family development appear impervious to experimental manipulation. It may be possible, however, to simulate developmental events covering a relatively long period of time and observe the ways in which reciprocal interaction in families changes. Some leads in this direction have been provided by Baltes and Goulet (1971), Tallman (Tallman, Wilson, & Straus, 1972), and Weick (1971, p. 16).

Another implication is that we can combine data sources more often than we generally do. For example, combining levels of experiential involvement should give a more comprehensive picture of the significance of developmental trends than the exclusive use of one source of information. If we are interested in how the birth of a child changes the quality of marital interaction between the parents and/or how the quality of marital interaction affects the likelihood of childbirth, we might draw on personal experience, the reports of both parents, the reports of other nuclear family members, as well as extended kin, neighbors, and friends.

The value of a pluralistic methodological framework can best be appreciated if it is contrasted with a critical appraisal of the methodological choices most often made by researchers. Therefore, we turn in the next section to examine the kinds of research designs most often used to study developmental reciprocity in families.

IV. Taking Stock of the Developmental Study of Family Reciprocity

Apart from the range of research methods that *could* be used to study the reciprocal effects of children on marriage and family life over time, it is desirable to examine the range, adequacy, and propriety of the research methods *commonly employed* to gather that knowledge. Such stock taking might actually prove to be a humbling experience if it is discovered that research evidence supporting pet theories or empirical generalizations is based upon inadequate or inappropriate methodological designs. From another viewpoint, however, an inventory and evaluation of research methods may function in a constructive manner by pointing to weaknesses or gaps in the way we gather our knowledge about the developmental nature of child, marital, and family interaction. This task will, we hope, signal new directions that researchers might take in the future to improve upon past efforts. Special attention will be given in this section to factors that family researchers should take into account in their assessment of the *developmental patterns* and *reciprocal influences* characterizing families as they move from one stage of the life cycle to the next.

Most of our knowledge about the effects of children on marital quality across the life span and the reciprocal effects of marital quality and parental behavior on children is based on two general research strategies: (*a*) the survey; and (*b*) direct observations in a field, laboratory, or clinical setting.

A. Survey Research

Survey research relies primarily on two reportage techniques: the questionnaire (administered face-to-face or by mail) and the interview. Data gathered by the survey method are usually represented numerically for purposes of quantitative analysis, although qualitative responses of respondents are often blended in to illustrate statistical findings. An extensive description of variations of these techniques can be found elsewhere (Nye, 1964). Of concern here is the extent to which investigators have employed these techniques in studies of developmental trends and reciprocal influences across the life-span and the adequacy of such techniques for assessing reciprocal influences over time.

1. The Survey Method and Developmental Analysis

The survey method is probably the most widely used to study marital quality over time, being the most suitable for tapping subjective data such as feelings, perceptions, normative standards, values, aspirations, and so on. To date, however, little use has been made of this method for studying the development of other relational networks in families across the life-span, such as parent–child and sibling relationships.

The tracing of developmental trends in marital quality with survey techniques has been attempted in two ways: cross-sectionally and longitudinally. Application of the cross-sectional survey method usually involves administering a structured questionnaire at a single point in time to married couples in various stages of the life cycle, thereby suggesting developmental trends in marital quality based upon the number and ages of children (cf., Blood & Wolfe, 1960; Miller, 1976; Rollins and Cannon, 1974; Rollins & Feldman, 1970; Spanier, Lewis, & Cole, 1975). There are advantages to this method that probably account for its widespread use. The cross-sectional method is efficient in terms of time and money. The researcher attempts to infer a developmental picture of family and/or marital interaction by having to secure respondent cooperation for only one small block of time, usually from 1 to 3 hours. Thus, the researcher does not have to be concerned about sample attrition.

Despite these advantages of convenience, however, this method has some serious shortcomings that confound valid research generalizations. The cross-sectional method does not control for the effect of history or cohort differences in value orientations between respondents of different ages (Baltes, 1968; Campbell & Stanley, 1963; Hill, 1964; Riley, 1973; Ryder, 1965; Schaie, 1965).

Not only might differential value orientations due to historical circumstances confound the developmental picture but cross-sectional studies of marital quality often overlook the existence of a selection process that gives us the impression that marital satisfaction and adjustment follow a U-shaped pattern over the life cycle. Such a pattern may actually be a methodological artifact in that many unhappy and unsatisfying marriages have dropped out of the population of marriages from which cross-sectional samples have been drawn, due to separation, divorce, and desertion (Miller, 1975; Spanier et al., 1975). Any developmental trend emerging from such data therefore has a definite synthetic quality that may distort our picture of marital reality in the middle and later stages of the life cycle.

Beyond this problem of self-selection, and closely related to problems of cohort socialization differences, is that of strictly age-correlated effects. Older respondents may be more likely than younger ones to answer questions in a socially desirable way rather than reporting a true picture of the marital relationship (Spanier et al., 1975). Marital satisfaction indices for these age groups will therefore be artifically inflated.

Despite these problems, the argument has been made that, due to the differential probabilities of marital dissolution over the life cycle, the U-shaped pattern may not be entirely artifactual (Leik and Leik, 1976). It can also be argued that socially desirable response sets reflect the very kind of conventional attitude and perception necessary for well-adjusted marriages.

Married couples are often assessed at a single point in time in terms of transitions into and out of specific stages of the marriage relationship. Such a design might be referred to as a short-term cross-sectional design. The research is based on a relatively homogeneous sample of couples, in that all of the marriages represent a single cohort in the family life cycle and, often, in marital duration and age of respondents. This type of design characterizes the long series of studies of the transition into parenthood (Dyer, 1963; Hobbs, 1965, 1968; Jacobby, 1969; LeMasters, 1957; Russell, 1974). Deutscher's (1964) analysis of couples at the other end of the parental career (the postparental stage) is lonely by comparison. There is little to recommend this approach other than its convenience.

The longitudinal survey method described by Hill (1964) attempts to overcome several deficits in the cross-sectional method but, in the process, encounters some serious problems of its own. The longitudinal design attempts to document developmental trends by following the same family members for a period of time and making repeated observations (Burgess & Wallin, 1953; deLissovoy, 1973b; Dizard, 1968; Feldman, 1964; Hill, 1970; Pineo, 1961). In this way the effects of history and generation can be better controlled. Developmental changes in family age and sex composition can be studied, role content and interaction patterns more carefully monitored from one stage of the life cycle to the next, and the problem of self-selection plaguing the cross-sectional designs reduced.

A "pure" version of this design would be a full-term longitudinal or panel study. Collecting data on marital quality from the onset of the couple's relationship to its demise through divorce or death would be analogous to studying individual human development from birth to death. However, so far as we are aware, there has been only one research project that has followed couples over an extended part of the marital career. This was the study begun by Burgess in 1939 with an availability sample of 1000 couples. The second wave of data collection began in 1942, but stretched into 1946, with usable questionnaires finally being received from 666 of the couples. The third wave of questionnaires went out in 1955, but it was 1960 before 400 couples had responded. The problem of "experimental mortality" or sample attrition is dramatically illustrated in this case (Campbell and Stanley, 1963). Attrition is likely to be more problematic in studies of marriage over time than in studies of individual human development. Marriage partners drop from the sample for the same reasons as in studies of individual development (residential mobility, noncooperation, accidents, death, etc.), but the chances of losing a sample element are doubled because when one spouse loses motivation to continue (due to marital problems, divorce, etc.) and drops out of this study, both are lost from the sample.

Furthermore, developmental changes monitored longitudinally are susceptible to the effects of "testing" (Campbell and Stanley, 1963). That is, the repeated crossing of marital or family boundaries by a research team may in itself cause changes in family organization and interaction over time that otherwise would not have occurred. Hill (1964) notes further complications when it comes to securing the cooperation and commitment of couples over a long time span, keeping track of the families over the years, and maintaining the morale of families who may tire of being studied at regular intervals. However, even with such cooperation, data from a longitudinal study are not necessarily generalizable to people from other than the one specific birth or event cohort being studied.

Financial cost is an additional problem. Even the best intentioned and most competent researchers often cannot muster the sizable research budget required by a long-term longitudinal method, rendering the less expensive but more artificial cross-sectional design an attractive alternative for studying marital and family interaction across the life span.

In order to avoid some of these deficits in the longitudinal method and still maintain the advantage of being able to follow family members over a period of time, some researchers have adopted a compromise strategy identified by Hill (1964) as the "segmented longitudinal panel," with or without controls (Bell, 1953, 1954; Feldman, 1971; Hill, 1970). This strategy provides more of a short-run view of developmental change than does a full-term longitudinal design. In the segmented longitudinal panel with controls, two or more groups of respondents are compared at two or more points in time to monitor the effects on one group of a shift in life cycle stage or other critical role transition, such as the transition to parenthood, the transition to postparenthood, or the transition to retirement status. This strategy most closely approaches the analytically powerful "pretest–posttest control group" and "nonequivalent control group" experimental designs described by Campbell and Stanley (1963). The "experimental group" is identified in advance by the researcher as one that will undergo a change in life cycle stage or other critical event, whereas the control group will not. The use of a randomly assigned control group, or, as in most cases of family research, one already assembled in the field and probably not equivalent to the experimental group, controls some of the effects of history, since both groups are exposed to similar influential events.

Effects due to "testing" are controlled because each group is observed the same number of times using the same instruments. The problem of experimental mortality or sample attrition is also lessened because in most cases respondents from the experimental group are no more likely than control group respondents to withdraw from the study. Also, compared to the lifelong longitudinal study, the short time span required by the panel study to make the necessary observations will minimize the proportion of the original sample dropping out of the study. Finally, the cost of the panel design is greatly reduced relative to the classical longitudinal study because of the shorter time that the researcher must maintain contact with respondents in the sample.

An example of the segmented longitudinal panel is that of Feldman (1971), who reports on a study of the effects of the arrival of children on marital quality (see also, Feldman and Rogoff, 1968; Meyerowitz and Feldman, 1966; Ryder, 1973). He compared the marital quality of primiparous, multiparous, and childless couples at three points in time. The primipara and multipara were interviewed once during pregnancy (during the second trimester) and twice following the birth of the child (at 5 weeks and 5 months of age). The childless couples were interviewed at the same chronological times but did not experience the transition to first-time or second-time parenthood, thus functioning as the control group. Therefore, several meaningful comparisons of marital satisfaction and role performance scores could be drawn between these three groups of married couples, some of whom were exposed to an "experimental treatment" (childbirth), whereas others were not.

By combining Feldman's findings with those of other possible segmented longitudinal studies of marital quality at various critical transition points throughout the life-span (e.g., family with adolescents, the
transition to postparenthood, retirement of the breadwinner[s], etc.), we
can begin a methodologically sound step-by-step linkage of the developmental nature of marital quality over the entire life cycle. The same
research process could be followed in the developmental study of other
reciprocal networks in families. This would involve identifying transition points that signal a discontinuity in role content or shift in the
structure of the relationship, comparing those who have completed each
transition with those who have not on key variables in a series of distinct
segmented longitudinal studies and then linking the findings of each
study to form a composite picture of the developmental nature of that
reciprocal network across the life-span.

Other researchers have utilized a segmented longitudinal design
without including a control group for comparative purposes (Luckey &
Bain, 1970). For example, deLissovoy (1973a, 1973b) twice interviewed a
sample of young couples married in high school (within 3 months after
marriage and again 30 to 38 months later) to document the tremendous
growth of financial and socioemotional strain as these teenagers moved
from the childless stage to the childbearing stage of family development.
Campbell and Stanley (1963) refer to this as a "one-group pretest–
posttest design." The interviews conducted by deLissovoy at two points
in time allowed him to show a marked trend of decreasing satisfaction,
companionship, cohesion, and overall adjustment due to the poor timing of marriage and parenthood in this group of teenage couples. Although a control group of couples marrying later and/or delaying the
transition to parenthood would have allowed a more valid assessment of
these negative effects on marital quality, deLissovoy's less complex
"before-and-after" design provided a basis for suggesting that premature marriage and parenthood are major contributors to a deteriorating
marital relationship.

A somewhat different solution to this issue is to combine cross-
sectional and longitudinal designs by following several cohorts across
modest periods of time and then linking the patterns of change into an
overall configuration. This procedure permits the researcher to assess
both developmental and historical effects. Under the name of "sequential analysis," this mixed design has been extensively treated elsewhere
by developmental psychologists (Baltes, 1968; Schaie, 1965). To our
knowledge, sequential analysis of this sort has never been employed by
family sociologists, nor has it been used to study reciprocal networks of
interaction in families. However, the sequential design is simply a logi-

cal extension of the segmented design. Instead of linking together several segmented longitudinal studies, the sequential design accomplishes the same result in a single study. Of course, this adds to the resources required for sequential research, and the "series of segmented studies" approach therefore remains attractive.

According to our dimensional analysis of research designs, we should not expect to find longitudinal analysis limited to verbal report media or surveys. The research by Ferreira (1960) is notable as an early attempt to use the questionnaire responses of pregnant mothers (about their motherhood attitudes) to predict deviant behavior patterns observed later in their newborn children. Thus, even though we have focused on the issue of cross-sectional versus longitudinal designs for survey research, the same considerations apply independent of the method of data collection.

2. The Survey Method and Reciprocal Influences in the Family

Although survey techniques have been used freely in the study of developmental trends, their usefulness for capturing reciprocal intrafamily influences is quite limited. The study of reciprocal processes virtually demands that family members be directly observed by the researcher in a laboratory or field setting. Validation of reciprocity is difficult to obtain by self-report techniques because respondents may be unaware of or insensitive to the nature of reciprocal causality in their day-to-day interactions. Family members may perceive the reciprocal nature of family interaction in quite different ways depending on their position in the family system, as Larson's (1974) evidence on multilevel perception would suggest. Hence, family members' reports of reciprocal effects may be distorted and lead to inconsistent or invalid generalizations on the part of the investigator. At best, we can only infer reciprocal effects when using survey techniques.

Such inferences relating to the family have been made by Aldous (1978) in her discussion of the research of Meyerowitz (1967), Feldman (1971), and Russell (1974). In each of these survey studies it was concluded that the infant has an active influence on the ability of new parents to cope with their new roles and maintain a satisfying and low-tension marital relationship. If parents reported that their babies were relatively quiet, ate well, slept through the night, were well-tempered, required relatively little care during the day, were generally healthy, and were not colicky, then they were likely to report greater frequency of laughing together, higher levels of marital satisfaction, less arguing, greater sensitivity to the child's physical and socio-emotional needs, more voluntary time spent with the child in nurturant socialization activities, less personal crisis and stress, and fewer child care problems than were other parents (Aldous, 1978).

Based on other research, we know that infants are born with certain individual differences in terms of activity level, crying, sleeping, etc. (Longstreth, 1974; Thomas, Chess, & Birch, 1970), and it may appear safe to assume that fetal and infant traits are the initial independent variables influencing marital and parental role performances and role satisfaction. (This theme is expanded in Chapter 6 by Lamb, in Chapter 10 by Howard, and in Chapter 11 by Korn, Chess, and Fernandez, this volume.) It seems quite logical to infer that the more satisfying and fulfilling nature of marital and parental roles resulting from "easy" babies has a beneficial feedback effect on the quality of the child's own behavioral and emotional development, as parents are more capable of effectively performing parental roles in raising well-socialized and intellectually competent children. On the other hand, if we ask what causes "easy" babies, we may discover that the history of marital and family interaction influences the interpretation of prenatal and newborn behaviors by other family members.

In a similar vein, Rollins and Cannon (1974) infer from their cross-sectional survey that children place a role strain on marriage during the middle years of the life span, accounting for the U-shaped curve of marital adjustment over the life cycle. This role strain may, in turn, influence parental behavior toward school-age and teenage children in the form of decreased tolerance and increased conflict, thereby altering developmental outcomes for the child. For example, a child experiencing a high level of conflict and restrictiveness at home may seek social support and approval outside of the family in the form of a delinquent peer group, early sexual intimacies, or early marriage. Indeed, the survey research literature strongly suggests that this type of reciprocal process is occurring (Bartz and Nye, 1970; Glueck and Glueck, 1968).

Thus, the survey method can provide a logical basis for inferring reciprocal intrafamily effects, although no such effects are directly observed in the data-gathering process itself. This method may also be useful as a precursory step before direct observations are made, thereby allowing the researcher to focus on a delimited number of behaviors and to make comparisons between reports and observations.

B. Direct Observation

The second general research strategy for studying the reciprocal nature of family interaction across the life span is that of direct observation in a field, laboratory, or clinical setting. Whereas the survey method is well-suited for obtaining subjective aspects of family interaction and development, the direct observation method is appropriate for observing the actual behavior of family members. Much discussion has centered upon the suitability of direct observational methods for family study, especially in a laboratory setting. Safilios-Rothschild (1970), Straus (1964), Sussman (1964), and Zelditch (1971) all make compelling arguments justifying the use of observational methods of various types, as opposed to survey techniques, for gathering information about family interaction. These writers also warn of potential problems with the validity of direct observational methods, such as artificiality of setting, behavioral sampling and coding difficulties, and reactivity due to experimeter effects.

Although the arguments in favor of utilizing direct observational methods are convincing and the general methodological issues important, the specific focus here is more on (a) the *extent* to which such methods have been used for studying the family across the life span and for studying reciprocal relationships involving family members; and (b) the *adequacy* of the direct observation method for studying these particular aspects of family life.

1. The Direct Observation Method and Developmental Analysis

In contrast to the survey technique, which has been used extensively as a tool for studying family interaction and marital quality over time, the direct observation method has been underutilized in the developmental study of family interaction. It is puzzling that investigators have not chosen to construct cross-sectional or segmented longitudinal panel designs for picturing developmental trends with direct observational methods. Several family interaction variables of theoretical and substantive importance can and should be studied to complement survey findings regarding shifts in marital quality over the life cycle. Marital and family power structure, communication structure, affection-support structure, conflict resolution techniques, and problem-solving methods and effectiveness are all subject to modifications and transformations as the family moves from stage to stage over the life cycle, and all involve the measurement of variables amenable to the direct observation method.

The limitations of the cross-sectional and longitudinal designs apply here as well and need not be repeated. They simply are not so severe as to preclude the use of observational methods for the study of developmental trends. Two examples of observational research will document the usefulness of these methods in family development research.

Raush *et al.* (1974) observed the process of marital conflict resolution and communication in a laboratory setting with a segmented longitudinal panel design. Married couples were observed in a sequence of four improvisational interchanges in which the investigators had created an incompatibility such that the husband and wife were working at cross-purposes. Some couples were observed at two points in time to monitor any changes that might have occurred in communication and conflict resolution. A portion of the married couples were expecting their first child during the first observation and had already made the role transition to parenthood for the second observation. The remaining couples, who were not expecting a child, served as a control group. Hence, a substantively important analysis of the developmental nature of the marital communication structure and conflict resolution process could be made with this "pretest-posttest control group design" using direct observation techniques.

A second example of the use of direct observational methods to study developmental trends is that of White and his colleagues (White & Watts, 1973). Their goal was to identify the factors distinguishing competent versus noncompetent 6-year-old children and then isolate antecedent environmental and experimental conditions to explain the growth of competence in childhood. They employed a "longitudinal natural experiment" strategy to accomplish the goal, utilizing interviews, questionnaires, and other paper-and-pencil tests (e.g., language ability, IQ, and abstract-thinking tests) to complement the direct observations. Because of previous research and theory suggesting a series of developmental stages in the first 6 years of life (Piaget, 1952; White, 1971), this research team made repeated observations on the behavior, mental abilities, and family interaction of children over a 1- to 2-year period. One year-olds were monitored for a 2-year period (until they were 3), whereas 2-year-olds were followed for a 1-year period.

What resulted from this sequence of observations was a carefully documented and extensive analysis of maternal and physical environmental factors associated with the development of competency over time in childhood. From the standpoint of methodological concerns, however, a more important contribution of this research may be the extent to which survey methods were combined with direct observational methods in a longitudinal design to give a broader picture of the factors involved in the social and intellectual growth of young children.

2. The Direct Observation Method and Reciprocal Influences in the Family

Whereas the survey method forces the investigator to infer reciprocity indirectly, the observational method allows more direct contact with family members such that act-by-act sequences of behavior and mutual effects are brought much closer to the investigator's own sensory capabilities. Hence, a more empirically sound basis exists for drawing valid generalizations about reciprocal, dynamic interactions using observational methods than by using survey methods.

Only a few attempts have been made to design observational research to tap family reciprocity in a developmental context (Lewis & Lee-Painter, 1974). Davids, Holden, and Gray (1963) measured attitudes of pregnant women toward the unborn child and mothers' anxiety levels during pregnancy and later observed them interacting with their children when they were 8 months of age. Mothers who held more negative attitudes toward child rearing and evidenced higher anxiety levels during pregnancy were less capable as caretakers of their children later on. As a consequence, these children scored relatively low on measures of motor and intellectual functioning. In sum, this observational evidence suggests that the arrival of the child influences the mother's emotional state and attitudes, which in turn affect the developmental growth of the child.

Based on their own studies with human infants and the observations of ethologists and others, Stayton, Hogan, and Ainsworth (1971) and Bowlby (1973) suggest that the child is born with physical adaptive capabilities that are activated to facilitate the adjustment process in a social environment. Likewise, mothers have a propensity (supposedly genetically based) to be sensitive to cues (sounds, sights, odors, etc.) emitted by the infant. Consequently, a bond of attachment between parent and child grows in a reciprocal and mutually reinforcing manner. Sensitivity to infant cries and cooperative and accepting behavior on the part of the mother leads to compliance with verbal commands on the part of infants (cooperation), as well as more contact-seeking and social proximity-seeking behavior, and greater responsiveness of infants. The infant's behavior results in even greater sensitivity to cues and levels of acceptance on the part of mothers, and so on in a spiraling and mutually reinforcing way.

Clark-Stewart (1973) observed mother–child interaction during seven in-home visits from the time the infants were 9-months old until they were 18 months of age. The observational data from this study corroborate those from Stayton et al., (1971). The degree to which mothers interacted with, were responsive to, and demonstrated positive emotion toward their infants was positively related to social development and language competency in the infant. A contributing factor here was the mother's role as mediator between the child and objects in the environment, as the child's interest in and ability to cope with surroundings was maximized by mothers who were sensitive to the child's needs for visual and auditory stimulation. Clarke-Stewart's direct observations show that verbally responsive and affectionate behavior of mother toward child led to the development of social skills and responsiveness in the child, which in turn fed back to the mother's behavior, making it even more responsive and sensitive to the needs of the child.

The studies considered in this section highlight two of the existing methodological problems in research on developmental reciprocity in families. First, because they are based on linear or cyclical models of reciprocity instead of a relational model, the identification of independent variables in these studies is not entirely convincing. We may ask what accounts for the mother's emotional state, attitudes, and behavior toward her child in addition to her own genetic propensities, her prepartum emotional state and attitudes, and her child's genetic endowments and behaviors. From a relational perspective, one would take the reciprocal relationship between mother and child as given and attempt to account for it at least partly in terms of the other reciprocal networks that exist in the family now and prior to the birth of the child. This does not mean that the findings of these investigators are flawed but only that a broader view of developmental reciprocity opens up a different set of questions and provides a more comprehensive explanatory framework.

The second methodological difficulty highlighted by these studies involves the selection of relational networks. No one would seriously question the importance of the mother–infant dyad, especially if the focus is on the development of children. However, if our attention is ultimately to broaden to the level of developmental reciprocity in families, we will need to achieve greater balance not only in the range of relational networks that are investigated but also in the slices and durations of development that are investigated (Bronfenbrenner, 1973; Lewis and Feiring, Chapter 3, this volume). To repeat these often-heard directives is not to deny the difficult choices that still remain. No single study can ever explore all the corners of family structure or development. We can expect, therefore, that pieces of the puzzle will be filled in slowly and in scattered fashion with the aid, perhaps, of larger scale, coordinated programs of interdisciplinary research.

An overview of the methods of research commonly employed by developmental psychologists and sociologists suggests a number of future directions that we can predict or at least hope will be taken. First, we can reach beyond marital and parent–child relationships with traditional survey and observational techniques. This requires that we find ways to transcend the image of marriage and parenthood as occurring in isolated dyads. Second, we can make greater use of the relatively sophisticated segmented and sequential designs for identifying the sources of variation in developmental change functions. Finally, we can go beyond the conventional dichotomy between survey and direct observational methods and not only employ novel methods such as the retrieval of archival and biographical materials but also combine methods for validation purposes and to provide complementary perspectives.

V. Conclusion

Little that we have written here points to the need for a methodological revolution or other significant breakthroughs in technique. Instead, our point has been that we can reconceptualize old issues and place them in new perspectives to facilitate decision making. Viewing research designs as multidimensional phenomena may permit us to seek out novel combinations of existing methods or at least alert us to the sacrifices that must be made in any choice of method. In many cases, all that is required is the application of existing methods to a wider range of developmental topics. Most important, we feel that continued attention to the theoretical and methodological implications of developmental reciprocity in families will serve to unite the behavioral sciences around a common developmental course of their own.

References

Aldous, J. Family careers: Development change in families. New York: Wiley, 1978.

Baltes, P. B., & Goulet, L. R. Exploration of developmental variables by manipulation and simulation of age differences in behavior. Human Development, 1971, 14, 149–170.

Baltes, P. B. Longitudinal and cross-sectional sequences in the study of age and generation effects. Human Development, 1968, 11, 145–171.

Bartz, K. W. & Nye, F. I. Early marriage: A propositional formulation. Journal of Marriage and the Family, 1970, 32, 258–268.

Bell, R. Convergence: An accelerated longitudinal approach. Child Development, 1953, 24, 145–152.

Bell, R. An experimental test of the accelerated longitudinal approach. Child Development, 1954, 25, 281–286.

Bell, R. Q. A reinterpretation of the direction of effects in studies of socialization. Psychological Review, 1968, 75, 81–95.

Black, K. D. & Broderick, C. B. Systems theory vs. reality. Paper presented at the annual meeting of the National Council on Family Relations, Portland, Oregon, 1972.

Blalock, H. M., Jr. (Ed.) Causal models in the social sciences. Chicago: Aldine-Atherton, 1971.

Blood, R. O. & Wolfe, D. M. Husbands and wives: The dynamics of married living. New York: Free Press, 1960.

Bossard, J. H. S. & Boll, E. S. *Ritual in family living*. Philadelphia: University of Pennsylvannia Press, 1950.

Bowlby, J. *Attachment and loss*. New York: Basic Books, 1973.

Bronfenbrenner, U. A theoretical perspective for research on human development. In H. D. Dreitzel (Ed.), *Recent sociology No. 5: Childhood and socialization*. New York: Macmillan, 1973, 337–363.

Burgess, R. L. & Conger, R. D. Family interaction in abusive, neglectful, and normal families. Unpublished paper, Pennsylvannia State University, 1977.

Burgess, E. W. & Wallin, P. *Engagement and marriage*. Chicago: Lippincott, 1953.

Campbell, D. T. & Fiske, D. W. Convergent and discriminant validation by the multitrait-multimethod matrix. *Psychological Bulletin*, 1959, 56, 81–105.

Campbell, D. T., & Stanley, J. C. *Experimental and quasi-experimental designs for research*. Chicago: Rand McNally, 1963.

Clark-Stewart, K. A. Interaction between mothers and their young children: Characteristics and consequences. *Monographs of the Society for Research in Child Development*. 1973, 38, No. 153.

Davids, A., Holden, R. H., & Gray, G. B. Maternal anxiety during pregnancy and adequacy of mother and child adjustment eight months following childbirth. *Child Development*. 1963, 34, 993–1002.

deLissovoy, V. Child care by adolescent parents. *Children Today*, 1973, 2, 22–25. (a)

deLissovoy, V. High-school marriages: A longitudinal study. *Journal of Marriage and the Family*. 1973, 35, 245–255. (b)

Denzin, N. K. *The research act: A theoretical introduction to sociological methods*. Chicago: Aldine, 1970.

Deutscher, I. The quality of postparental life. *Journal of Marriage and the Family*, 1964, 26, 52–60.

Dizard, J. *Social change in the family*. Chicago: Community and Family Study Center, University of Chicago, 1968.

Duvall, E. M. *Marriage and family development*. (5th ed.) Philadelphia: Lippincott, 1977.

Dyer, E. D. Parenthood as crisis: A restudy. *Marriage and Family Living*, 1963, 25, 196–201.

Feldman, H. *Development of the husband-wife relationship*. Ithaca: Cornell University, 1964.

Feldman, H. The effects of children on the family. In A. Michel (Ed.), *Family issues of employed women in Europe and America*. Leiden, Netherlands: E. J. Brill, 1971, 104–125.

Feldman, H., & Rogoff, M. Correlates of changes in marital satisfaction with the birth of the first child. Paper presented at the annual meeting of the American Psychological Association, Boston, 1968.

Ferreira, A. J. The pregnant woman's emotional attitude and its reflection on the newborn. *American Journal of Orthopsychiatry*. 1960, 30, 553–561.

Glueck, S., & Glueck, E. *Delinquents and non-delinquents in perspective*. Cambridge: Harvard University Press, 1968.

Hertel, R. *The Markov modeling of experimentally induced marital conflict*. Ann Arbor: University of Michigan, Ph.D. dissertation, 1968.

Hill, R. Methodological issues in family development research. *Family Process*, 1964, 3, 186–205.

Hill, R. *Family development in three generations*. Cambridge, Mass.: Schenkman, 1970.

Hill, R., & Rodgers, R. H. The developmental approach. In H. T. Christensen (Ed.), *Handbook of marriage and the family*. Chicago: Rand McNally, 1964, 171–211.

Hobbs, D. F. Parenthood as crisis: A third study. *Journal of Marriage and the Family*, 1965, 27, 367–372.

Hobbs, D. F. Transition to parenthood: A replication and an extension. *Journal of Marriage and the Family*, 1968, *30*, 413–417.

Jacoby, A. Transition to parenthood: A reassessment. *Journal of Marriage and the Family*, 1969, *31*, 720–727.

Kohn, M. L., & Schooler, C. Occupational experience and psychological functioning: An assessment of reciprocal effects. *American Sociological Review*, 1973, *38*, 97–118.

Larson, L. L. System and sub-system perception of family roles. *Journal of Marriage and the Family*, 1974, *36*, 123–138.

Leik, R. K., & Leik, S. A. Methodological paradigms for studying developing relationships. Paper presented at Conference on Social Exchange in Developing Relationships. The Pennsylvannia State University, 1976.

LeMasters, E. E. Parenthood as crises. *Marriage and Family Living*. 1957, *19*, 352–355.

Lerner, R. M. *Concepts and theories of human development*. Reading, Mass.: Addison-Wesley, 1976.

Lerner, R. M. Nature, nurture, and dynamic interactionism. *Human Development*, 1978, *21*, 1–20.

Lewis, M., & Lee-Painter, S. An interactional approach to the mother–infant dyad. In M. Lewis & L. A. Rosenblum (Eds.), *The effect of the infant on its caregiver*. New York: Wiley, 1974, 21–48.

Longstreth, L. L. *Psychological development of the child*. (2nd ed.) New York: Ronald Press, 1974.

Luckey, E. B., & Bain, J. K. Children: A factor in marital satisfaction. *Journal of Marriage and the Family*. 1970, *32*, 43–44.

Magrabi, F. M., & Marshall, W. H. Family developmental tasks: A research model. *Journal of Marriage and the Family*, 1965, *27*, 454–461.

Meyerowitz, J. H. The transition to parenthood and sources of satisfaction. Paper presented at the annual meeting of the American Sociological Association, San Francisco, 1967.

Meyerowitz, J. H., & Feldman, H. Transition to parenthood. *Psychiatric Research Reports*, 1966, *20*, 78–84.

Miller, B. C. Studying the quality of marriage cross-sectionally. Letter to the editor in *Journal of Marriage and the Family*, 1975, *37*, 11–12.

Miller, B. C. A multivariate developmental model of marital satisfaction. *Journal of Marriage and the Family*, 1976, *38*, 643–657.

Miller, S., Wackman, D. B., & Jorgensen, S. R. Couple communication patterns and marital satisfaction. Paper presented at the Visiting Scholars Seminar, Home Economics Center for Research, University of North Carolina at Greensboro, 1974.

Nye, F. I. Field research. In H. T. Christensen (Ed.), *Handbook of marriage and the family*. Chicago: Rand McNally, 1964, 247–272.

Piaget, J. *The origins of intelligence in children*. (2nd ed.) New York: International University Press, 1952.

Pineo, P. C. Disenchantment in the later years of marriage. *Marriage and Family Living*, 1961, *23*, 3–11.

Raush, H. L., Barry, W. A., Hertel, R. K., & Swain, M. A. *Communication, conflict, and marriage*. San Francisco: Jossey-Bass, 1974.

Riley, M. W. Aging and cohort succession: Interpretations and misinterpretations. *Public Opinion Quarterly*, 1973, *37*, 35–49.

Rodgers, R. H. *Improvements in the construction and analysis of family life cycle categories*. Kalamazoo, Mich.: School of Graduate Studies, Western Michigan University, 1962.

Rodgers, R. H. *Family interaction and transaction: The developmental approach*. Englewood Cliffs, New Jersey: Prentice-Hall, 1973.

Rollins, B. C., & Cannon, K. L. Marital satisfaction over the family life cycle: A reevaluation. *Journal of Marriage and the Family*, 1974, 36, 271–282.

Rollins, B. C., & Feldman, H. Marital satisfaction over the family life cycle. *Journal of Marriage and the Family*, 1970, 32, 20–27.

Russell, C. S. Transition to parenthood: Problems and gratifications. *Journal of Marriage and the Family*, 1974, 36, 294–301.

Ryder, N. The cohort as a concept in the study of social change. *American Sociological Review*, 1965, 30, 843–861.

Ryder, R. G. Longitudinal data relating marriage satisfaction and having a child. *Journal of Marriage and the Family*, 1973, 35, 604–607.

Safilios-Rothschild, C. The study of family power: A review, 1960–1969. *Journal of Marriage and the Family*, 1970, 32, 539–552.

Schaie, K. W. A general model for the study of developmental problems. *Psychological Bulletin*, 1965, 64, 92–107.

Spanier, G. B. Measuring dyadic adjustment: New scales for assessing the quality of marriage and similar dyads. *Journal of Marriage and the Family*, 1976, 38, 15–28.

Spanier, G. B., Lewis, R. A., & Cole, C. L. Martial adjustment over the family life cycle: the issue of curvilinearity. *Journal of Marriage and the Family*, 1975, 37, 263–275.

Spanier, G. B., Sauer, W., & Larzelere, R. Family development and the family life cycle: An empirical evaluation. Paper presented at the annual meeting of the National Council on Family Relations, San Diego, 1977.

Stayton, D. J., Hogan, R., & Ainsworth, M. D. Infant obedience and maternal behavior: The origins of socialization reconsidered. *Child Development*, 1971, 42, 1057–1069.

Straus, M. A. Measuring families. In H. T. Christensen (Ed.), *Handbook of marriage and the family*. Chicago: Rand McNally, 1964, 335–400.

Sussman, M. B. Experimental research. In H. T. Christensen (Ed.), *Handbook of marriage and the family*. Chicago: Rand McNally, 1964, 272–299.

Tallman, I., Wilson, L., & Straus, M. SIMCAR: A game simulation method for cross-national family research. Unpublished manuscript, University of Minnesota, 1972.

Thomas, A., Chess, S., & Birch, H. G. The origin of personality. *Scientific American*, 1970, 223, 102–109.

Weick, K. E. Group processes, family processes, and problem solving. In J. Aldous, *et al.*, (Eds.), *Family problem solving: A symposium on theoretical, methodological, and substantive concerns*. Hinsdale, Illinois: Dryden, 1971, 3–32.

White, B. L. *Human infants: Experience and psychological development*. Englewood Cliffs, New Jersey: Prentice-Hall, 1971.

White, B. L., & Watts, J. C. *Experience and environment: Major influences on the development of the young child*. Englewood Cliffs, New Jersey: Prentice-Hall, 1973.

Zelditch, M., Jr. Experimental family sociology. In J. Aldous, *et al.*, (Eds.). *Family problem solving: A symposium on theoretical, methodological, and substantive concerns*. Hinsdale, Illinois: Dryden, 1971, 55–72.

Influence of the Child on Marital Quality and Family Interaction During the Prenatal, Perinatal, and Infancy Periods[1]

Michael E. Lamb

6

I. Introduction

The devotion of an entire volume to consideration of the effects of children on marital quality and family interaction through the life-span is testimony to three enormously important changes in the way social scientists conceive of the process of psychosocial development. The topic implicitly represents commitment to the following notions:

1. Children have an influence on their "socializers" and are not simply the receptive foci for socializing forces.
2. Early sociopersonality development occurs in the context of a complex family system rather than in the context of the mother–infant dyad.
3. Social and psychological development is not confined to infancy and childhood but is a process that continues from birth to death.

All three of these notions represent significant conceptual advances. Unfortunately, developmental psychologists have traditionally assumed that infants play an essentially passive role in their socialization. Infants have typically been viewed as sensorily, affectively, and motorically incompetent organisms that have to be shaped by their environments into the type(s) of children or adults of which their society or culture approves. Until comparatively recently, in consequence, socialization was explicitly or implicitly believed to be a unidirectional process; no pro-

[1]The author is grateful to Ann M. Frodi and Marguerite B. Stevenson for their comments on an earlier draft of this chapter.

Child Influences on Marital and Family Interaction:
A Life-Span Perspective

grammatic or systematic attempts were made to elucidate the effects infants might have on their "socializers" (cf. Bell, 1968, 1974).

A second implicit assumption has also guided—I would prefer misguided—conceptualization and research on infant social develop-ment: The notion that the infant has only one significant relationship—that to the mother (cf. Ainsworth, 1969; Lamb, 1975, 1976e). In this respect too, therefore, research on infant social relations has been mis-directed inasmuch as researchers have attempted to validate unrealistic "explanations" of development. Only recently have we seen a growing realization that babies may have relations not only with their mothers but with peers, with fathers, and with siblings as well (see Lamb, 1976d, 1977a; Lewis & Feiring, Chapter 3, this volume). Alongside this realiza-tion, there has emerged an appreciation that individual mothers, like fathers and babies, each have discernibly characteristic styles of behavior and emotional expression. All mothers are not the same predictable composites of breasts and caresses that our major theorists depict.

Intimately related to the preceding notions is the final "guiding" assumption. Development psychologists have long posited that the sociopersonality styles developed in infancy established lifelong pat-terns and predispositions. This belief appears to have grown out of the pathology model, which has played an extremely influential role in di-recting theory building. Most impressive has been the pervasive influ-ence of the "maternal deprivation" literature, in which the psychoanaly-tic emphasis on the irreversibility of early socioemotional damage achieved prominence (cf. Rutter, 1972). Only recently has there emerged consensus that these earlier formulations—with their emphasis on early experiences—were incorrect (see Lamb, 1978b) and that the process of sociopersonality development is longer and more complicated than simplistic models postulate (Labouvie-Vief, 1978; Lamb, 1978a; Per-loff & Lamb, 1978; Rutter, 1977).

The traditional assumptions that these notions replace have led de-velopmentalists to a peculiarly misleading conception of the phenomena that they sought to explain. In essence, researchers and theorists have pondered how the mother shaped a passive tabula rasa in a way that would suitably and irreversibly direct it toward functioning as a compe-tent adult. The modifying influence of subsequent experiences, the ef-fect of the infant upon those around him or her, and the infant's poten-tial for relationships with persons other than primary caretakers were all ignored until a few years ago.

I stress the depressing narrow-mindedness of the major theories because their interpretations and heuristic formulations have had an enormous impact on the type of research conducted. As a result, this chapter will not contain a synthesis of a large body of respectable evidence because the available data are at best only tantalizing and tangentially relevant. Since conclusions cannot be drawn, I will strive instead to provide heuristic propositions.

II. The Prenatal Period

Proceeding chronologically, let us first consider the effects of pregnancy on family relations. Few studies have attempted to investigate the nature and extent of adjustments to pregnancy—and only one of these studies explicitly focused on *families* rather than upon pregnant *women*. Further, the studies by Davids and his colleagues (Davids, 1968; Davids & Holden, 1970; Davids, Holden, & Gray, 1963) and the more recent research by Bakow, Sameroff, Kelly, and Zax (1973) tell us more about the relation between maternal response and the later behavior of mother and infant than about the effects of pregnancy.

Some potentially important attitudinal changes in the prenatal period are suggested by the findings of a recent Yale dissertation (Arbeit, 1975). Interviewing a group of women during their first pregnancy, Susan Arbeit identified a number of significant themes common to most of the women's answers. One prominent theme concerned reevaluation of the women's relationships with their own parents—particularly their mothers. As they approached motherhood themselves, in other words, the women attained a more empathic view of their mothers' role and responsibilities. Increasingly, it seemed, they became aware that they would soon adopt similar roles. It would be interesting to know whether fathers-to-be go through a similar process of self-evaluation: A single clinical case report by Gurwitt (1976) suggests that they may. Whereas the women's reevaluations of mother–daughter relationships were characterized by "traditionalizing" identifications (Arbeit, 1975), however, Gurwitt's patient clearly aimed to perform *better* than his own father.

Two other themes discussed by Arbeit must surely characterize mothers-to-be more than fathers-to-be, since these themes were directly related to the physical symptoms of pregnancy, which are usually borne by women alone.[2] Many pregnant women began to ascribe personal

---

[2] Perhaps the *couvade* practice belies my presumption that the physical symptoms do not have a direct effect on men. Likewise, there is anecdotal evidence that some prospective fathers empathically share physical symptoms such as morning sickness and weight loss. Clearly, however, this is not the norm.

characteristics to their unborn fetuses (a theme that Arbeit (1975) describes as "the emerging definition of the fetus as child"). Accompanying this propensity, Arbeit delineated a conceptually related theme, characterized by insistence on maintaining personal identity (i.e., differentiating self from the unborn "other"). These themes may be especially relevant, since the extent to which pregnant women concern themselves with them and the manner in which they are resolved must surely have important implications for marital quality. Obsessive introspection may serve to distance husband and wife and cool their relationship; an inability to recognize the unborn child's individuality, meanwhile, may presage an unhealthily symbiotic and overprotective mother–infant relationship. This would be a pathological example of a complicated process whereby the child-as-fetus affects the mother's behavior, which in turn affects the formative social experiences of the child.

To the extent that they explicitly investigated the attitudes of prospective mothers and fathers, Leon Yarrow and his colleagues provided more information than Arbeit did concerning family responses to pregnancy, though their findings have been sketchily reported thus far (Soule, 1974). These researchers interviewed 67 pairs of parents-to-be during the eighth month of pregnancy concerning "their experiences and their general adaptation to the pregnancy, their expectation and feeling about the unborn child, and their relationship with each other. Husband and wife were interviewed separately [Yarrow, 1974, p. 3]." Soule's most important finding was the remarkable similarity between the attitudes expressed by the women and the attitudes expressed by their husbands. The implication, reasoned Soule, was that pregnancy is "a couple experience." It is not clear what this means, however. Pregnancy per se might not have influenced men and women directly in the same way; rather, the couples may have discussed their feelings about pregnancy, so that their responses to the interview represented a consensus. The consensual responding may obscure the fact, for example, that the pregnancy has a major *direct* effect on one spouse and an *indirect* effect on the other. Elucidation of direct and indirect effects will be necessary before we can claim to understand the nature and process of adjustments to pregnancy. Soule reported that differences between the husbands and wives were evident on very few items. In general, it seemed that the husbands were less ambivalent about the pregnancy than their wives and that they anticipated fewer life changes in the immediate future. These were realistic assessments, given the distribution of caretaking roles within the traditional nuclear family.

Unfortunately, Yarrow and his colleagues told us only that couples tended to feel the same way about pregnancy. They have reported disappointingly little evidence about *how* the couples felt, *how* pregnancy affected or changed the structure of the marital relationships, and *how* these effects in turn influenced the family in such a way that the child's development might be influenced. One might predict, for example, that the preparation for parenthood initiates a conservative or traditionalizing impact on childless couples' marriages. The wive's withdrawal from work in preparation for childbirth may facilitate a change from the more egalitarian values and role demands of dual-career couples to the more stereotyped role set of traditional nuclear families. Women who marry young and who have their first child soon after marriage are especially likely to be "locked into" traditional marital roles (Ahammer, 1973). I would predict similar trends among most types of couples—regardless of the egalitarianism or traditionality of their relationship. Clearly, this could be a significant cause of stress in some families, especially during the first pregnancy. It might be particularly interesting to determine whether the egalitarianism of the couples' relationships are positively related to the difficulty they encounter in adjusting to pregnancy. There is some evidence that this may have been so in the mid-1960s (Feldman, 1971). Much of the intracouple agreement that Soule noted may simply reflect reference to stereotyped notions and expectations about behavior that would be role appropriate in the last months of pregnancy. "Liberated" couples have recourse to fewer repositories of information concerning "appropriate" behavior and behavior change. Consequently, I would expect there to be less agreement during pregnancy and more marital stress within couples who claim allegiance to nontraditional attitudes than within "traditional" couples. These and other questions are currently being investigated by my colleagues and me, though no apposite data are yet available. Essentially, our belief is that pregnancy may trigger some fairly dramatic changes in the role structure of the existing family unit. Clearly, since marital roles are partially defined by complementarity, the role transitions brought about by pregnancy have implications for the person concerned as well as for his or her spouse. Thus, pregnancy affects the two parents-to-be and their relationship directly and indirectly.

It is unfortunate that the social implications of pregnancy have been explored so cursorily and that there have been so few systematic attempts to investigate the direct impact of maternal hormonal state on maternal personality, although this may play an important role in determining the quality of relationship established between mother and child or maintained between the spouses. The husband's ability to support his wife or tolerate her emotional lability, meanwhile, may also have long-term consequences for family adjustment. Perhaps future researchers will show greater appreciation of the biological and sociobiological aspects of the transition to parenthood.

Since the preparation for and transition to parental roles have already taken place, we should not expect second and subsequent pregnancies to have consequences similar to those encountered by primipari. I suspect that the responses of older siblings are critical determinants of the extent and nature of the impact of later pregnancies. Because of the intimate interrelations among family roles, meanwhile, one might predict primarily indirect influences on the parents. Each child's response is likely to be a function of his or her age, sex, and the quality of the relationships with the parents, whereas the parents' responses are likely to reflect changes in their behavior in response to the perceived needs of the child. Since indirect effects are mediated via attempts by a young child to prepare for the assumption of a new role within the family, second pregnancies must surely have a more complex (if less dramatic) effect on family relationships.

On the other hand, an old re-analysis of the Fels Longitudinal Study data (Baldwin, 1947) indicated that upon becoming pregnant, mothers changed their style of relating to their older children. Most notable were declines in (a) maternal warmth; (b) the intensity and duration of mother–child "contact"; (c) the effectiveness of the mothers' child-rearing policies; and (d) the mothers' infantilization of their children. By contrast, degree of restrictiveness, severity of punishment, and coercion all increased. In other words, the nature of mother–child relationships changed dramatically in anticipation of the expected births, and the new character was maintained after parturition. Interestingly, the changes that occurred were similar to the changes that occurred as children grew older (Baldwin, 1946). Thus, subsequent pregnancies appeared to accelerate the siblings' transition to "older child" roles. This may increase the siblings' vulnerability around the time of birth, since they are forced to adjust to several role changes at about the same time.

In sum, then, pregnancy can be viewed as a biosocial state that has two types of impact on family members and family relationships. There are, first, responses that are anchored in the present biological state and, second, those that relate to projected implications of that state. Both merit serious investigation by social scientists, and neither have been adequately explored in the past, despite their potential significance. In addressing these issues, furthermore, one might wish for serious consideration of the effects of the responses to pregnancy upon the formative experiences of the expected child.

III. The Perinatal Period

In all, we know little about the impact of pregnancy on family interaction and marital quality. Our understanding of childbirth is little better. Studies have confirmed what most people assumed—namely, that the birth of a baby is a profoundly moving experience for both parents (e.g., Greenberg, 1973; Greenberg & Morris, 1974; Klaus & Kennell, 1976). These feelings are not merely reported by the parents; they are also clearly evident in the initial interactions between parents and neonates (Parke & O'Leary, 1975).[3]

We know little about family interaction during childbirth, primarily because social scientists have only recently defined childbirth as a natural rather than a surgical process. In addition, as Barbara Anderson (Anderson & Standley, 1976) ruefully reported, pregnancies tend to terminate unpredictably, so that observations of family interaction during delivery are not easily made. In their preliminary pilot report, however, Anderson and Standley point toward some interesting statistical relationships between women's expressions of pain and tension and the husband–wife interactions during labor. It was found that "when the mother and father often talk about the course of labor, the woman's well-being and topics unrelated to the childbirth, the woman is unlikely to be in pain [p. 13]." A conclusion that the husband is serving as an effective analgesic rather than that women who are less distressed are more available for interaction is supported by other findings reported by Henneborn and Cogan (1974) and Tanzer (in Macfarlane, 1977).

Other studies have focused on *maternal* attitudes around delivery and their relation to subsequent behavior, but for methodological and conceptual reasons the merit of these investigations is debatable. Drawing their evidence exclusively from subsequent maternal recollections, for example, Doering and Entwisle (1975) reported significant relationships between the initial responses of mothers to their neonates and two

---

[3]On the other hand, it is important to remember that, in retrospect at least, some primiparous mothers describe their initial affective responses as involving feelings of strangeness, distance, and unfamiliarity (Robson & Moss, 1970; though see Macfarlane, 1977). According to Grey, Cutler, Dean, and Kempe (n.d.), the extent of such negative responses to first presentation of the neonate may be predictive of subsequent maladaptive patterns of interaction.

early "patterns of caretaking"—specifically, (a) whether the women chose a rooming-in arrangement; and (b) whether they chose to breast-feed or bottle-feed their babies. Unfortunately, though, the initial affective responses of the women were related to their "awareness" during delivery, which was, in turn, related to prenatal (Lamaze) childbirth preparation. It seems likely that all the characteristics that were significantly correlated were direct consequences of the prenatal training and the values therein encountered. In other words, the relationship between initial response and "caretaking style" may be entirely spurious. Clark and Alfonso (1976) have reported equivalently uninterpretable associations between women's feelings about their delivery and perceptions of their own caretaking competence.

These two studies focused exclusively on maternal attitudes. Paternal attitudes were explored by Greenberg and Morris (1974), but unfortunately these researchers could not examine the relationship between the initial responses (which were universally positive) and the subsequent behavior or attitudes of the men. The relationship between the nature of childbirth and subsequent marital quality, meanwhile, has not been explored—not even superficially. Presumably, information about the responses of mothers *and* fathers will together elucidate predictive relationships more reliably than data concerning the mothers alone. Certainly, one would expect that a relaxed environment in which the parents are able to share the childbirth experience and engage in some early interaction with the neonate may strengthen their own relationship (the perception of themselves as a family) and facilitate their bonding to the infant, although there is no evidence that paternal presence at delivery facilitates father–infant bonding (Greenberg & Morris, 1974).

In a series of observational studies, Parke and his colleagues (Parke & O'Leary, 1975; Parke, O'Leary & West, 1972; Parke & Sawin, 1976, 1977) have found that primiparous mothers and fathers both appear eager to hold and interact with their newborn babies. In these studies, fathers appeared particularly likely to monitor their babies visually when not interacting with them directly. Both parents appeared equivalently eager to interact with and show affection for their babies. It did not seem, furthermore, that the parents were simply "putting on shows" for one another, since they paid *more* rather than *less* attention to the infants when observed in parent–neonate dyads rather than mother–father–infant triads. Perhaps this occurred because the parents did not have to compete with their spouses for the opportunity to interact in the dyadic contexts (Parke & O'Leary, 1975). Despite the fact that mothers and fathers were equivalently affectionate with their babies, however, traditional role differentiation emerged quite early. Although male and female parents were equally sensitive to infant cues—for example, those implicit in feeding—mothers were far more likely to feed the babies than were fathers. This was the case even when the babies were bottle-fed and even when both parents were available and able to feed their infants (Parke & Sawin, 1976, 1977).

Beyond this, however, there is only limited and controversial evidence concerning the impact of childbirth (that is, incipient parenthood) on the style of interaction between husbands and wives and on their perceptions of the marriage. Sociologists have disagreed for years over how to characterize parents' responses to childbirth. LeMasters (1957) and Dyer (1963) have described the onset of parenthood as a "crisis" that is perceived as extremely stressful by most couples. By contrast, Hobbs (1965, 1968; Hobbs & Cole, 1976) found that few couples regarded parenthood as a crisis at all; in fact, most reported far greater marital satisfaction after the birth of the first baby than during the prenatal period. The data, unfortunately, were all gathered retrospectively. Curiously, Meyerowitz and Feldman (1966) found that whereas the majority of couples studied were more satisfied 5 months after delivery than before parturition, most anticipated a steady decline in marital satisfaction. The reason for this is obscure, but it is surely related to the concept of the "baby honeymoon" (Hobbs, 1965), which proposes that enthusiasm over the new baby fades with time as the novelty wears off. Researchers have been unsuccessful, however, in their attempts to validate the "baby honeymoon" concept (e.g., Wente & Crockenberg, 1976). In any event, Feldman's (e.g., 1971) more recent papers have concurred with the crisis notion, though the evidence cited is not convincing. Any role change is likely to involve transitional difficulties; describing these as crises is something of an exaggeration.

Interestingly, attendance at childbirth and parent preparation classes does not appear to be associated with any differences in the degree of difficulty encountered during the adjustment to parenthood (Wente & Crockenberg, 1976; Parke & O'Leary, 1975). However inadequate the preparation for parenthood, it is highly unlikely that parents-to-be (especially mothers-to-be) do not make some anticipatory adjustments prior to childbirth that would soften the impact of the baby's birth. These adjustments would mitigate against the occurrence of a response that could be described as a crisis. Nevertheless, inasmuch as the anticipatory changes are stylized rather than individualized and represent adjustments to hypothesized demands rather than realistic ones, it seems probable that further changes in marital relationships, roles, and attitudes will take place following the birth of the baby. Unfortunately, few researchers have investigated *how* families and couples are affected, and few have attempted to describe the specific behavioral, psychological, or role changes that underlie changes in marital adjustment or happiness. Conspicuously lacking are attempts to relate hormonal imbalances (which are likely to succeed parturition), postpartum depression in women, and indices of maternal and familial adjustment to childbirth and parenthood. Two-thirds of all postparturitional women experience some form of "postpartum blues" in the 10 days following delivery (Yalom, 1968). For most, the depression is transient. It seems likely that support networks are especially important at this stage, however, since women who fail to receive emotional support from spouses or family at this time may become isolated or may develop inappropriate social relationships. In such cases the brief depression may have long-term consequences.

Curiously, because of the long commitment to the "mother socializes passive baby" concept, we may know more about the nature and predictive importance of fathers' responses to childbirth than about mothers' responses. Extensive interviews of new fathers by Fein (1975) indicated that the adoption of a coherent role seemed to be the key to postpartum adjustment among men. Presumably, this is also important for mothers-to-be, although in the absence of good social supports, selection of and adjustment to a coherent paternal role may be particularly difficult.

As far as the *content* of the mother's role is concerned, I suspect that childbirth will have a conservative impact on gender and marital roles. The insistent and undeniable dependency of the baby makes equivocation or ambiguity about role demands more difficult to sustain than in the preparental phase, and our society's expectations regarding nurturant maternal roles are more clearly defined than any other. Notice, then, that responses to childbirth reinforce the "traditionalizing" impact of pregnancy. Analogously, most new fathers apparently experience pressures toward fulfillment of an economic provider's role (e.g., Benson, 1968; Lynn, 1974).

The paucity of the relevant data notwithstanding, it seems reasonable to predict that prospective and actual parenthood have a compounding conservative impact on gender roles. Inasmuch as complementary pressure on both mothers and fathers push both toward more traditional gender roles, one might predict changes in the individual personalities as well as changes in family relationships. Changes of both types would affect the formative experiences to which the newborn child was exposed and hence would affect his or her development. Needless to say, these are hypotheses (not conclusions), and they would benefit from detailed investigation, particularly as they have implications for our understanding of the development of gender roles (see Lamb & Urberg, 1978; Perloff & Lamb, 1978) as well as for our understanding of parent–infant relations, family dynamics, and sociopersonality development (Lamb, 1978b). It is unfortunate that so much attention has been paid to exploring the amorphous variable "marital satisfaction," whereas few attempts have been made to determine what changes in role demands and patterns of family interaction are taking place.

IV. The Infancy Period

Only with respect to postnatal family–infant transactions has there been considerable investigation. Unfortunately, it is easy to be misled by the number of published studies in this area. The bulk of the studies conducted have been aimed at answering rather different questions than those with which we are concerned. Investigators have explored interaction at the microanalytic level, ignoring the macroanalytic level almost completely. Most of the research simply points toward a conclusion that infants are capable of playing active roles in the modulation of individual bouts of interaction. In light of the traditional presumptions described in the preceding section, the research itself represents a virtual revolution in the way we view infancy, but it is no more than a promise that research focusing on the kinds of effects in which we are interested may be initiated soon. We still know relatively little about the influence babies have on their families, on their parents' relationships with one another and with older siblings, and on these siblings directly. Needless to say, we know even less about the influences that these effects have upon the formative developmental experiences of the child.

Active Participation in Interaction

Stimulated by a couple of papers by Richard Bell (1968, 1971), the concept of the passively socialized (plastic) infant has been most critically examined in recent years. The first wave of research related to Bell's proposition focused on the "effects" of very obvious infant characteristics. Several investigators attempted to exemplify the influence that children exert over parental behavior by showing that adults respond differently to children differing on dimensions such as sex (Condry & Condry, 1976; Lamb, 1977c, 1977d; Lewis, 1972; Lewis & Weinraub, 1974; Rubin, Provenzano & Luria, 1974; Moss, 1967) and state (Korner,

1974; Thoman, Becker, & Freese, 1978; Thoman, Acebo, Dreyer, Becker, & Freese, in press). These studies were important to the extent that they added empirical support to Bell's arguments, though their reported findings are of tangential interest in the present context.

Of greatest interest to us are those studies focused on the capacity of infants to exert voluntary or modulated control over adults during interaction sequences. Most of the relevant studies involve microanalyses of brief bouts of adult–child interaction and were undertaken in order to identify the roles of child and adult in maintaining the interaction. The bulk comprise fine-grained analyses of interactions involving infants younger than 4 months of age.

The research conducted by Brazelton and Stern has been most influential in effecting a revision of traditional preconceptions about infant social skills. Following their earlier work on mother–infant interaction during feeding sessions (Kaye & Brazelton, 1971), Brazelton and his colleagues (Brazelton, Tronick, Adamson, Als, & Wise, 1975) reported that one could discern rhythmic or cyclic qualities in early parent–infant interaction, with infants alternating from attention to nonattention. The cyclicity was evident in analyses of mutual gaze patterns, gross movements, and facial expression changes. Similar conclusions were reached by Jaffe, Stern, and Peery (1973), who found that a Markov chain model was at least partially successful in demonstrating that early gaze "conversations" had a reciprocal quality that mirrored the patterns of turn taking in adult conversation. In discussing their findings, Brazelton *et al.* concluded that the infants must be playing an active role in modulating interaction, although, as I have noted elsewhere (Lamb, 1977a), their data did not exclude the possibility that the apparent reciprocity resulted from the adults "filling in" the gaps in the infants' behavior. This would mean, of course, that the "reciprocity" was a product of adult, rather than infant, behavior. Either interpretation would be plausible. In addition, it is important to note that the cyclicity has not been found consistently, even within individual infants. Only gaze aversion reliably elicits maternal behavioral change (Brazelton, Koslowski, & Main, 1974).

Similarly inconclusive findings have emerged from other attempts to demonstrate the active role played by infants in modulating their interaction with adults. In constructing chain models for example, researchers have found it difficult to identify when an interaction begins and what constitutes "stimulus" or "response" (cf. Lewis, 1972; Lewis & Freedle, 1973). Similarly, the facts that neonates who were rated "alert" on the Neonatal Behavioral Assessment Scale (Brazelton, 1973) had mothers who were more attentive and sensitive than the mothers of less alert infants (Osofsky, 1975; Osofsky & Danzger, 1974) and that the mothers of alert newborns express more positive attitudes toward their babies (Bakow et al., 1973) only suggest, rather than prove, the role of infant characteristics in the modulation of social interaction.

Since Stern's design circumvented these problems, his description of patterns of dyadic gazing between mothers and infants is particularly important. Stern (1974a, 1974b) found that infants modulate interaction by averting their gaze when the stimulation provided by their mothers is too intense. This lends credence to Brazelton's claim that both adults and infants play active roles in their interaction. Comparable conclusions can be drawn from Fogel's (1975) study and from some recent experimental and naturalistic research. Notably, both Brazelton (Brazelton et al., 1975; Tronick, Adamson, Wise, Als, & Brazelton 1975) and (Carpenter 1974; Carpenter, Tecce, Stechler, & Friedman, 1970) have shown that when adults are unresponsive, infants intensify their efforts to elicit attention and reaction before crying or withdrawing from interaction. Sherrod (1976) failed to find this, perhaps because the artificial configural transformations he imposed overshadowed the effect of the behavioral transformations. In more naturalistic contexts, Strain and Vietze (1975) and Vietze, Strain and Falsey (1975) have shown that mothers and babies are more likely to start talking to one another when the other is already vocalizing and less likely to stop while the other continues to talk. This indicates that both adults and children actively direct the course of their interaction. On the other hand, the fact (Strain & Vietze, 1975; Vietze et al., 1975; Stern, Jaffe, Beebe, & Bennett, 1975; Tronick, 1977; Yogman, 1977) that states of simultaneous vocalization are most common is not consistent with Brazelton's hypothesis that there is reciprocal turn taking in early interaction.

Though his infant subjects were older (6 months), Kaye's (1975) research is also important because it indicates that infants use head turning as a signal to request assistance from their mothers while solving a task. Gaze and head aversion subsequently become important ways of modulating adult behavior in reciprocal games like peekaboo (Bruner & Sherwood, 1974).

In sum, the research discussed in this section lends scant support to the belief that infants are passive recipients of socializing stimulation. Infants direct the course of their development both by way of individual differences that are evident at birth and through the role they play in determining the nature of social interaction. The sensitivity of parents and infants to one another's signals determines the success of the early interaction, which, in turn, plays a crucial role in the facilitation of infant–adult bonding (Ainsworth, Bell, & Stayton, 1971, 1974; Lamb, 1975, 1976d; Schaffer & Emerson, 1964).

I should caution, though, that we do not yet know precisely what the infant's role involves. Some argue that infants simply emit behaviors that elicit responses from adults, whereas others claim that infants monitor their own behavior as well as that of adults in order to engage in reciprocal interaction sequences. There is strong evidence for the former and suggestive support for the latter. In any event, by 3 (and perhaps by 1) months of age, infants have developed expectations that adults will behave in a contingent and reciprocal fashion; babies are distressed when these expectations are violated. Presumably, these expectations about the behavior of adults develop out of interactional experiences. During the next 3 months, furthermore, we observe a dramatic unfolding of infant social capacity. Unfortunately, research involving infants of 6 to 24 months of age has focused rather narrowly on the emergence of attachment relations and "stranger anxiety." Considerably less attention has been paid to the microanalysis of adult–infant interaction.

Although we may quibble over the "innateness" of the capacities we have discussed and argue about the age at which they emerge or mature, all relevant studies point toward one conclusion: that infants have the skills necessary to monitor the behavior of others and the ability to apply this information in modulating, terminating, and initiating interaction with adults. These are not prerequisites for exerting influences on the nature of interaction within the family (e.g., the baby does not determine its gender, though gender may exert significant control over the types of interaction to which the baby is exposed), but they vastly increase the potential scope of the baby's impact. Infants affect patterns of interaction in a variety of ways—by being present or absent, because of constitutional characteristics over which they have no control, because others may label the infant's behaviors as "signals," and, most obviously, as active participant–members of their social environment.

Concepts of Family and Infant

Unfortunately, however, we do not know *how* this power is exercised, nor do we know *how* infants affect family relationships. The major reason for our ignorance, I suspect, is that theoretical conceptualizations to this day have viewed the infant social world as a two-person system—mother and infant—and have avoided consideration of the fact that the mother–infant dyad is embedded in a wider social context and that infants themselves have relationships with persons other than their mothers. It is unusual to study effects upon something whose existence is implicitly denied!

In fact, the empirical evidence suggests that most infants form relationships with both parents at around the same time (Lamb, 1976b, 1976c, 1977b), although they come to show clear but circumscribed preferences for their mothers toward the end of the first year of life (Lamb, 1976a; 1976e). Unfortunately, social scientists have a distressing tendency to leap from the fact that mothers may be the most important figures in their infants' lives to the conclusion that they are uniquely and exclusively significant. In the eyes of their infants they clearly are not. Furthermore, there is no obvious reason why the hierarchy among attachment figures need reflect the relative importance of these individuals as influences on the process of personality development. In fact, since mothers and fathers engage in different types of interaction with their infants, the two parents may be making independently significant contributions to the infants' personality development (Lamb, 1976b). In addition, among humans, as among monkeys (the parallel may be coincidental, but it is certainly provocative), fathers rather than mothers play the major role in channeling the infants' attention toward the appropriate (i.e., same sex) parental model (Lamb, 1977c, 1977d; Suomi, 1977). Human fathers achieve this by increasing the amount of interaction they have with their sons and temporarily reducing the amount of interaction they have with their daughters. Since mothers do not differentiate between sons and daughters in an analogous fashion, the net effect of the fathers' behavior is to maximize the salience of the same sex parent. This may play a crucial role in the early development of gender identity (Lamb, 1977d; Money & Ehrhardt, 1972) and signal the first stage in the more extended process of gender role acquisition (Lamb & Urberg, 1978).

Infants may have psychologically significant relationships not only with their mothers and fathers but with their siblings as well. Unfortunately, we know even less about sibling relations in infancy than about parent–infant transactions. In a recent study, we found that 18-month-olds engage in little direct interaction with preschool-age siblings, although they frequently monitored the other's whereabouts and activities, imitated the sibling's behaviors, and took over toys recently released by the older child (Lamb, 1978d). There are, obviously, vast individual differences in the extent of sibling interaction, but the determinants and antecedents of these have yet to be explored.

Effects of Infants on Their Families

Since students of infancy have only recently—and begrudgingly—acknowledged the relevance of the family to the infant's development, they have conducted few studies aimed at elucidating the infant's impact on the family. A few strands of evidence exist, however.

After the infant's birth, the person bearing the greatest proportion of the increased responsibilities the baby entails is the primary caretaker—the mother. As I have already suggested, the mother is pressured toward preparation for her role during pregnancy, though the preparation is unlikely to be adequate, since effective mothering does not involve merely the rote performance of learned caretaking behaviors. Instead, it demands affective commitment and the modulation of behavior patterns in accordance with the individual temperament and needs of each infant.

Feiring (1976; Feiring & Taylor, in press) has found that the emotional involvement of mothers (in their infants) is related to the extent to which they report receiving emotional support from "secondary parents" during this role transition. This suggests that the responses of mothers to their infants may be dependent on the nature of their marital relationships and the propensity of their spouses to assist and support them.

Feiring also reported a negative correlation between the perceived difficulty of the baby's temperament and the mother's emotional involvement with the baby. One might infer, then, that the more difficult the baby's temperament, the more support the mother is going to require from her spouse. Other infant characteristics, too, are likely to have a similar effect on the mother and her emotional needs. These must also be taken into account. In addition, the complexity of the problem multiplies when we consider that the infant may well have relationships with its father and siblings as well as with its mother. The nature of the relationship each forms with the baby may be dependent upon the adequacy of the various support relationships.

Another body of relevant research concerns "second-order effects." These occur when interaction within a dyad or triad is altered by the presence or absence of another individual (Lamb, 1976a, 1976b, 1978c, 1978d; Rosenblatt, 1974). Both the data and common sense predict that a baby's birth surely serves to limit the amount of interaction between spouses and between parents and older children (cf. Cohen & Beckwith, 1977; Rubenstein, 1967; Thoman, Barnett, & Leiderman, 1971; Thoman, Leiderman, & Olson, 1972). The family's long-term adjustment to an infant's arrival may be predicted best by the parents' response to the reaction of older children to their new sibling. Consistent with this, Legg, Sherick, and Wadland (1975) have reported that siblings' adjustment is facilitated by the increased involvement of fathers in interaction with them. In a traditional family context, it seems, the mother's attempts to interact sufficiently with an older child may not be sufficient to allay the sibling's realistic fears of displacement. The pilot study of Legg *et al.* suggests that the increased attention from fathers may serve to convince the older child that he or she is "special" for one parent too.

Since adjustment to the birth of a second (or subsequent) child involves modulating the impact of sudden maternal inaccessibility on an immature and dependent sibling, the demands on the parents are more complex than the demands imposed on them by the birth of their first child. One could speculate that whereas the first birth had a "traditionalizing" effect, the second may exert a more powerful pull toward interpersonal involvement in the family by fathers. Instead of being free to choose a level of involvement, as with the firstborn, there may be unambiguous demands for paternal involvement after subsequent births. Thus, responsible fathers may find themselves becoming more child centered than the stereotyped male role would predict. Since fathers are often less involved with young daughters than with sons (Lamb, 1977c, 1977d), the second birth may have an especially marked effect on families with firstborn daughters. Interestingly, Feldman (cf. 1971) has found that fathers want to be more involved in child care than their wives want them to be. The birth of a second child may reduce women's opposition to their husbands invading their preserve: This, too, would facilitate increased paternal involvement with laterborns.

V. Children's Contribution to Their Own Abuse

Let us turn now to consideration of some less obvious and certainly less desirable effects of children on their families. More specifically, I want to discuss briefly the role infants play in eliciting their own abuse, drawing upon a model currently being developed by Ann Frodi and myself. This topic provides an example of the way in which infant characteristics affect members of their families, thereby influencing the types of experiences to which they are exposed. The model also illustrates how the child's characteristics interact with other factors in determining its social experiences. This underscores the inadequacy of "single influence" models.

As Parke and Collmer (1975) demonstrated in their recent authoritative review, psychiatric and sociological models have dominated professional and lay conceptualizations of child abuse. Traditionally, child abuse has been attributed to mentally ill parents or parents who are driven to aggressive outbursts by intolerable social stress. Recently, we have witnessed a marriage of these two explanations. Despite its popularity, however, this combination of psychiatric and sociological concepts clearly does not comprise a satisfactory explanation of child abuse. Three facts about the incidence of child abuse show the social and/or psychiatric models, as commonly described, to be inadequate.

1. The psychiatric and sociological models both yield many false negatives. Most of the "potential abusers" never aggress against their children, and most parents living in stressful circumstances are never abusive.
2. Abusing parents do not abuse all their children—one is usually selected to be the victim.
3. The characteristics of infants and children partially determine the probability that they will be abused. Most impressive are the statistics indicating that premature and "difficult" infants are "at risk" for child abuse.

These three facts have led us to postulate that greater attention must be paid to the characteristics of children who are abused. We propose that the parents' personalities *and* the social–environmental milieu *and* the child's characteristics combine to determine when and where abuse will occur. In order to develop a comprehensive explanatory model of child abuse, then, we believe that one has to give careful consideration to the nature of caretaking, since this may permit us to clarify the contributions made by children to their own abuse. Consider the two major signals used by infants—smiling and crying. Intuitive and empirical considerations suggest that smiles elicit adult behaviors aimed at prolonging the baby's state because the interaction is pleasurable for both baby and adult, whereas cries elicit adult responses aimed at removing the cause of the distress, thereby terminating a signal that is perceived as aversive. Both self-report and psychophysiological evidence indicate that the appropriate behavioral propensities are established differentially by the sight and sound of smiling–cooing and crying infants (Frodi, Lamb, Leavitt, & Donovan, 1978). This implies that caretaking is motivated not only by adult altruism but also by the determination of adults to terminate signals they find unpleasant.

In other words, a crying infant is an arousing and aversive stimulus, and as such he or she increases the likelihood that aggressive behavior will occur (Berkowitz, 1974). Usually, the arousal is of a subthreshold nature, and the aversive stimulus is terminated simply by relieving the cause of the infant's distress. In the case of "difficult" infants, however, termination is not this simple. Despite the best intentioned ministrations of parents, these infants are relatively inconsolable, they cry extensively, and their moods are labile, unpredictable, and infrequently positive (Thomas, Chess, Birch, Hertzig, & Korn, 1963; Thomas, Chess, & Birch, 1968, 1970). As a result, we believe, the baby per se becomes an aversive stimulus *regardless of whether or not it is crying*, through a process of conditioning. Consistent with this notion, Donovan, Leavitt, and Balling (1978) found that the mothers of difficult infants failed to respond appropriately to changes in infant signals. Our prediction is that more veridical and prolonged stimuli than those used by Donovan *et al.* would lead to a more easily interpretable adult response, with the aversiveness of the infant dampening the adults' response to positive infant stimuli (e.g., smiles) and enhancing the perceived aversiveness of the infant's cries. The net effect would be to increase the probability of abuse.

Obviously, most difficult children are not abused, so some other factors must be incorporated into the model. In line with the sociological model (Garbarino, 1976, 1977; cf. Parke & Collmer, 1975), we believe that social stress plays a crucial role in determining when and whether a child will be abused. Once the child per se has become an eliciting stimulus for abuse, therefore, the likelihood that societal stress will take the caretakers over the "abuse threshold" is far greater (cf. the frustration–aggression literature reviewed by Berkowitz, 1969). In addition to demographic considerations and financial strain, two stressors are of particular interest in the present context: (a) insufficient opportunity to practice a parental role prior to being forced to assume such a role; and (b) unwanted pregnancy (Garbarino, 1977).

A somewhat analogous model may account for the "at risk for abuse" status of premature infants. Premature infants neither look nor sound like full-term babies, and my colleagues and I are currently attempting to determine whether the characteristics of premature infants (their high-pitched cry, their distorted head-to-body ratio, their fragility and size, their wizened appearance) make them less effective elicitors of the "cute response" (Jolly, 1972; Lorenz, 1935). In fact, these features may combine to make premature babies somewhat unappealing to their parents (cf. Blake, Stewart, & Turcan, 1975). Further compounding their risk status is the fact that premature infants are unable to smile for a good deal longer than full-term babies. Thus, their caretakers face the prospect of several months of interaction with infants who cannot emit strongly positively valenced signals yet frequently emit aversive signals (i.e., all babies cry). These factors may combine to make premature infants aversive in the eyes of their parents. As just noted, this increases the likelihood that they will elicit abusive aggression. Again, social stress surely plays a facilitatory role.

This "model," to be sure, is still being investigated and is by no means established. Whether or not research substantiates our predictions, however, I am fairly confident that any adequate explanation of child abuse must take into account the major factors included in our model. Maladaptive interaction patterns, like adaptive patterns, do not simply develop because of the predilections of the parents or the baby. Rather, they are dependent on the multiplicative and complex interaction among (a) infant characteristics and propensities (as in the characteristics of difficult or premature infants); (b) parental personalities and styles; (c) the history of interaction between the infants and their parents; and (d) the nature (be it stressful or supportive) of the wider social context in which the family system is embedded.

Child abuse is interesting in its own right, but it is also of interest because it illustrates in dramatic fashion the effect infants have on their families and the way that they themselves influence the nature of their experiences. Because there is a relatively quantifiable threshold involved, it allows me to emphasize that the various factors just enumerated should all be viewed as *necessary* considerations and that none can be viewed as *sufficient* in and of themselves. This "law of multiple necessary causes" is equally important whether we are considering infant social development, parental behavior, or marital quality as the dependent variable (Lamb, 1978a). The implication of this "law" is that conceptualizations of the effects of infants on their families will have to be more subtle and sensitive than those evident in the few investigations undertaken thus far. Clearly, theorizing and research in this area are both necessary and worthwhile. The data I have reviewed all point toward the conclusion that babies (real and anticipated) do influence their parents' behavior and personalities, although the nature of these changes and their importance remain incompletely determined.

VI. Conclusion

Most of the research I have reviewed has focused on the microanalytic level, whereas the issues with which we are concerned are formulated at the macroanalytic level. This has forced me to speculate about the complex interactions between microlevels and macrolevels and to grope toward inferences about macroprocesses on the basis of evidence derived from microanalyses. Investigation of microprocesses is certainly important, but I cannot help being disappointed by the propensity of developmental psychologists to ignore the fact that neither individual persons nor individual dyads exist apart from their social context. The index unit (whatever it is) is irretrievably anchored in its social context. The nature and relevance of the interactions within any target system are determined by the societal structure and its demands—in short, the unit can be *understood* only in its social context. It is painfully obvious that in their analyses of infant social relations, psychologists have ignored the societal factors almost completely. To my mind, this has rendered impossible any genuine explanation of infant sociopersonality development, and needless to say, it excludes the possibility of advancing understanding of family development. The best one can do is to point to the evidence I have reviewed and to note that our traditional formulations are both inadequate and incompatible with the available data. Although it seems certain that pregnancy and parenthood exert long-term influences on the family, we simply do not know *how*, *why*, and *to what extent*.

Developmental psychologists cannot bear all the responsibility for our current ignorance. Although it is the case that developmentalists have focused single-mindedly on a disembodied microanalytic level, family life researchers and sociologists have been similarly unhelpful, to the extent that they have focused on the macrolevel almost exclusively. In their search for culturally applicable generalizations, furthermore, they often tend to conceptualize the societal structure and its processes in monolithic terms, thereby glossing over the complexity of socializing agents and institutions and ignoring the interactions between individual characteristics and societal processes that serve to mediate most social influences on development.

Despite this depressing state of affairs, I believe there is cause for guarded optimism. One promising sign is the enthusiastic response that has greeted Urie Bronfenbrenner's (e.g., 1976, 1977) many pleas for ecologically valid research—that is, research on psychosocial development studied in meaningful social contexts. The number of papers devoted solely to consideration of these issues at the March 1977 convention of the Society for Research in Child Development confirmed that researchers are increasingly aware of the need to consider macroissues when addressing ostensibly microquestions.

Secondly, volumes such as this, which bring together representatives of a variety of disciplines, serve to stimulate debate and the exchange of ideas—and that is clearly what we need most. There comes a point when disciplinary specialization ceases to be functional and becomes counterproductive. As far as the study of sociopersonality development is concerned, I believe that that time has come. Fortunately, I think that increasing numbers of social scientists are aware of this. My prediction is that the most fruitful studies of the future will be interdisciplinary hybrids. Some of the more valuable will be those that look to sociologists for conceptualizations of the "socializing society" and to developmental psychologists for microquestions and notions about limiting conditions (e.g., are infants capable of doing what a theory demands of them?). In general, I would say that sociologists are asking many useful and provocative questions. Developmental psychologists, by contrast, have proven more sophisticated in the way they address these questions and the way they evaluate and interpret the answers. Let us hope for the reemergence of interdisciplinary respect and cross-fertilization that will presage the realistic evaluation of socially and individually relevant questions.

References

Ahammer, I. M. Social learning theory as a framework for the study of adult personality development. In P. Baltes & K. Schaie (Eds.), *Life-span developmental psychology: Personality and socialization*. New York: Academic Press, 1973.

Ainsworth, M. D. Object relations, dependency and attachment: A theoretical review of the infant–mother relationship. *Child Development*, 1969, 40, 969–1025.

Ainsworth, M. D., Bell, S. M., & Stayton, D. J. Individual differences in strange situation behavior of one-year-olds. In H. R. Schaffer (Ed.), *The origins of human social relations*. London: Academic, 1971.

Ainsworth, M. D., Bell, S. M., & Stayton, D. J. Infant–mother attachment and social development: Socialization as a product of reciprocal responsiveness to signals. In M. P. M. Richards (Ed.), *The integration of the child into a social world*. Cambridge: Cambridge University Press, 1974.

Anderson, B. J., & Standley, K. A methodology for observation of the childbirth environment. Paper presented to the American Psychological Association, Washington, D.C., September 1976.

Arbeit, S. A. *A study of women during their first pregnancy*. Unpublished doctoral dissertation, Yale University, 1975.

Bakow, H., Sameroff, A., Kelly, K., & Zax, M. Relation between newborn behavior and mother–child interaction at four months. Paper presented to the Society for Research in Child Development, Philadelphia, March 1973.

Baldwin, A. L. Differences in parent behavior toward three- and nine-year-old children. *Journal of Personality*, 1946, 15, 143–165.

Baldwin, A. L. Changes in parent behavior during pregnancy: An experiment in longitudinal analysis. *Child Development*, 1947, 18, 29–39.

Bell, R. Q. A reinterpretation of the direction of effects in studies of socialization. *Psychological Review*, 1968, 75, 81–95.

Bell, R. Q. Stimulus control of parent or caretaker behavior by offspring. *Developmental Psychology*, 1971, 4, 63–72.

Bell, R. Q. Contributions of human infants to caregiving and social interaction. In M.

Lewis & L. A. Rosenblum (Eds.), *The effect of the infant on its caregiver*. New York: Wiley, 1974.

Benson, L. *Fatherhood: A sociological perspective*. New York: Random House, 1967.

Berkowitz, L. A. A reexamination of the frustration-aggression literature. In L. A. Berkowitz (Ed.), *Roots of aggression*. New York: Atherton, 1969.

Berkowitz, L. A. Some determinants of impulsive aggression: Role of mediated associations with reinforcements for aggression. *Psychological Review*, 1974, *81*, 165–176.

Blake, A., Stewart, A., & Turcan, D. Parents of babies of very low birth-weight: Long-term follow-up. In *Parent-infant interaction*. Amsterdam: Elsevier, 1975.

Brazelton, T. B. *Neonatal behavioral assessment scale*. Philadelphia: Lippincott, 1973.

Brazelton, T. B., Tronick, E., Adamson, L., Als, H., & Wise, S. Early mother–infant reciprocity. In *Parent-infant interaction*. Amsterdam: Elsevier, 1975.

Bronfenbrenner, U. The experimental ecology of education. *Educational Researcher*, 1976, *5*, 5–15.

Bronfenbrenner, U. A theoretical model for the experimental ecology of human development. Paper presented to the Society for Research in Child Development, New Orleans, March 1977.

Bruner, J. S., & Sherwood, V. The game of peekaboo. Unpublished manuscript, Oxford University, 1974.

Carpenter, G. C. Visual regard of moving and stationary faces in early infancy. *Merrill-Palmer Quarterly*, 1974, *20*, 181–194.

Carpenter, G. C., Tecce, J. J., Stechler, G., & Friedman, S. Differential visual behavior to human and humanoid faces in early infancy. *Merrill-Palmer Quarterly*, 1970, *16*, 91–108.

Clarke, A., & Alfonso, D. D. Infant behavior and maternal attachment: Two sides to the coin. *American Journal of Maternal and Child Nursing*, 1976, *1*, 94–99.

Cohen, S. E., & Beckwith, L. Caregiving behaviors and early cognitive development as related to ordinal position in preterm infants. *Child Development*, 1977, *48*, 152–157.

Condry, J., & Condry, S. Sex differences: A study of the eye of the beholder. *Child Development*, 1976, *47*, 812–819.

Davids, A. A research design for studying maternal emotionality before childbirth and after social interaction with the child. *Merrill-Palmer Quarterly*, 1968, *14*, 345–354.

Davids, A., & Holden, R. H. Consistency of maternal attitudes and personality from pregnancy to eight months following childbirth. *Developmental Psychology*, 1970, *2*, 364–366.

Davids, A., Holden, R. H., & Gray, G. B. Maternal anxiety during pregnancy and adequacy of mother and child adjustment eight months following childbirth. *Child Development*, 1963, *34*, 993–1002.

Doering, S. G., & Entwisle, D. R. Preparation during pregnancy and ability to cope with labor and delivery. *American Journal of Orthopsychiatry*, 1975, *45*, 825–837.

Donovan, W. L., Leavitt, L. A., & Balling, J. D. Maternal physiologic response to infant signals. *Psychophysiology*, 1978, *15*, 68–74.

Dyer, E. D. Parenthood as crisis: A re-study. *Marriage and Family Living*, 1963, *25*, 196–201.

Fein, G. G. Children's sensitivity to social contexts at 18 months of age. *Developmental Psychology*, 1975, *11*, 853–854.

Feiring, C. The preliminary development of a social systems model of early infant–mother attachment. Paper presented to the Eastern Psychological Association, New York, April 1976.

Feiring, C., & Taylor, J. The influence of the infant and secondary parent on maternal behavior: Toward a social systems view of infant attachment. *Merrill-Palmer Quarterly*, in press.

Feldman, H. The effects of children on the family. In A. Michel (Ed.), *Family issues of employed women in Europe and American*. Leiden, The Netherlands: Brill, 1971.

Fogel, A. Developmental processes in mother–infant gazing behavior. Paper presented to the Society for Research in Child Development, Denver, March 1975.

Frodi, A. M., Lamb, M. E., Leavitt, L. A., & Donovan, W. L. Fathers' and mothers' responses to infant smiles and cries. *Infant Behavior and Development*, 1978, *1*, 187–198.

Garbarino, J. A preliminary study of some ecological correlates of child abuse: The impact of socioeconomic stress on mothers. *Child Development*, 1976, *47*, 178–185.

Garbarino, J. The human ecology of child maltreatment. Paper presented to the Society for Research in Child Development, New Orleans, March 1977.

Greenberg, M. First mothers rooming-in with their newborns: Its impact on the mother. *American Journal of Orthopsychiatry*, 1973, *45*, 783–788.

Greenberg, M., & Morris, N. Engrossment: The newborn's impact upon the father. *American Journal of Orthopsychiatry*, 1974, *44*, 520–531.

Grey, J., Cutler, C., Dean, J., & Kempe, C. H. The Denver predictive study from the National Center for the Prevention and Treatment of Child Abuse. Unpublished manuscript, (University of Colorado Medical Center), n.d.

Gurwitt, A. Aspects of prospective fatherhood: A case report. *Psychoanalytic Study of the Child*, 1976, *31*, 237–271.

Henneborn, W. J., & Cogan, R. The effect of husband participation on reported pain and the probability of medication during labor and birth. *Journal of Psychosomatic Research*, 1975, *19*, 215–222.

Hobbs, D. F. Parenthood as crisis: A third study. *Journal of Marriage and the Family*, 1965, *27*, 367–372.

Hobbs, D. F. Transition to parenthood: A replication and an extension. *Journal of Marriage and the Family*, 1968, *30*, 413–417.

Hobbs, D. F., & Cole, S. P. Transition to parenthood: A decade replication. *Journal of Marriage and the Family*, 1976, *38*, 723–731.

Jaffe, J., Stern, D. N., & Perry, J. C. 'Conversational' coupling of gaze behavior in prelinguistic human development. *Journal of Psycholinguistic Research*, 1973, *2*, 321–329.

Jolly, A. *The evolution of primate behavior*. New York: Macmillan, 1972.

Kaye, K. Gaze direction as the infant's way of controlling his mother's teaching behavior. Paper presented to the Society for Research in Child Development, Denver, March 1975.

Kaye, K., & Brazelton, T. B. Mother–infant interaction in the organization of sucking. Paper presented to the Society for Research in Child Development, Minneapolis, March 1971.

Klaus, M. H., & Kennell, J. H. *Maternal-infant bonding*. St. Louis: Mosby, 1976.

Korner, A. F. The effect of the infant's state, level of arousal, sex, and ontogenetic stage on the caregiver. In M. Lewis & L. A. Rosenblum (Eds.), *The effect of the infant on its caregiver*. New York: Wiley, 1974.

Labouvie-Vief, G. Personality and socialization in later life. In M. E. Lamb (Ed.), *Social and personality development*. New York: Holt, Rinehart & Winston, 1978.

Lamb, M. E. Fathers: Forgotten contributors to child development. *Human Development*, 1975, *18*, 245–266.

Lamb, M. E. Effects of stress and cohort on mother- and father-infant interaction. *Developmental Psychology*, 1976, *12*, 435–443. (a)

Lamb, M. E. Interactions between eight-month-old children and their fathers and mothers. In M. E. Lamb (Ed.), *The role of the father in child development*. New York: Wiley, 1976. (b)

Lamb, M. E. Parent-infant interaction in eight-month-olds. *Child Psychiatry and Human Development*, 1976, *7*, 56–63. (c)

Lamb, M. E. The role of the father: An overview. In M. E. Lamb (Ed.), *The role of the father in child development*. New York: Wiley, 1976. (d)

Lamb, M. E. Twelve-month-olds and their parents: Interaction in a laboratory playroom. *Developmental Psychology*, 1976, *12*, 237–244. (e)

Lamb, M. E. A reexamination of the infant social world. *Human Development*, 1977, *20*, 65–85. (a)

Lamb, M. E. Father-infant and mother-infant interaction in the first year of life. *Child Development*, 1977, *48*, 167–181. (b)

Lamb, M. E. The development of mother-infant and father-infant attachments in the second year of life. *Developmental Psychology*, 1977, *13*, 637–648. (c)

Lamb, M. E. The development of parental preferences in the first two years of life. *Sex Roles*, 1977, *3*, 495–497. (d)

Lamb, M. E. Psychosocial development: A theoretical overview and a look into the future. In M. E. Lamb (Ed.), *Social and personality development*. New York: Holt, Rinehart & Winston, 1978. (a)

Lamb, M. E. Social interaction in infancy and the development of personality. In M. E. Lamb (Ed.), *Social and personality development*. New York: Holt, Rinehart & Winston, 1978. (b)

Lamb, M. E. Infant social cognition and 'second order' effects. *Infant Behavior and Development*, 1978, *1*, 1–10. (c)

Lamb, M. E. Interactions between eighteen-month-olds and their preschool-aged siblings. *Child Development*, 1978, *49*, 51–59. (d)

Lamb, M. E., & Urberg, K. A. The development of gender role and gender identity. In M. E. Lamb (Ed.), *Social and personality development*. New York: Holt, Rinehart & Winston, 1978.

Legg, C., Sherick, I., & Wadland, W. Reactions of preschool children to the birth of a sibling. *Child Psychiatry & Human Development*, 1975, *5*, 5–39.

LeMasters, E. E. Parenthood as crisis. *Marriage and Family Living*, 1957, *19*, 352–355.

Lewis, M. State as an infant-environment interaction: An analysis of mother-infant behavior as a function of sex. *Merrill-Palmer Quarterly*, 1972, *18*, 95–121.

Lewis, M., & Freedle, R. Mother-infant dyad: The cradle of meaning. In P. Pliner, L. Krames, & T. Alloway (Eds.), *Communication and affect: Language and thought*. New York: Academic Press, 1973.

Lewis, M., & Weinraub, M. Sex of parent x sex of child: Socioemotional development. In R. Richart, R. Friedman, & R. Vande Wiele (Eds.), *Sex differences in behavior*. New York: Wiley, 1974.

Lorenz, K. Companions as factors in the bird's environment (1935). In *Studies in animal and human behavior*. Cambridge, Mass.: Harvard University Press, 1970.

Lynn, D. B. *The father: His role in child development*. California: Brooks/Cole, 1974.

Macfarlane, A. *The psychology of childbirth*. Cambridge, Massachusetts: Harvard University Press, 1977.

Meyerowitz, J. H., & Feldman, H. Transition to parenthood. *Psychiatric Research Report*, 1966, *20*, 78–84.

Money, J., & Ehrhardt, A. A. *Man and woman: boy and girl*. Baltimore: Johns Hopkins University Press, 1972.

Moss, H. A. Sex, age, and state as determinants of mother-infant interaction. *Merrill-Palmer Quarterly*, 1967, *13*, 19–36.

Osofsky, J. D. Neonatal characteristics and directional effects in mother-infant interaction.

Paper presented to the Society for Research in Child Development, Denver, April 1975.

Osofsky, J. D., & Danzger, B. Relationships between neonatal characteristics and mother-infant interaction. *Developmental Psychology*, 1974, *10*, 124–130.

Parke, R. D., & Collmer, C. Child abuse: An interdisciplinary analysis. In E. M. Hetherington (Ed.), *Review of child development research V*. Chicago: University of Chicago Press, 1975.

Parke, R. D., & O'Leary, S. Father-mother-infant interaction in the newborn period: Some findings, some observations, and some unresolved issues. In K. F. Riegel & J. Meacham (Eds.), *The developing individual in a changing world. Vol. 2. Social and Environmental issues*. The Hague: Mouton, 1975.

Parke, R. D., O'Leary, S., & West, S. Mother-father-newborn interaction: Effects of maternal medication, labor, and sex of infant. *Proceedings of the 80th Annual Convention of the American Psychological Association*, 1972, 85–86.

Parke, R. D., & Sawin, D. B. The father's role in infancy: A re-evaluation. *The Family Coordinator*, 1976, *25*, 365–371.

Parke, R. D., & Sawin, D. B. The family in early infancy: Social interactional and attitudinal analyses. Paper presented to the Society for Research in Child Development, New Orleans, La., March 1977.

Perloff, R. M., & Lamb, M. E. The development of gender roles: An integrative life-span perspective. Manuscript under editorial review, 1978.

Robson, K. S., & Moss, H. A. Patterns and determinants of maternal attachment. *Journal of Pediatrics*, 1970, *17*, 976–985.

Rosenblatt, P. C. Behavior in public places: Comparison of couples accompanied and unaccompanied by children. *Journal of Marriage and the Family*, 1974, *36*, 750–755.

Rubenstein, J. L. Maternal attentiveness and subsequent exploratory behavior in the infant. *Child Development*, 1967, *38*, 1089–1100.

Rubin, J. Z., Provenzano, F. J., & Luria, Z. The eye of the beholder: Parents' views on sex of newborns. *American Journal of Orthopsychiatry*, 1974, *44*, 512–519.

Rutter, M. *Maternal deprivation: Reassessed*. Harmondsworth: Penguin, 1972.

Rutter, M. Maternal deprivation, 1972–1977: New findings, new concepts, new approaches. Paper presented to the Society for Research in Child Development, New Orleans, La., March 1977.

Schaffer, H. R., & Emerson, P. E. The development of social attachments in infancy. *Monographs of the Society for Research in Child Development*, 1964, *29*, (Serial No. 94).

Sherrod, L. R. Recognition of facial configuration in 3-month-old infants. Unpublished manuscript, Yale University, 1976.

Soule, A. B. The pregnant couple. Paper presented to the American Psychological Association, New Orleans, August 1974.

Stern, D. N. Mother and infant at play: The dyadic interaction involving facial, vocal, and gaze behaviors. In M. Lewis & L. A. Rosenblum (Eds.), *The effect of the infant on its caregiver*. New York: Wiley, 1974. (a)

Stern, D. N. The goal and structure of mother-infant play. *Journal of the American Academy of Child Psychiatry*, 1974, *13*, 402–421. (b)

Stern, D. N., Jaffe, J., Beebe, B., & Bennett, S. L. Vocalizing in unison and in alternation: Two modes of communication within the mother-infant dyad. Paper presented at the Conference on Developmental Psycholinguistics and Communicative Disorders, 1975.

Strain, B., & Vietze, P. M. Early dialogues: The structure of reciprocal infant mother vocalization. Paper presented to the Society for Research in Child Development, Denver, April, 1975.

Suomi, S. J. Adult male-infant interactions among monkeys living in nuclear families. *Child Development*, 1977, *48*, 1255–1270.

Thoman, E. B., Acebo, C., Dreyer, C. A., Becker, P., & Freese, M. Individuality in the interactive process. In E. B. Thoman (Ed.), *Origin of the infant's social responsiveness*. Hillsdale, New Jersey: Lawrence Erlbaum Associates, in press.

Thoman, E. B., Barnett, C. R., & Leiderman, P. H. Feeding behaviors of newborn infants as a function of parity of the mother. *Child Development*, 1971, *42*, 1471–1483.

Thoman, E. B., Becker, P. T., & Freese, M. P. Individual patterns of mother-infant interaction. In G. P. Sackett (Ed.), *Observing behavior*. Baltimore: University Park Press, 1978.

Thoman, E. B., Leiderman, P. H., & Olson, J. R. Neonate-mother interaction during breast feeding. *Developmental Psychology*, 1972, *6*, 110–118.

Thomas, A., Chess, S., Birch, H. G., Hertzig, M., & Korn, S. *Behavioral individuality in early childhood*. New York: New York Universities Press, 1963.

Thomas, A., Chess, S., & Birch, H. G. *Temperament and behavior disorders in children*. New York: New York University Press, 1968.

Thomas, A., Chess, S., & Birch, H. G. The origin of personality. *Scientific American*, 1970, *223*, 102–109.

Tronick, E. The ontogenetic structure of face to face interaction and its developmental function. Paper presented to the Society for Research in Child Development, New Orleans, La., March 1977.

Tronick, E., Adamson, L., Wise, S., Als, H., & Brazelton, T. B. The infant's response to entrapment between contradictory messages in face-to-face interaction. Paper presented to the Society for Research in Child Development, Denver, April, 1975.

Vietze, P., Strain, B., & Falsey, S. Contingent responsiveness between mother and infant: Who's reinforcing whom? Paper presented to the Southeastern Psychological Association, Nashville, March 1975.

Wente, A. S., & Crockenberg, S. B. Transition to fatherhood: Lamaze preparation, adjustment difficulty and the husband-wife relationship. *The Family Coordinator*, 1976, *25*, 351–357.

Yalom, I. D. Postpartum blues syndrome. *Archives of General Psychiatry*, 1968, *28*, 16–27.

Yarrow, L. Parents and infants: An interactive network: Introduction. Paper presented to the American Psychological Association, New Orleans, La., August 1974.

Yogman, M. The goals and structure of face-to-face interaction between infants and fathers. Paper presented to the Society for Research in Child Development, New Orleans, La., March 1977.

Influences of Children on Marital Interaction and Parental Satisfactions and Dissatisfactions

Lois Wladis Hoffman and Jean Denby Manis

7

I. Introduction

In this chapter, data based on a national sample of married couples in the United States will be examined to shed light on the effects of children on their parents at different stages in the family cycle. In other chapters in this volume (e.g., Hartup, Chapter 2, this volume; Lamb, Chapter 6, this volume), it has been indicated that few studies have considered the child as independent variable and the parent as dependent variable. Lamb, in Chapter 6, has reviewed the one area that is a notable exception, the study of the infant in the parent–child interaction. The focus in these studies, however, is on the developmental process per se, and the object of analysis has been the child's development rather than the parents'.

There are also a group of studies and clinical papers that have examined the effects of the deviant child on the parents, sometimes with an eye to understanding the parents' state, sometimes with an eye to understanding that of the child, and, most often, with an interest in understanding the family dynamics themselves (Korn, Chess, & Fernandez, Chapter 11, this volume; Miller & Westman, 1964; Spiegel & Bell, 1959; Vogel & Bell, 1960). Studies of the effects of children on the parents, where the object is to understand the parents' state, usually have been carried out by sociologists and have focused on the effects of the number of children (Clausen & Clausen, 1973) or on the effects of the first child (Dyer, 1963; Hobbs, 1965, 1968; Hobbs & Cole, 1976; Hoffman, 1977; Meyerowitz & Feldman, 1966; LeMasters, 1957; Lamb, Chapter 6,

Child Influences on Marital and Family Interaction:
A Life-Span Perspective

this volume). As Hartup has pointed out in Chapter 2 (this volume), however, few of these studies have considered the effects of children developmentally. Rollins and Galligan, in Chapter 4 (this volume), have reviewed the studies of marital adjustment at different stages in the family cycle, but these studies have typically selected as the dependent variable the global concept of marital satisfaction, though some attention has been given to the more specific concept of companionship. Other studies have examined the relationship between family stage and the division of labor and power relationship between the husband and wife, or some general measure of stress. They have rarely tried to break these concepts down into their more specific components, and they have rarely examined the effects of the child on the parents' attitude toward the child. The research has often been based on samples limited with respect to social class or geographical area (Blood & Wolfe, 1960; Rollins & Cannon, 1974; Rollins & Feldman, 1970).

In this chapter, national sample data will be presented on the effects of children, at different stages in the family cycle, on the marriage relationship and on the satisfactions and dissatisfactions of the parents. These data, originally collected in 1975 as part of a cross-national study of the value of children to parents, are based on a sample of married couples in which the wife was under 40. The sample, which is representative of the 48 contiguous states, includes 1569 wives and a subsample of their husbands (456). Respondents were interviewed in their homes by members of the professional, nation-wide interviewing staff of the Institute for Social Research, University of Michigan. The interview was about 1.5 hours long and covered a range of topics but focused particularly on attitudes toward children. Although the data were collected for another purpose (Hoffman, 1975; Hoffman, Thornton, & Manis, in press), they are useful for exploring some of the issues raised in this volume. Since the data include measures of the traditionalism of the husband–wife relationship, attitudes toward the marriage and toward the effects of children on the marriage, and measures of the satisfactions and dissatisfactions of parenthood, and since the couples interviewed cover the range of family cycle stages during the years when parents are most involved in childbearing and child rearing, it is possible to contrast respondents' perceptions of these relevant variables at different family stages.

In considering these data, it is important to keep in mind two characteristics of the sample: First, all families included a husband and wife. The couple were not necessarily in their first marriage (12% are not), but there were no single-parent households. Second, the age range of the sample was limited. Thus, there were very few couples with children past adolescence.

The data are also limited for examining the effects of children at different stages in the family cycle in that this is a cross-sectional comparison and not a longitudinal study. When parents of preschool children are compared with parents of teenagers, it cannot really be assumed that the former will look like the latter in subsequent years, for they are also from different birth cohorts. The younger respondents may be more affected by newer viewpoints about marriage and children. For example, the younger couples in our sample, that is, those in an early stage of family life, were slightly more likely to have married at older ages. This is consistent with the current age-of-marriage trends and may have affected their reactions to children at the various points in the family cycle.

Furthermore, the data are subject to a number of the methodological criticisms pointed out in Chapters 1 and 5 (this volume). For instance, it is not possible to ascertain whether differences in the response patterns at different family stages are a function of the effects of children or some other aspect of the passage of time such as the duration of marriage or other maturation experiences of the parents. Older people answer questions differently, and the concept of satisfaction changes with time (Gurin, Veroff, & Feld, 1960). Furthermore, any comparison of married couples of different marital durations involves a special kind of sample attrition because of divorce. Thus, some characteristics of couples in the later stages may describe people whose marriages survive rather than changes that have occurred over time. These problems that involve ascertaining whether children are the independent variable or a spurious one plague both longitudinal and cross-sectional studies. A control group offers little help because childless couples, or those who postpone parenthood, are self-selected and different from the start.

Thus, the data reported here are limited for testing definitive hypotheses; but by examining the responses given by parents in the different stages of family life we can provide some insights into what the impact is of children on parents during the child-rearing period. These data should be useful for exploring some of the issues raised throughout this volume and as a source of ideas for subsequent empirical investigations. Most notably, they may provide a data base for further studies of the reciprocal feedback children receive as a consequence of their effects on parents. That is, another limitation of the present data is their unidirectional character. Yet, as described in Chapter 1, it is expected that children will evoke differential feedback as a consequence of the different contributions they make to their family's functioning. Since dimensions of individuality covary with ontogenetic change processes (Lerner & Spanier, Chapter 1, this volume), the data to be reported in this chapter make an initial contribution to understanding a primary component of circular functions, that is, the parameters of "initial" effects of children on parents at various stages of family development.

Family stage will be defined here in terms of the age of the oldest and youngest child, using four age groupings—preschool, elementary school, teenage, and over 18. Nine groups were studied (see Table 7.1). Three categories were combined in the over-18 group, and one was deleted. Couples with no children have been divided into two groups— those married less than 6 years and those married 6–10 years. Childless couples married longer than 10 years were deleted from this analysis because there were only 11, too few to examine. The family stages used are listed in Table 7.1 and subsequent tables. Of course, there are more children in the later stages, partly because the family is more likely to be complete and partly because family size desires have decreased recently and younger people will have smaller families even when family size is completed. The greater number of children, then, is partly a natural aspect of the more advanced stage and partly a by-product of using cross-sectional rather than longitudinal data.

The nine family stages will be compared with respect to the traditionalism of the husband–wife relationship, including the dominance pattern, the division of labor, and the ideology about these. Then the affectional relationship between the couple will be considered. And finally, the attitudes of the parents toward their children—their satisfactions and dissatisfactions at the different stages—will be examined.

In considering the traditionalism of the couple, there are a few fairly precise hypotheses that can be evaluated. But in examining the data for differences in the family stages with respect to the couple's affectional relationship and their attitudes toward their children, the analysis will be more exploratory, and thus, these data will be reported descriptively. They are rich data, based primarily on open-ended questions, and the range of answers is often more interesting than the pattern across the stages of the family cycle. Throughout the analysis, two levels of education—12 years or less, and some college—have been separated, since education seemed to be a particularly important factor affecting responses (Hoffman, Thornton, & Manis, in press). Where tables do not show this control, it is because the relevant results were not meaningfully different for the two groups, and the data could be presented more clearly in a single unit. Responses of men and women are always analyzed and presented separately.

II. Children and Traditionalism

In Chapter 6 of this volume, Lamb suggests that the advent of children, starting even with the first pregnancy, moves the couple toward more traditional sex roles. As the wife becomes oriented toward motherhood and, often, leaves employment, she becomes more involved in child care and household responsibilities (Campbell, 1970; Meyerowitz & Feldman, 1966). The husband, on the other hand, becomes more concerned with his responsibilities as economic provider (Benson, 1967). Lamb suggests that with subsequent children, the father becomes more active in child care, possibly diminishing the role segregation brought on by the first child. Furthermore, previous data, such as that collected by Blood and Wolfe (1960) in the 1950s, have indicated that the wife's power in family decisions diminishes with the birth of the first child but rises in later stages. A recent reanalysis of the Blood and Wolfe data and other subsequent findings by Quarm (1977) indicate that the presence and ages of children may be less important variables affecting family decision making than previously reported. However, Quarm also found in one additional sample, though not in another, that women with children under 6 report the least power, women with no children under 18 report the most, and women with children ages 6 to 18 but none under 6 report intermediate power.

Thus, previous research suggests that the first child moves the couple from more egalitarian and less differentiated family roles toward the more traditional sex role division. Though there is little evidence on how the ideology of the couple adapts to this change, the research on dissonance reduction (Wicklund & Brehm, 1976) suggests that this, too, would change toward the traditional view.

A. Power

Two questions used in previous research were repeated in this study as a simple and direct measure of husband–wife power:

When there's a really important decision that you and your husband (wife) disagree about, who usually wins out?

In your family, who usually makes the decisions about making an expensive new purchase, the husband mostly or the wife mostly?

When the responses to these questions were analyzed, singly or in combination, the results were consistent with the more recent work, Quarm's particularly, in that they indicate a slight increase in the husband's power during the early stage of parenthood, with a swingback thereafter, although these trends were not statistically significant. The effect of the first child on the wife's power is greater, however, if we consider also that the first child is often accompanied by the wife's leaving employment, for the two events in common do decrease her decision-making role more noticeably (Hoffman, 1977).

B. Division of Labor

To measure the extent to which husbands participated in the household tasks traditionally carried out by women, respondents were asked the following questions:

Has your husband (Have you) ever helped (your wife) with the housework? (If yes) These days, does he (do you) help regularly, occasionally, or only rarely?

Here the pattern was clear: Husbands were reported to help less with housework after the birth of the first child, and the drop continued throughout the family cycle. For the couples in this sample, the husbands were perceived as helping less in the later stages: Husbands with preschool children helped less than those with no children, and husbands with older children helped least of all. These findings were statistically significant whether the husband or the wife was the reporter, and they held with education and the woman's employment status controlled. As with power, the effect was most pronounced, however, when the first child was accompanied by the wife's leaving employment, since the husbands of the employed women helped more than the husbands of those not employed.

It is possible, of course, that the fathers did not in fact help less but that the work load increased, so that they were seen as helping less. In Robinson's (1977) study of how Americans spend their time, a study that used daily diaries of the hour-to-hour activities of husbands and wives, he concluded as follows:

Nor did the male contribution to housework appear to be affected by the arrival of children. While the housework time of both employed women and full-time housewives increased between 5 percent and 10 percent for each additional child in the household, fathers with more children often were found to do less housework than those with fewer children or no children.

Much the same conclusion held for child care. While each additional child may have meant between a 20 percent and 50 percent increase (depending on the number and age of the children) in direct child care activities for wives, in many instances husbands showed reduced time on direct child care activities as family size grew larger. This was particularly true for large families where at least one of the children was of preschool age [p. 149].

Thus, although one might speculate that with more children the husband would help more, this does not seem to be the case. And as children grow older, they are often enlisted as helpers rather than the father.

C. Ideology

In addition to the questions about who made the decisions and how much the husband participated in housework, two items in the questionnaire, both used in previous research (Hoffman, 1963), dealt with the ideology about these matters.

Respondents were asked to indicate their degree of agreement with the following statement:

Some equality in marriage is a good thing, but by and large the husband should have the main say-so.

Agreement with this view increased with the birth of the first child and never returned to the prechild levels. In fact, for the age range in our sample, agreement rose across the family cycle.

Agreement with the statement

Except in special cases the wife should do the cooking and housekeeping and the husband should provide the family with money.

showed a similar trend. Traditionalism increased with the age of the children. These results were also statistically significant for both men and women respondents, and they held with education and the woman's employment status controlled.

It is possible, however, that the pattern revealed is not an effect of parenthood but a function of the birth cohort problem mentioned earlier: The respondents further along in the family cycle were older and were socialized when sex role traditionalism was more prevalent. However, a close consideration of the data suggests that the respondent's age is not the sole explanation. For example, if we compare the women with only preschool children to those without children, we find that almost 44% of these mothers agreed strongly with the traditionalistic statement about the division of labor as compared with 26% of the childless married less than 6 years, and with 9% of the childless married 6–10 years. The age difference between these mothers and the childless, on the other hand, is slight: The mothers of only preschoolers were, on the average, only 1.5 years *older* than the childless women married less than 6 years and 3 years *younger* than those married 6–10 years. Although the women who have postponed childbearing for 6 or more years may be selectively distinct, the difference in attitude between the more recently married childless and the young mothers does not seem to be explained away by the age difference. The age range of the whole sample is relatively narrow, and a mean age difference of less than 2 years separates adjacent stages.[1]

D. Woman's Employment Status

A variable often seen as mediating the relationship between children and the sex role traditionalism of the couple, as well as an aspect of the pattern itself, is the woman's employment status. It has already been firmly established that the presence of young children is a deterrent to employment, though less so than in previous years (Hoffman & Nye, 1974). In our sample, 73% of the childless women, 43% of the mothers of preschoolers, and 59% of the mothers with no child less than 5 were employed. As can be seen in Table 7.1, it is the presence of preschool children that makes a difference rather than the stage in the family cycle as defined here or the age of the oldest child. To the extent that remarriage has become part of the family cycle in America, it should be noted that the data from this study, as in previous studies (Hoffman & Nye, 1974), showed that women who are in their second marriage are more likely to be employed than those in their first.

To summarize the data on the division of labor and power between the husband and wife and the accompanying ideology, the advent of children seems to move the couple in a traditionalistic direction. Whether or not there is a shift back in later stages is less clear from these data. There is a slight but not significant tendency toward a movement back to a more egalitarian power relationship in the later stages of family life and a definite increase in the maternal employment rates when there are no longer preschool children, but the husband's participation in housework and the ideology about these matters does not show a shift back with subsequent stages. Since the study did not include older couples, however, it is not possible to see whether there is a decrease in traditionalism in the later stages of family life as the children begin to leave the household.

III. The Marital Relationship

The review of the research on the effects of children on the affective aspect of the marital relationship in Chapter 4, this volume, suggests that marital satisfaction decreases with the birth of the first child and

[1]Mean age difference is based on the differences between the mean age for each of the eight stages—excluding the childless couples married 6–10 years because they cannot be ordered sequentially with the others.

TABLE 7.1
Employment Status of Women by Family Stage (in Percent)

	No children		Preschool children only (<5 years)	Oldest child 5–12 years; youngest <5 years	All children 5–12 years	Oldest child 13–18 years; youngest <5 years	Oldest child 13–18 years; youngest 5–12 years	All children 13–18 years	Oldest child >18 years; youngest 5 years or older
	Married <6 years	Married 6–10 years							
<13 years education									
Presently employed	60.9	80.0	40.8	39.2	53.5	43.8	55.6	55.3	50.0
Not employed now, worked since marriage	27.8	20.0	46.1	48.0	36.8	35.4	34.7	36.8	35.7
Worked before marriage or never worked	11.3	.0	13.1	12.7	9.7	20.8	9.8	7.9	14.2
N	115	20	267	204	155	48	144	38	28
>12 years education									
Presently employed	82.0	82.6	48.2	54.7	66.3	.0	70.2	66.7	66.7
Not employed now, worked since marriage	14.3	17.4	48.2	39.1	30.1	100.0	21.3	33.3	33.3
Worked before marriage or never worked	3.8	.0	3.5	6.2	3.6	.0	8.6	.0	.0
N	133	23	141	64	83	3	47	6	3

173

that a decline in marital companionship and an increase in stress may be important mediators of this effect. It has sometimes been argued that marital adjustment is curvilinearly related to family stage, but the upswing in the later stages has not been documented as convincingly as the initial drop with early parenthood (Spanier, Lewis, & Cole, 1975; Rollins & Galligan, Chapter 4, this volume).

As indicated in the reviews in other chapters in this volume (Lamb, Chapter 6; Rollins & Galligan, Chapter 4), the view of early parenthood as a strain on the marriage and even a crisis situation has not been supported in all studies (Hobbs, 1965, 1968; Hobbs & Cole, 1976), but it has been in many (Campbell, Converse, & Rodgers, 1976; Dyer, 1963; LeMasters, 1957; Rollins & Cannon, 1974; Rollins & Feldman, 1970; Rossi, 1968; Spanier, Lewis, & Cole, 1975). In the national sample data presented by Campbell, Converse, and Rodgers (1976), young parents described more tensions and anxieties than those at any other stage in the family cycle. They were more likely to report disagreements with their spouse about money and more likely to indicate a lack of mutual understanding. Young mothers were more likely than any other women to acknowledge that they have at some time thought of divorce.

The data from the present study are not inconsistent with the view that the early years of parenthood involve considerable stress, but they indicate a more complex picture. The first stage of parenthood is one when everything seems to be more intense. As will be discussed in the next section, preschool children are both more satisfying and more frustrating. The marriage relationship during the early years may also be more satisfying and more frustrating, and it is certainly more salient. For example, when open-ended questions about children were asked, answers were more often phrased by those in the early stages in terms of their effects—whether positive or negative—on the marriage. Thus, these data seem to suggest that although both marriage and parenting are stressful during the all-preschool stage, they are also in many respects a greater source of pleasure.

The data in Table 7.8, which will be considered more carefully later, seem to indicate that the advent of parenthood brings a slight drop in the percentage of men and women who indicate that marriage is the source of a great deal of satisfaction. Yet, parents' reports of how children affect their marriage are clearly positive.

Respondents were asked the following question:

Do you feel children have brought you and your husband closer together or further apart?

Most of the respondents, both men and women, felt that children brought them closer together. The less-educated respondents were more likely than those with some college to give this response; 75% of the less-educated women, 80% of the less-educated men, 63% of the college women, and 65% of the college men saw children as an asset to marriage. This pattern, that less-educated respondents evaluate parenthood more positively and report less dissatisfaction, showed up consistently throughout this sample of families with two parents present. In data reported by Zill (1977), less-educated parents indicated more dissatisfaction, but this reflects the large proportion of mothers without husbands in his less educated group.

The experience of having children increased the likelihood of saying that children bring the couple closer. Children were most often seen as assets to marriage in the early stages where there were preschoolers and before there were adolescents. For all groups, more parents of only preschoolers answered "closer together" than did the childless couples married less than 6 years, but the difference was most marked for the men. For uneducated men, 76% of the group who were childless and married less than 6 years gave this response, and 87% of the only-preschool group; for educated men, the figures were 51% and 73%. Least likely to give this response were women who were childless and married 6–10 years and the educated men in both the childless groups.

Respondents were also asked the reason for their views on this issue. The reasons given for how children bring the spouses closer are presented in Table 7.2. The most common reason given for this view is that having children gives them a shared task in which both parents are working together and mutually concerned with the children's welfare —that there is interdependence and a common goal. Sharing joys was also a frequent answer and was given by almost 25% of the women (both education groups combined). Another frequent reply was that children are "part of us," a "product of our love," and that they physically resemble and represent the two parents.

The most common reason given for the view that children move couples further apart is that it gives them less time to spend together as a couple. The second most frequent reason is that disagreements arise over child-rearing ideas or over a specific child. The third reason, given more often by parents in the first stage of parenting, is that the wife can get so absorbed in mothering that she shortchanges her role as wife.

The preponderance of the "closer together" response to the direct question about the effects of children on the marriage can, of course, be interpreted in terms of dissonance reduction. No one wants to acknowledge a mistake after it is too late to change the situation. Furthermore, since the work and responsibilities of parenthood seem heaviest early in the game, rationalization—dissonance reduction—seems most called for

TABLE 7.2
Responses Given to the Question of How Children Bring Husband and Wife Closer Together (in Percent)

	Women		Men	
	<13 years educ.	>12 years educ.	<13 years educ.	>12 years educ.
Common task	33.8	44.4	39.8	41.3
Sharing joys	25.8	21.7	21.5	16.7
Part of us	24.7	20.9	14.4	16.7
Do things like a family	18.6	13.6	14.9	12.3
Something in common	14.3	14.2	7.7	10.1
Both love them	14.0	10.0	13.8	10.1
Sharing troubles	11.5	10.6	9.4	10.9
A common bond	7.2	10.0	17.7	15.6
Something to talk about	3.0	6.7	4.4	5.1
Work harder at the marriage	4.1	2.4	6.1	3.6
Understand, appreciate each other more	1.6	5.7	2.8	3.6
Husband more settled, stays home more	1.6	.9	6.1	0.7
N^a	736	331	181	138

Note. Columns exceed 100% because a maximum of three responses were coded per respondent.
[a]N's include only respondents who indicated that children bring husband and wife closer, and percentages are based on these Ns.

during that period. However, the idea that children are functional to the marriage relationship came out in responses to questions that were not asking about the marriage at all, and as indicated earlier, they were given more frequently by men and women in the early stages of the family cycle. For example, the first question in the interview was

What would you say are some of the advantages or good things about having children, compared with not having children at all?

Of the mothers of only preschoolers, 19% indicated that the advantage of children was to strengthen the marriage or express the bond between the husband and wife. Of the childless women married less than 6 years, 21% said this, but it was not as common at any of the other stages.

Yet, at the same time, it was early in parenting that the negative effects of children on the marriage were voiced. The second question in the interview asked parents about the disadvantages of having children. Very few talked about marital strain as a disadvantage, but the parents with only preschoolers were more likely to say this than the other parents. Of the mothers in this first stage of parenting, 8% gave this answer (see Table 7.11). It was given as frequently by women who were as yet childless but not by mothers with older children. The most common disadvantage cited was the less specific response that children curtail your freedom, and this was given by 67% of the mothers of only preschoolers, more often than by any other group. As will be noted later, worries about the children rather than concerns about the marriage or the self came out more frequently as a disadvantage when the respondent had teenagers.

One dysfunction for marriage that was not most predominant at the preschool years is the loss of privacy between spouses. Asked in an open-ended question what children interfere with, the parents of teenagers were more likely to cite this problem (see Table 7.12). The teenagers, of course, stay up later at night, are present more and participate in the adult conversations, and seem more attuned to the parents' sexuality. Thus, although parents can go out without baby-sitters, their within-the-house privacy is diminished.

There is some indication in the data that the salience of the marriage relationship, so pronounced at the early stages, reemerges later when the children are older. Respondents were given a list and asked to indicate which item was most important to them. The list included being close to your husband (wife), having a happy family, being financially secure, having a sense of accomplishment, having fun and enjoying life, and other such items. The items most commonly chosen were "having a happy family," which was selected by 39% of the women and 34% of the men, and "being close to your spouse," which was selected by 30% of the women and 26% of the men (see Table 7.3). It is not surprising, of course, that "happy family" was more often chosen by parents, whereas being close to one's spouse was more often chosen by the childless couples, since for the childless the spouse was the family and for the parents the family included the spouse. More interesting, however, was the fact that among women, mothers with only adolescent children and those with children past adolescence were more likely than any of the other groups of women to select the marital relationship as the most important, and they rated it higher than having a happy family. It is as though the women at this stage in life are turning back toward their marriage. The men, on the other hand, did not show this pattern at all. The figures in Table 7.8 that indicate the percentage of respondents who reported that marriage was the source of a great deal of satisfaction are consistent with this pattern in that the last two columns for the women show the highest percentage of all the mothers, whereas the figures for the men do not. However, the percentage of women reporting marriage as a source of great satisfaction is so high for all groups that the variation across the family stages is slight.

One final change in the husband–wife relationship might be mentioned before turning to the more general effects of children: During the early stages of parenthood, there is a slight decrease in the percentage of women reporting they have the same friends as their husband. On the other hand, the data also show a pattern suggested in previous research (Hill, 1970; Litwak, 1968; Lamb, Chapter 6, this volume) that parenthood increases the contact with relatives, at least for the first stage or two.

In summary, when one examines the parents' views of how children affect their marriage, the evaluation is primarily positive. Despite the possibility that children may diminish the time the partners have for each other, children are seen as strengthening the marriage by providing a common goal, joys to share, and by symbolizing the parents' unity. During the early stages of family life, the marriage is particularly salient, and children are more likely to be evaluated, both positively and negatively, in terms of their effect on the marital relationship. There is some indication also that the salience of the marriage reemerges for women when their children are older. These data provide a somewhat different picture of the effect of children on the marital relationship than portrayed in most previous research. Measures of marital adjustment contrasted at various stages have suggested that the effect of children is negative, but there may be a change in the relationship rather than a deterioration.

TABLE 7.3

Responses Given, by Family Stage, to the Question of Which Values in Life Are Most Important (in Percent)

	No children		Preschool children only (<5 years)	Oldest child 5-12 years; youngest <5 years	All children 5-12 years	Oldest child 13-18 years		All children 13-18 years	Oldest child >18 years; youngest 5 years or older	Total[a]
	Married <6 years	Married 6-10 years				youngest <5 years	youngest 5-12 years			
Women										
Being financially secure	6.0	7.0	10.4	7.4	6.7	7.8	4.7	6.7	13.3	7.6
Feeling accepted by others	2.0	4.7	.5	.4	.8	3.9	2.6	.0	3.3	1.3
Having fun and enjoying life	13.5	14.0	6.5	5.2	5.0	3.8	5.2	4.4	3.3	7.0
Being close to spouse	38.5	34.9	30.0	27.0	24.2	25.0	26.2	44.4	40.0	30.1
Companionship—not being lonely	4.0	4.7	2.9	2.6	2.1	3.8	4.7	.0	.0	3.1
A sense of accomplishment	13.9	23.3	7.0	5.9	13.8	13.5	13.5	4.4	6.7	10.4
Having a happy family	21.0	7.0	41.7	50.0	47.7	42.3	41.1	40.0	30.0	39.4
N	252	43	417	270	240	52	192	45	31	1542

Continued

179

TABLE 7.3 (Continued)

	No children		Preschool children only (<5 years)	Oldest child 5-12 years; youngest <5 years	All children 5-12 years	Oldest child 13-18 years		All children 13-18 years	Oldest child >18 years; youngest 5 years or older	Total[a]
	Married <6 years	Married 6-10 years				youngest <5 years	youngest 5-12 years			
Men										
Being financially secure	9.2	5.9	10.4	19.0	12.7	12.5	17.6	6.7	25.0	13.1
Feeling accepted by others	.0	5.9	1.9	1.2	.0	.0	2.0	.0	.0	1.1
Having fun and enjoying life	14.5	29.4	12.3	8.3	11.3	6.3	3.9	6.7	.0	10.8
Being close to spouse	42.1	35.3	24.5	17.9	21.1	31.3	25.5	20.0	12.5	26.1
Companionship—not being lonely	.0	.0	1.0	.0	2.8	.0	4.0	6.7	.0	1.4
A sense of accomplishment	15.8	11.8	8.5	14.3	14.1	.0	17.6	20.0	25.0	13.3
Having a happy family	17.1	11.8	41.5	39.3	36.6	50.0	27.5	40.0	37.5	33.6
N	76	17	106	84	71	16	51	15	8	444

[a]Columns do not total 100% because values that were not chosen by at least 3% of one of the family stage categories were omitted.

IV. Satisfactions and Dissatisfactions of Parenthood

It has already been suggested that the first stage of parenting may be the most intense: The parent of preschoolers seems to feel more joys and more frustrations from the new role. The first child seems to introduce the greatest change into the lives of the couple. They may seem suddenly changed themselves from children to adults; they have responsibilities for others for perhaps the first time. This aspect of new parenthood comes through strongly whether the respondent is currently a new parent or a more seasoned one looking back.

Perhaps the most direct question about this was the following:

All in all, thinking about a woman's life, how is a woman's life changed by having children?

Men were asked the same question about a man's life. The answers to this question were rich and varied. Tables 7.4 and 7.5 list the major coding categories used to capture these responses, with the percentage of persons who gave each response.

One common response given by men and women was that having children changed one into an adult. Almost 20% of both women and men gave this response and worded it in such a way that it was clearly seen as a positive effect: "She becomes a mature woman, not just a silly school girl"; "It makes her feel more like an adult—more responsible"; "People accept you as an adult and treat you with respect."

The idea that the first child establishes adulthood is also borne out in Table 7.6, which shows the responses given to a direct question:

Which of these things do you think was—or might be—most important in making you feel you were really adult?

Respondents were given a checklist from which to answer, although they could add other events. Becoming a parent was the most common response for all parents—men and women. Nonparents most often chose "supporting yourself." For them to choose "becoming a parent," of course, would have indicated that they did not at present feel adult. Although some of the nonparents actually said they did not yet feel adult, the question was not designed to elicit this kind of response. Clearly, however, parenthood is seen by parents as an important sign of adulthood.

Returning to Tables 7.4 and 7.5, a number of other responses seem to be indirectly describing parenthood as moving into the adult role.

TABLE 7.4

Responses Given by Women, by Family Stage, to the Question "How Is a Woman's Life Changed by Having Children?" (in Percent)

	No children		Preschool children only (<5 years)	Oldest child 5-12 years; youngest <5 years	All children 5-12 years	Oldest child 13-18 years		All children 13-18 years	Oldest child >18 years; youngest 5 years or older	Total[a]
	Married <6 years	Married 6-10 years				Youngest <5 years	Youngest 5-12 years			
Positive responses										
You feel more adult, more mature, you become a woman	17.1	14.0	22.8	24.1	17.1	17.3	16.1	20.0	12.9	19.6
More stability	.0	2.3	1.7	3.7	2.5	.0	2.6	.0	.0	1.9
Feel needed, useful	10.3	4.7	12.5	10.4	9.2	11.5	8.9	11.1	12.9	10.5
Other "adult status"	9.5	.0	2.4	1.1	2.1	3.8	.5	2.2	3.2	3.0
A growth experience	5.2	9.3	10.1	9.6	10.4	3.8	7.8	8.9	16.1	8.8
Fulfillment, goal in life, meaning, enrichment	19.4	14.0	24.5	24.4	28.3	25.0	29.7	31.1	41.9	25.2
Become a better person	10.3	11.6	12.0	15.2	11.7	13.5	14.1	15.6	9.7	12.6
Marriage is enriched	.8	.0	1.4	.0	.0	1.9	.5	4.4	.0	.8

Response										
panionship	7.5	14.0	5.0	8.5	8.8	5.8	8.3	4.4	6.5	7.3
Bring happiness, joy, fun	5.6	9.3	12.9	9.6	11.3	9.6	13.5	15.6	16.1	10.9
Sense of achievement	6.0	2.3	7.4	5.6	7.1	9.6	10.4	6.7	12.9	7.2
Neutral or ambiguous responses										
More responsibility—not clear whether positive or negative	31.7	4.7	19.9	21.9	21.7	9.6	19.3	22.2	12.9	21.5
Role changes (more involved with the house, neighbors, or community)	6.3	7.0	2.9	5.9	6.7	3.8	3.6	2.2	.0	4.7
Change in priorities	5.6	7.0	2.4	1.5	2.5	1.9	2.6	.0	.0	2.8
Life style is changed	.4	2.3	3.4	2.6	1.7	7.7	1.0	.0	3.2	2.2
Negative responses										
Tie you down, can't act impulsively, can't do specific things	14.3	34.9	12.9	12.2	14.2	11.5	8.9	8.9	6.5	13.0

continued

TABLE 7.4 (Continued)

	No children		Preschool children only (<5 years)	Oldest child 5–12 years; youngest <5 years	All children 5–12 years	Oldest child 13–18 years		All children 13–18 years	Oldest child >18 years; youngest 5 years or older	Total[a]
	Married <6 years	Married 6–10 years				Youngest <5 years	Youngest 5–12 years			
Lose your individuality, life is not your own	11.9	23.3	9.8	11.1	9.2	7.7	7.3	4.4	6.5	10.1
Restrict woman's career or education	6.3	7.0	3.4	2.6	1.7	.0	3.1	2.2	6.5	3.4
More work, you're fatigued	4.0	2.3	5.0	5.9	5.0	5.8	3.1	4.4	3.2	4.7
Money problems	.8	2.3	1.4	1.5	.4	.0	1.6	.0	.0	1.1
Worries increase, responsibilities increase (negative)	9.1	4.7	6.2	4.1	3.8	9.6	4.7	.0	6.5	5.6
N	252	43	417	270	240	52	192	45	31	1542

[a]Columns total more than 100% because a maximum of three positive (or neutral) and three negative (or neutral) responses were coded per respondent.

TABLE 7.5

Responses Given by Men, by Family Stage, to the Question "How Is a Man's Life Changed by Having Children?" (in Percent)

	No children		Preschool children only (<5 years)	Oldest child 5–12 years; youngest <5 years	All children 5–12 years	Oldest child 13–18 years		All children 13–18 years	Oldest child <18 years; youngest 5 years or older	Total[a]
	Married <6 years	Married 6–10 years				Youngest <5 years	Youngest 5–12 years			
Positive responses										
You feel more adult	9.2	23.5	16.0	21.4	22.5	12.5	35.3	20.0	12.5	19.4
More stability	5.3	.0	7.5	9.5	5.6	12.5	9.8	6.7	.0	7.2
Feel needed, useful	.0	.0	3.8	1.2	2.8	.0	3.0	.0	12.5	2.0
Other "adult status"	19.7	17.6	12.3	8.3	11.3	18.8	19.6	6.7	12.5	13.7
A growth experience	3.9	5.9	7.5	4.8	2.8	12.5	3.9	13.3	12.5	5.6
Fulfillment, goal in life, meaning, enrichment	13.2	11.8	15.1	16.7	25.4	6.3	17.6	33.3	12.5	17.1
Become better person	3.9	17.6	10.4	15.5	15.5	18.8	7.8	13.3	.0	11.3
Marriage is enriched	1.3	.0	.0	.0	4.2	.0	.0	6.7	.0	1.1
Gives family feeling	2.6	5.9	1.9	.0	1.4	.0	5.9	.0	.0	2.0
Provides love and companionship	2.6	5.9	5.7	3.6	5.6	.0	3.9	13.3	12.5	4.7

Continued

TABLE 7.5 (*Continued*)

	No children		Preschool children only (<5 years)	Oldest child 5–12 years; youngest <5 years	All children 5–12 years	Oldest child 13–18 years		All children 13–18 years	Oldest child >18 years; youngest 5 years or older	Total[a]
	Married <6 years	Married 6–10 years				Youngest <5 years	Youngest 5–12 years			
Bring happiness, joy, fun	6.6	5.9	13.2	7.1	4.2	12.5	5.9	.0	.0	7.7
Sense of achievement, creativity	3.9	5.9	7.5	2.4	7.0	6.3	9.8	.0	.0	5.6
Influence on others, have an effect	.0	11.8	.0	3.6	2.8	.0	.0	.0	.0	1.6
Neutral or ambiguous responses										
More responsibility—not clear whether positive or negative	38.2	23.5	35.8	32.1	33.8	25.0	29.4	13.3	37.5	32.9
Role changes (more involved with the house, neighbors, or community)	3.9	.0	2.8	6.0	1.4	6.3	2.0	.0	.0	3.2

	1.3	.0	.9	1.2	1.4	6.3	.0	.0	.0	1.1
Life style is change	1.3	.0	.9	1.2	1.4	6.3	.0	.0	.0	1.1
Negative responses										
Tie you down, can't act impulsively, can't do specific things	19.7	.0	14.2	19.0	8.5	12.5	9.8	6.7	12.5	13.7
Lose your individuality, life is not your own	2.6	.0	8.5	2.4	.0	.0	2.0	.0	.0	3.2
Money problems	9.2	.0	3.8	3.6	4.2	.0	3.9	.0	.0	4.3
Worries increase, responsibilities increase (negative)	5.3	.0	2.8	1.2	2.8	.0	.0	.0	.0	2.3
N	76	17	106	84	71	16	51	15	8	444

[a]Columns total more than 100% because a maximum of three positive (or neutral) and three negative (or neutral) responses were coded per respondent.

TABLE 7.6

Responses Given, by Education and Family Stage, to the Question "In Every Person's Life There Is a Time When He Feels He Is Really an Adult. In Your Life, Which of These Things Do You Think Was—or Might Be—Most Important in Making You Feel You Were Really an Adult?" (in Percent)

	No children		Preschool children only (<5 years)	Oldest child 5-12 years; youngest <5 years	All children 5-12 years	Oldest child 13-18 years		All children 13-18 years	Oldest child >18 years; youngest 5 years or older
	Married <6 years	Married 6-10 years				Youngest <5 years	Youngest 5-12 years		
Women with <13 years education									
Becoming a parent	14.9	10.0	45.8	45.0	41.2	29.8	37.9	36.8	44.4
Supporting yourself	26.3	40.0	15.5	9.9	11.8	8.5	7.6	10.5	7.4
Getting married	26.3	20.0	20.7	20.8	20.9	23.4	26.9	26.3	14.8
Getting a job	8.8	20.0	7.4	6.4	9.8	12.8	6.2	10.5	3.7
Moving out of your parent's house	10.5	5.0	3.0	7.4	4.6	8.5	2.1	5.3	11.1
Finishing school	4.4	.0	3.3	5.0	6.5	6.4	9.0	2.6	11.1
Other	8.8	5.0	4.3	5.5	5.3	10.6	10.4	7.9	7.4
N	114	20	271	202	153	47	145	38	27
Women with >12 years education									
Becoming a parent	9.0	4.3	38.6	31.3	31.7	.0	25.5	20.0	.0
Supporting yourself	42.5	26.1	15.0	21.9	25.6	66.7	21.3	20.0	.0
Getting married	13.4	26.1	10.7	12.5	14.6	33.3	29.8	20.0	33.3
Getting a job	5.2	21.7	7.9	9.4	8.5	.0	6.4	.0	.0

Moving out of your parent's house	11.9	4.3	10.0	9.4	1.2	.0	6.4	.0	.0
Finishing school	10.4	4.3	7.9	9.4	11.0	.0	4.3	40.0	33.3
Other	7.4	13.0	9.9	6.3	7.3	.0	6.4	.0	33.3
N	134	23	140	64	82	3	47	5	3
Men with <13 years education									
Becoming a parent	3.4	.0	43.6	24.6	25.0	50.0	18.2	30.0	.0
Supporting yourself	41.4	40.0	21.8	26.3	25.0	8.3	18.2	40.0	33.3
Getting married	27.6	20.0	14.5	15.8	13.9	8.3	21.2	20.0	16.7
Getting a job	6.9	.0	7.3	15.8	11.1	16.7	9.1	.0	16.7
Moving out of your parent's house	6.9	.0	7.3	12.3	13.9	8.3	9.1	.0	16.7
Finishing school	6.9	.0	3.6	5.3	2.8	8.3	6.1	10.0	.0
Other	6.9	40.0	1.8	.0	8.4	.0	18.2	.0	16.7
N	29	5	55	57	36	12	33	10	6
Men with >12 years education									
Becoming a parent	8.5	.0	41.2	33.3	22.9	.0	16.7	.0	50.0
Supporting yourself	44.7	50.0	21.6	25.9	37.1	66.7	27.8	75.0	50.0
Getting married	8.5	.0	15.7	3.7	11.4	33.3	16.7	25.0	.0
Getting a job	8.5	8.3	5.9	3.7	5.7	.0	11.1	.0	.0
Moving out of your parent's house	4.3	25.0	5.9	14.8	2.9	.0	11.1	.0	.0
Finishing school	8.5	.0	3.9	7.4	11.4	.0	11.1	.0	.0
Other	17.0	16.6	5.9	11.1	8.6	.0	5.6	.0	.0
N	47	12	51	27	35	3	18	4	2

Thus, 22% of the women and 33% of the men answered the question by talking about "more responsibility," an ambiguous answer that was not clearly positive or negative. An answer such as "you are suddenly burdened with responsibilities" or "you have more worries and responsibilities" was coded in a different category as a clearly negative response. Of the women, 6% cited responsibilities as a clearly negative effect of children, as did 2% of the men.

Many of the other answers, the positive ones such as "feeling needed" and "becoming a better person" and all the negative ones, seem to indicate the end of carefree existence and the movement into a new status characterized by being responsible for others and by a diminishment of egocentrism.

One of the most common positive answers to this question was the idea that children were a fulfillment, that they gave life meaning. Of the women, 25% included this in their answer, as did 17% of the men. It is interesting to note that this answer was given more frequently by both sexes in the later stages of parenting, when there are no longer preschoolers in the family.

The answers to this question, it should be pointed out, were quite different from the answers to the questions "What would you say are some of the advantages or good things about having children, compared with not having children at all?" and "What are some of the disadvantages or bad things about having children, compared with not having children?" Although these questions produced some of the same answers as "How is a woman's life changed by having children?," the question about advantages brought forth more responses having to do with the love and joy children bring, whereas the question about disadvantages elicited more complaints about finances, loss of freedom, and worries.

In Table 7.7, data are reported that are based on a coding of the affect in the total answer to the question about how one's life is changed by children. Clearly the attitude toward motherhood becomes more positive after the first child, but it is interesting to note that for women, early parenthood still brought a mixed response, whereas mothers of older children—mothers with teenagers and no preschoolers—gave more all-positive responses. Data from previous surveys (Gurin, Veroff & Feld, 1960; Campbell, Converse & Rodgers, 1976) suggest that if our sample included older respondents, the percentage of all-positive responses would be still greater.

The mixed responses given by the parents of preschoolers were not amorphous. Both very positive and very negative changes were cited in the same answer, and throughout the interview, it was the couples in the early stage of parenting who reported the most satisfaction from children, even though they also registered severe complaints.

A. Satisfactions

In Table 7.8, for example, responses are reported for five separate questions in which the parent was asked how much satisfaction he or she obtained from particular areas of life—the job, spare-time activities, being married, the work done in and around the house, and being a parent. Women not currently employed were asked about their previous job, and nonparents were asked to anticipate how they would feel about parenting.

For both men and women with some college, the parents of preschoolers-only were most likely to report a great deal of satisfaction from parenthood—96% of the mothers and 98% of the fathers reported this. For the less educated, 96% and 95% said this, with a very similar percentage of the parents in the next stage (those with preschoolers and elementary-school-age children) also indicating a great deal of satisfaction from being parents.

Another indication of the joys of parenting preschoolers is that when parents were asked what age child brought the most happiness, the most common answer was the child in the preschool years. The majority of the women and men gave an age under 6. The data are reported in Table 7.9. It can also be seen from Table 7.9 that parents tended to like the age they have. That is, although the preschool age was generally the top choice, each age was more likely to be chosen by parents who have that age child currently than by any other group. Thus, parents of preschoolers were the most unanimous in choosing that age, parents of school-age children were more likely than any other parents to choose school age, and the only group of any size that chose teenagers were current parents of teenagers.

The data in Table 7.8 also show that for mothers at every stage, no area obtained as much unanimity as a source of high satisfaction as being a parent, though this was not true for fathers. Both men and women who did not yet have children cited marriage more than they did anticipated parenting.

The data presented in Table 7.8 were also analyzed for the women along a working–nonworking dichotomy. The working, educated women reported satisfaction from their jobs with greater frequency than either the men or the other women, but they still liked mothering more. Among the nonworking educated women, the marriage was a particularly important source of satisfaction. It is also interesting to note that

TABLE 7.7

Affect in Total Response Given, by Education and Family Stage, to the Question "How Is a (Woman's/Man's) Life Changed by Having Children?" (in Percent)

	No children		Preschool children only (<5 years)	Oldest child 5–12 years; youngest <5 years	All children 5–12 years	Oldest child 13–18 years			Oldest child >18 years; youngest 5 years or older
	Married <6 years	Married 6–10 years				Youngest <5 years	Youngest 5–12 years	All children 13–18 years	
Women with <13 years education									
Answered all positive	29.5	26.3	47.2	46.8	47.1	47.7	54.2	57.9	60.7
More positive than negative	19.6	26.3	10.8	9.4	11.1	11.4	7.7	15.8	14.3
Balance of positive and negative	.9	5.3	8.9	5.4	7.2	13.6	5.6	2.6	3.6
Neutral	22.3	5.3	17.8	22.2	17.6	15.9	17.6	10.5	14.3
More negative than positive	16.1	21.1	8.2	5.9	6.5	.0	5.6	5.3	.0
Answered all negative	11.6	15.8	7.1	10.3	10.5	11.4	9.2	7.9	7.1
N	112	19	269	203	153	44	142	38	28
Women with >12 years education									
Answered all positive	21.4	4.5	35.5	42.2	38.6	.0	50.0	66.7	33.3
More positive than negative	24.4	9.1	13.5	17.2	20.5	.0	9.1	16.7	.0
Balance of positive and negative	7.6	18.2	8.5	7.8	8.4	33.3	6.8	.0	.0
Neutral	18.3	27.3	22.0	18.8	20.5	.0	22.7	16.7	.0
More negative than positive	15.3	13.6	6.4	7.8	7.2	66.7	6.8	.0	33.3

Answered all negative	13.0	27.3	14.2	6.3	4.8	.0	4.5	.0	33.3
N	131	22	141	64	83	3	44	6	3
Men with <13 years education									
Answered all positive	15.4	75.0	40.0	32.7	41.7	61.5	39.4	60.0	33.3
More positive than negative	23.1	.0	14.5	27.3	16.7	7.7	21.2	.0	16.7
Balance of positive and negative	.0	.0	1.8	.0	.0	.0	6.1	10.0	.0
Neutral	46.2	25.0	29.1	23.6	38.9	30.8	27.3	30.0	50.0
More negative than positive	7.7	.0	10.9	9.1	.0	.0	6.1	.0	.0
Answered all negative	7.7	.0	3.6	7.3	2.8	.0	.0	.0	.0
N	26	4	55	55	36	13	33	10	6
Men with >12 years education									
Answered all positive	21.3	18.2	36.0	37.0	51.4	33.3	38.9	50.0	.0
More positive than negative	14.9	45.5	28.0	18.5	20.0	33.3	27.8	25.0	50.0
Balance of positive and negative	8.5	.0	6.0	.0	8.6	.0	5.6	.0	.0
Neutral	25.5	27.3	12.0	22.2	14.3	33.3	22.2	.0	50.0
More negative than positive	17.0	9.1	14.0	18.5	5.7	.0	5.6	.0	.0
Answered all negative	12.8	.0	4.0	3.7	.0	.0	.0	25.0	.0
N	47	11	50	27	35	3	18	4	2

TABLE 7.8
Percentage Reporting a Great Deal of Satisfaction from One of Five Areas in Life (by Education and Family Stage)

| | No children | | Preschool children only (<5 years) | Oldest child 5–12 years; youngest <5 years | All children 5–12 years | Oldest child 13–18 years | | | Oldest child >18 years; youngest 5 years or older |
	Married <6 years	Married 6–10 years				Youngest <5 years	Youngest 5–12 years	All children 13–18 years	
Women with <13 years education									
Job	42.6	50.0	37.1	39.4	48.9	52.8	38.6	51.6	30.0
Spare-time activities	58.8	65.0	51.1	61.7	60.8	68.1	59.3	63.9	63.0
Being married	94.7	90.0	88.9	87.7	91.0	87.8	85.1	91.7	96.3
Work in house	44.7	45.0	48.9	51.5	45.8	40.8	51.4	58.3	55.6
Being a parent	92.9	85.0	96.0	96.6	93.5	93.9	89.9	94.4	96.3
N	115	20	272	204	155	49	148	36	27
Women with >12 years education									
Job	58.9	69.6	62.0	58.2	59.3	66.7	61.9	33.3	33.3
Spare-time activities	69.4	90.9	64.8	69.8	68.7	66.7	78.3	66.7	66.7
Being married	95.5	95.7	89.4	87.5	86.7	100.0	76.6	100.0	100.0

194

Work in house	33.8	31.8	39.4	32.8	45.1	66.7	36.2	16.7	66.7
Being a parent	90.7	59.1	95.8	92.2	90.4	100.0	87.0	100.0	33.3
N	134	23	142	64	83	3	47	6	3

Men with <13 years education

Job	55.2	40.0	52.7	63.6	61.1	53.8	51.5	66.7	50.0
Spare-time activities	82.8	100.0	65.5	55.4	77.8	76.9	57.6	66.7	66.7
Being married	96.6	100.0	87.3	82.1	88.9	92.3	85.3	77.8	100.0
Work in house	51.9	100.0	40.0	42.9	36.1	69.2	67.6	44.4	66.7
Being a parent	82.8	80.0	94.5	94.6	86.1	84.6	79.4	77.8	100.0
N	29	5	55	57	36	13	34	9	6

Men with >12 years education

Job	60.5	58.3	51.0	48.1	62.9	66.7	61.1	100.0	100.0
Spare-time activities	74.5	66.7	68.0	70.4	77.1	66.7	83.3	75.0	.0
Being married	91.5	91.7	90.2	74.1	94.3	100.0	83.3	75.0	100.0
Work in house	46.8	25.0	37.3	37.0	40.0	33.3	38.9	50.0	.0
Being a parent	80.0	66.7	98.0	85.2	97.1	100.0	61.1	100.0	100.0
N	47	12	51	27	35	3	18	4	2

TABLE 7.9

Responses, by Education and Family Stage, to the Question "What Age Child Provides the Most Happiness?" (in Percent)

Age (in years)	No children Married <6 years	No children Married 6–10 years	Preschool children only (<5 years)	Oldest child 5–12 years; youngest <5 years	All children 5–12 years	Oldest child 13–18 years Youngest <5 years	Oldest child 13–18 years Youngest 5–12 years	All children 13–18 years	Oldest child >18 years; youngest 5 years or older	Total[a]
				Women with <13 years education						
0–5	70.5	75.0	79.7	73.5	58.4	60.9	44.3	48.7	46.2	66.1
6–12	14.3	15.0	7.7	10.2	26.8	19.6	20.7	12.8	26.9	15.1
13–17	2.7	.0	.8	1.0	.7	4.3	12.1	17.9	7.7	3.6
18 or older	6.3	5.0	5.0	2.6	4.7	2.2	1.4	2.6	7.7	3.9
N	112	20	261	196	149	46	140	39	26	989
				Women with >12 years education						
0–5	57.6	66.7	67.7	63.8	30.3	.0	41.9	.0	33.3	54.2
6–12	11.2	16.7	8.9	15.5	34.2	33.3	23.3	16.7	.0	16.4
13–17	3.2	5.6	2.4	.0	3.9	33.3	14.0	33.3	.0	4.4
18 or older	16.8	11.1	6.5	5.2	7.9	.0	9.3	16.7	66.7	10.3
N	125	18	124	58	76	3	43	6	3	456

196

Men with <13 years education

	0–5	6–12	13–17	18 or older	N
	55.6	29.6	.0	7.4	27
	[80.0	20.0	.0	.0]	5
	80.8	5.8	1.9	7.7	52
	48.2	26.8	5.4	.0	56
	40.0	37.1	5.7	2.9	35
	[25.0	50.0	.0	.0]	12
	54.8	19.4	16.1	.0	31
	[40.0	30.0	20.0	.0]	10
	[50.0	16.7	.0	.0]	6
	55.1	23.9	5.6	3.0	234

Men with >12 years education

	0–5	6–12	13–17	18 or older	N
	41.5	24.4	7.3	12.2	41
	[57.1	28.6	.0	.0]	7
	64.4	20.0	2.2	2.2	45
	54.2	12.5	.0	.0	24
	37.1	31.4	2.9	5.7	35
	[66.7	.0	33.3	.0]	3
	29.4	23.5	11.8	17.6	17
	[25.0	50.0	25.0	.0]	4
	[.0	50.0	.0	50.0]	2
	47.2	23.6	5.1	6.7	178

*a*Columns do not total 100% because the "Other" category—those who gave more than one age—has been omitted.

197

educated mothers obtained more satisfaction from their jobs than did less educated mothers and men, whether or not they were currently employed.

The satisfactions and dissatisfactions anticipated by as yet childless couples did not always match the views of those who are parents: In many of the tables the biggest difference separates the first two from the remaining columns. In Table 7.10, for example, the many specific answers to the question about what the advantages are of having children have been grouped according to the psychological needs that were implied in the response. One of the most commonly cited advantages of children is that they are fun. Although this response was frequently given by both the childless respondents and the parents, it increases considerably with parenthood. Conversely, the view that children satisfy a need for achievement and creativity drops with parenthood, particularly for men and mothers of preschoolers.

B. Disadvantages and Concerns

Table 7.11 presents the data for the parallel question about disadvantages. The most commonly cited disadvantage, as already noted, was loss of freedom, usually expressed as "they tie you down." This was mentioned most frequently at the first stage of parenting by both men and women but declined steadily thereafter. Financial disadvantages, the second most frequently cited response, showed a drop with parenthood but rose again in the later stages, particularly for the men. Interference with the mother's employment, which has a little bit of both of these concerns in it, was mentioned by about 10% of the mothers of only preschoolers. However, it dropped when the youngest child hit school age, the point at which many mothers in fact return to work.

Concerns about "this troubled world," as we might expect, did not particularly engage *parents* with young children, though these concerns were cited by the childless couples. The parents, however, couched their concerns about world conditions in terms of the dangers and uncertainties these represent for their children. The childless talked more about whether they should bring children into the world when it is "such a mess." Concern about the child's health and safety was also voiced quite often by parents of teenagers as a disadvantage of children, reflecting a kind of general shift from seeing the disadvantages of young children in terms of their inconvenience or restraints on the parents to seeing the disadvantages of older children in terms of the parents' anxieties about the children themselves. It is as though the interference of children in the parents' lives lessens over the years, and, in fact, the respondents who reported no disadvantage were more likely to be the parents of the older children. At the same time, the anxieties about the child increased as the child became more independent and was on the verge of leaving the parental home.

Consistent with this picture are the responses to the following question:

Some people say having children does not leave them enough time for other things they want to do. Would you say that having children prevents (would prevent) you from doing other things you want to do very often, sometimes, or not at all?

The percentage of parents who said that children do not interfere at all rises across the stages of the family cycle as the age of the children increases. For example, 28% of the less-educated mothers of preschoolers-only answered "not at all," whereas 63% of the less-educated mothers with adolescents-only gave that response. The more-educated women showed the same pattern but were less likely to say "not at all" at each stage. This education difference shows up throughout the data—the less-educated women were less likely to report dissatisfactions with parenthood. For this particular question, as perhaps for the pattern in general, it seems likely that the difference was because the educated women had more alternative things they wanted to do. It seems unlikely that the educated women were more bereft of substitute child care, and in addition, the educated women had fewer children. If the responses of fathers reflect in any way their participation in child care, the educated fathers would be seen as being more involved. Of the educated fathers of preschoolers-only, 18% said "not at all," the same percentage as the mothers in this group. On the other hand, 40% of the less-educated fathers of preschoolers said "not at all," as compared with the 28% of the mothers in that group.

Respondents who said children do interfere were asked to specify what they interfered with. These answers are listed in Tables 7.12 and 7.13. The most commonly stated interference was just the very general feeling of being tied down, of being unable to go out spontaneously and of having to get baby-sitters. Socializing with friends, that is, going out with them in the evening or going to visit in their homes, was also frequently mentioned.

Respondents were also asked the following question:

Some people say that children cause a lot of worry and emotional strain. Do you think that they cause a lot of worry and emotional strain, would you say they cause only a moderate amount, would you

TABLE 7.10

Responses Given, by Family Stage, to Question "What Are the Advantages of Having Children?" (in Percent)

	No children		Preschool children only (<5 years)	Oldest child 5-12 years; youngest <5 years	All children 5-12 years	Oldest child 13-18 years		All children 13-18 years	Oldest child >18 years; youngest 5 years or older
	Married <6 years	Married 6-10 years				Youngest <5 years	Youngest 5-12 years		
Women									
Adult status and social identity	15.1	9.3	21.1	25.9	18.3	23.1	23.4	17.8	29.0
Expansion of the self	32.5	39.5	32.1	33.7	42.5	36.5	37.0	33.3	32.3
Morality	6.3	9.3	7.2	8.1	6.7	1.9	6.8	6.7	3.2
Primary group ties and affection	63.1	74.4	69.8	64.1	69.6	55.8	60.4	68.9	54.8
Fun and stimulation	42.5	34.9	60.9	64.8	57.9	42.3	60.4	48.9	74.2
Achievement and creativity	13.1	16.3	9.4	12.2	12.9	3.8	13.5	11.1	6.5
Power and influence	2.8	2.3	3.1	1.9	2.5	3.8	1.0	.0	.0
Security and economic help	7.5	7.0	3.1	3.7	5.8	19.2	9.9	8.9	16.1
N	252	43	417	270	240	52	192	45	31

Men

Adult status and social identity	9.2	11.8	20.8	13.1	22.5	12.5	31.4	6.7	.0
Expansion of the self	30.3	17.6	26.4	22.6	45.1	37.5	37.3	53.3	25.0
Morality	1.3	5.9	7.5	3.6	4.2	12.5	3.9	26.7	.0
Primary group ties and affection	56.6	47.1	55.7	67.9	60.6	50.0	62.7	53.3	50.0
Fun and stimulation	36.8	29.4	58.5	59.5	56.3	50.0	47.1	53.3	62.5
Achievement and creativity	21.1	17.6	11.3	7.1	11.3	.0	11.8	6.7	12.5
Power and influence	2.6	.0	3.8	2.4	1.4	.0	.0	6.7	.0
Security and economic help	6.6	11.8	6.6	8.3	9.9	.0	15.7	13.3	12.5
N	76	17	106	84	71	16	51	15	8

Note. Columns exceed 100% because a maximum of four responses were coded per respondent.

201

TABLE 7.11

Responses Given, by Family Stage, to the Question "What Are the Disadvantages of Having Children?" (in Percent)

	No children		Preschool children only (<5 years)	Oldest child 5–12 years; youngest <5 years	All children 5–12 years	Oldest child 13–18 years		All children 13–18 years	Oldest child >18 years; youngest 5 years or older
	Married <6 years	Married 6–10 years				Youngest <5 years	Youngest 5–12 years		
Women									
Loss of freedom	56.0	62.8	67.4	58.5	49.2	38.5	33.9	26.7	22.6
Financial costs	57.1	41.9	34.8	40.4	41.3	40.4	46.4	33.3	54.8
Worries about children's health and safety	19.4	20.9	15.3	21.9	20.4	19.2	22.9	22.2	29.0
Specific aspects of child rearing unpleasant	4.8	11.6	11.0	11.5	4.2	3.8	15.1	6.7	6.5
Worries about "troubled world"	10.7	16.3	3.8	4.8	7.5	7.7	10.4	13.3	3.2
Interfere with mother working	9.5	9.3	10.1	8.9	4.6	3.8	1.6	2.2	.0
Marital stress	9.9	4.7	8.2	3.7	5.8	3.8	3.6	2.2	.0
Worries about own ability as parent	6.0	11.6	3.4	4.1	5.4	5.8	6.3	6.7	9.7
Children may disobey, not respect parents	1.2	.0	2.6	2.2	1.3	5.8	5.2	.0	.0
Concern about over-population	1.6	7.0	.0	.4	.8	.0	.5	.0	.0
Vague—a burden, trouble	2.4	.0	1.4	1.1	1.7	.0	1.0	.0	3.2
No disadvantages	7.1	2.3	10.1	11.5	18.3	15.4	16.7	22.2	25.8

Men

Loss of freedom	46.1	41.2	63.2	48.8	46.5	18.8	43.1	33.3	12.5
Financial costs	53.9	70.6	40.6	51.2	39.4	31.3	45.1	53.3	62.5
Worries about children's health and safety	22.4	35.3	18.9	19.0	18.3	6.3	19.6	46.7	.0
Specific aspects of child rearing unpleasant	6.6	5.9	12.3	9.5	7.0	6.3	7.8	6.7	.0
Worries about "troubled world"	11.8	11.8	7.5	2.4	4.2	12.5	13.7	20.0	25.0
Marital stress	7.9	11.8	6.6	2.4	5.6	.0	5.9	.0	12.5
Worries about own ability as parent	2.6	17.6	2.8	3.6	4.2	.0	3.9	6.7	.0
Children may disobey, not respect parents	2.6	5.9	.9	2.4	2.8	.0	2.0	.0	.0
Concern about over-population	5.3	5.9	.0	.0	.0	.0	.0	.0	12.5
Interfere with mother working	.0	.0	1.9	1.2	1.4	.0	.0	.0	.0
Vague—a burden, trouble	3.9	5.9	.9	1.2	1.4	6.3	2.0	.0	.0
No disadvantages	6.6	.0	10.4	15.5	22.5	37.5	15.7	6.7	25.0
N	76	17	106	84	71	16	51	15	8

Note. Columns exceed 100% because a maximum of four responses were coded per respondent.

203

TABLE 7.12

Responses Given by Women, by Education and Family Stage, to the Question "What Do (Would) Children Interfere With or Prevent You from Doing?" (in Percent)

	No children		Preschool children only (<5 years)	Oldest child 5-12 years; youngest <5 years	All children 5-12 years	Oldest child 13-18 years		All children 13-18 years	Oldest child >18 years; youngest 5 years or older
	Married <6 years	Married 6-10 years				Youngest <5 years	Youngest 5-12 years		
Women with <13 years education									
Freedom to go places, do as you want (generally tied down)	42.5	27.8	39.6	35.3	41.4	28.1	30.9	42.9	30.8
Socializing, going out with friends	30.0	50.0	32.5	32.4	35.4	21.9	28.4	21.4	23.1
Sports, recreation, hobbies	20.0	16.7	17.3	18.0	5.1	12.5	19.8	7.1	.0
Travel, vacations	21.3	16.7	7.6	9.4	22.2	9.4	18.5	21.4	23.1
Work, career	12.5	27.8	14.2	15.1	11.1	12.5	4.9	.0	.0
Time for self	3.8	16.7	10.7	5.0	9.1	25.0	13.6	14.3	23.1
Education	1.3	5.6	4.6	5.0	6.1	.0	3.7	.0	.0
Housework, shopping	2.5	.0	9.6	5.0	3.0	3.1	2.5	.0	.0
Privacy with spouse	3.8	.0	4.1	1.4	3.0	3.1	7.4	.0	7.7
Spending money	2.5	.0	.5	.0	1.0	6.3	3.7	.0	15.4
N^a	80	18	197	139	99	32	81	14	13

204

Women with >12 years education

Freedom to go places, do as you want (generally tied down)	34.7	33.3	33.3	21.8	29.3	.0	31.0	25.0	33.3
Socializing, going out with friends	24.0	14.3	28.2	23.6	19.0	33.3	6.9	.0	33.3
Sports, recreation, hobbies	20.7	23.8	27.4	40.0	22.4	.0	24.1	50.0	33.3
Travel, vacations	35.5	28.6	10.3	14.5	34.5	.0	31.0	50.0	.0
Work, career	24.8	38.1	16.2	20.0	15.5	33.3	17.2	.0	.0
Time for self	10.7	19.0	15.4	20.0	8.6	33.3	20.7	.0	.0
Education	6.6	.0	9.4	7.3	8.6	.0	3.4	.0	66.7
Housework, shopping	3.3	9.5	2.6	7.3	.0	33.3	.0	.0	.0
Privacy with spouse	7.4	.0	1.7	3.6	1.7	.0	6.9	.0	.0
Spending money	5.8	.0	.9	.0	1.7	.0	6.9	.0	.0
N^a	121	21	117	55	58	3	29	4	3

Note. Columns exceed 100% because a maximum of three responses were coded per respondent.

[a]N's include only respondents who indicated that children interfere, and percentages are based on these N's.

TABLE 7.13

Responses Given by Men, by Education and Family Stage, to the Question "What Do (Would) Children Interfere With or Prevent You from Doing?" (in Percent)

| | No children | | Preschool children only (<5 years) | Oldest child 5-12 years; youngest <5 years | All children 5-12 years | Oldest child 13-18 years | | All children 13-18 years | Oldest child >18 years; youngest 5 years or older |
	Married <6 years	Married 6-10 years				Youngest <5 years	Youngest 5-12 years		
Men With <13 years education									
Freedom to go places, do as you want (generally tied down)	20.8	.0	33.3	22.5	35.0	40.0	31.6	25.0	50.0
Socializing, going out with friends	33.3	50.0	51.5	40.0	25.0	40.0	21.1	.0	25.0
Sports, recreation, hobbies	37.5	100.0	18.2	22.5	45.0	.0	31.6	50.0	25.0
Travel, vacations	16.7	.0	3.0	15.0	10.0	20.0	26.3	50.0	25.0
Work, career	.0	.0	3.0	2.5	.0	.0	5.3	.0	.0
Time for self	4.2	.0	9.1	.0	10.0	.0	.0	.0	.0
Education	.0	.0	.0	.0	.0	.0	.0	.0	.0
Housework, shopping	.0	.0	3.0	7.5	.0	.0	.0	.0	.0
Privacy with spouse	12.5	.0	15.2	.0	15.0	20.0	.0	.0	.0
Spending money	8.3	.0	3.0	.0	5.0	.0	5.3	.0	.0
N^a	24	2	33	40	20	5	19	4	4

Men with >12 years education

Freedom to go places, do as you want (generally tied down)	27.9	27.3	28.6	33.3	25.0	50.0	25.0	.0	.0
Socializing, going out with friends	34.9	27.3	42.9	50.0	29.2	50.0	8.3	25.0	.0
Sports, recreation, hobbies	27.9	9.1	35.7	38.9	16.7	50.0	8.3	25.0	.0
Travel, vacations	46.5	63.6	19.0	27.8	41.7	50.0	66.7	25.0	100.0
Work, career	11.6	.0	.0	5.6	.0	.0	8.3	25.0	.0
Time for self	.0	9.1	11.9	5.6	4.2	.0	.0	25.0	.0
Education	2.3	.0	2.4	.0	.0	.0	.0	.0	100.0
Housework, shopping	.0	.0	2.4	.0	4.2	.0	.0	.0	.0
Privacy with spouse	2.3	.0	2.4	5.6	4.2	50.0	.0	.0	.0
Spending money	7.0	.0	9.5	11.1	.0	.0	16.7	.0	100.0
N^a	43	11	42	18	24	2	12	4	1

Note. Columns exceed 100% because a maximum of three responses were coded per respondent.

[a]N's include only respondents who indicated that children interfere and percentages are based on these N's.

say they cause a little worry and emotional strain, or would you say none at all?

The answers to this question further support the view that teen-agers are seen, at least by their mothers, as less interfering but more worrisome. It is in the families where at least one child has reached adolescence that mothers were most likely to indicate that children are "a lot of worry," whereas mothers of preschoolers were least likely to do so.

As with the previous question about interference, an open-ended follow-up question asked the respondents to specify their worries. The worries most commonly mentioned by all parents were the anxieties when the child is ill, general worries and self-doubt about their child rearing (whether or not the parent was doing the right thing), and concern about accidents. Among these three, however, some were more characteristic of one stage than another. The mothers of preschoolers were particularly likely to mention the worries connected with having a sick child; over 50% of the mothers of preschool children cited this as a major anxiety. These parents, as well as the parents of school-age children, voiced a great deal of concern about whether or not they were doing the right thing. And the parents of teen-agers were the most worried about accidents.

Most of the worries connected with teenagers had to do with the fact that they are out of the range of the parental spotlight and more vulnerable to peer and other outside influences. Thus, worries about negative peer influences were frequently mentioned by parents of teenagers. At this stage, parents often simply said that they worried whenever the children were "away from home," "out late," or when the parent did not know exactly where the child was. Drugs, alcohol, sex, and "getting into trouble" complete the list of major parental worries that were particularly geared toward teenagers.

Girls were seen as more of a worry than boys in general, and this was particularly true when the children were teenagers. Parents still voiced considerable concern with the daughter's sexuality—sometimes in terms of her reputation, sometimes in terms of her vulnerability to sexual attack, and sometimes in terms of concern about premarital pregnancy.

Another shift in the orientation toward children between the preschool and the adolescent years has to do with the perceived requirements of parenthood. Respondents were asked a series of questions about themselves and their spouses concerning the ways in which they thought they had been good parents and the ways in which they felt they had failed. The overall positive or negative evaluation did not show variation from stage to stage, but the areas discussed did. Parents of preschoolers talked about love and attention, but at the teenage stage this concern was less, and parents evaluated themselves and their spouses in terms of whether or not there was communication with the children and understanding of them.

In summarizing the data on parental satisfactions and dissatisfactions, it appears that preschool children particularly provide an abundance of both. Most parents cited this age as the one that brings the most happiness, and yet the parents of preschoolers were more likely to see children as interfering with the other things they want to do. Although the vast majority of mothers see children as a source of a great deal of satisfaction, this was particularly true of those with preschoolers. Still, when asked how children change one's life, it was the mothers in the more advanced stages who were more likely to report only positive changes. Predominant among the changes reported by all parents is that becoming a parent means responsibility and the end of egocentrism and a relatively carefree life. For some, this change was conceptualized in positive terms as a sign of maturation and adulthood, but for others it was described more as a burden. Whereas parents in the early stages were more likely to see children as blocking their freedom, parents in the later stages were more likely to report worries about the child.

V. Conclusions

The responses of subjects at the different stages of family life have not been markedly different, and for the most part observations have been based only on trends. The data primarily document the impact of becoming a parent, in that they describe the first stage most clearly. It is difficult to say whether this is because the first child has a greater impact on the parents' lives or whether it is because the change from nonparent to parent is the one with the most universal or generalizable impact. Every parent goes through this transition from nonparent to parent, and every parent at some point has only preschool children. The only other stage that may be almost as clearly marked is when the children leave home, and none of our subjects had reached this point. In between there is a mixture: The families were of different sizes, the distribution of the children's ages differed, and perhaps most important, the qualities of the children varied widely. That is not to say that there are not uniform effects that can be teased out, but to do so would require more empirical controls than it was possible to exercise here.

If one considers, for example, the change that is introduced by the first child, one can come up with a long list of effects that are not particularly restricted by the nature of the relationship between the parents, the quality of the child, or the social class of the family. Even in very diverse families, the first child means adulthood, new responsibilities, a new status in the community and among relatives and friends, a readjustment of tasks, and a transformation from "couple" to "family." A dependent, irrational, highly demanding, important person enters the scene, and his or her future depends on the parents.

So pervasive is this change that in one recent study of young couples it was reported that friendships were strained when one couple preceded the other into parenthood (Bram, 1974). Those without children felt uncomfortable in social relations with new parents because of the constant intrusion of the new baby into conversations and interactions: "Instead of talking politics we were talking dirty diapers" or "We'd go shopping like we used to, but while I was looking at dresses, she wanted to go to the infant department." This does not mean that the specific effect of the first child is not mediated by many other aspects of the situation, but some of the impact cuts through the individual variations.

To illustrate, consider instead the effects on the parents of children reaching adolescence. It is a change that happens more gradually. The experience is not even marked by a specific age. Here it has been operationally defined as 13, but it can happen at 11 or at 15. The particular child may be rebellious or conforming, sexually precocious or immature, socially competent or awkward and isolated; and the meaning these traits have for the parents will vary. As parents see the almost finished product of their efforts, they may feel confident and reaffirmed in their child rearing or disappointed and guilty or eager to blame the spouse. The child's growing independence may be threatening because they feel a decrease in their own importance, or it may be welcome as an opportunity to turn, less restricted, to other interests. If the child brings into the home new views about work, sex, drugs, and social and political relationships, parents may feel threatened and may dig in to do battle, may become emotionally seduced and themselves experiment in previously unexplored behaviors, or may learn and expand from these encounters.

Thus, although the effects of the adolescent child can be studied, they require consideration of many conditioning variables or concentration on a homogeneous population, possibly including just the one stage. The child's reaching adolescence simply may not have the kind of universal impact that the first child does. For this reason, survey data of the kind presented here, which include couples across a range of family stages, do not yield a delineated picture of any but the first encounter with children.

But even when one looks at the transition to parenthood that these data reveal, it is a set of apparent contradictions. The first child seems to bring about a separation of roles for the husband and wife: The mother is likely to give up outside employment; the husband helps less with household tasks; the parents move more toward a traditional ideology; there is an increased likelihood that they will have separate friendships. Yet, most couples see children as bringing them closer together, primarily because of the interdependence of functions and the sharing of a common goal. Parenthood establishes the couple's adulthood and increases their responsibilities, but these changes are not necessarily evaluated negatively. The description our respondents gave of parenthood during the early years was fraught with polarities. Children restricted the couple's freedom, but they were almost unanimously seen as providing enormous satisfaction, and both views were expressed particularly during the early years when the children were young.

When the children reached school age, the mother was likely to return to work, and the restrictions of parenthood were lessened. By adolescence, the restrictive effects were reduced still further, but the worries about the children's safety and their future increased.

There is some indication in the data of a swing back toward the prechild situation in certain respects when the *youngest* child reaches adolescence. For example, the wife's decision-making power may rise somewhat, though the ideology and the division of household tasks remain traditional. Friends are shared again, the slight temporary increase in separate friendships, noted earlier, perhaps resulting from the greater amount of time women spend with other young mothers in the neighborhood during the preschool stage. Contact with relatives is reduced to prechild levels. And there is some indication that the mothers, though not the fathers, become more oriented toward their marital relationship when the youngest reaches adolescence than during the previous years of motherhood.

The extent to which there is an eventual return to the prechild situation, however, cannot be fully explored with these data, since all of the wives were under 40 and none of the families were in the so-called "empty nest" stage. The "empty nest" stage may involve a return to the two-person household, but the experience of parenthood (as well as various aspects of aging) will have had an impact. Thus, some of the earlier interactions and orientations might be reactivated but in modified form. And new patterns might emerge. It is possible that the effect of the last child leaving is as great as the arrival of the first, but the present study has dealt only with the childbearing years.

The focus in this analysis has not been on marital adjustment per se, and satisfaction and dissatisfaction have not been conceptualized as though they were two ends of a continuum. It is this aspect of the analysis that has allowed us to see the two-sided nature of the effects of the first child. Marital relationships and attitudes toward children are complex phenomena and may require this kind of differentiated approach. The pitfalls of relying on global, unidimensional concepts have been pointed out in other chapters (e.g., Hartup, Chapter 2, this volume) and the follow-up study of the Burgess and Wallin couples by Dizard (1968) has shown that what might look like "marital adjustment" at one stage might include qualities that make for marital discord at a later one.

Perhaps some of the data discussed in this chapter will indicate the value of further exploratory work and suggest new conceptualizations. A more adequate understanding of the effects of children across the family cycle requires a reconsideration of both methodology and concepts.

References

Benson, L. *Fatherhood: A sociological perspective*. New York: Random House, 1967.

Blood, R. O., & Wolfe, D. M. *Husbands and wives: The dynamics of married living*. New York: Free Press, 1960.

Bram, S. *To have or have not: A comparison of parents, parents-to-be, and childless couples*. Unpublished doctoral dissertation, University of Michigan, 1974.

Campbell, A., Converse, P., & Rodgers, W. *The quality of American life*. New York: Russell Sage Foundation, 1976.

Clausen, J. A., & Clausen, S. R. The effects of family size on parents and children. In *Psychological perspectives on population*, J. T. Fawcett (Ed.). New York: Basic Books, Inc., 1973.

Dizard, J. *Social change in the family*. Chicago: Community and Family Study Center, University of Chicago, 1968.

Dyer, E. D. Parenthood as crisis: A restudy. *Marriage and Family Living*, 1963, *25*, 196–201.

Gurin, G., Veroff, J., & Feld, S. *Americans view their mental health*. New York: Basic Books, 1960.

Hill, R. *Family development in three generations*. Cambridge, Massachusetts: Schenkman Publishing Company, 1970.

Hobbs, D. F. Parenthood as crisis: A third study. *Journal of Marriage and the Family*, 1965, *27*, 367–372.

Hobbs, D. F. Transition to parenthood: A replication and an extension. *Journal of Marriage and the Family*, 1968, *30*, 413–417.

Hobbs, D. F., & Cole, S. P. Transition to parenthood: A decade replication. *Journal of Marriage and the Family*, 1976, *38*, 723–731.

Hoffman, L. W. Effects of the first child on the woman's role. In *The first child and family formation*, W. Miller & L. Newman (Eds.). North Carolina Press, Chapel Hill, 1977.

Hoffman, L. W. Parental power relations and the division of household tasks. In F. I. Nye & L. W. Hoffman (Eds.), *The employed mother in America*. Chicago: Rand McNally & Co., 1963, 215–230.

Hoffman, L. W. The value of children to parents and the decrease in family size. *Proceedings, American Philosophical Society*, 1975, Vol. *119*, 6.

Hoffman, L. W., & Nye, F. I. *Working mothers*, San Francisco: Jossey-Bass, 1974.

Hoffman, L. W., Thornton, A., & Manis, J. D. The value of children to parents in the United States. *Population: Behavioral, social, and environmental issues*, in press.

LeMasters, E. E. Parenthood as crisis. *Marriage and Family Living*, 1957, *19*, 352–355.

Litwak, E. Extended kin relations in an industrial society. In E. Shannas and G. Streib (Eds.). *Social structure and the family, generational relations*, 1968.

Meyerowitz, J. & Feldman, H. Transition to parenthood. *Psychiatric Research Reports*, 1966, *20*, 78–84.

Miller, D. R. & Westman, J. C. Reading disability as a condition of family stability. *Family Process*, 1964, *3*, 66–76.

Quarm, D. E. A. The measurement of marital powers. Unpublished doctoral dissertation, University of Michigan.

Robinson, J. P. *How Americans use time—A social-psychological analysis of everyday behavior*. New York: Praeger Publishers, 1977.

Rollins, B. C. & Cannon, K. L. Marital satisfaction over the family life cycle: A reevaluation. *Journal of Marriage and the Family*, 1974, *36*, 271–283.

Rollins, B. C., & Feldman, H. Marital satisfaction over the family life cycle. *Journal of Marriage and the Family*, 1970, *32*, 20–28.

Rossi, A. Transition to parenthood. *Journal of Marriage and the Family*, 1968, *30*, 26–39.

Spanier, G. B., Lewis, R. A., & Cole, C. L. Marital adjustment over the family cycle: The issue of curvilinearity. *Journal of Marriage and the Family*, 1975, May, 263–275.

Speigel, J. & Bell, N. The family of the psychiatric patient. In S. Arieti (Ed.), *American handbook of psychiatry*. New York: Basic Books, 1959.

Vogel, E. F. & Bell, N. W. The emotionally disturbed child as the family scapegoat. In N. W. Bell & E. F. Vogel (Eds.), *A modern introduction to the family*. Glencoe: Free Press, 1960.

Wicklund, R. A. & Brehm, J. W. *Perspectives on cognitive dissonance*. Hillsdale, N.J.: Lawrence Erlbaum Associates, 1976.

Zill, N. Reports on American family life from a national sample of children and parents. Presented at the Bienniel Meeting of the Society for Research in Child Development, New Orleans, May, 1977.

Youth and Their Parents: Feedback and Intergenerational Influence in Socialization[1]

Vern L. Bengtson and Lillian Troll

8

I. Introduction

This chapter questions two assumptions frequently underlying discussions of parent–youth interaction. The first concerns the inevitability of generational differences, if not conflict, between generations (Bettleheim, 1965; Davis, 1940; Mannheim, 1952) as each new cohort of youth comes of age, loosens its ties to parents and becomes autonomous and independent adults. The second assumption concerns the direction of influence in socialization. Most studies that have examined similarity between youth and parents adopt a unidirectional model of transmission, in which influence is seen as passing down the generations from parent to child, from elder to youth. In large part, this assumption is based on an earlier one: that individuals' potential for change and development is highest at the beginning of life and virtually comes to an end after adolescence.

Our perspective in this chapter is based on an opposite assumption, that the interactions involved in socialization affect all participants, whatever their time of life. If youth adopt new behaviors and values, for example, it is plausible that these will influence and perhaps modify the prior orientations of their parents. Thus each interacting generation will

[1]Partial support for preparation of this paper was furnished by National Science Foundation, Grant No. ERP-75-21178, and by the Administration on Aging, Grant No. 90-A-1297(01) and 90-A-1009. Portions of this paper are drawn from a review drafted earlier (Troll and Bengtson, 1978).

We wish to acknowledge the invaluable contributions of Jan Wolverton to the production of this manuscript, and to Neal Cutler for his reactions to an earlier draft.

change, develop, or be socialized anew. In looking for evidence for such bidirectional influence, we first examine data on parent–child similarity (sometimes labeled transmission) in four areas—politics, religion, sex roles, and work–achievement orientations. Second, we examine parent–child affect (sometimes termed attachment, solidarity, or conflict) as an element in such bilateral socialization. Third, we discuss the probable effects of social change processes upon socialization, adopting the concept "generation units" (Mannheim, 1952) as a possible mediating mechanism between individual development and societal process. Finally, we suggest a feedback model of intergenerational influence using concepts of "forerunner" and "keynote" effects and apply this model to the four content areas listed above.

We take the perspective that socialization can best be seen as a process of ongoing negotiation between generations representing complementary roles, a process which can be viewed both within and outside the family. Relations between parents and children at each stage of the life course reflect influence processes that are both bilateral and continuously changing. The patterns of such influence within families are altered directly or indirectly, by societal processes that themselves can be viewed in generational themes, and which derive from period and cohort themes on the one hand and the family themes on the other. In the process of transition into adulthood, each new cohort of youth, or at least the band of forerunners in that cohort, strikes a unique keynote to set itself off from its parents and elders. This keynote, however, derives from the salient themes of its families and the power and persistence of its message within the culture depends upon its congruence with the salient thrusts of ongoing historical processes.

II. Transmission: Intergenerational Contrast and Similarity

Transmission has the connotation of sequentially passing on information in a linear fashion from one unit of a system to another (such as generations within a family). But it is important to note that transmission also implies exchange—that the actions of each unit in the sequence are influenced by the actions of the others; in short, that there is feedback among elements of the system. Under such conditions sequence or causal ordering may be difficult to ascertain.

This is the case when we attempt to answer questions concerning intergenerational transmission or contrast. Indications of similarities or differences between parents and children compared at one point in time can be used to examine three issues involved in generational analysis (Bengtson, Furlong, & Laufer, 1974). The first involves descriptions concerning the degree of similarity or difference between generations. This may be phrased as follows: To what extent do people of different generations appear to replicate each other, in behaviors, attitudes, and orientations? A second issue is what might cause generational contrast or similarity. Can differences between generations be attributed to contrasts in developmental or ontogenetic status, or can they better be traced to their being born and coming of age at different points of history, that is, to the differential influence of sociohistorical trends? The third issue is sequence. Is it at all possible to infer "transmission" from evidence for "similarity"? If so, who influences whom—do parents not learn from youth, as well as the reverse?

These three key questions have seldom been addressed systematically in the parent-child socialization literature. However, a number of recent reviews highlight perspectives on generational analysis (Braungart, 1974; Bengtson & Starr, 1975; Bengtson & Cutler, 1976; Elder, 1975; Cutler, 1976a).

A. Perceptions of Distinctiveness and Influence

Two theoretical extremes are suggested by similarity or contrast among generations (Bengtson, 1970; Mannheim, 1952). One emphasizes the inevitability of differences because of different locations in developmental and historical time. Each cohort must deal anew with issues of identity, intimacy, values, and appropriate behaviors as it moves into adulthood, and comes into "fresh contact" with established configurations of culture. This is especially true in periods of rapid social change (Davis, 1940; Reich, 1970). Friedenberg (1969) summarized the perspective most popular in the 1960s in his oft-quoted aphorism: "Young people today aren't rebelling from their parents; they're abandoning them." Mead (1970) suggested that in the "prefigurative" culture that is emerging, the old must learn from the young, since the pace of contemporary technosocial change is so rapid.

The opposite position minimizes generational contrasts. Apparent differences between generations are temporary; children differ from their parents primarily because of ontogenetic developmental status (Adelson, 1970). To be adolescent is to be different from older adults, but when youth in turn become middle-aged or old, they will then presumably resemble their parents and grandparents.

An accurate picture of generational distinctiveness probably lies between these two extremes. But relevant to both extremes is the concept of the "generational stake" each cohort has in maximizing or minimizing its perception of continuity (Bengtson & Kuypers, 1971). The perspective of middle-age parents on the next generation is in part a product of their own life-span status (as postulated in Erikson's [1950] Stage 7 concerning "generativity" needs). The effort and commitment parents have invested in raising their children, their present diminished influence on them, as well as the recognition of their own mortality, make it important that the next generation "carry on." Their children, on the other hand, are looking forward to an independently constructed life ahead. Needing to express their uniqueness, they view their parents' goals from a different perspective. (See discussions of this point in Lerner, 1975; and Lerner & Knapp, 1975).

The issue of perception—of attribution to the other—is important in exploring apparent generational dissimilarities. Several studies (Bengtson & Kuypers, 1971; Lerner, 1975; Bengtson & Acock, 1977; Gallagher, 1976) demonstrate the difference between *actual* attitudes or values expressed by youth and parent respondents and the attitudes and values each *perceives* the other to have. Each generation warps the attitudes of the other, though in opposite directions. Late-adolescent children exaggerate the difference between their own attitudes and those of their parents; their parents minimize this difference. The actual differences fall between these two extremes. The discrepancy between actual and perceived orientations may indeed enter into the negotiation of differences involved in cross-generational influence during socialization (Bengtson & Black, 1973).

Evidence of bidirectional influence is found in Hagestad's (1977) analysis of role changes in the "empty nest" transition. Her sample of 119 mothers of college-age children were asked whether they felt their children had tried to influence them during the past 2 or 3 years and whether such efforts had been successful. Three-fourths of the sample recalled such attempts, and about two-thirds of these reported them to have had an effect. For example, a number suggested that without such influence they would have found the events of the late 1960s to be much more foreign and threatening. One woman volunteered, "You think that boys with long hair are a strange and dangerous species until your own son becomes one of them and you discover that he is still the same kid—honest, concerned about the world around him, not wanting to hurt anybody [p. 19]." Thus, perceptions of distinctiveness are not incompatible with perceptions of bidirectional influence.

B. Evidence of Parent–Child Similarity or Contrast

The question remains: What, if anything, appears in contemporary society to be transmitted across generations? Although many studies of adolescents reflect this question, methodological flaws in many of the earlier—and some of the recent—ones have led us to ignore two general kinds in the discussion to follow. The first kind involves group instead of pair comparisons, where data from each generation are aggregated and contrasts between generations are based on group means instead of lineage comparisons. The second kind of study not included in this review is that in which one generation provides the information about the other or others—where there is no examination of different generations independently. Unfortunately, these two criteria eliminate a large proportion of the relevant research. For example, Hyman (1959), reviewing the early literature on political orientations, did not critically screen the methodology. Thus, most of the correlations he reports are suspect (Connell, 1972). Since Hyman's book influenced subsequent theorizing on the subject of political socialization, he may have unwittingly contributed to a somewhat biased view of the effect of parents on the formation of their children's political values and attitudes (Cutler, 1976; Tedin, 1974).

Four topics or areas have received most attention in the empirical literature, presumably because of their central role in current generational concerns. These are politics, religion, sex roles, and work or achievement orientations. How similar are youth to their parents in these areas of behavior or attitudes? What can be ascertained regarding bidirectional influence processes, that is, the influence of children over their parents, as well as the reverse?

1. Politics

Substantial parent–child similarity in *political party affiliation* has been noted in numerous studies (Levin, 1961; Jennings & Niemi, 1968; Blumfeld, 1964; and Dodge & Uyecki, 1962). There is evidence of some parent–child similarity in *general political orientations*—liberalism, political cynicism, egalitarianism, humanitarianism–materialism, collectivism-individualism, and dedication to causes (Bengtson, 1975a, b; Cutler, 1976; Troll, Neugarten & Kraines, 1969; Thomas & Stankiewicz, 1974; Angres, 1975). Similarity in *specific political attitudes* (Friedman, Gold, &

Christie, 1972; Lerner & Knapp, 1975; Jennings & Niemi, 1968; Troll & Bengtson, 1978; Gallagher, 1974) has mixed support.

Little evidence is available concerning bidirectionality of socialization influences, that is, the degree to which children influence their parents in political orientations. However, in Hagestad's (1977) data, about one-third of the mothers reported their college-age daughters had affected their own views on political issues. Kenniston's (1968) sample of "young radicals" pointed to many instances of confrontation on political topics between themselves and their parents, leading the latter to modify their views. Jennings and Niemi (1975) point to changes in both generations' political orientations, possibly as the result of direct influence, or perhaps as a result of both generations changing in response to societal shifts.

2. Religion

Parent–child agreement on religion seems to be even higher than on politics. Three studies found at least 70% agreement on *denominational affiliation* (Jennings & Niemi, 1968; Hill, Foote, Aldous, Carlson, & MacDonald, 1970; Acock & Bengtson, 1975). Congruence on *general religious orientation*, though lower than for denominational affiliation, is also substantial (see Troll & Bengtson, 1978). Congruence on *specific religious attitudes and behavior* can also be found (Weiting, 1975; Acock & Bengtson, 1975). No studies appear to have examined children's influences on parents in this area.

3. Sex Roles and Sexual Behavior

Most investigators agree that there has been a notable generational shift in definition of appropriate *sex role behaviors* as well as in orientations and attitudes toward *sexual behavior* (Bengtson & Starr, 1975; Zelnick & Kantner, 1977). However, there have been very few intrafamily comparisons on these variables (see Spanier, 1976a). Most information comes from surveys of nonrelated individuals in which age cohorts are contrasted. These suggest a generational trend toward greater permissiveness—but also that older cohorts are more permissive today than 10 years ago. Is this evidence of socialization by the young of the old? Possible clues as to reciprocal socialization in "forerunner" families (to be discussed later in this chapter) come from incidental data acquired in such depth interviews as those of Angres (1975) with mothers of former college radicals. These mothers acknowledged that they had changed their attitudes toward nonmarital sexual cohabitation as a consequence of the impact of their children's attitudes and behavior.

4. Work-Achievement Orientations

It appears that there is considerable parent–child similarity in both occupational attainments and motives regarding achievement. In the face of an occupationally upwardly mobile society over the past century, the fact that Hill *et al.* (1970) found three-generational continuity in husband's occupation (47% over three generations) is notable. One might expect to find even greater similarity in orientation toward achievement than in actual educational or occupational attainment, since the latter is contingent upon economic opportunity. As Hill *et al.* (1970) state, "Under conditions of rapid economic and social change, each generational cohort encounters... a unique set of historical constraints and incentives [p. 322]." The Hill study did not measure achievement orientation or motivation as such. Those studies that did look at interest, plans or motivation (Kandel & Lesser, 1972; Troll *et al.* 1969; Switzer, 1974) report substantial parent–child agreement in these characteristics. In fact, the only deviant results are those of Thomas and Stankiewicz (1974) and of Angres (1975). Because their samples are more "avant-garde," they may be picking up the beginnings of a new historical shift away from the "Protestant ethic." This will be discussed later as part of the "forerunner effect."

Life styles may be the area in which there is least accord between adolescents and their parents (see review in Troll & Bengtson, 1978). There are, however, some aspects of life-style that show cross-generation similarity: consumership style (Hill *et al.*, 1970); order of life values (Clausen, 1974; Bengtson, 1975; Kalish & Johnson, 1972); and cognitive style (Troll *et al.* 1969; Troll & Smith, 1972). Although these areas may appear most open to parent–child conflict, they also may be the arenas of significant child-to-parent influence (Hagestad, 1977).

Two conclusions may be drawn here. First, we might rank adolescent–parent agreement on the four areas we have reviewed from highest to lowest as follows: religion, politics, work–achievement orientations, and sex roles and sexual behavior. We will consider possible implications of this ranking in Section V with respect to the topic of "keynote characteristics" in generations. Second, we might note that evidence is beginning to accumulate for bidirectionality of socialization influence in these areas. As Hagestad (1977) concludes, young adult children appear to serve as important mediators of wider social and cultural change to the mothers in her study, "making human sense out of what may otherwise seem alien to a parent [p. 11]." She also notes that children were seen as bridges to nonfamily spheres such as work, education, or leisure; several women quoted conversations with a son or daughter as factors in making decisions to go back to work or school. Perhaps in a different decade, the influence of their children might lead to other kinds of decisions, depending on dominant themes in the keynote constellation.

III. Feelings: Solidarity, Affect, and Attachment

In the preceding section, we briefly reviewed the evidence for similarities in orientations and beliefs between adolescents and their parents that could be the products of reciprocal or bilateral socialization. In the present section, we will focus upon affective components of the intergenerational relationship that might be related to such similarities.

A. Measuring Intergenerational Solidarity

A variety of labels have been used to conceptualize family interrelationships. Most of these deal with the concepts of closeness and affect. For example, "solidarity" between generations has been conceptualized in terms of three components: interaction, affect, and consensus (Bengtson, Olander, & Haddad, 1976). The latter, consensual solidarity, has been discussed in the preceding part of this chapter as "transmission." The focus in this section is upon the first two elements—association and affect—which in turn involve such topics as attachment, conflict, interaction, and communication.

Unfortunately, data available on this subject are even less adequate than those regarding intergenerational transmission in adolescence. There are even fewer studies, and most suffer from many of the same methodological problems discussed earlier. They tend to rely on reports of only one family member. Almost all involve self-report rather than observational or experimental data. Few look beyond social expectations and surface behavior to more complex dimensions of interaction or affect. In an area most needy of creative design and measurement—that of long-standing affective bonds between clinically normal people—little application of clinical expertise or theory has been evident. Where clinical approaches have been used, they are too often from a dogmatic rather than an empirical perspective, as, for example, the body of studies dealing with "schizophrenic" or "problem" families (see review by Riskin & Faunce, 1972).

Moreover, there has been little direct study of conflict (and its resolution) between youth and parents. Concepts and operationalized measures differ so widely that it is often hazardous to generalize across studies. Sampling also makes it difficult to generalize. Finally, the dimensions in which we are interested—family closeness and affect, and the extent of bilateral socialization—have been treated primarily as independent or intervening variables (for example, the use of "closeness" as an intervening variable for examining variations in between-generation similarity) rather than as dependent variables in their own right.

Thus, it is difficult to make generalizations from the available literature (for one review, see Troll & Bengtson, 1978). Perhaps the primary difficulty is insufficient clarity in the concepts involved, defining "solidarity" or "attachment" between generations. We will focus on the construct of "affect" as a dimension of intergenerational solidarity, noting that although this is a dyadic property of any social bond, its perception appears to vary between members of the dyad.

B. Evidence of Parent–Child Affect

The major generalization from studies available indicate high attributions of positive affect between generations in the family. Just as it may be argued that it is rare to find a young child not attached to his or her parents (Ainsworth, 1972)—and vice versa, presumably—so does it seem to be rare to find a high school student who does not report feeling close to his or her parents. In comparisons of Danish and and American adolescents (Kandel & Lesser, 1972), only 11% of American high school students and 13% of the Danish students did not report feeling "close" to their mothers, while 13% of Americans and 14% of Danes did not feel close to their fathers. Over one-third of both groups said they enjoyed doing many things with their parents and wanted to be like them in many ways. Anderson (1973) found that only one-quarter of Swedish youth stated that they did not have warm feelings for their parents. Several other studies of high school students indicate that parent–child relationships are usually perceived as satisfying (Douvan & Adelson, 1966; Larson & Myerhoff, 1965; Lubell, 1968). However, it should be pointed out that different generations may have contrasting definitions of the situation regarding affect.

In support of the "generational stake" hypothesis (Bengtson & Kuypers, 1971) described earlier in this chapter, middle-age parents appear consistently to overestimate the degree of attachment, understanding, and communication compared to the responses of their college-age children (Bengtson & Black, 1973; Lerner & Knapp, 1975). Mothers expressed more concern for their children's welfare than their children expressed for their mother's welfare (Angres, 1975). Nonetheless, Hill *et al.* (1970) report that in their three-generation study, the youngest adult generation was the strongest endorser of kinship obligations and contact, whereas the oldest generation was the weakest endorser of these values. Studies of college students (Freeman, 1972) and youth (Bengtson, 1971) show that they may think there is a significant generation gap in our society, at least so far as warmth and communication are concerned, but they less often perceive a serious one in their own family. This is as true of student radicals as it is of more general samples (Troll, 1971; Angres, 1975). Parents may be concerned about their children living up to normative expectations for young adults (Troll & Turner, 1978), and their young-adult or late-adolescent children may be focused upon differentiating themselves as unique identities (Lerner, 1975).

Nevertheless, parents and youth remain important to each other (Troll, 1972; Hagestad, 1977), and their feelings about each other are rarely cool or neutral. Often this may lead to open conflict, since where affect runs high, it is rarely only positive or only negative (Lowenthal, Thurner, & Chiriboga, 1975; Troll & Smith, 1976). Where love is to be found, its converse can also be prevalent. Bengtson and Black (1973b) found high correlations between positive and negative affect, particularly in youth, and similar findings have been reported by Lowenthal *et al.* (1975). On the whole, we are faced with a growing body of data on adult kinship interactions that suggest that there is lifelong persistence of some parent–child bonds in the face of geographic separation, socioeconomic differences, and even value conflicts (Gewirtz, 1972; Kalish & Knudsen, 1976; Troll, 1971; Troll & Smith, 1976).

Bengtson and Black (1973b) report a developmental trend in perception of family solidarity among four age groups of adolescents and young adults; the older groups perceived greater affectual solidarity than the younger, who were perhaps still trying to achieve independence from parents and thus minimized their ties to them. The older youth, having achieved job and marriage, could feel freer to recognize their feelings of closeness—or to once more feel close to parents.

This generalization is supported by Angres (1975), who found that when the younger generation of the Chicago families interviewed 7 years earlier had been in college, they reported more differences with their mother than the mothers themselves reported. These overt conflicts had tended to center on apparently superficial concerns, such as style of dress or hair length, rather than apparently major issues, like political and social values. Incidentally, it is these "superficial" or perhaps "keynote" concerns that adolescents say they would refer to peers rather than to parents (Brittain, 1963; Larson, 1972). It may be that there is a displacement of anger into areas where it can be handled without disrupting family relations.

Angres noted that in the follow-up interviews 7 years later, however, the reports of differences between the two generations were no longer discrepant. Newlyweds surveyed by Feldman (1964) had reported that their relations with their parents had improved since they left home. On the other hand, a San Francisco sample of newlyweds (Lowenthal *et al.* 1975) showed some rejection of their parents. Only further investigation can show whether we are dealing with different "generational units," since the San Francisco sample consisted of mostly "traditional" working-class subjects, whereas the Chicago sample (Angres, 1975) was more middle-class. We are not equating "generation units" with social class but suggesting that social class differences may provide one element of diversification in the age group experience.

Three general points may summarize the data on intergenerational feelings. First, parent–child attachment, solidarity, or affect does not appear to decrease markedly at the end of adolescence. Parents remain important to their children and children remain important to their parents even when the children are young—and older—adults. Second, perceptions of this affect may vary with developmental status in accord with the construct of the "generational stake," and the nature of the relationship may also shift. Third, feelings do not seem to be related directly to the degree of similarity in values, attitudes, or life styles, but rather may motivate acceptance by parents of their children's values and thus reverse socialization.

IV. Generation Processes:
Societal and Individual

We have noted that similarity between generations may be attributed to true "transmission," either unilateral or reciprocal, or to other factors that offer equally plausible explanations. An obvious consideration involves the effect of societal processes on transmission. Here we must consider the interface among several generational processes—those outside the family in society at large as well as those within the family and even within the individual (Troll, 1970). Some writers (e.g., Bengtson, 1975a, b; Connell, 1972; Jennings & Niemi, 1975; Thomas, 1974) have concluded that similarities between parents and children are more likely the result of their joint exposure to what goes on around them (societal generational processes) than of specific within-family socialization. The present section briefly describes these various generational processes. For a more comprehensive discussion see, for example, Troll (1970).

A. Temporal Processes and Generation Units

In considering this issue, three kinds of societal generation processes could be differentiated: a period effect, a cohort or age group effect, and a "generational unit" effect. To illustrate a period effect, Bengtson and Cutler (1976) point out that trends in expressions of alienation can be attributed to historical events that reflect changes in the population as a whole, changes that cannot be attributed to identifiable age, region, sex, education, or income group. Mannheim (1952) related social change to age cohort effects. Because there is a "continuous emergence of new participants in the cultural process [p. 293]," one "comes to live within a specific, individually acquired, framework of useable past experience, so that every new experience has its form and its place largely marked out for it in advance [p. 296]." He further pointed out that "members of any one generation can only participate in a temporally limited section of the historical process [p. 296]." It is because each new age cohort comes afresh upon the social scene and can see it with new perspective that new variations of old themes can occur.

Mannheim (1952) also proposes the independent effect of the generational unit. Not all people born at the same time share the same socialization or perceive historical events in the same way. "Only where contemporaries are in a position to participate as an integrated group in certain common experiences can we rightly speak of community of location of a generation [p. 298]." Laufer and Bengtson (1974) note that no single characterization of youth in the 1960s would be completely descriptive of all members of that cohort. Rather, a range of styles can be discerned, including activists, revivalists, communalists, and freaks. Although all of these youth may be considered members of the same generational cohort, they are clearly not of the same generational unit. Such other social structural variables as social class, race, and geographic location would be expected to influence generational unit membership.

Bengtson and Cutler (1976) argue that all three of these generation-in-society processes interact with each other (as well as with generation-in-the-family processes) to influence values, attitudes, and behaviors. For example, public opinion poll data on political alienation and on attitudes toward government support of medical care show the effects of both period and cohort. Persons born at different times, and thus of different age cohorts in 1968, when alienated feelings permeated our country, showed correspondingly different levels of susceptibility to the alienated mood (cohort effect). However, all the cohorts were more alienated in 1968 than in 1952 and 1960 (period effect). Similarly, both people in their 20s and in their 60s were more in favor of federal medical aid in 1960 than they were at other times (period effect), although the older cohort liked the idea better than the younger one all along (age effect).

B. Individual Developmental Levels

Not only is intrafamily reciprocal socialization affected by extrafamily processes but it is also affected by the differential susceptibilities to influence at different stages of the life course, as we touched on early in our discussion of the generational stake. Mannheim (1952) recognized this when he spoke of the "fresh view" that each new age cohort of youth brings to its interactions both with its parents and with other members of society. Human developmentalists generally start from the assumption that although there is always reciprocity and mutuality of influence between child and parent—even from before birth—there are times when the influence vector is likely to be stronger in one direction and other times when the strength of the vector is reversed. In times of rapid developmental change, particularly when this change is associated with processes traditionally labeled as maturational, the individual is more likely to be open to new influences than during times of relatively slower change. Thus, the "fresh view" Mannheim speaks of is supplemented by a greater readiness for assimilation of new ideas and practices, to use a more Piagetian (Piaget, 1950) vocabulary. And the convergence of both factors of developmental change and "fresh contact" in adolescence makes this period one of particularly strong impetus for change. New attitudes eventually adopted by all members of a family as if they were responding independently to outside influences in society are more likely to have been adopted first by the youth and then transmitted to their parents.

In conclusion, it is likely that different generational processes interact to affect the strength of the influence of one generation upon another. As will be discussed in the following sections, period, cohort, and generational-unit effects arising from societal processes may mediate parental or youth influences. Similarly, differential time of life effects may influence the strength of reciprocal flow of socialization pressure, or at least the perceptions by members of each generation of the strength of this pressure. At one point in individual development, the greater influence may be from parent to child. At another point, the greater influence may be from child to parent. There is, furthermore, no reason to believe that this alternation is either all-or-none in nature or not likely to reverse again many times throughout life.

V. Feedback: A Model of Reciprocal Effects Between Generations

The reciprocal influence between generations of youth and their parents that characterizes the process of adopting new ways and attitudes is neither uniform nor unimodal. Such complex interplays can at this time only be approximately understood. Two of these processes are suggested in the following paragraphs. The first, deriving from the "family themes" described by Hess and Handel (1959), may be called the forerunner effect. The second, derived from hypotheses of youth's need to differentiate from its parents, we may call the keynote effect.

A. The Forerunner Effect

In *Family Worlds*, Hess and Handel (1959) delineate an idiographic model in which each family is describable in terms of its unique family theme that pervades the assumptions, beliefs, and behaviors of its members. Haan, Smith, and Black (1968) found striking differences among kinds of families in the way family ideology, specifically moral judgment levels (as in Kohlberg, 1968), is transmitted from middle-age parents to their late-adolescent offspring. In some families, particularly those with "principled" moral levels, the transition to adulthood is accompanied by mutual upheaval and conflict; in others—chiefly those with more "conventional" moral levels—the transition seems to be relatively uneventful. Similarly, Angres (1975) found that the families of left-wing student activists expressed different kinds of reciprocal transmission from the families in the matched nonactivist subsample.

We are proposing here that the impact of societal change upon family members—adolescents and their parents—varies with the degree of openness to change in their family theme. Those most receptive to change we will call (after Mannheim) *forerunners*. Mannheim (1952) remarks that the "nucleus of attitudes particular to a new generation is first evolved and practiced by older people who are isolated in their own generation (forerunners) [p. 308]." Adelson (1970) has made a similar point.

B. The Keynote Effect

The keynote effect is related to period effects in that it deals with the fact that cohorts or generation units differ in the area of life that they attempt to challenge or change. We noted in our brief review of the empirical data on family similarities collected within the past 20 years that the least generational differences seem to be in religion and the most in sex roles and sexual behavior. Of special interest in this regard is the general finding (Troll & Bengtson, 1978) that in three-generation studies there is more difference between the middle generation and youngest adult generations than between the oldest and middle ones. These data further suggest that one of their youthful keynote areas of the now middle-aged cohort was religion, whereas that of the youth of the 1960s was more in the area of sexual behavior. There is even a suspicion from recent developments in our population that the next youth cohort may move back into the area of religion again for its keynote (Balswick, 1974).

Why age cohorts or generational units adopt the keynotes they do is difficult to explain. Undoubtedly, there is some relation between youth keynotes and the temper of the times in which they "come of age," as suggested by Reisman (1950). On the other hand, so far as particular families are concerned, the keynote theme must be congruent with the family theme as well.

In this regard, we are hypothesizing the following three-step sequence of socializing interactions. (See Bengtson & Black, 1973a, for a similar formulation based on systems theory and focusing on generational cohorts instead of on the family.)

Step One

Within forerunner families, a new cohort of adolescents "comes of age." Because they are at a time of life very open to change and, in addition, come from families whose theme embraces the goodness of change, they embrace a keynote issue which emerges from the current historical condition. This may be a shift from a religious orientation to life to a secular or rational one if, perhaps because of a proliferation of mechanical inventions that give men the feeling they are gaining control over their lives as never before, they feel religion has become irrelevant. Such may have been the case with the forerunner youth in the 1920s and 1930s. Then when energy crises and awesomely lethal weapons make people feel more powerless than they did before, a new generation of youth may—as now—turn again to more fundamentalist religions. Or there may be, instead, an emphasis—or deemphasis—on political action. Or a new perspective on sexual behavior, on work and achievement, or on other issues which may today be of minimal salience.

Whatever the keynote issue adopted by particular adolescents, however, it is likely to be "in tune" with the family theme to which they and their parents were socialized. If a keynote issue is adopted by a large number of youth, its force is felt in many directions. Among the first to be influenced would be the parents of these forerunner youth, as well as other members of their generational unit who are more likely to be followers than forerunners. However, before such reciprocal socialization takes place, the degree of similarity between the forerunner youth and their parents will be less than that between nonforerunner youth and *their* parents. Also, at this first step, the similarity between one generation unit and other generation units in the same cohort will be lessened.

Step Two

If the keynote issue truly "fits" the conditions of the times, both forerunner parents who are more attuned to change than others of their age cohort and nonforerunner age mates of the forerunner youth may be influenced to adopt it. This should then increase the similarity between forerunner youth and their parents and age mates while decreasing the similarity between the nonforerunner youth and *their* parents.

Step Three

If the keynote issue continues to have relevance for current historical–economic conditions, the nonforerunner parents in their turn may be influenced by their children. At this point one might say that society is moving in this new direction. Of course, at the same time, a new cohort of forerunner youth will be trying out a new keynote issue, so that the process is a continuous and an overlapping one. In effect, each lineage generation plays both a mediator role and a recipient role. This multiple generation effect becomes manifest in political or other social change in the society as a whole.

C. Applications of the Model

Let us now consider some examples of the forerunner effect in the areas reviewed earlier: For example, religion, politics, work and achievement, and sex roles and sexual behavior, to put them in order of current youth–parent differences summarized in Section II.

1. Politics

Parent–child congruence in political party affiliation has fluctuated over the 20 years it has been studied. These fluctuations seem to be synchronized with fluctuations in the political climate of the country. From the 1950s to the 1970s, the voting majority shifted from Democrat to Republican to Democrat to Republican, loosely corresponding to a left–right–left–right alternation. In times of Republican or conservative victory, conservative parents were more likely to have children who were in political agreement with them. In times of Democratic victory, it was the children of the Democrats who were more likely to vote like their parents. During the late 1950s, more children of Republicans voted Republican than children of Democrats voted Democrat. Dodge and Uyeki (1962), who collected their data at that time found that 96% of Republicans' children voted Republican and 51% of Democrats' children voted Democrat. Note that a majority of the Democrats' children still voted like their parents, though.

The converse was true in the more liberal 1960s. Jennings and Langton (1969) found that 68% of Republican offspring called themselves Republican and 85% of Democratic offspring were Democrats. Thomas (1971) reports that in 1965 the college-age children of politically active liberal parents were somewhat more congruent with them than were the children of conservative parents like their parents. The left-wing college students investigated by the University of Chicago Youth and Social Change Project in 1965 (Goldsmid, 1972) were, as a group, more in political agreement with their liberal parents than were the less active, more conservative students with their more conservative parents.

2. Religion

Since the early 1960s, there has been a historical shift in this country away from organized religion (Bengtson & Starr, 1975). Middle-age parents showed wide differences in religiosity from their college-age children as a group (Acock & Bengtson, 1975a, b; Armstrong & Scotzin, 1974; Payne, Summers, & Stewart, 1973; Weiting, 1975; Yankelovich, 1970, 1972).

As noted earlier, family continuity in religious beliefs and practices, although substantial, is not as great as in denominational affiliation. The younger generation mostly adheres to the religious identity of its parents and grandparents but gives the actual working out of practices new meanings and new structure (Acock & Bengtson, 1975; Braun &

Bengtson, 1972; Jennings & Niemi, 1968; Kalish & Johnson, 1972; Linder & Nahemow, 1970). Thus although the area of religion has not been one of the most salient keynote issues in the last few decades, it is still important. If current speculations about a trend toward a new fundamentalism are accurate, we may designate the forerunner families in this case to be those that remained religiously conservative—just as in conservative political times, the forerunner families appear to have been the Republicans. It would be dangerous to equate forerunner status with radicalism, because in times that arouse conservative keynotes, forerunners will come from families with a conservative family theme.

3. *Sex Roles and Sexual Behavior*

A shift toward liberalization of both sex roles and sexual behavior appears to have taken place in this country since the middle 1960s. Both acceptance of premarital sex in general and admission of having engaged in it has increased significantly (Spanier, 1976b; Zelnik & Kantner, 1977). Actual experience with premarital sex increased from 10% in 1958 to 23% in 1968 in a dating relationship, and from 31% to 39% in an engagement (Bell & Chaskes, 1970). Over this same period, the rate of premarital sex had remained at about 50% for male undergraduates but had increased from about 34% to 50% for female undergraduates (Christensen & Gregg, 1970). Attitudes of acceptance increased even more rapidly than did experience. In the Bell and Chaskes study, those Temple University coeds who thought they had "gone too far" decreased from 65% in 1958 to 36% ten years later. A Purdue Public Opinion survey of high school students in 1952 found that 56% of high school boys and 67% of high school girls "would not consider them good friends any more" if their friends did not follow morals and rules for behavior of unmarried people; in 1965, the proportions had dropped to 22% for boys and 38% for girls (Christensen & Gregg, 1970). The prevalence of sexual activity among never-married teenage women increased by 30% between 1971 and 1976, so that by age 19, 55% of a national probability sample reported having had sexual intercourse (Zelnik & Kantner, 1977). Comparisons between aggregates of parental and youth generations show wide differences (Armstrong & Scotzin, 1974; Freeman, 1972; Steininger & Lesser, 1974; Walsh, 1970; Yankelovich, 1972). Changes between 1969 and 1973 suggest a period effect is as noticeable as a cohort effect.

Little data on parent–child comparisons of sexual norms are available, but those which we do have point to greater lineage differences in this area than in either politics or religion. This is true both for sexual permissiveness (Lerner & Knapp, 1975; Thomas & Stankiewicz, 1974) and for sex-role stereotyping (Aldous & Hill, 1965; Angres, 1975; Thomas & Stankiewicz, 1974; Troll et al., 1969). Angres' findings are a good illustration of the influence of historical trends working through adolescent forerunners in changing the attitudes the parents held before social change. When they were college students, the political activists (forerunners in politics) the Chicago youth in the sample had been as ready to espouse a liberal view of sex-role equality and, to a lesser extent, sexual permissiveness, as they were to espouse a liberal political view. At this time they tended to differ more from their parents than did the nonactivists, who agreed with their parents' more conservative views. Seven years later, though, both the activists' parents and other people their own age were shifting to greater liberalization of sexuality and sex-role views.

In summary, cohort and period effects seem to be more overriding of lineage (family socialization) effects in sex-role ideology and sexual behavior than in orientations concerning politics or religion. However, some family continuity is apparent, partly because liberal children, even in this area, tend to come from the most liberal parents. Again the concept of a "keynote" issue, in conjunction with "family themes," appears a useful way to conceptualize observable trends.

4. Work and Achievement Orientations

The forerunners of the mid-1960s not only adopted a different orientation toward politics, sex roles, and sexual permissiveness, but also toward work (Bengtson & Starr, 1975; Flacks, 1968). Flacks observed that "the dissatisfaction of socially advantaged youth with conventional career opportunities is a significant social trend, the most important single indicator of restlessness among sectors of the youth population." While only a small portion of that cohort actually evidenced a rejection of job-holding, most of the cohort reflected a change in orientation. Over three-fourths of students surveyed by Yankelovich in 1969 said that "commitment to a meaningful career is a very important part of a person's life." However, they did not endorse inevitable rewards for hard work (only 39% said they did in Yankelovich's 1971 survey) and were more concerned with personal fulfillment and social service than with financial rewards. In 1969, only 56% of college youth agreed that "hard work will always pay off" as opposed to 76% of their parents, 79% of noncollege youth, and 85% of parents of noncollege youth (Yankelovich, 1972). Angres (1975) noted significant aggregate generational differences in work ethic attitudes in the re-test data of 1972. However, attitudes toward work seem to have changed more than achievement motivations, suggesting that persistent genotypic personality characteristics were being expressed in new phenotypic ways (see Kagan & Moss, 1962). Again, the process is analogous to the way earlier family themes in political and religious areas are not discarded so much as reworked into new modes (Furstenberg, 1967; Hill et al., 1970; Kandel & Lesser, 1972; Kerkckhuff & Huff, 1974; Switzer, 1974; Troll & Smith, 1972; Troll et al., 1969).

Hill's (1970) data on 3-generational families (all of whom, even the youngest couples, predate the cohort shift described above) point sharply to the strong influence of sociohistorical conditions in providing differential climates for achievement. Noted upgrading in education and income of the husbands over the three generations is allied to greater opportunity. Even so, what Hill calls "consumership achievement level" (purchases of major appliances, for example) showed 80% continuity over three generations relative to the level of each cohort.

The aggregate generational differences in work ethic attitudes reported by Angres (1975) were duplicated in lineage generational differences. Thomas and Stankiewicz (1974) found similar lack of agreement between parents and college-age children on work achievement values, although Troll et al. (1969) and Switzer (1974) found more similarity in orientation to work.

The discussion in this section has focused upon the way keynote generational themes derive from a complex network of persistent family themes, ontogenetic developmental pressures, and sociohistorical salient issues and how the reciprocity of intergenerational influences results in changes in these themes that are translated into changes in historical issues. In the past few decades, we have witnessed changes in issues currently salient: politics, religion, sex roles and behaviors, and work and achievement values. We have even seen reversals or alternations in the dominance of such thematic areas. We could predict that future keynotes may shift the salience of these areas again or even bring new ones on the social scene.

VI. Conclusion

This chapter has described a complex feedback system of transmission and differentiation involving generations of youth and their parents. Components of this system include: parent–child similarity; parent–child affect; family themes; the generational stake; forerunner effects; generation and period effects in the broader society; and keynote generational themes. We have suggested that a cybernetic feedback model can help to explain the family's contribution to enabling social change, as well as its role in acting as a brake to such social change.

Basic to this model is the position that families constitute cultural units, differing from each other in value systems and world perspectives which pervade the assumptions and behaviors of its members (Hess & Handel, 1959). Furthermore, we propose that these cultural units have integrity over time—over generations from parent to child to grandchild—and that this integrity is maintained by transmission of general family themes. Depending on current societal conditions, a given family may be what can be termed a "forerunner" or not. If its family theme is congruent with dominant social trends, it emerges as a forerunner; if its theme is incongruent, it does not.

In some historical periods, dependent on contemporary ideological conditions, forerunner families may be labeled "radical" or "conservative." When the mood of a society is swinging toward "radical" ideologies, for example, those families that have long tended to espouse similar "radical" perspectives are likely to become forerunners. The "left-wing" middle-aged parents and their college-age children who were interviewed by the Chicago Youth and Social Change Project (Flacks, 1967; Troll et al., 1969) and the Harvard youths described by Keniston (1968) were in tune with the "movement" mood of the 1960s. Their "Protestant ethic" counterparts in the same samples were not so in tune. These positions can be reversed from decade to decade—or even faster.

When families are in tune with the dominant societal mood, the spearhead of this effect may be manifest in their children who are in the process of transition into adulthood. These children would modify their family theme so as to set themselves off from their parents, a process described by Bengtson and Kuypers (1970) as the "generational stake." The keynotes of their unique contribution, though adapted from the theme of their parents and forebearers, would be sufficiently different to emphasize, if not exaggerate, this uniqueness.

Since keynote characteristics are in tune with dominant social trends, they should spread both laterally, to the children of nonforerunner families and vertically, to the parents of the forerunner youth. Presumably, however, these characteristics would be "watered down" in this transmission process since they would need to be assimilated into systems that would be less consistent with them than those of the forerunner youth. Conversely, the forerunner youth would present, in their keynote characteristics, an exaggerated form of these attributes that would become less "deviant" in the process of general acculturation.

The keynote characteristic of the youth of the late 1960s that represented defiance of the prevailing emphasis upon fashion and cleanliness and affluence by untidiness of hair and clothes and general sloppiness and disregard of "personal hygiene" became transmuted into new fashions of expensive blue jeans, unisex hair styles, and floor-hugging furniture. But note that both other youth and middle-aged parents adopted these new fashions, as they did some of the antiwar and populistic political ideologies.

Because forerunner youth tend to socialize their parents into new modes of expressing older themes, social (and individual) change proceeds slower than it would if only a cohort of youth existed (as imagined in Golding's fictional *Lord of the Flies*). Because forerunner youth retain the essence of their family themes, societal change is at best gradual.

While the model presented here is intended to clarify the process of intrafamily bidirectional socialization, it is of course only a preliminary step in the study of individual, cohort, and social change. The delineation of the suggested elements of forerunners, family themes, and keynote themes should help focus future research.

References

Acock, A. C., & Bengtson, V. L. Intergenerational transmission of religious behavior and beliefs. Paper presented at the Pacific Sociological Association Annual Meeting, Victoria, 1975.

Acock, A. C., & Bengtson, V. L. On the relative influence of mothers and fathers: A covariance analysis of political and religious socialization. Paper presented at the Annual Meeting of the American Socialization Association, New York, 1976.

Adelson, J. What generation gap? *New York Times Magazine*, January, 1970, *18*.

Ainsworth, M. Attachment and dependency: A comparison. In J. Gewirtz (Ed.), *Attachment and Dependency*. Washington, D.C.: Winston, 1972.

Aldous, J., & Hill, R. Social cohesion, lineage type, and intergenerational transmission. *Social Forces*, 1965, *43*, 471–482.

Andersson, B. The generation gap: Imagination or reality? Paper presented to the Biennial Meeting of the International Society for the Study of Behavioral Development, Institute of Education, Goteborg, Sweden, 1973.

Angres, S. Intergenerational relations and value congruence between young adults and their mothers. Unpublished Ph.D. dissertation, University of Chicago, 1975.

Armstrong, B., & Scotzin, M. Intergenerational comparison of attitudes toward basic life concepts. *Journal of Psychology*, 1974, *87*, 293–304.

Balswick, J. A. The Jesus people movement: A generational interpretation. *Journal of Social Issues*, 1974, *30*, 23–42.

Bell, R. R., & Chaskes, J. B. Premarital sexual experience among coeds 1958–1968. *Journal of Marriage and the Family*, 1970, *32*, 81–84.

Bengtson, V. L. The generation gap: A review and typology of social–psychological perspectives. *Youth and Society*, 1970, *2*, 7–32.

Bengtson, V. L. Inter-age differences perceptions of the generation gap. *The Gerontologist*, 1971, 85–89.

Bengtson, V. L. Generation and family effects in value socialization. *American Sociological Review*, 1975, *40*, 358–371.

Bengtson, V. L., & Acock, A. C. Socialization and attribution processes: Actual vs. perceived similarity among parents and youth. Paper presented at the annual meetings of the American Sociological Association, Chicago, 1977.

Bengtson, V. L., & Black, K. D. Intergenerational relations and continuities in socialization. In P. Baltes and W. Schaie (Eds.), *Life-span developmental psychology: Personality and socialization*. New York: Academic Press, 1973.

Bengtson, V. L. Solidarity between parents and children: Four perspectives on theory development. Paper presented at the Theory Development Workshop, National Council on Family annual meeting. Toronto, Canada, October 16, 1973b.

Bengtson, V. L., & Cutler, N. Generations and intergenerational relations: Perspectives on age groups and social change. In R. Binstock and E. Shanas (Eds.), *Handbook of aging and the social sciences*. New York: Van Nostrand, Rinehold, 1976.

Bengtson, V. L., Furlong, M. D., & Laufer, R. Time aging and the continuity of social structure: Themes and issues in generational analysis. *Journal of Social Issues*, *30*, 1974, 1–31.

Bengtson, V. L., & Kuypers, J. A. Generational differences and the developmental stake. *Aging and Human Development*, *2*, 249–260.

Bengtson, V. L., Olander, E., & Haddad, A. The 'generation gap' and aging family members; Toward a conceptual model. In J. F. Gubrium (Ed.), *Time, roles, and self in old age*. New York: Human Sciences Press, 1976.

Bengtson, V. L., & Starr, J. M. Contrasts and consensus: A generational analysis of youth in the 1970's. In Havighurst, R. J. (Ed.), *Youth. The Seventy-fourth Yearbook of the National Society for the Study of Education*, Part 1. Chicago: University of Chicago Press, 1975.

Bettelheim, B. The problem of generations. In E. Erikson (Ed.), *The challenge of youth*. New York: Anchor Press.

Blumfeld, W. S. Note on the relationship of political preference between generations within a household. *Psychological Reports*, 1964, *15*, 976.

Braun, P., & Bengtson, V. Religious behavior in three generations: Cohort lineage effects. Paper presented at the Gerontological Society meetings, San Juan, 1972.

Braungart, R. G. The sociology of generations and student politics: A comparison of the functionalist and generational unit models. *Journal of Social Issues*, 1974, *30*, 31–54

Brim, O. G. Socialization through the life cycle. In O. G. Brim and S. Wheeler (Eds.), *Socialization after childhood*. New York: John Wiley and Sons, 1966.

Brittain, V. Adolescent choices and parent-peer cross-pressures. *American Sociological Review*, 1963, *28*, 385–391.

Christensen, T., & Gregg, F. Changing sex norms in America and Scandinavia. *Journal of Marriage and the Family*, 1970, *31*, 612–627.

Clausen, J. Value transmission and personality resemblance in two generations. Paper presented at American Sociological Association meeting, Montreal, 1974.

Connell, R. W. Political socialization in the American family. *Public Opinion Quarterly*, 1972, *36*, 323–333.

Cutler, N. E. Generational analysis and political socialization. In S. A. Renshon (Ed.), *Handbook of political socialization. Theory and research.* New York: Free Press, 1976.

Davis, K. The sociology of parent–youth conflict. *American Sociological Review*, 1940, 5, 523–535.

Dodge, R. W., & Uyeki, E. S. Political affiliation and imagery across two related generations. *Midwest Journal of Political Science*, 1962, 6, 266–276.

Douvan, E., & Adelson, J. *The adolescent experience*, New York: Wiley, 1966.

Elder, G. L. Age differentiation and the life course. In A. Inkeles, J. Colemen and N. Smelser (Eds.), Annual Review of Sociology. Palo Alto: *Annual Reviews*, Inc., 1975.

Erikson, E. H. *Childhood and society.* New York: Norton, 1950.

Feldman, H. Development of the husband–wife relationship. Preliminary report, Cornell studies of marital development: Study in the transition to parenthood. Ithaca, New York: Cornell University, 1964.

Flacks, R. The liberated generation: An exploration of the roots of student protest. *Journal of Social Issues*, 1967, 23, 52–75.

Freeman, H. The generation gap: Attitudes of students and of their parents. *Journal of Counseling Psychology*, 1972, 19, 441–447.

Friedenberg, E. Current patterns of a generation conflict. *Journal of Social Issues*, 1969, 25, 21–38.

Friedman, L. N., Gold, A. R., & Christie, R. Dissecting the generation gap: Intergenerational and intrafamilial similarities and differences. *Public Opinion Quarterly*, 1972, 36, 334–346.

Furstenberg, F., Jr. Transmission of attitudes in the family. Unpublished doctoral dissertation, Columbia University, 1967.

Gallagher, B. J. An empirical analysis of attitude differences between three kin-related generations. *Youth and Society*, 1974, 4, 327–349.

Gallagher, B. J. Ascribed and self-reported attitude differences between generations. *Pacific Sociological Review*, 1976, 19, 317–332.

Gewirtz, J. L. Attachment and Dependency. J. L. Gewirtz (Ed.), Washington, D.C.: Winston, 1972.

Goldsmid, P. Intergenerational similarity in political attitudes: The effects of parent–child relations and exposure to politics. Unpublished doctoral dissertation, University of Chicago, 1972.

Haan, N., Smith, M. B. and Black, J. Moral reasoning of young adults: Political-social behavior, family background, and personality correlates. *Journal of Personality and Social Psychology*, 1968, 10, 183–201.

Hagestad, G. O. Role change in adulthood: The transition to the empty nest. Unpublished manuscript, Committee on Human Development, University of Chicago, 1977.

Hess, R., & Handel, G. *Family worlds.* Chicago: University of Chicago, 1959.

Hill, R., Foote, N., Aldous, J., Carlson, R., & MacDonald, R. *Family development in three generations.* Cambridge, Mass.: Schenkman, 1970.

Hyman, H. *Political socialization.* Glencoe, Illinois: Free Press, 1959.

Jennings, M., & Niemi, R. The transmission of political values from parent to child. *American Political Science Reivew*, 1968, 42, 169–184.

Jennings, M. & Niemi, R. Continuity and change in political orientations: A longitudinal study of two generations. *American Political Science Review*, 1975, 69, 1316–1335.

Kagan, J., & Moss, H. A. *From birth to maturity.* New York: John Wiley and Sons. 1962.

Kalish, R., & Johnson, A. Value similarities and differences in three generations of women. *Journal of Marriage and the Family*, 1972, 34, 49–54.

Kalish, R., & Knudsen, F. W. Attachment vs. disengagement: A life span conceptualization. *Human Development*, 1976, *19*, 171–181.

Kandel, D., & Lesser, G. *Youth in two worlds*. San Francisco: Jossey-Bass., 1972.

Keniston, K. *Young radicals: Notes on committed youth*. New York: Harcourt, Brace, Jovanovich, 1968.

Kerkhoff, A. C., & Huff, P. Parental influence on educational goals. *Sociometry*, 1974, *37*, 307–327.

Kohlberg, L. *Stage and sequence: The cognitive-developmental approach to socialization*. Harvard University, 1968.

Larson, L. E. The influence of parents and peers during adolescence: The situation hypothesis revisited. *Journal of Marriage and the Family*, 1972, *34*, 67–76.

Larson, W. R., & Myerhoff, B. Primary and formal family organization and adolescent socialization. *Sociology and Social Research*, 1965, *50*, 63–71.

Laufer, R., & Bengtson, V. L. Generations, aging, and social stratification: On the development of generational units. *Journal of Social Issues*, 1974, *30*, 181–205.

Lerner, R. M. Showdown at the generation gap: Attitudes of adolescents and their parents toward contemporary issues. In H. D. Thornburg (Ed.), *Contemporary adolescence: Readings*. Belmont, California: Wadsworth, 1975.

Lerner, R. M., & Knapp, J. R. Actual and perceived intrafamiliar attitudes of late adolescents and their parents. *Journal of Youth and Adolescence*, 1975, *4*, 17–36.

Levin, M. L. Political climates and political socialization. *Public Opinion Quarterly*, 1961, *25*, 596–606.

Linder, C., & Nahemow, N. Continuity of attitudes in three-generation families. Paper presented at the Gerontological Society Meeting, Toronto, 1970.

Lowenthal, M. F., Thurnher, M., & Chiriboga, D. *Four stages of life*. San Francisco: Jossey-Bass. 1975.

Lubell, S. That generation gap. *The Public Interest*, 1968, *13*, 52–60.

Mannheim, K. The problem of generations. In K. Mannheim, *Essays on the sociology of knowledge*. London: Routledge and Keagen, (originally published 1923.), 1952.

Mead, M. *Culture and commitment: A study of the generation gap*. New York: Basic Books, 1970.

Neugarten, B. (Ed.), *Middle age and aging*. Chicago: University of Chicago Press, 1968.

Payne, S., Summers, D., & Stewart, T. Value differences across three generations. *Sociometry*, 1973, *36*, 20–30.

Piaget, J. *The psychology of intelligence*. London: Routledge and Kegan Paul. 1950.

Reich, C. A. *The greening of America*. Random House, 1970.

Riesman, D. *The lonely crowd*. New Haven: Yale University, 1950.

Riskin, J., & Faunce, E. E. An evaluation review of family interaction research. *Family Process*, 1972, *11*, 365–455.

Spanier, G. B. Perceived parental sexual conservativism, religiosity, and premarital sexual behavior. *Sociological Focus*, 1976, *9*, 285–298. (a)

Spanier, G. B. Formal and informal sex education as determinants of premarital sexual behavior. *Archives of Sexual Behavior*, 1976, *5*, (1), 39–67. (b)

Steininger, M., & Lesser, H. Dogmatism, dogmatism factors, and liberal-conservativism. *Psychological Reports*, 1974, *35*, 15–21.

Switzer, K. A. Achievement motivation in women: A three generational study. Unpublished master's thesis, Wayne State University, 1974.

Tedin, K. L. The influence of parents on the political attitudes of adolescents. *American Political Science Review*, 1974, *68*, 1579–1592.

Thomas, L. E. Family correlates of student political activism. *Developmental Psychology,* 1971, *4,* 206–214.

Thomas, L. E. Generational discontinuity in beliefs: A exploration of the generation gap. *Journal of Social Issues,* 1974, *30,* 1–21.

Thomas, L. E., & Stankiewicz, J. F. Family correlates of parent–child attitude congruence: Is it time to throw in the towel? *Psychological Reports,* 1974, *34,* 10–38.

Troll, L. E. Issues in the study of generations. *Aging and Human Development,* 1970, *1,* 199–218.

Troll, L. E. *Development in early and middle adulthood.* Monterey, California: Brooks/Cole, 1975.

Troll, L. E. The family of later life: A decade review. In C. Broderick (Ed.), *A decade of family research and action.* Minneapolis, Minnesota: National Council on Family Relations, 1971.

Troll, L. E. Salience of family members in three generations. Paper presented at the meeting of the American Psychological Association, Honolulu, Hawaii, 1972.

Troll, L., & Bengtson, V. L. Generations in the family. In W. Burr, R. Hill, I. Reiss, and I. Nye (Eds.), *Handbook of contemporary family theory.* New York: The Free Press, 1978.

Troll, L. E., Neugarten, B. L., & Kraines, R. J. Similarities in values and other personality characteristics in college students and their parents. *Merrill-Palmer Quarterly, 15,* 323–336.

Troll, L., & Smith, J. Three-generation lineage changes in cognitive style and value traits. Paper presented at Gerontological Society meeting, San Juan, 1972.

Troll, L. & Smith, J. Attachment through the life span: Some questions about dyadic bonds among adults. *Human Development,* 1976, *19,* 156–170.

Troll, L. E., & Turner, B. Impact of changing sex-roles upon the family of later life. In Constantine Safilios-Rothschild (Ed.), *Impact of changing sex roles upon the family.* In press.

Walsh, H. The generation gap in sexual beliefs. Paper presented at the American Sociological Association, Washington, D.C., 1970.

Wieting, S. G. An examination of intergenerational patterns of religious belief and practice. *Sociological Analysis,* 1975, *36,* 137–149.

Yankelovich, D. Generations apart: A study of the generation gap. A survey conducted for CBS News, 1970.

Yankelovich, D. *The changing values on campus.* New York: Simon and Schuster, 1972.

Zelnik, M., & Kanter, J. F. Sexual and contraceptive experience of young married women in the United States, 1976 and 1971. *Family Planning Perspectives,* 1977, *9,* 55–71.

Parent and Child in Later Life: Rethinking the Relationship

Beth B. Hess and Joan M. Waring

9

I. Introduction

This is an opportune moment, historically, to rethink the nature of intergenerational relations in later life, and a volume devoted to parent–child interaction through the life course provides the appropriate forum for such a discussion. It is our contention that these relationships are on the threshold of change and that very different and more fundamental questions than those that have shaped much of the social science literature to date must be addressed. This assertion is predicated on the fact that adult offspring are now largely emancipated from the obligation to provide basic care to their elderly parents within the kinship system. Our purpose here is to survey the large but not yet fully relevant literature in search of at least partial answers to such important and impertinent questions as: Why should any special relationship exist at all between parents and offspring in later life? In what way is life satisfaction enhanced or diminished by such a relationship? Are voluntary intergenerational ties viable?

In the pages to follow we shall discuss how intergenerational relations in later life differ from those at earlier stages in family development and earlier historical epochs; the particular demographic characteristics of the cohorts of interest; factors that undermine or threaten to rupture such relationships, as well as those that strengthen and preserve generational ties; and lastly, new issues and trends that could signify the emergence of a "new breed" of aged parents and adult offspring.

Child Influences on Marital and Family Interaction:
A Life-Span Perspective

II. Characteristics of Intergenerational
Relationships in Later Life

A. Historical Changes

What we observe in intergenerational relations in later life today is the consequence of trends underway well before the Industrial Revolution but certainly accelerated by the changes it brought about. With the shift from a family system based on consanguine values to one held together by the bonds of conjugality and sentiment, the obligations and influences of kinship have been minimized and the older parent placed outside the children's circle of privatized domesticity (Hareven, 1976).

More recent trends in the political economy of modern industrial nations have further eroded filial obligations. These trends have culminated in the extension of public responsibility to matters of health and welfare previously left to families and the private sector. Although the United States has been a comparatively late and often reluctant purveyor of such services, those who are now middle-aged nonetheless represent the first cohort of offspring fully released from the need to provide minimal income maintenance or health care for aged parents. Born around the time Social Security was enacted, the middle-aged also witnessed the enactment of Medicare and the Older Americans Act in time to coincide with or precede their parents' entry into the boundaries of old age. Thus, current cohorts of the elderly are totally dependent neither on savings nor on their children for basic subsistence or medical attention. They have known virtually from the time their children were born that they could make claims against the state for some income in old age, and more recently for health care, yet many undoubtedly still have lingering expectations of care based on the values to which they themselves were socialized as children.

The expanding sphere of social welfare entitlements both continues and reinforces the generational differentiation and nucleation of family units just noted. We may safely conclude that responsibilities to kin in older generations must now be defined differently and be based on considerations other than those that have operated over most of human history (and that sociobiologists might argue have worked to ensure survival of lineage genes by ensuring that care will be reciprocated by the child in the parents' old age). For the present it seems fair to say that relations between aged parents and adult children—and between aged children and ancient parents—are "anomic" in the sense that clear normative prescriptions are lacking at the same time that the range of choices of what to do is expanding. We are seeing emergent, fluid, often ad hoc arrangements—which may remain precisely that.

B. Family Stage Differences

Our contention that relations between the generations in later life should be considered problematic rather than given is bolstered by comparisons presented in this volume with parent–child relations at the other stages of the life cycle. The crucial difference is that, at the distal end of the life course, parents and children are both adults, and in some ways social equals. For many decades, both parties to the relationship have claimed the prerogatives of adult status among their peers and in the community. Gone is the earlier socially sanctioned power imbalance based on the minority position of the child and his or her economic dependence. With the public entitlements of Social Security, Medicare, and the Older Americans Act, gone also is the reverse situation of complete economic dependence of an elderly parent on offspring. The autonomy and equality conferred by adulthood, however, places a commensurate burden on the generations. They must voluntarily undertake the initiatives necessary to maintain the relationship if it is to be preserved. They must also be held responsible for behaviors that increase or decrease the satisfaction derived from the relationship.

Another major distinction is that members of both older generations, if still married, have primary emotional investments in and obligations to their marriage partners. For the elderly generation, concerns for the welfare of the spouse supersede concerns for grown children. In addition, for the middle generation, responsibilities to one's parents are secondary to obligations to one's own children, who, even as young adults, may require some nurturance and financial support. The primacy of conjugal bonds introduces still another complication: the matter of in-laws. Elderly parents must deal with offspring as members of a loyal pair, whereas the married adult offspring typically must manage relationships with two sets of parents. Attitudes and behavior toward kin thus become an integral part of the relations between the child and parent.

A further distinction is that parent–child interaction in later life typically is not part of a daily routine but increasingly part of leisure schedules. Neolocality plus the financial independence and autonomous family status of elderly individuals, as well as the increasing probability of joint survival for the older couple, mean that separate residences will be maintained for a considerable portion of later life. By this time, members of both generations usually will have lived as many years outside as within the original parent–child household, lacking opportunities to create the intimacies that earlier day-to-day, face-to-face contact provided.

C. The Sum of Differences

These distinctive characteristics of parent–child relationships in later life today add up to what we have called the voluntaristic assumption of intergenerational ties. Generational autonomy and financial independence direct our attention to qualitative dimensions, particularly the affectional valence of the relationship. As Kreps (1977) asks: "Except for periods of psychological stress, illness and the like, will there be sufficient mutuality of interest to hold [them] together on a continuous basis? [p. 23–24]" Thus, the best model for examining intergenerational relations in later life may not lie in the family system but in friendship patterns—relationships based upon mutual respect, common interests, affection, and emotional support. "Homophily," the tendency for liking to be based on shared traits and attitudes, may be the process underlying the degree of contact and satisfaction derived from it (Hess, 1972; Lazarsfeld & Merton, 1954). To assess the bases for homophily and other factors that might enhance or detract from a satisfying intergenerational relationship in later life, we must first examine particular characteristics of the cohorts of interest at this moment in history.

III. Age and Cohort Differences

Regardless of time or social context, two factors ensure that the middle-aged and old—either as kin or as social aggregates—will bring different motivations, capacities, aspirations, and expectations to their relationships with one another. They are necessarily of different ages and thus face different life stage exigencies. As members of different cohorts, they have grown older subject to distinctive concatenations of social influences. Even when they experience the same historical event (e.g., war, depression), the impact of the event on their lives is likely to vary because of their different age locations and cohort membership. These inevitable sources of differentiation come into clearer focus in Figure 9.1.

Viewed macroscopically, as social aggregates, the middle-aged and old are distinguished by varied sets of social characteristics. As a result of their cohort membership, they have undergone unique life course

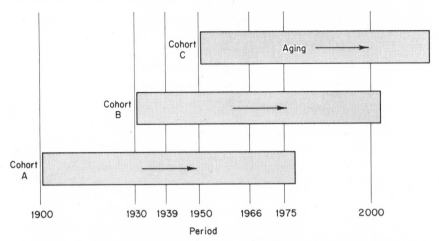

FIGURE 9.1. *Sources of differentiation due to age location and cohort membership. (Adapted from Riley, M. W., Johnson, M. & Foner, A.,* Aging and sociology, Volume III: A sociology of age stratification. © *1972, Russell Sage Foundation, New York, p. 16, Figure 1-3.)*

experiences. They also have different age dependent needs related to the biological risks of advancing age as well as to the way chronological age is currently used to provide or prohibit access to various social desiderata. Consequently, the middle-aged and old have "self-interests" that are potentially productive of conflict in the societal arena—and of strain in the intergenerational relationship.

Within the cohorts that now comprise the elderly, however, there is considerable diversity. This variety is the result of differences in national origin, length of exposure to urbanism, available opportunities, etc. These differences, along with additional ones deriving from greater age itself, have led Neugarten (1974) to distinguish the "old-old" from the "young-old." The "old-old," those 75 and over, differ in capacities, needs, and resources from the "young-old," those 55 to 74, who may not even define themselves as old, especially if they have living parents (which is increasingly the case) and if they are in good health. Nonetheless, the present situation of the "traditional" old is one of lessened likelihood of being in the productive sector of the economy, lower income, less education, and poorer health than that which characterizes other adult strata.

Those who are middle-aged, on the other hand, are more homogeneous in terms of nativity and experience but have had a distinctive cohort biography: Born about the time of the Great Depression and reaching adulthood during World War II or soon thereafter, they became the beneficiaries of a trend toward higher levels of educational attainment and the expanding economy of postwar America. The women married young and almost universally and proceeded to produce the largest cohorts of offspring on record. The men underwent an unprecedentedly rapid transition to adulthood: completing school, going to war, getting married, finding a job, and becoming a parent—all within a very short span (Winsborough, 1975). The present situation of the middle-aged is one of continuing and high demands on time and resources and often decreasing energies. Although relatively privileged economically and socially, they carry the burdens of familial and societal dependencies. For those in blue collar occupations, moreover, it is the period of the "life cycle squeeze," when the cost of raising and educating children continues to increase, whereas income is leveling off, sending many women back to work (Oppenheimer, 1974).

There are additional, often overlooked differences that are crucial to understanding intergenerational and interstratum relations today: cohort differences in fertility and the relative size of the cohort of which one is a member (Waring, 1956). Differential fertility affects not only the number of dependents one has early in life but, in old age, the number of potential interpersonal resources. For instance, there is some indication that women with few or no children run a higher risk of institutionalization in old age (Soldo & Myers, 1976), a risk especially threatening to those now old who restricted childbearing during the depression years.

More important to the commonweal is the issue of dependency ratios, the proportion of wage earners to both dependent children and nonproductive old people. Although the labor force will be absorbing the large number of "baby boom" children in coming decades, the propensity toward earlier retirement and longer life expectancy will keep the ratio high, even under conditions of zero population growth (USGPO, 1976). What will change is the composition of the dependency burden, with old people accounting for an increasing share and requiring greater amounts of income transfers (Harootyan & Rosenberg, 1976). The biggest problem is yet to come: when the large birth cohorts of 1947–1957 become retired early next century and must depend upon a labor force composed of their own very small number of offspring. This development, it is argued, can only accelerate the trend toward public assumption of income maintenance throughout the life course (Shanas & Hauser, 1974).

The impact of old-age dependency and medical requirements is already being felt in pressures on the Social Security system, with consequent resentment among younger labor force members (Kreps, 1976). The greater burden, however, is being born by today's middle-aged with surviving parents and a large number of closely spaced children, many of whom are undergoing expensive educations. Their interest in securing their own old age may give then an "anticipatory stake" in such measures and so quell vociferous complaint.

Societal Strain or Generational Solidarity

In emphasizing the pressures for dissensus and change in the society arising from differences in the past history and current status of the middle-aged and old (Foner, 1974), we must not overlook the possibility that these strains in the social system may deflect strain from the family. For example, dissatisfaction with the burdensome dependency ratio is registered against a universalistic bureaucracy rather than against the dependency of particular family members, thus defusing a possible source of tension in intergenerational relationships. Moreover, the removal of responsibility for income maintenance and health care from the interpersonal system can be viewed as conducive to positive affect in intergenerational relations. Resentment and hostility between generations may be lessened to the extent that these responsibilities are perceived as societal concerns (Kreps, 1977). The offspring are relieved of excruciating choices between their parents' needs and those of their own children, and the aged parent is spared being placed in the position of petitioner for favors from those for whom they were once responsible.

The essential change has been that the adult child now provides for an aged parent in the *citizen* role rather than the familial one. Similarly, the "politicization" of needs of old people permits them to press demands and express intergenerational hostility also in the role of citizen. Perhaps some crucial dimension of caring is lost, but these developments do not preclude either ordinary or extraordinary displays of concern and devotion. Rather, it is in this fashion that intergenerational exchanges have shifted from the fulfillment of instrumental needs (with certain exceptions we shall discuss later) to expressive ones, which require the active participation of family members in both generations.

IV. Factors Tending to Attenuate Intergenerational Bonds

The question of why relationships between elderly parents and their children are voluntarily continued becomes more challenging given the inevitable differences in age and cohort membership and the often opposing self-interests indicated earlier. These differences in past experience and present concern reduce the probability of homophily and contain potentials for indifference, if not strife. But a number of other conditions also inhibit initiatives on behalf of preserving the relationship. Among these are decreasing opportunities to help, new roles for middle-aged women, psychological barriers, and the timing of life course transitions.

A. Diminishing Opportunities

A considerable body of research reports frequent contact and helping patterns between elderly parents and at least one of their offspring (Hill, 1970; Riley, Foner, Hess & Toby, 1968; Sussman, 1976a, b). However, the need, occasion, and ability to share personal and material resources in mutually gratifying ways in later life are often diminished. For example, geographic distance creates impediments to spontaneous, casual, or convenient gestures of help. The availability of social services in some communities, for example, senior citizen minibuses and day care, provides an alternative to seeking such assistance from family members and thus reduces occasions for face-to-face interaction. Absorption in the marriage may exclude the other generation.

Further, the earlier initiation and compressed period of childbearing among the current cohorts of middle-aged make it likely that elderly parents will outlive the grandparent role. No longer useful as providers of regular or intermittent child care, they lose a mechanism that kept contact with their children alive and appreciated. Further, the middle-aged offspring may themselves be entering the grandparent role and, if they are among those who gladly espouse the role, could view their own parents' attempts at great-grandparenting as competitive. The fact that great-grandparents now more nearly approach the stereotypical image of "grandmother" and "grandfather" may add to the competition (Troll, 1971). By contrast, some elderly parents will resist undertaking grandparenting activities when asked and so violate the "extended expectations" of their children and increase intergenerational tensions.

Although opportunities for a mutually gratifying exchange of services are limited in number, the transfer of gifts and money is also constrained by the need of each generational unit to maintain resources for an increasing period of nonearning. Retirement incomes and assets must now be stretched over a decade or more, with widows subject to the disadvantage of partial benefits. In addition, some elder parents wish to keep funds aside for nursing-home expenses in the event that such placement becomes necessary. The middle-aged offspring may also be trying to accumulate a retirement nest egg sufficient to ensure independence and an adequate standard of living when old. Thus, the economics of long life expectancy do not encourage intergenerational transfer of income, except through inheritance.

The financial independence of the generations, however, enables them to maintain the separate residences that most prefer until such arrangements are no longer feasible or possible (Kobrin, 1976). Thus, when elderly parents need to call upon children for assistance, they are apt to be frail, greatly disabled, gravely ill, or mentally incompetent. Although ill health typically increases the number of contacts between parents and offspring, these frequently fail to engender feelings of closeness and satisfaction between the generations. Rather, family members are often reluctant and feel ill-prepared to take on such responsibility, regardless of a value commitment to the desirability of home-based health care (Litman, 1971). Some children define such care taking as a sacrifice.

Generally, institutionalization is not considered a desirable alternative by either parent or child. Not only is there a stigma attached to the perceived "dumping" of a parent—evidence of persisting obligation norms—but it also tends to limit intergenerational contacts. However, intergenerational stress may be alleviated through transfer to a nursing home when the condition of the parent becomes physically and emotionally difficult to manage. This advantage, however, is offset by the high cost of such care over a long period (Kent & Matson, 1972; Miller, Bernstein & Sharkey, 1975).

B. The Demands of Middle Age

Role allocation in our society is such that those now in middle adulthood easily fall victim to overcommitments. High performance demands from work as well as numerous family and community obligations converge during the middle years. Vincent (1972) speaks of the "Caught Generation," Goode (1960) of "role strain," and Brim (1976) of a male "mid-life crisis"—all denoting the pressures now characteristic of this period in the life course. Although these difficulties may be peculiar to, or most pronounced in, the current cohort of middle-aged (the small number of depression children who now must deal with the needs of the larger cohorts on either side), the consequence is to limit the time and emotional energy that adult male children can expend on the needs of aged parents.

Since the middle-aged male has been more likely to be perceived as burdened by multiple role obligations and the female less involved in nonfamily roles and more responsible for the conduct of intergenerational relations, parents could continue to hope for attentions and expect help when necessary. But several trends are now underway to change the pattern of a woman's life course and her availability for and interest in tending to elderly relatives: earlier nest emptying, increasing rates of labor force participation, and entry or reentry into higher education. Involvement in these new roles by the middle-aged woman, however, may coincide with the time of greatest need for her services and physical presence by the elderly parents—hers and her husband's.

It is one of those demographic ironies that whereas one set of trends promises increased freedom from family responsibilities and hence new opportunities for satisfying alternatives in later life, another set makes it difficult for many women to pursue such possibilities with total commitment. They are at risk of having their nest refilled. Whatever plans the middle-aged couple may have had for their newfound decades of life together are increasingly likely to be upset by instabilities in the lives of either their children or their aged parents, which may require financial or personal attention and often an investment of emotional energy. The middle-aged woman seeking a new set of role obligations in the world of work or education must be prepared to reassume the maternal or daughter role when the once emptied nest begins to refill. Similarly, the middle-aged man may find decisions regarding retirement and residence affected by the need to provide a temporary refuge for a grown child or elderly relative (Shepard, 1976).

The rule of reciprocity plus norms of filial obligation, and a touch of noblesse oblige (Hill, 1970), may ease, somewhat, the strain of housing an aged parent. But the middle-aged offspring may also find their own adult children returning to the nest following some failure in their lives. For these returnees to the nest, there are very few ameliorating norms; to the contrary, the children's disappointments may be perceived as reflecting on some flaw in the parents. At the moment we know very little about these refilled nests, but given the increased survivorship in both older generations and the high rates of divorce, desertion, unwed motherhood, and singleness in general among younger cohorts, the possibility of temporary, shifting multigeneration households anchored by the middle-aged cannot be ignored.

C. Psychological Barriers

There has been a persistent assumption in the literature on the family of later life that parental caretaking is a "good thing," that the volume of visiting and help are signs of vitality and viability in the family system. When analyzing the relationship between parents and adolescent children, it is presumed that earlier hostilities and envies are re-solved though not forgotten, and much is made of the high level of value congruence and basic trust that characterizes these two generations (see Bengtson & Troll, Chapter 7, this volume). But growing older does not necessarily carry with it the promise that the conflicts and problems between parents and children while growing up will disappear. Al-though years of separate residence and greater self-knowledge may erase some of the minor difficulties and blunt the edge of some of the major ones, struggles for control, patterns of blaming, and disappoint-ments about achievement, etc., may linger to undermine the possi-bility of a comfortable relationship between parents and children in the later years. Or they may be transferred onto the in-law relationship, creating a different but no less difficult kind of strain. As a result, there can be considerable emotional distance between the generations.

Meeting as adult equals serves to mitigate earlier problems of subordination–superordination but by the same token does not ensure the achievement of authentic equality. Perhaps this is why so many elderly prefer their intimacy "at a distance" (Shanas, 1973), maintain independent households as long as possible, and make demands on adult offspring as a last resort. Conversely, those old people who were socialized into a traditional set of expectations regarding children's obli-gations for care may not be able to understand the child's resistance to these "legitimate" demands for dependence (Lopata, 1976; Seelbach & Sauer, 1976).

In other words, more than just competing demands impinge on the middle generation. Both the prospect of reviving an original depen-dency relationship and the prospect of reversing it can be equally abhor-rent to the adult child (Clark & Anderson, 1967; Streib, 1965; Simos, 1970). The expressed reluctance to take on primary care of an ailing parent (Sussman, Vanderwyst & Williams, 1976; Wake & Sporakowski, 1972) may not reflect "hardheartedness" so much as a strong reality orientation—the situation may be more emotionally stressful than the offspring can cope with. From the point of view of the old person, becoming dependent upon the largesse of a former subordinate cannot be easily reconciled with a self-image constructed out of active mastery over a lifetime—which could explain why older men are often more reluctant than women to seek help from children.

None of this is new or especially modern. We are reminded of the observation of Homans (1961) that interaction is often easier among members of nonadjacent or "alternative statuses" than among those whose status characteristics are so comparable as to generate envy or acute awareness of inferiority. This is often cited as the source of "avoidance" taboos between adult offspring and in-laws, as well as the "joking relationships" between grandchildren and grandparents in situations where the elders do not reside in the same household or remain at the top of the family hierarchy (Appel [Sweetser], 1956; Goode, 1964; Olsen, 1976). This is certainly characteristic of contemporary America. Here, also, may lie the source of that resentment on the part of grandparents who are routinely expected to take care of grandchildren (Lopata, 1973)—the task must be voluntarily assumed.

In recognition of many of these difficulties, it has been proposed by Blenkner (1965; see also, Troll, 1971) that the developmental challenge of middle age is the achievement of "filial maturity," that is, to become a "dependable resource" for an aged parent without falling into the pattern of role reversal, thereby also allowing the parent to accept dependency without loss of self-worth. As is the case with so many prescriptions for mental health and personal development, it is easier to describe what a positive outcome should be than to detail how one gets there. Surely, the forces we have mentioned earlier that erode the bases of homophily, and whatever residues remain from psychic struggles of the past, all render problematic the attainment of intergenerational harmony, much less filial maturity.

D. Transitions

Other threats to intergenerational relationships are related to the nature and timing of the transitions of later life. Most status passages of middle and old age involve losses, which is not to say that opportunities for growth are not also present. But the aging individual must first deal with the negative impacts of, for example, the empty nest, widowhood, retirement, and the death of a parent or child. It is difficult enough for an individual to negotiate any one of these transitions, that is, to learn to give up a former role that was part of the definition of self, and then to learn the new role which carries with it a status decrement. And it is difficult enough for significant others to provide the emotional support necessary to ease the transitions, as well as to experience their own "counterpart transitions" of learning to relate to the other in terms of the new role instead of the old one (Riley & Waring, 1976). In these circumstances, reciprocal aid is also possible; for example, in helping the aged parent, the offspring rehearse for their own future, and conversely, the older person, having already lived through middle-age transitions, can serve as a role model and source of advice, but there are other difficulties.

Within the intergenerational system of later life, some transitions are joint ones. The mother's loss of her husband, for example, means the loss of a father for the child. Although this may provide the opportunity for closeness and sharing mutual grief, it may likewise deny each the help needed in managing the private grief, with consequent strain and possible recriminations. Similarly, some of the transitions in later life might occur simultaneously, or nearly so, as when the middle-age daughter reaches the postparental stage or is divorced at the same time that her mother is widowed, or when a son's retirement coincides with a parent's terminal illness. The self-absorption of each generational member undergoing his or her own transition may preclude providing the affective support the other requires, or it may generate resentment at the imposition of additional demands during a period of stress and so encourage mutual withdrawal.

The potential for strain is also present when the learning of a new role, as well as the "counterpart transition" on the part of others, takes an extended period and makes unaccustomed demands on the relationship. Widowhood, for example, often requires long-term supportive gestures, "presence" from the typically overextended middle-age child and spouse, perhaps financial liability, and sometimes sharing of residence on the part of the adult child (Adams, 1968; Chevan & Korson, 1972; Cosneck, 1970; Lopata, 1973; Morgan, 1976).

Yet, for all the difficulties of dealing with a widowed parent, the offspring are often inhibiting influences on the parent's desire to remarry (McKain, 1972; Treas & Van Hilst, 1975). To be sure, from an adult child's point of view, there are very practical objections related to inheritance. Although the newlyweds are not likely to produce new heirs, there are stepchildren to consider as potential claimants. There is also the fear that one's parent is being swayed by irrational feelings and that someone is taking advantage of his or her loneliness. The inability to perceive that one's parent could be sexually active makes it difficult for middle-age children to contemplate a parent's remarriage. Realizing this, many old people do not perceive remarriage as a legitimate alternative; they may avoid the issue by idealizing the dead spouse (Lopata, 1973) or elect to cohabit, preferably without their children's knowledge.

In general, the transitions of later life, whether joint, simultaneous, sequential, or involving "normal" (Neugarten, 1968), as contrasted with unexpected, losses, are paradigmatic of the questions raised in this chapter: What are the centripetal and centrifugal forces operating on the generations? The possibilities of anticipatory socialization, role modeling, mutual support, and renewed closeness are inherent in these events, even as they generate strain and dissensus. In the following section we shall examine the sources of continuity, closeness, and consensus in the parent–child relationship.

V. Factors Tending to Preserve and Prolong the Intergenerational Bond

We have argued in the preceding that in the absence of any imperative need or obligation to maintain intergenerational ties, such behavior becomes increasingly dependent upon the voluntary initiatives of the parties. Steps must be taken to engage in exchanges of goods and services, visiting, and other mutually maintained contacts. Since most family groups are characterized by such sustained gestures of concern (Riley & Foner, 1968; Sussman, 1976), powerful consolidating forces are obviously at work. Primary among these, we suggest, is the operation at long range of the norm of reciprocity (Gouldner, 1960), whereby the gift of caring from parent to child during infancy is returned through the adult child's tendering of care for the aged parent. Sussman (1976) speaks of an implicit bargain struck during the years of dependency. Reinforced by childhood caretaking, provision of an education, and transfers of gifts throughout the child's minority, this original sense of obligation could serve to generate anxiety and guilt over a poor performance as a dutiful offspring decades later. Moreover, there is an audience of "others"—friends, social work and health care personnel, neighbors—who monitor the way the family members deal with one another, thus enforcing norms of filial piety through the evocation of shame.

Solidarity between generations is also enhanced by many aspects of socialization: moral and religious upbringing; role modeling, expectations, and learning; anticipatory rehearsals; and the reciprocal flow of information that often produces value congruence. Further, the provision of gifts and services, and the needs that elicit them, are also a means of affirming the integrity of a family line, even though they often entail strain or resentment. Finally, but of utmost importance, is the fact that for many individuals of both generations, continued interaction is the expression of genuine caring, rewarding in and of itself. The impetus may be simply that of affection.

As we review the material on socialization, visiting, and parental caretaking and their consequences for life satisfaction of old people, several points will become increasingly obvious: that preservation of a relationship may or may not be conducive to maintenance of morale or some other indicator of well-being; that we cannot infer mutuality of interest and affection from visiting patterns, or the quality of the relationship from quantity of gifts. Our emphasis here is on the mix of forces affecting the interaction, with results as ambiguous, ambivalent or idiosyncratic as those that describe the feelings any one family member has for another.

A. Socialization

Whatever other tasks are—or are not—performed by the family, role learning, value transmission, and identity formation remain ineluctable by-products of intimate interaction. But examination of the socialization process has typically focused on the infancy stage, when dependence and attachment are most obvious. What of the later years? For one, earlier family socialization for adulthood does have some *durable* effect; part of what is learned while growing up, either through instruction or observation of parental behavior, creates images of what adult behavior is like or ought to be like. For another, socialization is *enduring*; information is often exchanged among family members throughout their lives, and opportunities for role modeling continue as well.

1. Values

Generally high levels of value congruence have been reported by a number of investigators both for adolescents and their parents and for three-generation lineages (Bengtson, 1975; Bengtson & Acock, 1976; Hill, 1970; Jacobsen, Berry & Olson, 1975; Kalish & Johnson, 1972; Thomas, 1971; Troll, 1972). However, much of this intergenerational similarity in orientation and attitude could be an artifact of similarities in social placement, with the differences attributable to cohort specific sources of divergence (Yoels & Karp, 1976). Nonetheless, there does seem to be a "tent of values" (Jacobsen *et al.*, 1975) under which family members can gather and communicate and perhaps increase their liking of one another, as the principle of homophily would suggest. Yet, the association between agreement and affection would tend to remove from data bases those relationships in which disagreement was extreme, especially in research designs where the parent selects the respondent child.

The channels of value transmission along three generations are sufficiently complex that generalizations are hazardous, as Bengtson and Acock (1976) attest. Moreover, dissonance reduction mechanisms may distort the amount of agreement or divergence. Bengtson and Kuypers

(1971) have proposed the concept of "developmental stake," whereby members of different generations interpret value congruence in terms of their own identity needs; thus, old people minimize differences, whereas the young emphasize their own uniqueness. But what we really do not know is whether values of the middle-aged move closer to those of their now-old parents as the former approach retirement and their own old age, or whether each generation defines its own value content for later life. For the moment it is safe to say that despite many differences of style and appearance, and perhaps of substance, there remain enough areas of basic agreement to permit family members of different ages to share a consciousness of kind and to feel responsible for one another.

2. Role Modeling, Expectations, and Care of the Old

With regard to the value placed upon caring for elderly relatives, certain expectations may be more deeply rooted in some subcultures than in others (Fandetti & Gelfand, 1976; Lopata, 1976; Seelbach & Sauer, 1976; Wake & Sporakowski, 1972; Sussman, et al. 1976). But parents in the majority culture as well as in these subcultures are often reluctant to articulate specific claims for themselves; rather, the more generalized message "honor thy father and mother" is conveyed early under religious auspices—the commencement of a long socialization to filial maturity. Explicit exhortation is reinforced when the adult is observed caring for an elderly relative, although such role modeling, of course, may have a negative impact ("she wasted her life caring for her father"). In one of the very few attempts to distinguish the effects of role modeling from those of role expectations, Johnson (1976) found that expectations are more easily registered, often regardless of the congruence of the role model projected. Nonetheless, we suspect that many middle-age parents attempt to "set an example for the children" when they tend the needs of an aged parent. They hope that such care, in turn, will secure their own future from abandonment.

3. Reciprocal Socialization

Since roles are acquired and relinquished throughout the life course, the need for continuing socialization endures for both generations (Riley, et al. 1969). Thus, parents do not necessarily lose their usefulness as socializers upon the child's entry to adulthood. As the old person experiences the transitions of later life, for example, the child is invited to undergo anticipatory rehearsal. Since many of these conditions involve status decrements, however, some offspring will decline the opportunity to assist or to learn other than negative lessons ("I'll never carry on like my father"). If the children are able to help the parent adapt and cope with retirement, widowhood, residential changes, or death of friends, the parents then become positive, successful role models, and in this exchange each generation will have served the other well. Given the probability that the middle-age couple will have three or four such parental role models, a variety of coping patterns might be observed and evaluated.

As for the reciprocal socialization of the parent by the child, the process is more one of conveying expectations than providing role models. However, the injunction to "stay youthful," which is widespread in the culture, involves elements of both. Perhaps children are really asking their parents to set an example for their own ultimate aging. However, it is certainly possible that the longer the old parent remains "young," the less likely he or she is to become a burden on the adult child. In many ways, the offspring have an "anticipatory stake" (Waring, 1975a) in the parents' successful outcomes. That remaining youthful might place a great strain on old people, in the absence of more age appropriate models of behavior, is suggested by Cleveland (1976) with regard to sexual activity; with the discovery of gerosexuality, too much may now be expected of elderly lovers.

Because of their command over resources, the balance of socializing power appears to reside in the middle generation. They serve as relay stations in transmitting the "new ideas" from the youngest generation and as sources of information about matters of crucial importance to parents, for example, medical services and entitlements (Shanas & Sussman, 1977). Their direct influence probably extends to all areas of their parents' lives. Especially influential would be the middle-age child who lives closest. In addition, most research indicates that daughters are more likely than sons to be in contact with older parents from both lineages.

This "special relationship" between female offspring and aging mothers stems from a number of sources: Women in our society are socialized to assume the nurturant role and to be responsible for kin caring in general. Moreover, there are probably more parallels in the lives of women of different generations than is the case for men, so that the basis of homophily is broader. Nor can we overlook the psychological dimensions: The women presumably have long since reconciled their antagonisms in a common commitment to femininity, whereas the men's lives may remain infused with the echos of rivalry and claims of mastery. Whatever the source, Neugarten (1968) has proposed that mothers and daughters provide particularly salient referents to one another throughout life. Certainly, from an actuarial standpoint, the widowed mother is a more relevant role model for her daughter than either she or a widowed father would be for the son. The comparable situation for males would be retirement, but since most old men are still living with a spouse, it seems unlikely that they would need to intensify the father–son bond or that sons would necessarily reciprocate (Streib, 1965; though Lowenthal, Thurnher & Chiriboga, 1975, found, in their small and selective sample, a closeness to an oldest son).

Among the working class, sons do appear to maintain strong ties to aging parents (Aldous, 1967; and in Great Britain, Townsend, 1963; Young & Willmott, 1957). Both Townsend (1963) and Koller (1974) further remark on the tendency for a youngest child, especially if this is a daughter, to become responsible for the parent, thus freeing older siblings to meet the demands of their own growing families or for upward mobility. Adams (1968) reports that sons and daughters maintained similar levels of contact while their aging parents remained married, but when the mother became a widow, the son's attentions declined, whereas those of the daughter increased (see also, Chevan & Korson, 1972; Cosneck, 1970; Lopata, 1973; Riley & Foner, 1968).

In general, reciprocal socialization, role modeling, and value transmission are more likely to produce similarities and encourage closeness between female members of a lineage than between males, but this may change if the life course patterns of females continue to depart in major ways from those of their mothers.

B. The Helping–Caring Network

Intergenerational integration or involvement is frequently inferred from patterns of visiting or the exchange of goods and services. Often associated with these initiatives is the added assumption that such patterns reflect positive affect. It seems to us equally plausible that negative feelings could determine the frequency and duration of contact. For instance, it is not altogether clear that contact can be equated with emotional closeness. Brown (1969) reports that relatively few elderly parents say they enjoy a close affectional relationship with the children whom they visit, and other research indicates that although most parents are likely to cite children as important resources and to have visited with them recently, strikingly smaller proportions consider these contacts close and rewarding (Berghorn, Schafer, Steere & Wiseman, 1977). Visiting patterns and intergenerational exchanges, as with all types of system transaction, both unite and separate; that is, the exchange between units is a form of connecting, but at the same time, an acknowledgment of the boundaries that exist between the two. In this latter sense, Aldous (1967) proposes that intergenerational contacts are governed by the need to maintain the integrity of both units.

Although some old people may complain of too much interference from offspring (e.g., "live-in" widows interviewed by Lopata, 1973, and Cosneck, 1970) and others of being abandoned by children (e.g., inner-city Polish Americans; see Lopata, 1976), there remains another 20% in most surveys who either do not have offspring or do not wish to have any contact with their children. Feelings of isolation or social deprivation are, of course, highly subjective: Some old people will never feel they are receiving enough attention, and others will have learned to live without. There is also evidence of what can be called a Goldilocks effect, whereby both too many and too few family contacts are perceived as stressful, so that there is a level of "just right"—enough to satisfy needs without evoking resentment (Kerchkoff, 1976; Ross, Rowe, McArdle, Yeracaris & Carrel, 1976; Stinnett, Collins & Montgomery, 1970). Satisfaction with parent–child relations in later life is obviously based upon the experiences of two lifetimes, each with its own trajectory, but also undergoing the myriad vicissitudes of any relationship lasting 5 decades or more. For many old people, levels of expectation will be adjusted toward congruence with reality. Those whose expectations remain "extended" without hope of realization will feel deprived (Seelbach & Sauer, 1976). Role bargains struck at earlier stages may require renegotiation as the relative distribution of needs and resources shifts dramatically over time.

1. The Flow of Assistance

The two-way transfer of advice, help in emergencies, goods, and services is well-documented (Cantor, 1975; Hill, 1970; Jackson, 1972; Kerckhoff, 1966; NCOA, 1974; Riley & Foner, 1968; Sussman, 1976). Among the urban poor, parents are more likely to be recipients of material support from their children and to reciprocate in the form of services (baby-sitting, advice). This diffusion of resources among members of low-income families serves in many ways to reduce mobility potential, but the needs of group members may be such that only an extended family in mutual aid relationships can survive.

At the other extreme, a large proportion of adult children do *not* provide any material support at all to parents; (of those who have living parents) 81% of the married men, 84% of the nonmarried men, and 88% of the nonmarried females in a recent Social Security Administration survey of pre-retirees (Murray, 1973) did not provide any such support. These data undoubtedly represent financial self-sufficiency on the part of many older parents, but even so, other evidence suggests that old people are reluctant to request assistance when needed. For instance, although in a national probability sample, two-fifths of respondents 65 years and older reported "not having enough to live on" as a very or somewhat serious problem, very few indicated that financial support from their children was an important interest or need (NCOA, 1974). We suspect that the reluctance to articulate this need not only reflects a norm of generational independence but also a fear that gifts of money may substitute for other attentions and gestures of caring.

If accepting gifts of money has a "cost" for the elderly recipient, it may also be perceived as a sacrifice on the part of the offspring and, as such, is associated with low morale (Robinson & Thurnher, 1976). The expenses associated with a parent's protracted illness are a financial as well as an emotional drain (Kent & Matson, 1972; Miller, Bernstein & Sharkey, 1975). But demands for companionship can be even more trying (Simos, 1970).

On the other hand, although few might articulate it directly, some parents, particularly those socialized in ethnic or religious patterns of strong familism, will resent *not* being cared for by a child. In a poignant sense, these older parents are victims of their very success in instilling "modern" values in the offspring. In another study of ethnic whites' attitudes toward care of an aged relative, support for family assumption of this task was attentuated over the three generations (Fandetti & Gelfand, 1976). And variation by age strata was reported by Wake and Sporakowski (1972), with the adolescents more willing to care for such a relative than are their middle-age parents, who are faced with the realistic probability of having to do so.

Attitudes, of course, are not necessarily reliable indices of behavior, and to express willingness to provide a home for an aged parent when it is not an immediate prospect is relatively easy. Attitude data, however, do allow us to gauge the strength of some norms, which in this case indicate overwhelming endorsement of independent living by people of all ages. Old people consider sharing a home with one's child as a last resort (NCOA, 1974; Riley & Foner, 1968; Sussman *et al.* 1976), undertaken only when alternative costs and risks exceed those of dependency on one's child. In the Sussman *et al.* (1976b) study, however, most respondents approved some government incentive for the care of elderly relatives, with monthly checks being favored over tax credits or public assumption of physical maintenance needs. The old person can define the monthly check as a legitimate return for a productive lifetime, and the child can perceive the payment as an independence–enhancing contribution of the parent. The reality of the moment, however, is that it is with great reluctance that an old person moves in with an adult child, however much the child is depended on for social supports. Often, the old person refers to herself or himself as a "guest" in the child's home (Cosneck, 1970; Lopata, 1973); but with suitable arrangements, open communications, and much tolerance and goodwill, multigeneration living can be mutually beneficial (Lynn, 1976).

VI. Consequences, Issues, and Trends

Before turning to emergent issues and trends in intergenerational relations, we need first to assess the importance of existing patterns of interaction to the well-being of both generations, but primarily to that of old people. To arrive at any balanced view requires us to avoid the extremes of both the romanticism with which Americans view family life and the cynicism with which descriptions of its current state are often imbued. As for the former stance, the pervasive assumption is that parents are always and in every way devoted to their children. This view recently received its fullest expression in the words of a judge who returned adults to the care of their parents for the purpose of religious deprogramming: "We are talking about the essence of civilization . . . mother, father and children. I know of no greater love than parents for their children. The child is the child even though a parent may be 90 and the child 60 [*New York Times*, March 25, 1977]." Curiously, there is no such assumption of invariant goodwill on the part of children. To the contrary, many Americans believe, erroneously, that old people are being regularly "abandoned" or "dumped" into nursing homes and other institutional hiding places. This belief further fosters talk about the disintegration of family life.

From the literature reviewed so far, however, we have seen that most elderly parents and at least some of their middle-age offspring engage in activities that serve to preserve intergenerational ties. These voluntary efforts on behalf of maintaining contact occur in the face of various structural and situational contraints, much as the proffering or provision of help occurs despite a value system that stresses generational independence except in the case of extreme need. As intergenerational contacts in later life increasingly call for the sharing of leisure time, it becomes important to ask whether such interaction confers related benefits: Does the interaction contribute to feelings of life satisfaction, morale, or whatever other measure of well-being might be proposed? We must also ask about the degree to which alternative relationships serve to contribute to such feelings and to integrate the old, especially, into ongoing social life.

A. The Well-Being of the Generations

A survey designed to assess the quality of life in America found that the middle-aged were, on the whole, both less happy and less satisfied with their lives than people of other ages (Campbell, Converse & Rodgers, 1976). We have suggested earlier that these negative assessments might be, in part, an outcome of their overcommitments. Indeed, other polls have found that the middle-aged are more likely to complain that they lack time to do the things they would like to do. And other studies generally indicate that an improvement in marital satisfaction accompanies the departure of grown children from the household, which also implies a reduction in role demands (see, however, Spanier, Lewis & Cole, 1975). Whether ordinary involvements with aging parents, however voluntary, are viewed as yet another claim on their leisure time and are thus resented, is not reliably known, although major responsibility for care is often considered a sacrifice.

Studies attempting to assess the well-being of the old, although abundant, are not necessarily comparable or consistent. Researchers, for example, seldom use the same measure, and samples vary widely in representativeness. Nonetheless, after reviewing the relevant literature, Palmore and Luikart (1972) conclude that the most frequent correlates of life satisfaction among old people are lesser age and greater health, activity, income, and education.

There is little agreement, however, as to the contribution of children to parental feelings of well-being. Medley (1976), for example, notes that "satisfaction with family was found to make the greatest single impact on life satisfaction [p. 448]" for both men and women 65 years and older, with standard of living and health next, and finances having no direct effect. Yet, Edwards and Klemmack (1973) found that socioeconomic status eliminated other effects; and Spreitzer and Synder (1974) found this also, using perceived health and financial status as variables. But Stinnett, Collins and Montgomery (1970), and Stinnett, Carter and Montgomery (1972) report that aged parents receiving five to seven visits a year had higher need satisfaction scores than those whose children visited either only once a year or more than eight times a year.

Nor are children absolutely necessary to perceived satisfaction with life in old age or mature adulthood, especially for women who derive pleasure from work (Sears & Barbee, 1977; Campbell, Converse & Rodgers, 1976). With income-producing work and full careers becoming more characteristic of women's lives, the incoming cohort of elderly women will be higher than the current one in both work experience and fertility. Thus, work and children, along with the marital relationship may provide alternative bases of satisfaction for women in later life.

And what about fathers? It is so frequently assumed that family variables impact largely on mothers that research on fathers at any stage in life has been relatively rare.[1] The grandfather role has not been considered very important for either generation because we do not typically associate males with caregiving (Havinghurst, 1954). Watson and Kivett (1976) almost reluctantly conclude that intergenerational relationships are not all that important to the morale of old men, and that health and social class are better predictors of satisfaction in old age.

We do know, however, that old men bereft of family ties are more vulnerable to suicide, motor vehicle and pedestrian death, and accidents of all types than are similarly deprived females of the same age (Gove, 1973). The special advantage of the female probably reflects her socialized abilities to seek out substitutes for missing kin and to develop deeper relationships with whomever remains in the social networks (Hess, 1976a).

1. Children and Nonfamily Associations

Again, the evidence is complex and findings mixed about the relationship between family integration and other social networks. Some find integration into community life more related to friendship than to family networks (Spakes, 1976); and other researchers find that respondents living alone, without strong family ties or opportunity to play traditional family roles, tended to compensate through community activity (Trela & Jackson, 1976, see also Rutzen, 1977). This pattern of dependency on family versus friends or neighbors was also found among old people in Kansas City: Where relatives were nearby, especially children, the old people preferred to depend upon these when necessary, but where no children lived in the area, old people were likely to depend upon friends and neighbors when in need (Berghorn et al. 1977).

Still other studies show that persons with high levels of kin interaction are also high interactors with nonkin, and those with low rates of contact with relatives have similarly depressed investments in other social networks (Biesty, DiComo & Hess, 1977; Booth, 1972; Croog, Lipson & Levine, 1972). Clearly, there is no simple relationship between family and other social networks: Some people may be generally high or low interactors, whereas others may compensate for losses in one area with enhanced involvement in different groups. Such substitutability, however, may be governed by considerations of fit; that is, one network may operate to meet a certain set of needs and a different one a different set, so that there are limits to how these can be used (Weiss, 1973; Litwak & Szelenyi, 1969). But there is agreement on one point: Social

[1]A recent exception is the October 1976 issue of *Family Coordinator*, on fatherhood.

isolation is emotionally stressful for both old and young. The existence of even a single "confidant" has been found to reduce risks of suicide or mental illness (Lowenthal & Haven, 1968). Bock and Webber (1972), in their study of suicide among isolated widowed people, explain the higher rate for widowers by the intervening variable of social isolation. Moreover, contrary to Roberts and Roberts (1975), Bock and Webber (1972) suggest that widows and widowers with social networks are lower suicide risks than married old people who depend solely on one another and whose social resources will be totally depleted upon the death of their spouse.

Thus, although having children on whom to depend may hinder some old people's integration into nonfamily networks, it is no bar for others who seem to be high socializers on all dimensions. The absence of offspring on whom to call in need, though, has a profound effect on those whose other interpersonal resources were never very ample. Given the support and satisfaction that nonfamilial associations provide, it behooves children to encourage their parents' participation in such networks.

2. Children and the Marriage Relationship

For those middle-age and older people who are still married, the conjugal relationship remains primary. Most recent studies have shown that marital satisfaction is heightened among couples who have negotiated the transition to the empty nest. This satisfaction appears to persist, if not increase, for those who remain married through the final stage of the family cycle (See Rollins & Galligan, Chapter 4, this volume). Along the way, efforts have often been made to enrich the marriage, and aged spouses tend to be more tolerant and accepting of the other than in their younger years (Clausen, 1972; Lowenthal et al., 1975; Miller, 1976). In addition, for the older pair, an independence from kin coupled with enhanced interdependence has been associated with greater marital adjustment in a number of studies (Gilford & Bengtson, 1976; Lowenthal et al., 1975; Miller, 1976; Roberts & Roberts, 1975; Smart & Smart, 1975). These aged parents often cite their offspring as a source of satisfaction, but rather in the sense that the children have been safely launched than as current purveyors of gratification. We might add, parenthetically, that since few older couples have a child residing permanently in their home, whatever satisfactions or tensions derive from the day-to-day marital relation are either not directly elicited by adult children or occur because these latter are *not* there. Obviously, however, there is the possibility of children indirectly affecting the relationship by generating conflicts over frequency of visiting, gift giving, etc.

Although most of the data in this volume have involved parental couples, the demographic facts of old age are that most old women are not members of a married pair. As we have already noted, the widowed parent's relationship to the child depends upon role adjustments for both generations, with the "counterpart transition" (Riley & Waring, 1976) often requiring extensive changes in patterns of help and contact. Although most widows live alone and prefer it, they often move nearer one of their children, and in advanced old age are quite likely to be living in the home of one, most often a daughter. On the one hand, a lifetime of socialization to dependency and family intimacy should make it easier for a widow than widower to impinge upon the lives of the offspring, but there is evidence suggesting that elderly males are less resentful than females at having to make a home with the adult child (Cosneck, 1970). It seems safest to conclude that having children on whom to rely in widowhood must confer some benefit, although these contacts can also be unsatisfying in terms of what the adult child may perceive as excessive demands (Simos, 1970) and the old person may see as indifference (Lopata, 1973). One study of widowed and married old people found that family interaction was associated with greater morale for both, but the scores of married people were higher than those of the widowed at each level of kin contact (Morgan, 1976).

B. New Issues

The proliferation of programs for the aged following the passage of the Older Americans Act, as well as their entitlements under Medicare and the Social Security Act (whose provisions are continually being revised), have created a new role for adult offspring, that of manager or guide through the bureaucracy. The requirements of this role are that children become sources of information about bureaucratic services and procedures so that the parents can become aware of the full range of options and resources available and are able to secure that to which they are entitled. Further, children are likely to be called upon to initiate the process that links old persons to governmental institutions and to handle bureaucratic authorities as the need arises (Kreps, 1977; Sussman, 1976). It is rather ironic that the quintessential duty of the child should now be to humanize the increasingly depersonalized arrangements for care of the aged. The so-called "demystified" world of the modern welfare state itself requires demystification. But the imper-

sonal is also impartial, and this guarantee of at least minimal maintenance works to the advantage of both generations.

There remains one last task in the life course: preparation for death.
Today, because it often takes so long to die, the middle-age child frequently has the responsibility of negotiating and supervising an extended terminal illness and the ultimate demise of parents. Involved
here are decisions regarding medical care, residential placement, and
sometimes whether or when to cease heroic measures to preserve life.
Since such questions rarely confronted earlier cohorts who had lower
life expectancy, less sophisticated medical technology, and fewer options, clear-cut guidelines do not exist, and decisions are frought with
anguish, doubt, and even guilt. Furthermore, old people today are more
likely than in the past to die in public, that is, in hospitals or nursing
homes rather than at home behind the veil of domestic privacy. For all
these reasons, then, issues of life and "death with dignity" have become
matters of public concern, debated in many forums. Yet, both parent
and child are in the situation of working out their own adjustments and
reconciliations individually or together. It is always possible that this
aspect of their relationship may lead to a new state of intimacy, in which
the giving of life to the one is reciprocated through the tendering of care
at the end of the life of the other.

C. The "New Breeds"

From all the foregoing, it should come as little surprise that both old
people and their adult children have recently been giving unexpected, or
at least nontraditional, answers to researchers' questions. Many of these
"new" attitudes were presaged by the findings reported in Riley and
Foner (1968), which effectively destroyed a number of stereotypes. But it
remained for the aged themselves to define their strengths and expectations, and the past decade has seen an accumulation of data that testify
to the vitality and independence of most old people. Especially notable
are the findings of the Harris survey for the National Council on the
Aging (NCOA), "The Myth and Reality of Aging in America" (1974); the
reality being that the older respondents felt much more positively about
themselves and perceived fewer conditions as being "problems" than
did younger respondents when asked about old people. Stereotypes
remain powerful, however, as many of those 65 years and older believe
that other old people are more incompetent and less interesting than
themselves.

If, through mandatory or willing retirement, more of the "young-
old" identify themselves with other elderly as "senior citizens" with a

stake in expanded entitlements, the meaning and image of being old will have to change to accommodate reality. Further, incoming cohorts of old people will be less likely than those now old to have been socialized to familistic expectations; they will have higher educational attainment and greater lifetime earnings; the women will have had some work experience and their own retirement benefits in many cases. The "old-old" may exhibit those characteristics commonly associated with old age but might also be using their intermediate juniors as models for successful aging. In essence, although a two-tiered old age seems likely for the near prospect, there may be less disjunction in the extended view. The years from 55 to the late 70s will be lived independently of children by politically and socially active, and probably healthier, men and women (Neugarten, 1974).

As for their children, two recently published surveys hail a "new breed" as well. Yankelovich, Skelly, and White (1977) report that over two-thirds of young and middle-age parents agree with the statement "Children don't have an obligation to their parents regardless of what the parents have done for them"—and this included 64% of the "traditionalists" as well as 73% of the "new breed." Similar proportions (64% and 68%) endorsed the statement "It's important for parents to have their own lives and interests—even if it means spending less time with their children." In a more limited survey of Hawaiian parents, over 90% of middle-class white parents and 73% of lower income white parents said that they "did not expect to rely at all on their children in old age" (Espenshade, 1977).

VII. Conclusion

From our review of the relevant literature, we may safely conclude that no single prescription can guarantee mutually satisfactory relations between the generations in later life. With the passage of time, so much diversity arises in family groups that possibly no two sets of parents and children in the society—or even in the same family—have traveled parallel paths.Let us eschew prescriptions about what intergenerational relationships should be and instead respond to the diversity by encouraging the broadest spectrum of social supports and services to aging parents and their offspring, so that they may work out their singular solutions to singular problems in the best way possible.

However limited the contributions each generation can make to the well-being of the other and however minimized the needs or opportunities for family caretaking, reports of the demise of the family are greatly exaggerated. A need for community, intimacy, and solidarity based on kinship remains a compelling impulse of the human spirit. For the middle generation, attention to kin as a voluntaristic undertaking may be the essential condition for the development of filial maturity and self-acceptance. For the elderly parent, being able to depend on offspring when necessary, without regression to childlike behaviors or impossible demands, may be the surest bulwark against Eriksonian despair (Erikson, 1959). If parent–child relationships are initially founded on mutual respect, there is every reason to expect them to become firmer over time as the dependency-based relationship moves to one of equality. Resentment and guilt should be minimized with the transfer of financial and service burdens to the state. Under these circumstances, far from seeing the death of the family, we may witness authentic solidarity between the generations across the life-span.

Acknowledgments

Thanks are due to the many colleagues who have commented on earlier versions of the chapter: Ann Foner, Matilda Riley, Harry Bredemeier, Karen Schwab, Reuben Hill, and Kathleen Bond.

References

Adams, B. N. The middle-class adult and his widowed or still-married mother. *Social Problems*, 1968, *16*, 50–59.

Aldous, J. Intergenerational visiting patterns: Variations in boundary maintenance as an explanation. *Family Process*, 1967, *6*, 235–251.

Appel (Sweetser), D. The social structure of grandparenthood. *American Anthropologist*, 1956, *58*, 656–663.

Bengtson, V. L., & Acock, A. C. On the influence of mothers and fathers: A covariance analysis of political and religious socialization. American Sociological Association meetings. New York City, 1976.

Bengtson, V. L. Generation and family effects in value socialization. *American Sociological Review*, June 1975, *40*, 358–371.

Bengtson, V. L., & Kuypers, J. A. Generational difference and the developmental stake. *Aging and Human Development*, 1971, *2*, 249–260.

Berghorn, F. J., Schafer, D. E. Steere, G. H., & Wiseman, R. F. *The urban elderly: A study of life satisfaction*. Montclair, N. J.: Allenheld Osmon & Co., 1977.

Biesty, P., DiComo, W. G., & Hess, B. B. The elderly of Morris County, New Jersey: Findings of Senior Citizen Assessment of Needs (SCAN) Survey. Office on Aging, Morristown, N. J., mimeo 1977.

Blenkner, M. Social work and family relationships in later life with some thoughts on filial maturity. In Ethel Shanas and Gordon Streib (Eds.), *Social structure and the family: Generational relations.* Englewood Cliffs, N. J.: Prentice Hall, 1965.

Booth, A. Sex and social participation. *American Sociological Review*, 1972, 37, 183–192.

Brim, O. G., Jr. Male mid-life crisis: A comparative analysis. In B. B. Hess (Ed.), *Growing old in America.* New Brunswick, New Jersey: Transaction Books, 1976.

Brown, R. Family structure and social isolation of older persons. *Journal of Gerontology*, 1969, 15, 170–174.

Campbell, A., Converse, P. E., & Rodgers, W. J. *The quality of American life. Perceptions, evaluations, and satisfactions.* New York: Russell Sage Foundation, 1976.

Cantor, M. Life space and the social support system of the inner city elderly of New York. *The Gerontologist*, 1975, 15, No. 1, Pt. 1, 23–27.

Chevan, A., & Korson, J. H. The widowed who live alone: An examination of social and demographic factors. *Social Forces*, 1972, 51, 45–52.

Clark, M., & Anderson, B. G. *Culture and aging.* Springfield, Illinois: Charles C. Thomas, 1967.

Clausen, J. The life course of individuals. In M. Riley, M. Johnson, & A. Foner, *Aging and society, Volume 3: A Sociology of age stratification.* New York: Russell Sage Foundation, 1972.

Cleveland, M. Sex in marriage: At 40 and beyond. *The Family Coordinator*, July 1976, 25, No. 3, 233–240.

Cosneck, B. J. Family patterns of older widowed Jewish people. *Family Coordinator*, 1970, 19, 368–373.

Croog, S. H., Lipson, A., & Levine, S. Help patterns in severe illness: The roles of kin network, non-family resources and institutions. *Journal of Marriage and the Family*, 1972, 34, 32–41.

Edwards, J. N., & Klemmack, D. L. Correlates of life satisfaction: A reexamination. *Journal of Gerontology*, 1973, 28, 497–502.

Erikson, E. H. Identity and the life-cycle. *Psychological Issues*, 1959, 1, 18–164.

Espenshade, T. J. The value and cost of children. The Bulletin of the Population Reference Bureau, Inc. Washington, D.C., April, 1977.

Fandetti, D. V., & Gelfand, D. E. Care of the aged: Attitudes of white ethnic families. *The Gerontologist*, 1976, 16, 545–549.

Foner, A. Age stratification and age conflict in political life. *American Sociological Review*, 1974, 39, 187–196.

Gilford, R., & Bengtson, V. L. Measuring marital satisfaction in three generations; Positive and negative dimensions. Gerontological Society Meetings, New York City, October, 1976.

Goode, W. J. *The family.* Englewood Cliffs, New Jersey: Prentice Hall, 1964.

Goode, W. J. A theory of role strain. *American Sociological Review*, 1960, 25, 483–496.

Gouldner, A. The norm of reciprocity: A preliminary statement. *American Sociological Review*, 1960, 25, 161–178.

Gove, W. Sex, marital status and mortality. *American Journal of Sociology*, 1973, 79, No. 1, 45–67.

Hareven, T. K. The last stage: Historical adulthood and old age. *Daedalus*, Fall, 1976, 13–28.

Harootyan, R. A., & Rosenberg, E. Old age dependency: The next half-century. Gerontological Society Meeting, New York City, 1976.

Havighurst, R. Flexibility and the social roles of the retired, *American Journal of Sociology*, 1954, 59, 309–311.

Hess, B. B. Age, gender role and friendship, Gerontological Society Meeting, New York City, October, 1976. (a)

Hess, B. B. Friendship. In M. Riley, M. Johnson & A. Foner, *Aging and society, Volume 3: A sociology of age stratification*. New York: Russell Sage Foundation, 1972.

Hess, B. B. *Growing old in America*. New Brunswick, New Jersey: Transaction Books, 1976.

Hill, R. *Family development in three generations*. Cambridge, Massachusetts: Schenkman Company, 1970.

Homans, G. C. *Social behavior: Its elementary forms*. New York: Harcourt, Brace and World, 1961.

Jackson, J. J. Marital life among aging blacks. *Family Coordinator*, 1972, *21*, 21–27.

Jacobsen, R. B., Berry, K. J., & Olson, K. F. An empirical test of the generation gap: A comparative intrafamily study. *Journal of Marriage and the Family*, 1975, *37*, 841–852.

Johnson, M. The role of perceived parental models, expectations and socializing behavior in the self-expectation of adolescents from the U.S. and West Germany. Unpublished Ph.D. Dissertation, Rutgers University, 1976.

Kalish, R. A., & Johnson, A. I. Value similarities and differences in three generations of women. *Journal of Marriage and the Family*, 1972, *34*, 49–53.

Kent, D. P., & Matson, M. B. The impact of health on the aged family. *Family Coordinator*, 1972, *21*, 29–36.

Kerckhoff, A. C. Family patterns and morale in retirement. In I. H. Simpson & J. C. McKinney, (Eds.), *Social aspects of aging*. Durham, North Carolina: Duke University Press, 1966.

Kerckhoff, R. K. Marriage and middle age. *Family Coordinator*, 1976, *25*, 5–11.

Kobrin, F. E. The primary individual and the family: Changes in living arrangements in the United States since 1940. *Journal of Marriage and the Family*, 1976, *38*, 233–239.

Koller, M. R. Families: A multigenerational approach. New York: McGraw-Hill, 1974.

Kreps, J. M. Social security in the coming decade: Questions for a mature system. *Social Security Bulletin*, March, 1976.

Kreps, J. M. Intergenerational transfers and the bureaucracy. In E. Shanas & M. B. Sussman, (Eds.), *Family, bureaucracy and the elderly*. Durham, North Carolina: Duke University Press, 1977.

Lazarsfeld, P. F., & Merton, R. K. Friendship as social process: A substantive and methodological inquiry. In M. Berger, T. Abel, & C. H. Page (Eds.), *Freedom and control in modern society*. Princeton, New Jersey: D. Van Nostrand, 1954.

Litman, T. J. Health care and the family: A three-generational analysis. *Medical Care*, 1971, *9*, 67–81.

Litwak, E., & Szelenyi, I. Primary group structures and their functions: Kin, neighbors and friends. *American Sociological Review*, 1969, *34*, 64–78.

Lopata, H. Z. *Polish Americans*. Englewood Cliffs, New Jersey: Prentice Hall, 1976.

Lopata, H. Z. *Widowhood in an American City*. Cambridge, Massachusetts: Schenckman Company, 1973.

Lowenthal, M. F., Thurnher, M., & Chiriboga, D. *Four stages of life*. San Francisco, California: Jossey-Bass, 1975.

Lowenthal, M. F., & Haven, C. Interaction and adaptation: Intimacy as a critical variable. *American Sociological Review*, 1968, *33*, 20–30.

Lynn, I. Three-generation household in the middle class. In B. B. Hess, (Ed.), *Growing old in America*. New Brunswick, New Jersey: Transaction Books, 1976.

McKain, W. C. A new look at older marriages. *Family Coordinator*, 1972, *21*, 61–69.

Medley, M. L. Satisfaction with life among persons sixty five years and older. *Journal of Gerontology*, 1976, *31*, 448–455.

Morgan, L. A. A re-examination of widowhood and morale. *Journal of Gerontology*, 1976, *31*, 687–695.

Miller, B. C. A multivariate developmental model of marital satisfaction. *Journal of Marriage and the Family*, 1976, *38*, 643–657.

Miller, M. B., Bernstein, H., & Sharkey, H. Family extrusion of the aged patient. *The Gerontologist*, 1975, *15*, 291–296.

Murray, J. Family structure in the preretirement years. Social Security Administration, U.S. Dept. of Health, Education and Welfare Publication No. (SSA) 74–11700. Retirement History Study Report No. 4, October, 1973.

National Council on the Aging. *The myth and reality of aging in America*. 1974.

Neugarten, B. L. The awareness of middle age. In B. L. Neugarten (Ed.), *Middle age and aging: A reader in social psychology*. Chicago, Illinois: University of Chicago Press, 1968.

Neugarten, B. L. Age groups in American society and the rise of the young-old. *Annals of the American Academy of Social and Political Science*, September 1974, 187–198.

Olsen, N. J. The role of grandmothers in Taiwanese family socialization. *Journal of Marriage and the Family*, 1976, *38*, 363–372.

Oppenheimer, V. K. Life cycle squeeze: The interaction of men's occupational and family life cycles. *Demography*, May 1974, *11*, 227–245.

Palmore, E., & Luikart, C. Health and social factors related to life satisfaction. *Journal of Health and Social Behavior*, 1972, *13*, 68–80.

Riley, M. W., & Foner, A. *Aging and society, Volume 1: An inventory of research findings*. New York: Russell Sage Foundation, 1968.

Riley, M. W., Foner, A., Hess, B., Toby, M. Socialization for the Middle and Later Years. In D. A. Goslin (Ed.), *Handbook of Socialization Theory and Research*. Chicago, Illinois: Rand-McNally, 1969.

Riley, M. W., Johnson, M., & Foner, A. *Aging and society, Volume 3: A sociology of age stratification*. New York: Russell Sage Foundation, 1972.

Riley, M. W., & Waring, J. Age and aging. In R. K. Merton, & R. Nisbet (Eds.), *Contemporary Social Problems*, 4th edition. New York: Harcourt, Brace, Jovanovich, 1976.

Roberts, W. L., & Roberts, A. E. Factors in lifestyles of couples married over fifty years. Gerontological Society Meetings, Louisville, Kentucky, 1975.

Robinson, B., & Thurnher, M. Parental care-taking of family-cycle transition. Gerontological Society Meeting, New York City, 1976.

Ross, J. E.. Rowe, S. K., McArdle, J. L., Yeracaris, C. A., & Carrell, S. D. Patterns of interaction with significant others among rural, suburban and urban elderly populations. Gerontological So...ty Meeting, New York City, 1976.

Sears, P., & Barbee, A. H. Career and life satisfaction among Terman's gifted women. In J. Stanley, W. George & C. Solano (Eds.), *The gifted and the creative: Fifty year perspective*. Baltimore: Johns Hopkins University Press, 1977.

Seelbach, W., & Sauer, W. Filial responsibility expectations and morale among aged parents. Gerontological Society Meeting, New York City, 1976.

Shanas, E. Family-kin networks and aging: A cross-cultural perspective. *Journal of Marriage and the Family*, 1973, *35*, 505–511.

Shanas, E., & Hauser, P. M. Zero population growth and the family life of old people. *Journal of Social Issues*, 1974, *30*, 79–92.

Shanas, E., & Sussman, M. B. (Eds.), *Family, bureaucracy and the elderly*. Durham, North Carolina: Duke University Press, 1977.

Sheppard, H. L. Factors associated with early withdrawal from the labor force. American Institutes for Research, Center on Work and Aging, Washington, D. C. (Paper, 1976)

Simos, B. G. Relations of adults with aging parents. *The Gerontologist*, 1970, *10*, 135–139.

Smart, M. S., & Smart, R. C. Recalled, present and predicted satisfaction in stages of the family life cycle in New Zealand. *Journal of Marriage and the Family*, 1975, *37*, 408–415.

Soldo, B. J., & Myers, G. C. The effects of total fertility on living arrangements among elderly women. Gerontological Society Meeting, New York City, 1976.

Spakes, P. Social integration, age, and family participation. Gerontological Society Meeting, New York City, 1976.

Spanier, G., Lewis, R. A., & Cole, C. L. Marital adjustment over the family life cycle: The issue of curvilinearity. *Journal of Marriage and the Family*, 1975, *37*, 263–275.

Spreitzer, E., & Synder, E. E. Correlates of life satisfaction among the aged. *Journal of Gerontology*, 1974, *29*, 454–458.

Stinnett, N., Carter, L., & Montgomery, J. E. Older persons' perceptions of their marriages. *Journal of Marriage and the Family*, 1972, *34*, 665–670.

Stinnett, N., Collins, J., & Montgomery, J. E. Marital need satisfaction of husbands and wives. *Journal of Marriage and the Family*, 1970, *32*, 428–434.

Streib, G. F. Intergenerational relations: Perspectives of the two generations on the older parent. *Journal of Marriage and the Family*, 1965, *27*, 469–476.

Sussman, M. The family life of old people. In R. Binstock & E. Shanas, (Eds.), *Handbook of aging and the social sciences*. New York: Van Nostrand Reinhold, 1976.

Sussman, M. B., Vanderwyst, D., & Williams, G. K. Will you still need me, will you still feed me when I'm 64? Gerontological Society Meeting, New York City, 1976.

Thomas, E. L. Political attitude congruence between politically active parents and college-age children: An inquiry into family political socialization. *Journal of Marriage and the Family*, 1971, *33*, 375–386.

Townsend, P. *The family life of old people*. Baltimore, Maryland: Penquin Books, 1963.

Treas, J., & Van Hilst, A. Marriage and remarriage among the older population. Gerontological Society Meeting, Louisville, Kentucky, 1975.

Trela, J. E., & Jackson, D. Family life and substitutes in old age. Gerontological Society Meeting, New York City, 1976.

Troll, L. E. The family of later life: A decade review. *Journal of Marriage and the Family*, 1971, *33*, 263–290.

Troll, L. E. Is parent–child conflict what we mean by the generational gap? *Family Coordinator*, 1972, *21*, 347–349.

U.S. Government, Department of Commerce, Bureau of the Census. Demographic aspects of aging and the older population in the United States. CPR Special Studies Series. May, 1976, P-23, No. 59.

Vincent, C. E. An open letter to the "Caught generation." *Family Coordinator*, 1972, *21*, 143–150.

Wake, S. B., & Sporakowski, M. J. An intergenerational comparison of attitudes toward supporting aged parents. *Journal of Marriage and the Family*, 1972, *34*, 42–48.

Watson, A. J., & Kivett, V. R. Influences on the life satisfaction of older fathers. *Family Coordinator*, 1976, *25*, 482–488.

Waring, J. M. Conflict between the middle aged and old: Why not? American Sociological Association Meeting, San Francisco, 1975a.

Waring, J. M. Social replenishment and social change: The problem of disordered cohort flow. *American Behavioral Scientist*, 1975b, *19*, No. 2, 237–256.

Weiss, R. S. The fund of sociability. In H. Z. Lopata (Ed.), *Marriage and families*. New York: D. Van Nostrand, 1973.

Winsborough, H. H. Statistical histories of the life cycle of birth cohorts: The transition from school boy to adult male. Center for Demography and Ecology, University of Wisconsin, Madison. CDE Working Paper 75-19, 1975.

Yankelovich, Skelly & White, Inc., Raising children in a changing society. Minneapolis, Minnesota: General Mills, Inc., 1977.

Yoels, W. C., & Karp, D. A. A social-psychological critique of oversocialization: Dennis Wrong revisited. American Sociological Association Meeting, New York City, 1976.

Young, M., & Willmott, P. *Family and kinship in East London*. London: Routledge and Kegan Paul, 1957.

The Influence of Children's Developmental Dysfunctions on Marital Quality and Family Interaction

10

Judy Howard

I. Introduction

My intent is to present a life course picture of families into which a handicapped child is born and grows to adulthood. This event produces one of the most stressful experiences that a family can endure. Conventional guidelines concerning how normal babies develop motorically, cognitively, and socially are seemingly of little value. Instead of appreciating the developing baby's abilities, the family will see instead evidence of his deficiencies and each member of this unit, including the handicapped child, influences marital quality and family interaction.

The material presented is divided into six sections. The first part deals with the parents' emotional responses to the initial recognition that their hoped-for normal child is abnormal. Following this, there is a discussion of parental attachment to their handicapped young child and the roles of each in this family triad of mother–father–child. Some pertinent aspects of the handicapped person's childhood, adolescence, and adulthood are discussed. Personality characteristics of the parents of handicapped children and their marital situation are presented, as well as the effect upon the siblings and extended family of the handicapped child. This presentation is based on a review of the recent literature and on my personal experiences as the medical director of a comprehensive intervention program for handicapped children and their families.

II. Parental Reactions to the Recognition of Their Child as Handicapped

Parental reaction to the recognition of having a disabled offspring is, in general, the same whether this disability is recognized at birth or in the early years of development. More often than not, the handicap is not detected at birth. For instance, mental retardation, congenital deafness, cerebral palsy, or a severe visual handicap are generally not confirmed at the time of birth (Parmelee, 1962). In those conditions apparent at birth, such as Down's syndrome and spina bifida, the degree of severity of the impairment often cannot be immediately ascertained. This element of unpredictability further complicates the emotional responses of the family and adds to their anxiety (Call, 1958; Heisler, 1972). The parental emotional responses to the realization of their child's handicap are described by Klaus and Kennell (1976) and include shock, depression, guilt, denial, anger, sadness, and anxiety.

Depression is the commonest and most predictable reaction, often presenting itself as grief similar to mourning, as if the child had died. According to Solnit and Stark (1961), the mourning process cannot be as effective when the damaged child survives. D'Arcy's (1968) interviews with 96 mothers of anencephalic infants who were stillborn or had died shortly after birth reveals that the mothers' sense of loss and grief was more acute than that of mothers whose congenitally deformed babies survived. However, these mothers recovered sooner from their mourning than did the mothers whose abnormal babies lived. The day-to-day impact of such a child on the mother is unrelenting and makes heavy demands on her.

Feelings of depression are often accompanied by feelings of shame, an anticipation of social rejection, pity, or ridicule. Parents see the handicapped infant as an ego extension of themselves (Illingworth, 1967; Kohut, 1966). The majority of parents of cerebral palsy children who attended a group discussion expressed feelings of alienation and isolation from their families and society in general (Call, 1958). Withdrawal from social participation is not unusual.

Guilt is another common response of parents. For example, those parents who did not want the baby may regard this situation as a punishment. The mother who has attempted to self-abort and then delivers a baby with multiple congenital defects may see the baby's abnormalities as an extension of her "bad" self. Sex behavior could be another important source of guilt feelings. Guilt about sexual thoughts, deviant sexual acts, or even childhood fantasies about sex can reemerge if the child is impaired (Jamison, 1965).

Denial, a third emotional response, is a protective mechanism that defends the parents against the problems they must face. Many will deny that the infant is abnormal (Klaus & Kennell, 1976; Taichert, 1975). Long-term problems are denied because, "someday the baby will grow out of his handicap." Anger can occur simultaneously with the denial process (Legeay & Keogh, 1966). This can be projected in many different directions. The parents often feel it is the physician's fault. This transference spares their blame of each other or themselves. Marital conflict is an obvious result when parents accuse each other.

It should be recognized, however, that the nature of parental responses depends on a complex of several factors, including personality traits and socioeconomic status. The personality of the parents involved will in great part determine their emotional response (Heisler, 1972). Lobo and Webb (1970) interviewed 10 sets of parents who had a Down's syndrome child. Of these families, 2 completely rejected the infant and placed him or her out of the home, 3 "emotionally rejected" the infant but kept him or her at home, and 5 "emotionally accepted" the infant. The profile of the 2 families who completely rejected their child is as follows: Both fathers were self-employed, and intellect was of great importance to them. The mothers were perfectionists and had periods of depression. Both couples had problems communicating with each other and felt that God was punishing them for this problem. There were infrequent contacts with relatives who were socially beneath them. And both couples had had previous contact with Down's syndrome children.

The three families who "emotionally rejected" their infant but kept him at home had the following characteristics: The fathers had little educational background; two were self-employed and one was unemployed. Physical appearance was important to them. Two of the mothers had a history of depression, and the third mother has been hospitalized in a mental institution. All three marriages were unstable even prior to the birth of the Down's syndrome child; all of the parents had had poor, insecure homes as children.

The profile of the five families who accepted their infants revealed fathers with steady employment who were content with their social status; mothers had no history of emotional illness; all five marriages were stable; all had strong support from extended families and had stable home backgrounds; and all had had little contact with Down's syndrome children.

Even though the numbers are small in the previous study, it is one of the rare reports that describes a handicapped child's family characteristics. My clinical experience with five families with Down's syndrome children is similar in certain respects. Two families, who had had previous experience with Down's syndrome children through their work experiences in state institutions and hospitals, placed their infant at the time of birth. One family, in which both parents had spent considerable time with Down's syndrome children in a day care setting, have kept their child and are very active in providing "the best experiences" for him, so that he may become an independently functioning adult. The remaining two families had never had experiences with Down's syndrome children other than seeing them in public places accompanied by their care givers. These parents have kept their child at home, are "not expecting too much" from him or her and plan to place the child out of the home when he or she "becomes too difficult to handle."

Parental realization of their infant's handicap may also bring into play conflicting emotional factors, ambivalent feelings, and even death wishes (Heisler, 1972). The distressed parents begin to ponder the realistic problems of the handicap and how it will influence their life. If placement is their decision, they have had to accept the apparent hopelessness of the child's condition. Parents who have made the decision to place their infant or child in an institution have tended to express greater overall concern for the welfare of the family, whereas parents who have kept the child at home express greater concern for the welfare of that child (Marcellus & Hawke, 1966; Skelton, 1972). This is usually a very agonizing time (Fackler, 1968), which is often complicated by a belief that society's attitude stresses the parental obligation of caring for their handicapped infant.

The point at which parents recognize the handicap is an important time for professionals to interact with these parents. To the extent that if they can be helped to express themselves and come to some understanding of their feelings at the time of the diagnosis, the better they are able to deal with their feelings and the questions of siblings and relatives (Call, 1958). The more inhibited the parents are in questioning those professionals, the less likely are they to create an atmosphere that permits the handicapped child to know that he or she is acceptable to them and to the rest of the family (Gurney, 1961). Family members' attitudes toward the handicapped child usually are related to the parent's response (Call, 1958; San Martino & Newman, 1974).

The first stage of emotional disintegration, which is characterized by depression, denial, anger, and sadness, is followed by a period of adjustment (Molony, 1971) or equilibrium (Klaus & Kennell, 1976). The parents report a gradual lessening of both anxiety and emotional reactions. There may be partial acceptance and partial denial of the handicapping condition. As they await the developmental milestones of sitting, walking, and talking, there may be fresh disappointment when a stage is delayed. The precarious balance of emotions with which they have learned to live may be shattered. Anger, depression, displacement, and somatic problems may result with each crisis they face (Bentovim, 1972). New defense mechanisms begin to assert themselves but rarely relieve the stress of the situation. An appropriate example of a recurring crisis is the one that parents of cerebral-palsied children face when the orthopedic surgeon tells them that their 6-year-old child needs a second operation. Three years previously, the first surgery lengthened the heel cords. Subsequently, the muscles in the thighs have become tight and need lengthening. The parents and child once again face the stresses of hospitalization, possible complications from the general anesthesia and/or surgery, and the difficult postsurgical care due to the heavy leg casts.

Let me conclude this first section by summarizing a family's emotional response to the recognition that their child has a handicap. Interspersed with feelings of depression and denial is anger. Parental anxiety is expressed about the future, the child's role in the family, the extent of his or her disability, and social adjustment. Hopefully, the family can begin a reparative process that will involve a partial acceptance of the problem. McAndrew (1976) found that the majority of 116 parents of handicapped children who had had previous knowledge and experience in bringing up normal children were unable to apply this to their handicapped child. It seems unrealistic to expect parents to accept their situation fully and to have the same confidence in parenting their handicapped child that they did in parenting their normal children.

III. Parental Attachment and Parental Roles

Attachment, or mutual bonding between parents and their infants, is an area of much current interest. Klaus & Kennell, (1976) have written a book entitled *Mother–Infant Bonding*, which stresses the importance of early attachment. These authors have stressed that a mother's or father's behavior toward the infant is derived from personal family experiences, cultural background, genetic endowment, and previous pregnancies. Detailed studies have been done by Condon and Sander (1974) of the normal neonate's capacities to see, hear, and move in rhythm with the mother's voice in the first minutes and hours of life. Therefore, the infant's behavior and parent's behavior both contribute to the establishment of a lifelong relationship. Lamb's chapter in this volume, (Chapter 6) on the influence of the child on marital quality and family interaction during the prenatal, perinatal, and infancy periods, assesses the studies to date that have examined the reciprocity of interaction between a normal infant and his or her family.

When parents are depressed and anxious about their abnormal child's condition, it is obvious that their interaction with the infant will be disturbed. The mother, out of her sense of shame and grief, may reject the child and not respond to his early attempts to communicate, whether it be turning his head toward her voice and quieting or patiently waiting for eye contact. She may handle him perfunctorily and isolate him from others as well as from enriching experiences. Also, the infant may have deficiencies in his "signaling system," which interfere with his ability to imitate or return a positive interaction (Connor, Williamson, & Siepp, 1975). For instance, when he cries and mother picks him up, he may be unable to adjust his body to her handling, and instead of being soothed, he continues to cry. Eye contact may be difficult if the infant has a problem maintaining a head position. Fraiberg (1974) has found that parents of blind infants are frequently emotionally indifferent to their child because of his lack of facial expression and contingent smiling.

Alternatively, the 3-month-old deaf infant as well as the infant with normal hearing eagerly looks with his eyes for social interaction. However several months later, the deaf infant does not turn toward the sound of his parents' voices. In addition, because of lack of auditory feedback, he ceases to babble around 6–9 months of age (Schlesinger, in press). Thus, as noted by A. Harris (in press), the deaf infant may be a limited or atypical participant in social exchange with the parent, with the result that parent–child interaction may be out of phase long before appropriate diagnosis is made and mutual development of attachment is seriously compromised. R. Harris (in press) states that the deaf infant's failure to respond to the parents could cause them to feel a sense of dissatisfaction or incompleteness. He maintains that parents often feel rejected and deprived, possibly without being aware of it. It would seem reasonable to propose that these feelings, in turn, may gradually result in a lack of parental stimulation and, hence, a decrease in overall parent–child interaction. Thus, when the infant's irritable or passive temperament is compounded with a physical and/or mental handicap, the strain on the parent's skill and, hence, the establishment of a strong bond of attachment, may be enormous (Connor et al. 1975).

There is a lack of research that looks specifically at attachment behaviors between parents and their abnormal children. D'Arcy's (1968) study of 90 families with Down's syndrome infants perhaps gives us a clue as to how difficult it is for some mothers to establish a relationship with their infants. Most of the 90 mothers felt it took months to get used to the idea that their babies were not normal. Eleven claimed it took years. The fathers seemed more distraught if the Down's syndrome child was a boy rather than a girl.

Gumz and Gubrium (1972) report on the concerns of 50 parents of mentally retarded young children during a series of crisis periods. This study reveals the influence these youngsters can have on their parents' present and future concerns. Most mothers were initially concerned about the emotional strain of caring for the handicapped infant, the readjustment of a family's daily routine, the additional time involved in caring for the child, the possibility of neglecting other family members, and the ability to maintain harmony and integration. Their second concern dealt with the infant's eventual ability to get along well with others, to make and keep friends, and to believe that even if one does not attain the highest levels of achievement, one may still be happy. Their third area of concern dealt with the child's future. Mothers reported that they believed it important that their child be accepted by others, be protected from emotional stress, and be happy regardless of academic achievement or job success.

The concerns reported by the fathers tended to be different. Most were initially concerned about the family budget and the cost of providing help for the child. Their next area of concern had to do with the handicapped infant's eventual role as a leader, his or her ability to be a winner and to assert himself or herself outside the home. The fathers' third area of concern involved hopes that the child would become academically successful, would have the ability to obtain training for a good job, and would be able to support himself or herself. The authors did not obtain information regarding the fathers' perceptions of their retarded son versus their perceptions of their retarded daughter and whether or not working mothers perceive their retarded child differently than nonworking mothers.

If the hopes and expectations of parents with handicapped children are not met, one of the results may be a very close emotional relationship. Call (1958) described the close emotional tie that developed between the parents attending his group discussions and their cerebral palsy children. Their relationship was so close that the child's independence was interfered with and other relationships for the parents and child were nonexistent, even to the exclusion of siblings.

The process of attachment is often made more complex by the necessity of the parents to recast their anticipated roles. New responsibilities must be undertaken and certain personal goals forfeited (Adams, 1968; Kohut, 1966).

Farber (1959), a sociologist who has done extensive research into the functioning of families with mentally retarded children, pictures the normal family as a "series of triads of mother–father–child whose continued existence as a group depends upon the successful attainment of certain primary goals. The relative importance of these goals is ranked by family members as a basis for making decisions and establishing family routines [pp. 5–6]." Stevenson (1968) found that most families are able to change with time and readjust their individual roles. However, if a retarded child is present within this triad and he or she never progresses beyond the preadolescent stage of development, there is an arrest in the usual cycle of necessary family changes. Parental goals are frustrated, their parents' domestic and community careers are affected, and there may be changes in the role expectation of one or both of them.

IV. The Childhood Years

I have chosen to designate the ages of 2–12 years as the childhood years. This span of approximately 10 years is most significant for an individual's development. The normal 2-year-old begins to seek independence from his or her care giver. Locomotion allows the child to move easily away from the parent, and the acquisition of speech gives him or her a sense of controlling the environment. A reciprocal chain of events occurs. As the child demonstrates increasing ability to care for himself or herself both personally and socially, the parents allow the child more and more independence for his or her growth as an individual. The child's experiences during childhood prepare him or her to assume greater responsibility during the years of adolescence and, eventually, adulthood.

For the handicapped child and his or her family, this is a time of further stress. Parents tend to shield their handicapped child from experiences and infantilize the child as well. They frequently are so struck by perceived limitations that activities the child could perform independently or with a minimum of help are not offered (Connor et al., 1975).

Call (1958) found three major problems that parents of cerebral palsy children face. First, they have difficulty in perceiving the child's actual handicap and actual abilities; second, there is considerable difficulty in psychological separation of child and parent; and third, there is an extended mutual interdependence of parent and child. These parental misperceptions are further explored by E. Shere and Kastenbaum's (1966) study of 13 mother–child pairs. They report on the attitudes of the mothers as well as on the quality of their interactions with their 2–4-year-old severely physically handicapped children. The mothers' concerns centered on their child's motor development and its improvement. They felt justified in not concerning themselves with the child's delayed speech and social development, since all medical advice was concerned with the physical handicap. They felt that "good mothers" were able to keep their children happy, and a "happy position" was one in which the child was placed supine on the floor, had ceased to cry, and demanded nothing. None of the mothers perceived that their child was in need of an object or toy to play with. They tended to overestimate their child's level of understanding and expressed feelings of "shame" in having a handicapped child.

M. Shere (1955) studied 30 twins, of whom 1 of each pair had cerebral palsy. Using home visits and a question–answer method, she observed that the mothers tended to overextend help to the twin with cerebral palsy, babied him or her, discouraged curiosity, and overprotected the child from real and imagined danger. The mother appeared to be more patient and accepting of the afflicted twin than she did of the normal twin.

A report by Marshall, Hegrenes, and Goldstein (1973) offers further insight into the problems parents face as they try to manage their handicapped child's development. They observed two groups of 20 mother-child pairs, one group with retarded and one with nonretarded 3–5-year-olds. The mothers of the retarded children were more demanding and commanding in their verbal exchange with their children. They described the retarded child as limited mentally and socially, thus requiring greater external control by the parent. The retarded child's decreased verbal ability extinguishes the mother's opportunity and incentive to respond by labeling objects or by repeating what the child has said. Schlesinger and Meadow (1972) found that mothers of deaf children exert more control over their child's environment than do those of hearing children.

There appears to be a lack of appreciation by the parents of handicapped children of the effects of overprotection and infantilization on the involved child. As this pattern continues during childhood, we find evidence of emotional problems during the handicapped child's preadolescent years. Block (1955), using a variety of projective psychological tests and interviews, evaluated 38 preadolescent children with cerebral palsy. He found six areas of major psychological problems. These children had unresolved dependency feelings and excessive need of affection; excessive submissiveness and compliance, with underlying hostility; egocentricity, with emphasis on expansive self-concepts; compensation for feelings of inferiority and inadequacy by fantasy; resignation to rather than recognition of limitations imposed by their disability; and superficial conscious recognition of the handicap and unconscious rejection of the self.

In a more recent investigation by Minde, Hackett, Killou, and Silver (1972), 39 out of 41 parents of 6-year-old physically handicapped children were optimistic that normalcy would come in time. This positive attitude was reflected in the children's hopeful statements of "getting better in time." However, by 10 years of age, the reality that a cure was not forthcoming became evident when 50% of the children demonstrated a depressed affect.

My own professional experience has made me aware of the young child and his or her parents' acute sensitivities to the handicapping conditions. Recently, the parents of an 8-year-old boy with ataxic cerebral palsy asked me, "What have we done wrong?" They were distressed that the social worker in the school he was attending had referred the family for guidance and counseling. As one of the few handicapped children within a large population of normal children, he had become openly depressed and hostile because he was different in that he was unable to keep up physically with the other children. The parents interpreted the referral for counseling as an indication that they might have caused their son's current adjustment problem. I reassured them that it was a natural emotional response by a sensitive child to be depressed as he faced some real problems.

Emotional disorders are also a complication of the mentally retarded. The impairment of reasoning abilities reduces the child's adaptive capacities, adding emotional stress within the family. The mentally retarded child will tend to misinterpret and overreact to ordinary stimuli, and such behavior contributes to his limited tolerance to stress. As the child approaches adolescence, the "cute behaviors," such as snuggling up to the opposite sex, become intolerable to both the family and society (Hammer & Barnard, 1966). The child is reprimanded and asked to behave like an adult, even though his mental age might be that of a 7-year-old. These problems become compounded by society's lack of acceptance of immature behavior by the physically large child. Parents and siblings are embarrassed when confronted repeatedly by stressful situations that are more difficult to control in the older retarded child. Often, the final result is placement of the misbehaving retarded child out of the home. This will relieve the immediate family situation but may also aggravate reappearance of parental guilt feelings (Hofstatter & Hofstatter, 1969). Parents often identify with their handicapped child's emotions to the point of feeling personally responsible for the child's failures.

Parental sensitivities about causing their handicapped child's problems may have some relevance. Seidel, Chadwick, and Rutter (1975), using a standardized psychiatric interview (Rutter & Graham, 1968) and a standardized behavioral questionnaire (Rutter, 1967) with 33 physically disabled children, found that 25% had psychological problems. Those children demonstrating emotional problems differed consistently from the remainder of the group; the disturbed children frequently came from broken or overcrowded homes, homes with marital discord, or clinically apparent maternal psychiatric disorders.

V. The Adolescent and Adult Years

The basic needs of a handicapped adolescent are no less than those of a normal teenager during this time of development. In order to achieve even a limited degree of maturity, the adolescent must develop a personal identity, establish his sexual role, develop some degree of independence, and decide on a vocation. Hammer & Barnard (1966) reviewed the characteristics and problems of 44 noninstitutionalized adolescent retardates. Their parents' main concerns related to their pubertal development and sexual behaviors. Excessive dependence, demonstrated by the adolescents' inability to develop self-help skills and follow simple directions, was usually accepted by the parents and not perceived as a problem. The families failed to recognize the changing needs of the maturing retardate, with a resultant increase in the family's problems. The retardate had trouble in adapting to changes in his environment and tended to react to strange and unfamiliar situations in an infantile manner. The moderate and severely retarded adolescent exhibited limited sexual drives and interest. The most frequent complaints from the family and school personnel involving the moderately retarded males were those of masturbation, genital exposure, and overly affectionate behavior, whereas the moderately retarded females presented problems with respect to caring for their menstrual periods and to masturbation.

The physically handicapped adolescent also has to face new issues of independence, work, and sexual relationships. Practically nothing is known of how he proceeds in solving these problems. Dorner (1976) interviewed 46 adolescents with spina bifida to find out how they felt about their situation. As compared with 50% in a normal group of adolescents, 85% of these handicapped adolescents were tearful and/or wanted to "get away from it all." As compared with 8% in the normal population, 25% were suicidal. The majority of those adolescents who were suicidal were girls. The handicapped group felt that their ideas about sex and feelings of depression were the most difficult topics to discuss at home. They complained that their parents were "too protective." About two-thirds of the group hoped to get married. The girls were particularly worried about their capacity to conceive and the boys had understandable concerns about potency.

Minde (1977) has followed a group of children with cerebral palsy from 1967 through 1975. The results from his interviews with 34 adolescents on how they see their development are consistent with Dorner's findings. All 25 nonretarded adolescents talked openly about their handicap and seemed to conceptualize at least part of its consequences. The 9 physically handicapped retardates mentioned they were not like other children, and 6 of these had no idea or plans for a later occupation. The 3 who had plans for their future were unrealistic in the goals they were setting for themselves. Of the 34 adolescents, 23 who were attending a school for the orthopedically handicapped, had not thought of a life beyond school. Of the 11 adolescents attending a regular school, 70% had specific, realistic occupational plans, for example, secretary, housekeeper.

Minde (1977) also explored the incidence of psychiatric disturbances in this group of 34 physically handicapped adolescents. Using the standardized psychiatric symptom inventory (Rutter & Graham, 1968) he found that 7 out of 34 had definite psychopathology. Severe family discord and the absence of friends outside of the school situation were the common experiences in this group demonstrating psychological problems.

To be more specific about the handicapped person's struggle with himself and his relationship to others, Ogden (1974), a psychiatrist, recounts the story of an adult with cerebral palsy, who underwent 2 years of psychotherapy. A 29-year-old employed engineer with spastic diplegia and above average intelligence, he presented himself as emotionally denying that he had cerebral palsy and as trying to contain his angry feelings toward his mother, who was rejecting him. Furthermore, he wanted desperately to have a romance with a young lady who was also rejecting him. After months of therapy, he finally was able to say, "Who could stand this monstrous body? I can't. Who could even give me a chance to get to know them before they got scared away? I've wanted to die just to be able to get out of this body. I'm trapped alone inside of it." Following this outburst, he began to learn to integrate his feelings of self with his body representation. As he did this, he began to understand and cope with his angry feelings.

Let us shift from this lonely account of one person's struggle to a group discussion by three adults with cerebral palsy (Richardson, 1972). It was an open discussion, which began with complaints concerning the stereotyped reactions these persons received regarding their disability. "My whole identity as a person was defined as a CP." Schools were preoccupied with the handicap at the expense of the individual's educational and social development. "I would be in arithmetic class, and someone would come and say, 'It's time for therapy!' "

The segregation and lack of social activities at school were sometimes compensated for by the parents, who encouraged their handicapped child to bring home friends. However, whereas communication problems are perhaps characteristic of all parent–child relationships, the parents of a handicapped child may see him or her as less than a whole person and avoid the topic of the handicap. Lack of preparation for understanding their sexuality was particularly distressing to these adults. Parents and schools failed to provide information about sex. These adults also mentioned that during late adolescence they wanted nothing to do with handicapped people. "They were those funny people who walked around on the TV screen and got us money, but that wasn't me."

Mowatt (1965) studied the emotional conflicts of handicapped young adults and their mothers. Following a series of separate group discussions for mothers and for their handicapped young adult sons and daughters, a comparison of the discussions of the two groups was made. The mothers, who had accomplished the difficult task of raising a physically handicapped child, expressed attitudes of restraint, whereas the young adults freely expressed anger toward their parents, siblings, and roommates. Mowatt speculates that the mothers may have been less spontaneous because they were dealing with inner conflicts—the "continual" mourning of the unborn normal child. Another reason for their attitude may be related to the chronicity of the problem and their inability to sustain a high emotional state. Minde (1977) observed an emotional distancing of the parents from their handicapped adolescents as compared with their previous close relationship when the child was at a younger age.

As the adolescent becomes an adult, responsibilities of independent living, marriage, and children occur. Floor, Baxter, Rosen, and Zisfein (1975) provide us with some information concerning 54 marriages of handicapped adults who were previously institutionalized. The adults were moderate to mildly mentally retarded. They were described as having a lower than average income and job status, minimal social and sex education and experience, and an absence of a family model or family support. All of these individuals were either orphans or had families who were unwilling to accept them after discharge from an institution. Also characteristic of these persons was lack of foresight in future planning, an inability to make long-term decisions, and a struggle to exist on a day-to-day basis. Of the couples 50% were able to sustain a marriage of several years' duration, and, at least in the first few years, their children did not seem to be an overwhelming burden.

The social role of the adult retardate who has not been institutionalized was studied by Charles (1957). Of 151 subjects with IQs less than 70, 24 had died and 11 had been institutionalized. Among the survivors, 80% had married and four-fifths of those had families. The majority were self-supporting and able to function in a reasonably satisfactory manner in society. The outcome for 336 adults with cerebral palsy was not as optimistic. Of these, 30% were employed, 30% were in institutions or had died, and 40% were at home without productive activity (O'Reilly, 1975).

VI. Parental Personalities and Marital Integration

A more detailed review of the literature of parents who have experienced the initial shock of recognizing their child's handicap elucidates a certain amount of information concerning their personalities, family, and marital situations. Interpretation of information pertaining to the former concern is complicated by the fact that "before-sketches" of the parents' personalities and responses to previous stressful situations such as the one they are presently enduring with their handicapped child are not available. The personality characteristics of 76 parents of young retarded children were indexed by the Minnesota Multiphasic Personality Inventory (MMPI) in a study by Erickson (1968). The mean profile patterns for both mothers and fathers suggested problems in impulse control. They had greater than average physical symptoms of psychogenic origin, anxiety, and depression. However, the majority of the individual parent profiles were within normal limits. According to Erickson, this study also correlated with the results from the MMPI on parents of older retarded children, as well as on parents with young and older emotionally disturbed children.

The effects of the child's deficiency on the mother (Cummings, Bayley and Rie, 1966) and the father (Cummings, 1976), using the Edwards Personal Preference Schedule (EPPS), a standardized personality inventory that profiles 15 manifest psychological needs, have been studied. Mothers of mentally retarded children differed from those of normal children in the following seven areas: (a) increased occurrence of depressed feelings; (b) increased preoccupation with the involved child; (c) increased difficulty in handling anger at the child; (d) feelings of increased possessiveness toward the child; (e) decreased sense of maternal competence; (f) decreased enjoyment of the child; and (g) feelings of rejection toward the handicapped child. The fathers of the mentally retarded children demonstrated eight characteristics that were different from those in fathers of normal children. They (a) were more depressed; (b) were more preoccupied with the involved child; (c) experienced decreased enjoyment from the child; (d) had decreased self-esteem; (e) experienced decreased interpersonal satisfaction with their wife and other children; (f) had a need for more order and routine; (g) had less assertiveness; and (h) had less sexual interest in the opposite sex. The authors expressed concern that the father, relative to the mother, has fewer opportunities to help his handicapped child directly, as in the daily care-giving activities. With fewer opportunities for counterbalancing the sense of loss, frustration, and anger, the father seemed to demonstrate more expressions of psychological stress. Fathers as well as mothers need opportunities for mourning the partial loss of their ideals for their children when confronting a child's permanent handicap.

Instruments like the MMPI, EPPS, and Farber's Indices of Marital Integration and Sibling Role Tension are useful in that individual personality and marital and family interaction patterns can be documented statistically. Individual interviews are more difficult to analyze and report because the data are not as concise. However, the description that Minde et al. (1972) and Minde (1977) report, based on information obtained in interviews, of the changes in general patterns of thought of parents of physically handicapped youngsters over an 8-year span, is most revealing. In his first interview with the parents, he found that they could not deal with thoughts concerning the long-term development of their children. Out of 41 parents, 21 refused to contemplate the future. Twenty-six felt everything would eventually be normal, as compared with 14 parents interviewed 8 years later. During the first interview, 34 parents mentioned that their child had attempted to discuss the future of his or her handicap. Twenty-five avoided the issue entirely, and most of these believed that handicapped children ran no higher risk of psychological difficulties than normal children. Of the 9 parents who had answered the child's questions, 2 had reassured the child and 7 had offered a factual explanation. Eight years later, 60% of the parents did not know how their child perceived his or her handicap and did not mention it to the child. There were no discussions of the child's future occupations, and the parents assumed that their child did not think of it either. Yet, as mentioned in the previous section of this chapter, a majority of these children had talked openly about their handicap during interviews with Minde.

Parental concerns also changed over time. Eight years previously, 32% of the parents wanted help for their child's physical disability and only 3% were concerned about their child's education. The results of follow-up interviews demonstrated that 47% of the parents wanted educational help for their child and only 4% were concerned about the future. The parental concern ranked last was the child's capability to cope emotionally with the handicap and his or her future.

Minde (1977) describes a pattern in which the parents of the physically handicapped adolescents were emotionally distancing themselves from the involved son or daughter. In 14 of 19 families with other children, the parents claimed that the nonhandicapped sibling had suffered psychologically by being deprived of attention and care, especially in the early years. The parents were vocal that they should not allow this to continue. Fewer parents discussed with each other, or anyone else, current difficulties they were having with their handicapped child. Several mothers mentioned that their husbands were unwilling to think of the emotional needs of the adolescent. These mothers found that they were also withdrawing from their child in an attempt to maintain their marital relationship. It seems reasonable to assume that parents of adolescent children would normally begin to withdraw physically and emotionally from their children as they allow them to prepare for their independent adult roles. Unfortunately, the theme of many reports (Call, 1958; Dorner, 1976; Freeman, 1970; Hammer & Barnard, 1966) has emphasized the handicapped person's inadequate preparation for adulthood. One of the primary reasons has been the close interdependent relationship that has developed since infancy between the handicapped child and the parents. It must, therefore, be a most frustrating and frightening experience for the handicapped adolescent as he or she becomes aware of the withdrawal of the parents.

There have been several attempts to study the effects of a handicapped child on the parents' marital relationship. Gath (1972) reports the effects of Down's syndrome children on families. In the 2 years following the birth of the handicapped child, two-thirds of the families either had a parent with depressive psychiatric illness or displayed obvious marital conflicts. On the other hand, an investigation by D'Arcy (1968) revealed that 73 of 90 mothers who had Down's syndrome children claimed that their marriage remained happy and unchanged, three happy marriages changed for the worse, and the others, unhappy to begin with, remained unhappy. The majority of 116 families with a physically handicapped child reported "good marital relationships." Only 17 of the mothers felt that their marriages had deteriorated as a result of having a handicapped child (McAndrew, 1976). Fowle (1968), using Farber's Index of Marital Integration, found no significant difference in marital integration between parents caring for a mentally retarded child at home versus parents who had such a child in an institution. The children living at home were enrolled in a day care center, and thus, this probably eased the daily burden of care by their families. Farber (1959) concluded at the end of his study of families with mentally retarded children that the dominant feature determining marital integration was simply the degree of integration achieved prior to the introduction of the handicapped child.

VII. The Handicapped Person's Siblings and Family

The mother of a 2-year-old child with spastic hemiplegia and normal intelligence recently asked me for psychiatric referral for her 4-year-old normal daughter. Her concern was that her daughter was having frequent episodes of intense crying and depression because her brother may need braces and eventual surgery. Following several sessions with a child psychiatrist, the daughter's behavior improved and the mother was able to explain the probable cause. As I had expected, the mother acknowledged that she had been extremely upset and depressed in front of her daughter regarding the visits to an orthpedic clinic.

Gath (1973, 1974), through observations of the siblings of Down's syndrome children, has found that the oldest sister demonstrates more psychiatric symptoms than the brothers. These symptoms are difficulty with peer relationships, often manifested in unpopularity, restlessness, disobedience, misery, and temper tantrums. Rutter, Tizard, and Whitmore (1970) report that unpopularity, restlessness, and misery are behavioral items most commonly associated with psychiatric disorders in children. The explanation for the increased amount of behavioral disturbances in the oldest sisters of handicapped children no doubt relates to their parents' expectations that they assume more responsibilities to help at home (Farber & Jenne, 1963; Fox, 1975). Gath (1973) also found a trend indicating that the children of women who were over 40 at birth of the affected child were more vulnerable to behavioral problems than those children whose mothers were under 40 years of age. It is hypothesized that older mothers feel more responsible for causing the handicap and thus attend less to the needs of their other children.

Even though previous studies (Rutter, 1970) have failed to find any association between social class and psychiatric disturbances in the siblings, Gath's (1973) study revealed more antisocial behavior in the siblings of the lower class as compared with siblings of the higher social classes. Results indicated that for boys, the social class of the family and the general kind of environment in which the boy was growing up was more precisely predictive of deviant behavior than was his age or ordinal position. There also was a suggestion that families with more than six children have increased problems with siblings, a finding that is consistent with those of other studies (Davie, Butler, and Goldstein, 1972; Douglas, 1964; Rutter, 1970). However, peculiar to Gath's findings is that the rate of deviation in the siblings' behavior is also increased in the two-child family. This is not difficult to understand, for if there is one normal child and one handicapped child, it is reasonable to suppose that the normal child will have more pressure to succeed and may be isolated from his peer group. Schreiber and Feeley (1965) reported that parents of mentally retarded children expressed concern about the normal child's feelings of being overburdened by the care of the retarded sibling, of responsibility for the retardation, of an obligation to make up to the parents for what the mentally retarded brother or sister could not give them, and of guilt for being the normal child.

Grossman (1972), after an extensive review of the literature, found that siblings of the retarded are more likely to show signs of emotional disturbance than are siblings of normal children. They are also likely to develop a variety of misconceptions about their retarded brother and sister or to develop avoidance strategies. San Martino and Newman (1974) suggest that the normal sibling becomes a scapegoat, particularly when the parental guilt over having given birth to a retarded child is substantial and has not been dealt with effectively. When excess attention is given to the abnormal sibling, the normal sibling may take on some of the behavioral characteristics of the retarded child in order to get attention, or there may be great anger on the part of the normal child toward the handicapped child, either expressed overtly or turned inward into guilt or self-punishment. Not infrequently, siblings of the handicapped child become mother figures and assume an air of maturity beyond their years. They do not allow their own dependency needs to be met (Adams, 1968; Hawke, 1967; Poznanski, 1969).

Fowle (1968), using Farber's Sibling Role Tension Index, compared sibling role tension in families in which severely mentally retarded children had been retained in the home with that in families in which similar children had been placed in an institution. Two groups of 35 families each were involved. The findings indicated that the role tension of the retardate's siblings was higher when the affected child was kept at home. Again, the oldest female sibling was more adversely affected by the presence of the retarded child in the home than was the oldest male sibling, a finding that supports those of Gath (1973, 1974). Such findings indicate that parental counseling should include information concerning the importance of the siblings' role within the family interaction.

An effort to enhance siblings' understanding of their handicapped brother or sister was made by Weinrott (1974). Older siblings of retarded children were invited to attend the special camp that the abnormal youngsters attended. The siblings were given 5 days of training in behavior modification techniques to use with their own retarded brother or sister and the other retarded children in the camp. Siblings were also provided with information about how to help the retarded children improve language skills and motor coordination. After the termination of the camp program, most siblings showed some behavior change at home, which was indicated by, for example, a tendency to spend more time with their retarded brother or sister in play and in specific tasks. In addition, the parents reported that the siblings were less likely to respond emotionally to some of the disruptive or aggressive behavior of the retarded family member. These gains did not persist, probably because of lack of continual guidance and support for the siblings. Even so, the camping program did indicate that siblings were interested in being involved in the care of their retarded brother or sister.

Schreiber and Feeley (1965) report on the feelings of teenage siblings of mentally retarded children who attended approximately 18 group sessions under the leadership of a professional group worker. These normal siblings related their concern about how to tell their friends about their retarded sibling, how to deal with parents who did not discuss the problems of the retarded family member with them, whether the parents' expectations concerning their role in the continued care of the retarded sibling were real and fair, whether they were betraying their family's confidence by sharing their thoughts, did the retardation in their family lessen their chances of marriage, and would their future children inherit the retardation. Following the conclusion of the group sessions, the authors felt that the young person with positive family relationships is often capable of enduring the emotional hurt and anxiety of having a retarded sibling without severe disruption of his or her family and social life. These teenagers summed up their group experience by saying: "We helped each other. We learned how to talk about retardation and felt free to discuss our problems. We helped each other to be better prepared for any unexpected behaviors of our brothers and sisters. We knew that we were not alone [p. 225]."

VIII. The Extended Family

Due to a lack of recorded information, the impact of a handicapped child on the extended family can be scanned only superficially. Davis' (1967) discussion about the role of the maternal grandmother when a retarded child is present is one of the few studies available. The maternal grandmother usually plays an important part in the life of the new family. She adds to the security of the family. Fifty families with retarded children were compared with 30 normal families in order to determine the support given by the maternal grandmother. Support is described as "intimate" if the maternal grandmother lives nearby and visits frequently, as "effective" when she is available on call, as "ineffective" when there is little or no contact, and as "unfamiliar" when she is not available. Less than one-half of the families with a retarded child had "effective" support from the maternal grandmother. In contrast, the normal control families received "effective" support three-quarters or more of the time. The reason given for this finding probably lies in the quality of the families' relationships, which tended to be strained in those with a retarded child, rather than in geographical factors.

There is no literature concerning the role of paternal grandparents and the maternal grandfather or aunts and uncles. McAndrew (1976) found that 33% of the 116 parents interviewed felt that there were adverse changes in their relationships with grandparents and friends following the birth of their physically handicapped child, and 75% were disturbed by the public's expressions of thoughtlessness and unkindness toward their child.

My personal experience has been that the extended family is supportive irrespective of the severity of the handicap. However, these observations are biased in that I work with young, motivated families who actively seek help in the care of their handicapped child. The mothers provide their own transportation, whether it be by car or bus. Grandparents are often brought to the preschool intervention program to observe their handicapped grandchild. Siblings and friends of the family, both adults and children, enthusiastically come to observe the handicapped child in the program. It is my hope that this extended family support system will continue even when the handicapped person becomes an adult.

IX. Conclusion

I have attempted to discuss some of the experiences of a family with a handicapped child and some of the feedback the child receives as a consequence. From the initial parental response of emotional disintegration there evolves a period of adjustment and reorganization of the family's daily activities and plans. We have tried to follow the course of the handicapped person's reaction to his problem through childhood into adulthood. Many family crises occur during this time. There may be multiple involvements with professional specialists, surgeries, special equipment, special schools, peer group problems, vocational training, and ultimately recognition of the chronicity of the handicap. Family roles may not develop along conventional guidelines when the individual family members must adjust to the problems posed by a handicapped child's atypical development. Adulthood for the handicapped is probably the worst crisis for the family unit. This period of life seems aided least by support systems available for the family. One can only speculate that when parents are unable to care for their handicapped adult child, they place him with other family members, in foster homes, or in institutions. Does this final crisis of placement meet with the same amount of parental grief and depression as that described with the initial recognition of the problem at birth? We do not know.

This chapter has given a brief selective review of the available literature concerning the family and its handicapped offspring. Over 700 references were examined, and only a small percentage of them were found to be appropriate for this discussion. Tremendous gaps of knowledge are present. What we have are glimpses into select groups of families at certain points in time. These are clustered about the infancy and early childhood periods. There are no longitudinal studies comparing handicapped children and their families with normally matched control groups. There is even an absence of short-term studies observing the changing emotional behaviors of the handicapped person and those with whom he or she is intimately involved. Perhaps in the future, we will begin to fill these gaps and study more intimately the longitudinal course of the handicapped person within the family. Important to record are observations regarding the handicapped child's beginning awareness of the problem and how he or she and the family cope with the inevitable crises that ensue. Such information is crucial if appropriate preparation of the handicapped child for independent living is to occur.

References

Adams, M. E. Problems in management of mentally retarded children with cerebral palsy. *The Cerebral Palsy Journal*, 1968, March–April.

Bentovim, A. Emotional disturbances of handicapped pre-school children and their families—Attitudes to the child. *British Medical Journal*, 1972, 3:579–581.

Block, W. E. A study of somatapsychological relationship in the cerebral palsy children. *Exceptional Children*, 1955, 22, No 2.

Call, J. Psychological problems of the cerebral palsied child, his parents and siblings as revealed by dynamically oriented small group discussions with parents. *Cerebral Palsy Review*, 1958, September–October.

Charles, C. C. Adult adjustment of some deficient American children. *American Journal of Mental Deficiency*, 1957, 62:300–310.

Condon, W. S., & Sander, L. W. Neonate movement is synchronized with adult speech: Interactional participation and language acquisition. *Science*, 1974, 183, 99–101.

Connor, F., Williamson, G., and Siepp, J. Social-emotional development in atypical children. *A program guide for infants and toddlers with neuromotor and other developmental disabilities*. Experimental Edition. United Cerebral Palsy Association, 1975. Pp. 251–259.

Cummings, S. The impact of the child's deficiency on the father: A study of fathers of mentally retarded and of chronically ill children. *American Journal of Orthopsychiatry*, 1976, 46:2, 246–255.

Cummings, S., Bayley, H., and Rie, H. Effects of the child's deficiency on the mother: A study of mothers of mentally retarded, chronically ill and neurotic children. *American Journal of Orthopsychiatry*, 1966, 36:4, 595–608.

D'Arcy, E. Congential defects: Mothers' reactions to first information. *British Medical Journal*, 1968, 3:796–798.

Davie, R., Butler, N., & Goldstein, H. *From birth to seven*. Longman, London, 1972.

Davis, D. Family processes in mental retardation. *American Journal of Psychiatry*, 1967, 124:3, 340–350.

Dorner, S. Adolescents with spina bifida. *Archives of Disease in Childhood*, 1976, 51:439–444.

Douglas, J. *The home and the school*. London: MacGibbon and Kee, 1964.

Erickson, M. MMPI comparisons between parents of young emotionally disturbed and organically retarded children. *Journal of Counseling and Clinical Psychology*, 1968, 32:6, 701–706.

Farber, B. Effects of a severely mentally retarded child on family integration. *Monograph Society for Research in Child Development*, 1959, 24:2, 1–112.

Farber, B., & Jenne, W. Family organization and parent–child communication: Parents and siblings of a retarded child. *Monographs of the Society for Research in Child Development*, 1963, 28:7.

Fackler, E. The crisis of institutionalizing a retarded child. *American Journal of Nursing*, 1968, July, 1508–1512.

Floor, L., Baxter, D., Rosen, M., & Zisfein, L. A survey of marriages among previously institutionalized retardates. *Mental Retardation*, 1975, April, 33–37.

Fowle, C. The effect of the severely mentally retarded child in his family. *American Journal of Mental Deficiency*, 1968, 73:3, 468–473.

Fox, A. Families with handicapped children—A challenge to the caring professions. *Community Health*, 1975, 6:217–222.

Fraiberg, S. Blind infants and their mothers: An examination of the sign system. In: M. Lewis, & L. A. Rosenblum (Eds.), *The effect of the infant on its caregiver*. New York: Wiley, 1974.

Freeman, R. Psychiatric problems in adolescents with cerebral palsy. *Developmental Medicine and Child Neurology*, 1970, 12:1, 64–71.

Gath, A. The mental health of siblings of congenitally abnormal children. *Journal of Child Psychology and Psychiatry*, 1972, 13:211–218.

Gath, A. The school age siblings of Mongol children. *British Journal of Psychiatry*, 1973, 123:161–167.

Gath, A. Sibling reactions to mental handicap: A comparison of the brothers and sisters of mongol children. *Journal of Child Psychology and Psychiatry*, 1974, 15:187–198.

Grossman, F. *Brothers and sisters of retarded children*. Syracuse, New York: Syracuse University Press, 1972.

Gurney, W. The influence of professional personnel on parents of infants born with anomalies. Unpublished report, 1961.

Gumz, E., and Gubrium, J. Comparative parental perceptions of a mentally retarded child. *American Journal of Mental Deficiency*, 1972, 77:2, 175–180.

Hammer, S., and Barnard, K. The mentally retarded adolescent, *Pediatrics*, 1966, 38:5, 845–857.

Harris, A. E. Language in the deaf community and the deaf individual: Communicative competence and control. In L. S. Liben (Ed.), *Theoretical and practical implications of the development of deaf children*. New York: Academic Press, in press.

Harris, R. I. Research in impulse control: Diagnostic and training implications for deaf children. In L. S. Liben (Ed.), *Theoretical and practical implications of the development of deaf children*, New York: Academic Press, in press.

Hawke, W. Impact of cerebral palsy on patient and family. *The Canadian Nurse*, 1967, January, 29–31.

Heisler, V. *A handicapped child in the family*. New York: Grune and Stratton, 1972.

Hofstatter, Leopold and Hofstatter, Lilli. Emotional problems of the child with mental retardation and his family. *Southern Medical Journal*, 1969, May, 583–586.

Illingworth, R. Counseling the parents of the mentally handicapped child. *Clinical Pediatrics*, 1967, 6:6, 340–347.

Jamison, J. The impact of mental retardation on the family and some directions of help. *Journal of the National Medical Association*, 1965, 57:2, 136–138.

Klaus, M., & Kennell, J. *Maternal-infant bonding*. St. Louis, Missouri: C. V. Mosby, 1976.

Kohut, S. The abnormal child: His impact on the family. *Journal of the American Physical Therapy Association*, 1966, 46:2, 160–167.

Legeay, C., & Keogh, B. Impact of mental retardation on family life. *American Journal of Nursing*, 1966, 66:5, 1062–1065.

Lobo, E., & Webb, A. Parental reactions to their mongol baby. *The Practitioner*, 1970, 204:412–415.

Marcellus, D., & Hawke, W. Survey of attitudes of parents of children with cerebral palsy in Windsor and Essex County, Ontario. *Canadian Medical Association Journal,* 1966, 95:1242–1244.

Marshall, N., Hegrenes, J., & Goldstein, S. Verbal interactions: Mothers and their retarded children versus mothers and their non-retarded children. *American Journal of Mental Deficiency*, 1973, 77:4, 415–419.

McAndrew, I. Children with a handicap and their families. *Child: Care, Health and Development*, 1976, 2:4, 213–238.

Minde, K. Coping styles of 34 cerebral palsied adolescents. Paper presented at the American Psychiatric Association, 1977.

Minde, K., Hackett, J., Killou, D., & Silver, S. How they grow up: Forty-one physically handicapped children and their families. *American Journal of Psychiatry*, 1972, 128:12, 1554–1560.

Molony, H. Parental reactions to mental retardation. *The Medical Journal of Australia*, 1971, April 24, 914–917.

Mowatt, M. Emotional conflicts of handicapped young adults and their mothers. *The Cerebral Palsy Journal*, 1965, July–August, 6–8.

Ogden, T. Psychoanalytic psychotherapy of a patient with cerebral palsy: The relation of aggression to self and body representations. *International Journal of Psychoanalytic Psychotherapy*, 1974, 3:4, 419–433.

O'Reilly, D. Care of the cerebral palsied: Outcome of the past and needs for the future. *Developmental Medicine and Child Neurology*, 1975, 17:2, 141–149.

Parmelee, A. The doctor and the handicapped child. *Children*, 1962, September–October, 190–193.

Poznanski, E. Psychiatric difficulties in siblings of handicapped children. *Clinical Pediatrics*, 1969, 8:4, 232–234.

Richardson, S. People with cerebral palsy speak for themselves. *Developmental Medicine and Child Neurology*, 1972, 14:4, 524–535.

Rutter, M. A children's questionnaire for completion by teachers, preliminary findings. *Journal of Child Psychology and Psychiatry*, 1967, 8:1–9.

Rutter, M. Sex differences in children's responses to family stress, In E. Anthony and C. Koupernik. (Eds.), *The child in his family*. London: International Yearbook of Child Psychiatry, 1970.

Rutter, M. & Graham, P. J. The reliability and validity of the psychiatric assessment of the child: I. Interview with the child. *British Journal of Psychiatry*, 1968, 114:563–579.

Rutter, M., Tizard, J., & Whitmore, K. *Health, education and behavior*. London: Longman, 1970.

San Martino, M., & Newman, M. Siblings of retarded children: A population at risk. *Child Psychiatry and Human Development*, 1974, 4:168–177, 1974.

Schlesinger, H. S. The effects of deafness on childhood development: An eriksonian perspective. In L. S. Liben (Ed.), *Theoretical and practical implications of the development of deaf children*, New York: Academic press, in press.

Schlesinger, H. S., & Meadow, K. P. *Sound and sign*. Berkeley, California: University of California Press, 1972.

Schreiber, M., & Feeley, M. Siblings of the retarded: A guided group experience. *Children*, 1965, 12:6, 221–229.

Seidel, U., Chadwick, O., & Rutter, M. Psychological disorders in crippled children: A comparative study of children with and without brain damage. *Developmental Medicine and Child Neurology*, 1975, 17:563–573.

Shere, M. Social-emotional factors with families of the twins with cerebral palsy. *Exceptional Children*, 1955, 22:5, 197–199.

Shere, E., & Kastenbaum, R. Mother-child interaction in cerebral palsy: Environmental and psychosocial obstacles to cognitive development. *Genetic Psychology Monographs*, 1966, 73:255–335.

Skelton, M. Areas of parental concern about retarded children. *Mental Retardation*, 1972, February, 38–41.

Solnit, A., & Stark, M. Mourning the birth of a defective child. *Psychoanalytical Study of the Child*, 1961, 16:523–537.

Stevenson, K. The reactions of parents to their retarded children. *North Carolina Medical Journal*, 1968, April, 150–160.

Taichert, L. Parental denial as a factor in the management of the severely retarded child. *Clinical Pediatrics*, 1975, 14:7, 666–668.

Weinrott, M. A training program in behavior modification for siblings of the retarded. *American Journal of Orthopsychiatry*, 1974, 44:3, 362–375.

The Impact of Children's Physical Handicaps on Marital Quality and Family Interaction

11

Sam J. Korn, Stella Chess, and Paulina Fernandez

I. Introduction

Early in our work on the New York Longitudinal Study of temperament in young children (Thomas, Chess, Birch, Hertzig, & Korn, 1963), we indicated our interest in "the interplay of organismic and environmental forces in the development of the child [p. v]." This interactive point of view has been extended to our continuing investigation of the adjustment patterns found among children with congenital rubella (Chess, Korn, & Fernandez, 1971). Neither the child, the parents, nor the physical environment can be viewed as *the* significant determinant of any specific adaptive outcome. Each child, with his or her particular pattern of characteristics, is continuously being affected by the family and is reciprocally having an impact on the family. We are dealing with multidetermined, interacting systems that are also undergoing changes over time. The child grows, the parents age, the marriage and family develop, and the environment is never static.

One may examine selected variables at one point in time to determine their relationship to phenomena under consideration. For example, we can search for indices of children's characteristics or socioeconomic variables that may help predict the likelihood of a particular developmental outcome at some point in the life span. However, the *interactive* and *developmental* aspects of all of the factors involved must be heavily weighed, and any generalizations drawn must be tempered by these considerations.

The study of physically handicapped children requires attention to patterns of interaction in the family. The birth of a handicapped child in

299

any family can be viewed as a strain on the already existing patterns of social interactions and adjustments in the family. Whether the stress results in familial disorganization is dependent on an interwoven set of complex individual, familial, sociocultural, and historical phenomena. The events that are of concern to us continue to unfold from the parents' first recognition that their child is physically disabled to their ongoing concern for the child's well-being and the well-being of their family and marriage. The course of events, as they affect the parents, must be followed from the parents' initial emotional reactions to the handicapped neonate to the day-to-day impact of the ordinary and extraordinary demands that the chronically handicapped child imposes on the family, to the point when the handicapped adult may become independent of the family.

Parents are often shocked and depressed (Klaus & Kennel, 1976) and may become withdrawn and isolated (Illingworth, 1967). The parents' reactions are important for several reasons. Professional help for the parents must deal with these reactions, and supportive services are crucial. In addition, these parental reactions also have a reverberating impact on the child. The handicapped child often experiences disruptive child care practices, and mother–child interactions may be mutually distressing. The young blind child, for example, is more likely to encounter emotional indifference by the parents because of the child's reduced facial expressiveness and the absence of contingent smiling (Fraiberg, 1974). The young cerebral palsy child is more likely to experience a diminishing amount of maternal warmth during his or her second and third years—especially if the child is not yet walking (Kogan & Tyler, 1973). Jacobs and Pierce (1968) found that handicapped children are more likely to be rejected by nonhandicapped children in social situations.

The handicapped child imposes continuous strain on his or her caretakers. These are chronic, long-term, and changing stresses that the family must respond to. The handicapped child's reduced sensory and/or response capacity often makes the child appear to be "unresponsive" to parents' care. The demands for special care, the higher frequency of emotional disorders, the difficulties in getting along with others, etc., impose an added physical and emotional strain on the parents and siblings. Family routines have to be continuously readjusted, and the siblings are frustrated in their competition for the parents' attention and care. Most of these general issues are more completely elucidated in other chapters of this volume. Howard (Chapter 10, this volume) has also summarized a large number of studies involving the impact of a child's physical handicaps on the child and on the family. In this paper we will examine in depth data from one study of the impact of a child's physical handicap on the child and on the family. This evaluation will provide a basis for ascertaining if the effects of a handicap lead to the reciprocal parent–child interplay just noted and discussed in earlier chapters in this volume. In addition, some of the methodological and data analytic problems encountered in doing research on the impact of child handicaps may be illustrated from this examination.

II. The Rubella Birth Defect Evaluation Project

Following the 1964 rubella epidemic, the Rubella Birth Defect Evaluation Project was established at New York University Medical Center (Cooper, Ziring, Ockerse, Fedun, Kiely, & Krugman, 1969). Since 1967, under the directorship of Stella Chess, the behavioral, psychological, and psychiatric implications of congenital rubella have been studied. Part of this investigation dealt with the impact of the birth and rearing of the congenital rubella child on the family. We were concerned about the kinds of disruption that might follow the birth of a handicapped child, so that professional help might be recommended when it was called for. We also felt that it was important to take these factors into account in formulating recommendations for the care of the children.

This report will describe some of the effects on the families that we found, as well as the particular characteristics of the children and the families that were associated with marital discord and family disruption. At this stage of our investigation the children ranged in age from 3 to 6 years. This age probably follows the parents' initial reactions to the birth of the handicapped child, and their first series of adjustments. Although the specific characteristics of the marital relationships and the developmental stages of the marriages involved are relevant issues, these were beyond the scope of this investigation, and such data are unfortunately not available. However, tentative information on the impact of the handicapped child on the family, albeit at single points in time, will be offered.

III. Characteristics of the Sample

The study sample consisted of 243 children who were part of the Rubella Birth Defect Evaluation Project. All of these children had a diagnosis of congenital rubella confirmed by either virus isolation or serological procedures. There is no suggestion that our sample was a random sample of rubella children. Many unknown selective factors may have operated for, or against, a child's being brought to the project and his or her subsequent participation in our research.

Of the 243 children, 124 were boys and 119 girls. They ranged in age from 3 to 6 years (median = 56.5 months) when this phase of the investigation was conducted. A more complete summary can be found in Chess *et al.* (1971).

In this rubella sample, almost three-quarters of the children had a hearing handicap, about one-third had visual defects (unilateral and bilateral microphthalmia, esotropia, cataracts, glaucoma, strabismus, etc.), about one-third had neurological "hard signs" (spasticity, cerebral palsy, seizures, paresis, encephalitis, etc.), and about one-third had cardiac defects (congenital heart disease, patent ductus arteriosis, pulmonic stenosis, etc.). Within the framework of these four areas of physical handicap, less than one-third of the children had only one area of handicap, 19% had a handicap in two areas (e.g., hearing and vision), 19% had three areas of handicap (e.g., hearing, vision, and cardiac), and 11% had defects in all four areas. The remaining 21% had no physical defects. A few examples of the "defect histories" of some rubella children will give some idea of what was faced by the children and their parents.

Arthur: born 11/19/64, age 4:1

Vision: rubella retinopathy, bilateral moderate; myopia right eye; abnormal pigment deposit in retina
Hearing: 1/68 profound hearing loss; 9/66 hearing aid—no response without aid, with aid will dance and clap hands
Cardiac: congenital heart disease, ventricular septal deficit; sinus rhythm, 1A
Neurologic: psychomotor retardation with moderate spasticity in both lower extremities; 1/68 right and left spastic paresis; left leg with incipient flexia contractive of calf muscle; hydrocele left

Ellen: born 1/1/65, age 5:5

Vision: bilateral congenital cataracts, postcataract extraction in both eyes; visual impairment; rubella retinopathy; probably microphthalmia both eyes; capsule remnants both eyes
Hearing: 11/69 deafness severe; aids, responds to few words—same with or without aids
Cardiac: congenital heart disease; lesion undetermined, sinus rhythm 1A; pulmonic stenosis NSR
Neurologic: retarded neuromotor development; psychomotor retardation equivocal

David: born 12/15/64, age 3:5

Vision: cataract left eye; postcataract removal left eye; right eye congenital severe myopia; cataract removal 4/67
Hearing: deafness severe to profound; hears radio when played loudly, vocalizes more with aids
Cardiac: congenital heart disease PDA; possible perceptual pulmonic stenosis 1A; three times cardiac catherization
Neurologic: 8/67 tight external hip rotators, X ray both hips negative; psychomotor retardation

Everett: born 11/13/64, age 4:10

Originally classified as a "well baby" (without defect)
Vision: rubella retinopathy (mild) both eyes
Hearing: right ear moderate hearing loss

Dora: born 12/25/64, age 5:1

Vision: cataract right eye; rubella retinopathy left eye; microphthalmos right eye
Hearing: bilateral serous obitis, no response left labyrinth; severe to profound hearing loss 6/66; severe loss 1/69
Cardiac: congenital heart disease; pulmonary stenosis; probably pulmonary artery coarctation; ventricular septal defect; cardiac catheterization 6/65

Formal intelligence assessment (Stanford–Binet Form L-M or Cattell Infant Scale) was obtained for 171 of the children; 43% were found to be of average to superior intelligence, 23.4% were dull, normal, or borderline, 9.9% were mildly or moderately retarded, 12.9% were severely or profoundly retarded, and for the remaining 10.5%, no estimate of intelligence based on formal testing was possible.

The extent of the children's physical defects and their intellectual levels were not unrelated. Of the 74 children with average to superior intelligence, 28 (38%) had no physical defects, 28 others (38%) had only one defect area, only 6 (8%) had three defect areas, and none of these children had four defect areas. On the other hand, among the 56 children assessed to be retarded, 16 (29%) had four defect areas, 16 (29%) had three defect areas, 12 (21%) had two defect areas, and only 2 children (4%) had no physical defects.

Among our rubella children we have an additional overlay of psychiatric diagnoses that included 18 (7%) children who were also autistic or who manifested a partial syndrome of autism, 28 (12%) with reactive behavior disorders, 8 (3%) with cerebral dysfunction, in addition to 89 (37%) children diagnosed as mentally retarded. Of the sample, 118 (49%) had no psychiatric disorder, and a number of children had more than one psychiatric disorder.

The families of our rubella children varied considerably. The mothers of most of the children were white (62%), and the next two largest groups were black (19%) and Puerto Rican (15%). The largest proportion of the mothers were Catholic (57%), and the remainder were mostly Protestant (16%) and Jewish (12%). The children's fathers were occupied, for the most part, as skilled workers (35%), 18% were professionals, 19% were in clerical or sales positions, and 22% were either semiskilled or unskilled workers. Only 4% of the fathers were unemployed. Most of the mothers (77%) described themselves as housewives, although many had also worked at one time or another. Of the mothers who were working at the time the data were collected, 7% were professionals, 4% were in clerical or sales position, 2% were skilled, and 7% were semiskilled or unskilled workers.

IV. Procedure for Collecting Data

The basic procedures for collecting data are described in an earlier report (Chess et al. 1971). Physical, psychiatric, and psychological assessments were made on the basis of direct examination of the child, as well as through interviews with the parents, teachers (where applicable), and staff of the project at New York University Medical Center. Demographic data were updated from interviews with the parents.

Information on the child's impact on the family was extracted from a parent interview specifically designed for this purpose that was conducted by a social worker on our research staff. The open-ended interview was designed to provide information on the following: (a) parents' understanding of the nature of the children's defects; (b) parents' handling of the child, including attitudes toward training, discipline, etc., as well as parents' expectations for the child's future; (c) changes in family life-style attributed to the handicapped child; and (d) stress in the family before and/or after the birth of the handicapped child, including marital discord, family relationships, etc. These special interviews were able to be completed on 162 families in our rubella sample.

V. Impact of the Child on Marital Quality and Family Interaction

Description of the reciprocal impact of the handicapped child on marital and family interaction requires historical (e.g., longitudinal) analyses. We will eventually obtain such data as a part of our project. At this writing, however, our data essentially reflect patterns of covariation derived from unitemporal assessments. Nevertheless, we may see if the data are consistent with the notion that child-handicapping conditions contribute to marital quality and family interaction. Consideration of the reciprocal feedback the child may receive must await a second wave of data collection.

Parental discord and severe deterioration of the marriage that, to some extent, could be specifically attributed to the presence of a handicapped child in the family were found in 6 instances (3.7%) of the 162 families interviewed. Of course, there were many other instances of marital discord in our sample of families, but in these other cases, the difficulties were neither attributed to the handicapped child nor intensified by the child. Only those families in which the problems reported are directly related to the birth and presence of the rubella child are included here. In 4 of the 6 families, there is evidence that parental disagreements existed before the handicapped child was born, but the child did aggravate the difficulties.

James: age 4:2

We did not get along before James came, but our disagreements increased in intensity. . . .After we realized his handicap, I became very depressed. . . .My husband also suffered. . . .We drifted apart, and he took to alcohol more. I withdrew. . . .We blamed each other for James's condition. . . .After our next baby was born, we also fought about money.

Mildred: age 3:9

We used to fight all the time about money and his running around. He said the child [Mildred] was my fault. . . .With a child that did not grow normal, he left and is with someone else now.

Laura: age 4:7

Laura's coming made matters worse. He denied he was the father, saying he could never produce a sick or damaged child. . . .He hated Laura and hit her often, and one day he threatened to kill Herman [a younger child]. . . .He is a heavy drinker and hit me and the children. . . .I had to leave him.

In only 2 of the 162 families did we find that the onset of marital discord occurred *after* the handicapped child was born. The child is seen as the precipitator of the difficulties.

Michael: age 4:1

We got along well before Michael was born. . . .separated first when the baby was 3 years old—for about a month. Most recent separation lasted 5 months so far. . . .I think he's egotistical and can't stand an imperfection in his child, and that's why he left. . . .I can't definitely say; he might have wandered off even if Michael was normal.

Nora: age 5:4

After Nora was born, we began to quarrel a great deal. She didn't sleep at night, and we argued about who should wake up to take care of her. . . . We became touchy and irritable with one another. We don't go out together anymore. [Mr. P was a factory worker but says that he left his job because Mrs. P cannot handle Nora and the other children. Mrs. P says that he actually gives her no help in the house.]

We see in these examples the kinds of emotional distress, guilt, and rejection that may be experienced by one or both parents of a handicapped child. These reactions may be redirected at the child or displaced onto the husband or wife. In some cases, no doubt, the handicapped child is the scapegoat for the marital discord. What the underlying personal or family dynamics might actually be in these cases cannot be reliably inferred from these reports. However, in each of these instances, the handicapped child is at the center of the immediate cause of marital discord.

A more common problem found in families of rubella children is the disruption of family routines. The handicapped child is seen by the parents as interfering with activities they would ordinarily be engaged in as a couple or as a family with their nonhandicapped children. We found 36 families, 22.2% of the 162 cases, in which such disruption in family life was attributed to the rubella child.

The kinds of stresses experienced by the families and the intensity of the reactions can best be appreciated from a sample of interview reports.

Dora: age 3:9

I had to take Dora to so many doctors, hospitals, and clinics that the household routines were very much confused. I was hardly able to stay home to take care of the house.

James: age 4:4

We had disagreements about disciplining him. The older girls are understanding, but I feel that they are really burdened by him. I don't feel that I can take him everywhere. He creates a scene and stir wherever we go. Cindy was confirmed the other day—I took him to church. We wanted to take the family out to a restaurant afterward but couldn't. He will scream, gestures wildly, doesn't speak clearly. . . . carries on so loudly that he's embarrassing—can cause a crowd to gather. He makes a circus out of a restaurant eating experience.

Charles: age 5:2

Sometimes people are cruel, siblings can get embarrassed. We have to spend so much more time on Charles because of his impairment. I do have a large family, and there are many places where we cannot take him—like when the children are performing. We can't participate in many family functions because he doesn't behave well. He can make loud noises, will get stares, and the children can't always be comfortable with it.

Ellen: age 4:11

Our lives are not normal. We avoid socializing with parents of normal kids. No vacations, and its difficult to get sitters. We don't entertain friends. I can't organize household work because of doctor and clinic visits.

All too often, there is the impression that these accounts barely reflect the complex distresses experienced by these families.

Among the 36 families in which the parents did complain that the handicapped child disrupted their family life, the most frequently cited problems involved (a) intense emotional reactions to the handicapped child, by one or both of the parents, that persisted over time and spilled over into their personal interactions; (b) inability to go on vacations, visit friends or places as a family because the handicapped child was disruptive or embarrassing; (c) limited social life for the parents as a couple because of the inability to find baby-sitters willing and able to care for the special needs of the handicapped child; (d) neglect of other children because of the excessive demands made by the handicapped child, often leading to the siblings resenting the handicapped child. Parents also complained that their friends abandoned them, they had less time and money for their own interests, could not organize or else neglected their housekeeping routines, and spent too much time arguing about the care of the handicapped child. On the average, each of the families involved in this group cited about two such complaints or family problems that they attributed directly to the handicapped child.

However, it must be remembered that marital discord or family disruptions explicitly due to or related to the handicapped child occurred in only 42 (25.9%) of the 162 families studied. In the remaining 74.1%, we find that the parents, either by themselves or with help, adequately cope with the added stress. In some cases, the handicapped child and the challenges involved were seen as a rewarding experience that actually strengthened the marriage and family. Accordingly, these data on prevalence must be placed in proper perspective. All too often, the helping professions focus on pathology and the need for helping services. Perhaps this is as it must be. However, although we do find that the impact of a handicapped child *adds to the stresses of child care and family life*, the impact is *not necessarily severely distressing or degenerating*.

Lillian: age 5:1

There isn't anywhere we don't go because of Lillian, or don't do because of her. The two girls play together and are included in family outings. Lillian's defects do not interfere in any way with family life.

Anne: age 5:9

We take Anne everywhere. She enjoys the theater; we go sailing. There is no place or family activity that she cannot participate in like her sister.

Martin: age 3:10

We were told to treat Martin like a normal child, and we do. All the children fit into our pattern of living; we don't revolve around them. As a family, we take him on excursions, as with the other children.

Alan: age 4:2

We have worked Alan in, worked our life around him. The children love him, want him to be part of our life. We take him to Little League, etc. Everyone participates; the older children help. They love him.

And at the extreme end of this range of responses we find a very positive effect expressed.

James: age 4:10

Our lives are enriched by James. He's delicious, a cute kid. . . .baby of the family. We get a lot of pleasure from him. We enjoy watching him grow. The older boys love him.

Quite clearly, the impact of a handicapped child is, for most families, not an impairing one. And this should be emphasized especially for those who help families plan for a handicapped child. The assumption of distress could very well become a self-fulfilling prophecy.

What, then, is the overall impact of a congenitally handicapped, often multihandicapped child, on marital quality and family interaction? In about three-fourths of our families, the child, at least during the preschool years, does not impair marital quality or family patterns. In the remaining one-fourth, we find evidence of adverse effects of stress: serious parental disagreements and/or disruption of family routines. These data must also be viewed in the light that in about 15% of our families most intensely studied (24 of 162) the parental relationship was an impaired, stressful one before the advent of, and therefore unrelated to, the handicapped child.

Our data are more consistent with the findings of D'Arcy (1968) than with those of Gath (1972). D'Arcy reported that 19% of 90 families with a Down's syndrome child became less happy or changed in a "negative" way. Gath, on the other hand, reported a distress rate of about 67% in families by the second year after the birth of a Down's syndrome child. The distresses reported included serious depressive reactions in one or more of the parents and/or obvious marital conflict. It is difficult to reconcile these data with the fact that we found that only about 25% of the families with handicapped children did experience marital discord or serious family disruption. D'Arcy's more modest findings seem to be confirmed. However, it is possible that the overall differences in distress rates may be a function of the definitions of "distress" that were used, as well as the degree of support services made available to help parents maintain personal and marital integration. In our sample, the project staff provided the parents with considerable supporting services, including counseling, carefully detailed information on the child, and contact with schools.

With all of this in mind, we must point out that the chronically handicapped child seems to impose a unique kind of stress on the family. It is quite likely that a family's ability to cope with a handicapped child is not, as suggested by Farber and Jenne (1963), simply a function of its ability to integrate potentially disorganizing stresses prior to the birth of the child. Although many of the problems cited by parents may occur in the rearing of nonhandicapped children, the stresses involved in coping with a nonhandicapped child are seen as finite—as stages that the child will pass through—with a less stressful period expected to follow. The same can be said for the vicissitudes of economic misfortune, acute illness, etc., that may be cited by parents.

However, the stresses involved in rearing the handicapped child are often seen as persistent, long term, frequently changing as the child grows, and a problem from which many parents find no relief. Often there is no extended family or helping service to provide respite. Personal and family values may have to be sacrificed for the constant, demanding care of the handicapped child. The future is most often seen by the parents as bleak, with hopes of improvement diminishing when the child does not quickly "outgrow" the handicap. With no such improvement to fuel hopes and no periodic help to provide respite and regeneration, we can see how the pressure can become disruptive and degenerating, regardless of the family's ability to cope with the ordinary stresses of child rearing and family organization.

This distressing impact of the child on the family has another important feature that must be considered—its reverberating effect on the handicapped child. Even if the parents' apparent reaction was only indifference, we would have cause for concern in terms of the impact on the child's development. Indifference conceals many other emotions. However, in these families, the parents attribute their marital difficulties and family disruptions to the child. The handicapped child is viewed as the source of their guilt and interpersonal discord, as overdemanding, an embarrassment to the parents and to the other children in the family, and a serious economic drain that results in a wide range of family sacrifices. Given this array, it is obvious that these negative reactions will have a disturbing effect on the growing handicapped child. The impact on attachment and on the child's self-concept and interpersonal development can only be estimated, but a number of reports strongly suggest that the reciprocal impact on the growing handicapped child can be serious and long lasting (Chess *et al.* 1971; Ogden, 1974; Mowatt, 1965; Richardson, 1972).

VI. Characteristics of Handicapped Children and Their Parents in Families with Marital Discord and Family Disruptions

Are there particular characteristics that are prevalent among impaired families due to the handicapped child? Our emphasis here is not on a theoretical elaboration of family dynamics; our approach will primarily be an actuarial one. We will also be concerned with the usefulness of a family distress index based on variables related to the likelihood of impaired family life. This discussion might be valuable in that, for those most vulnerable, services may be mobilized to help reduce the stressful impact of the handicapped child and to minimize any consequent impairment in family life.

Toward this goal we will compare two groups of children with sequelae of congenital rubella for whom our records were most complete; 40 children from families in which impairing stress due to the handicapped child was found (Distress Group) and 40 children selected at random from the remaining families in which no impairment in family life style was found (No Distress Group). Impairment would include parental discord, serious disruption in such family routines as social and recreational activities, or the deterioration of interpersonal relations. This conclusion is based on the parent interview reports that were conducted as part of our investigation.

Since our outcome variable is dichotomous—distress versus no distress—and our groups were of equal size, a variable that is not specifically related to one of these outcomes would be equally distributed—with a relative frequency of 50% in each of the two groups of families. Our major concern is with risk estimation so that service needs may be anticipated. Thus, we will describe our results in terms of the percentages of families of children with particular attributes that do fall in the Distress Group, as contrasted with the percentage remaining in the No Distress Group.

VII. Sociofamilial Attributes: Demographic and Attitudinal

The following section presents the results of analyses relating demographic variables and attitudinal responses to vulnerability to distress. Such linkages are useful as first approximations in a search for processes involved in vulnerability. That is, variables such as race and religion may covary with underlying processes. Thus, the establishment of such linkages will provide clues as to where, in future research, search for such process will be profitable (see Lerner & Spanier, Chapter 1, this volume).

A. Race

Does a child's race provide us with an index of increased vulnerability to family distress? We recognize that race, per se, cannot be construed as a cause of distress in families of handicapped children, yet if found to be related to vulnerability, it may be established as a marker variable for covarying processes. In our samples, we find that distress is least likely to occur in white families. Among 54 such families, 46% were found to be in the Distress Group; the remaining 54% of the white families were in the No Distress Group. Among the 12 Puerto Rican families, 50% were in the Distress Group. Among the black children, 58% were in the Distress Group, with 42% of the black children falling in the No Distress Group. Quite clearly, race alone is not a particularly powerful index of vulnerability, probably because by itself it conveys little about the significant family processes.

B. Religion

Within the major religious groups among our families, the highest rate of distress is found among our Jewish mothers. Of the 12 Jewish mothers in our two samples, 67% were in the Distress Group, and only 33% were in the No Distress Group. Among the 15 Protestant mothers, 60% were in the Distress Group, and in the group of Catholic mothers we found 44% with impairment in family life. If we compare the Catholic and non-Catholic mothers in terms of relative frequency of distress versus no distress, we find 44% in the former group and 60% in the latter group. Perhaps the distress rate is lower among the Catholic mothers because of their religious resignation—as expressed, for example, in their attitudes against abortion. This reaction would also reduce any personal guilt about the handicapped child that they might otherwise experience. However, the 2×2 χ^2 for these data is not statistically significant ($p > .05$).

C. Education

There is a slightly greater likelihood that we will find impairment in family life among families of handicapped children in which the parents' educational level is not higher than completion of high school. In the two groups of children, 43 of the fathers did not go beyond high school. Of these, we find 54% in families with distress. Of the 32 fathers who had at least some college, only 41% are in the Distress Group. The same pattern can be seen when we examine the educational levels of the mothers; of the 51 mothers with no schooling beyond high school, 57% are in the Distress Group. Mothers who had at least some college are less likely to be in the Distress Group—41%. The lower frequency of distressing impact of the handicapped child on the family among those parents with higher education may reflect some aspect of marital organization specific to this group. It might also be that this group is better informed about their children's handicaps and can muster their resources to obtain better services for the child's and family's needs. However, the χ^2 analyses of these relationships, for mothers and for fathers, were not statistically significant ($p > .05$).

D. Occupational Level

With regard to parents' occupational level, a more complex relationship to the incidence of distress in the family exists. The lowest rates of impaired family relationships occur in families in which the fathers are in either the *lowermost* or the *uppermost* occupational levels. Of the 19 fathers who are unskilled or semiskilled, 6 (or 32%) are in the Distress Group, and for the professionally occupied fathers the proportion in the Distress Group is 40% (6 of 15 cases). On the other hand, of 14 fathers in clerical or sales positions and 29 in skilled occupations, the proportions in the Distress Group are 64% and 55%, respectively.

Among the mothers, 60 described themselves as housewives, and for them, 50% were in the Distress Group. Among the remaining working mothers, we find the same pattern. There is one aspect of the mothers' occupational data that is of special interest. Of the 6 women who were classified as housewives and who were previously skilled or professional workers, 17% (1 of 6) were in the Distress Group; of the 8 women who were classified currently as skilled or professional workers, rather than housewives, 50% were in the distress group (4 of 8). Of course, the sizes of these samples are quite small, but the trends are of more than casual interest in terms of the dynamics of family life under stress. Perhaps the women who have given up their earlier careers invest more of themselves to make their family role more satisfying; alternatively, they may simply deny more of their real disappointment.

E. Prior Distress in the Family

In the two groups of families, we found 20 families in which some degree of family stress was reported as existing before the birth of the handicapped child and as not being related to the particular pregnancy.

> He was 26 years older than me, was very restrictive, didn't let me wear makeup, dictated how I should wear my hair . . . very possessive of me. He threatened to kill me.
>
> Our marriage is full of stress and friction . . . incompatible natures. He says that I am inefficient and that the house is unroutinized. Family life is bedlam.
>
> We are constantly fighting because of his gambling and drinking. He often stays out all night.

We found that such prior distress was not a factor predictive of the incidence of impaired family relationships related to the birth and care of the handicapped child. Exactly one-half of the 20 families with such prior distress were in our Distress Group and one-half in the No Distress Group. The handicapped child may present a totally new set of pressures. These may not alter patterns of earlier stress or may be factors that are additive and affect fragile families more than stable families. We can see that some of our families were already stabilized in a chronically distress state.

F. Identification of Child's Defects by Parents

In almost all of the cases, 37 of the 40 in the No Distress Group and 36 of 40 in the Distress Group, the parents reasonably accurately identified their children's defects. Obviously, this variable does not relate to the likelihood of finding impaired family patterns.

G. Parents' Opinion of Available Services

During the course of the interviews with parents, we discussed with them whether they felt that the services available to them were adequate for their needs.

We're very happy with what is done for us. . . .He gets periodic evaluation at the school, we come [to the hospital] every year. Everything is checked.

We are delighted. They are concerned and offer all kinds of help—we really don't even make use of all they offer for parents . . . a marvelous, all-around place.

Karen gets all the therapy she needs—very convenient—all have been wonderful to us.

On the other hand, some parents reported that services to the child and family were incomplete and unsatisfactory—family seldom included, inadequate counseling, limited therapy for child, etc.

I feel that Charles needs more than 2 hours of school a day. He seems happier after a full day's stimulation. I wish they could extend the school day.

He doesn't go to school now. I have to wait until next year.

I need free dental care for him. I can't afford a private dentist.

Among the 51 parents who felt that services were at least "adequate," the proportion in the Distress Group was 45%, and for the 20 parents who felt that services were inadequate, the proportion was 75%. The 2 $\times$ 2 χ^2 for these data was significant ($p < .05$).

H. Attitude toward Abortion

Mothers were also asked about their attitudes toward medical abortion. The question was intentionally left general and somewhat ambiguous—abortion in general? at the time of the pregnancy with this child? after the rubella alert? if the current situation could have been anticipated? None of this was specifically delineated. In the discussions, the mothers often gave lengthy, sober, and thoughtful responses that conveyed a particularly sensitive view of their feelings.

I don't feel anyone has a right to take a life. God gave me what he wants to. We wanted a child very much [had a miscarriage earlier]—we would and did take our chances.

Even if I didn't have a religious reason, I would still take a chance that everything would turn out right. If you think that something will happen, you probably wouldn't have any children at all.

Today my attitude toward abortion is positive knowing what the results are . . . although we love him very much. But at the time of my pregnancy I was sure that everything would turn out all right.

It's not fair to a child to be brought into the world with handicaps like that. We do, of course, love him.

I was in favor of abortion and feel hurt that I was assured that all would be well and gave birth to this kind of child.

I would have regretted not having him—but I think that I would have agreed to a legal abortion.

Our findings relating attitudes toward abortion and the incidence of impaired family life show that of the 37 mothers who expressed a favorable attitude toward medical abortion, 23 (or 62%) were in the Distress Group. Of the mothers who are opposed to abortion, no matter what the grounds, only 14 (41%) were in the Distress Group. The $2 \times 2 \chi^2$ analysis of these data was not significant at the .05 level.

Perhaps the mothers who said that they do favor abortion were more likely to be in the Distress Group because their expressed attitude toward abortion was reactive to their current marital and/or family difficulties that they attribute to the handicapped child. On the other hand, those who oppose abortion may be more accepting of "God's will" or fate and feel less personal guilt regarding the birth of the handicapped child. For those who favor abortion but did not choose this option, these palliatives are not as directly available. The relationship between a favorable attitude toward abortion and the likelihood of finding an impaired family situation was fairly similar in all of the major religious groups. That is, whether the mother was Catholic, Protestant, or Jewish, those who favored abortion were more likely to be found in the Distress Group. Among the Catholic mothers, it was 8 out of 12; among the Protestants, it was 6 of 8; and for the Jewish mothers, 7 of the 10 who favored abortion were in the Distress Group.

I. Summary of Sociofamilial Indices

Regardless of the issue of statistical significance, it appears that the incidence of impaired marital quality and family interaction is disproportionately high among the black children, Jewish mothers (ignore the paradox), fathers in clerical and sales occupations, where services for the family and child are seen as inadequate by the parents, and where there is a favorable attitude toward medical abortion. We suggest that each of these can be viewed as an indicator variable related to the greater likelihood of distress in families of handicapped rubella children. Even more so, the concurrent incidence of a number of these factors in a family may provide us with a useful index of potential for marital discord or family impairment. We shall call this Family Distress Index-S, where the components are sociofamilial factors. The number of such factors actually found among our 80 families varied from 0 to 4. There were 36 families with not more than one Family Distress Index-S factor, and among these, the proportion in the Distress Group was 28%—10 families in the

TABLE 11.1
Family Distress Index-S: Sociofamilial Attributes and the Incidence of Family Distress

| Family Distress Index-S | Group | | | Proportion with family distress (in Percent) |
	No Distress	Distress	Total	
0	8	3	11	27
1	18	7	25	25
2	8	13	21	62
3	6	15	21	71
4	0	2	2	100
Total	40	40	80	

Note. Chi square analysis comparing children with 0–1, 2, and 3–4 factors and incidence of distress versus no distress ($df = 2$) was statistically significant beyond the .05 level of confidence.

Distress Group, and 26 families in the No Distress Group. Of the 21 families with 2 signs and of the 23 families with 3 or 4 signs, the proportions in the Distress Group were 62% and 74%, respectively. In fact, 75% of the families in the Distress Group had two or more factors on the Family Distress Index-S, while 65% of the No Distress Group had not more than one sign. These data are summarized in Table 11.1.

Obviously these demographic and attitudinal factors, by themselves, do not cause an impaired family situation, nor are they a complete picture of relevant factors. We will go on to add a consideration of types and severity of handicap, because these, too, are related to impaired family relationships. However, the cluster of factors that thus far make up our index of vulnerability can serve as an effective alerting signal. The value of clustering the separate factors lies in the fact that such a pooling increases reliability. We need indices that are effective and can be applied to a fairly large segment of cases.

VIII. Demographic and Physical Attributes of the Handicapped Child

What are the characteristics of the handicapped children themselves that are associated with marital discord or family disruption?

A. Age

The children in our samples varied in age from 36 to 73 months, with most of the younger children in families falling into the Distress Group. Of the 33 children below the age of 60 months, 24 (73%) are in families in the Distress Group. On the other hand, the 34% of the 47 families with rubella children who are at least 60 months old are in the Distress Group. The 2 × 2 χ^2 analysis of these data is significant (p < .05).

Since the older children were less than 60 months old at one time, the data are at first glance puzzling. However, the parent reports deal with distress at the time the study was conducted. We must assume that the distresses that may have been present earlier were resolved and that by the time the children are 5 years old or so, a stable period ensues. The evaluation of this interpretation will be part of our continuing longitudinal study of rubella children and their families.

B. Sex

We do find slightly more families with distress when the handicapped child is a boy. Among the 39 male children, we find a 54% in the Distress Group, and for the 41 female children, the proportion is 46%. Whether this is a function of some sex-related attributes per se or a function of differential parental attitudes and expectations is not clear from our data.

C. Ordinal Position and Size of Family

These two variables are considered together because the combination gives a more complete perspective. As ordinal position of the handicapped child increases, there is a decrease in the number of distressed families—from a high of 57% among the 28 firstborn to a low of 41% among the 17 children who were fourth or more in birth order. For those born second or third, there were 47% and 44% in the Distress Group, respectively.

Furthermore, the highest proportion of distress occurs among families with two children—70% of the 23 families with two children are in the Distress Group. For the 7 families in which the handicapped child is the "only child," the figure was 57%, for the 25 families with three children, it was 28%, and for the 23 families with four or more children; it was 48%.

Are the distressed families likely to have no more children after the birth of the handicapped child? The answer is no, since only 47% of the 34 families in which the rubella child is the "last child" were in the Distress Group.

The two-child family may provide an important clue to some aspects of family dynamics and to the distresses related to the handicapped child. Of the 23 two-child families in our study, 17 were families in which the handicapped child was the firstborn. Of these, 11, or 65%, were families with distress, and only 6 were in the No Distress Group. In these families, it is as if the second child is added to an already distressed family. Perhaps the parents have to prove their ability to have a normal child, or perhaps they believe that a normal child will actually stabilize their marriage and family. However, such two-child families are at great risk for the distressing impact of the handicapped child. The risk is even greater than where the handicapped child is the only child (4 of 7, or 57%) or where he or she is the last child in a family of more than two children. Of the 26 families in which there are more than two children and the handicapped child is the last child, only 9, or 35%, are families in the Distress Group.

D. Visual Handicap

In the samples of children, there are 49 children with no visual defect and 11 others whose vision is normal with eyeglasses. Twenty children have some visual handicap that is uncorrected, and 15 of these, or 75%, are in families in the Distress Group. Among the children with normal visual functioning, the proportion in the Distress Group is 42% (25 of 60 children).

E. Hearing Handicap

A much larger proportion of the rubella children suffer from a hearing handicap. Only 23 of the 80 children have no hearing defect at all or hear at the normal level with the help of aids. Of these children, 30% are in families in the Distress Group. On the other hand, we find 57 children with some degree of hearing loss uncompensated for by aids. Here, too, as with the children with visual handicap, the proportion of families in the Distress Group is disproportionately high (58%). The milder the functional hearing handicap, the less likely are we to find a family with impaired marital or family relations due to the handicapped child. Where the functional hearing level is moderate (response only to loud speech), 30% (3 of 10) of the families are in the Distress Group. When the children can only respond to loud sounds, the proportion is 62% (13 of 21), and when there is no response at all to sound, the proportion is 75% (9 of 12). A 2×2 χ^2 comparing the last two categories of hearing handicap with the others in terms of distress—no distress is significant $(p < .05)$.

F. Neurological Handicap

The analysis of neurological handicap is limited to a comparison of children with hard neurological signs and those without hard signs. There are 38 children with hard signs and 42 with no neurological signs, hard or soft. In the former group, 74% of the families are in the Distress Group, and in contrast, the proportion among the other children is 29%. The $2 \times 2\ \chi^2$ for this set of contingencies is also significant ($p < .05$).

G. Cardiac Handicap

We found 33 of our 80 children to have some cardiac defect, and 21 (64%) of these children are among the families in our Distress Group. Of the remaining 47 children, those without cardiac defect, the proportion in this group is 40%.

H. Number of Defect Areas

Another way to look at the relationship between physical handicap and the impairment of family circumstances is to consider the range of multiple handicaps. Given these four defect areas (vision, hearing, neurologic, and cardiac), each child can be classified as having one to four defect areas. There are 14 children with defects in all four areas, 13 with defects in three areas, and 53 children with defects in two or fewer areas. The proportion of families in the Distress Group among those with the largest number of multiple handicaps was 86%. For the next group it is 62%, and for those with two or fewer areas of handicap the rate is 38%. The $2 \times 2\ \chi^2$, comparing those with three or four defect areas and those with two or fewer defect areas in terms of distress—no distress is significant ($p < .05$).

I. Summary of Attributes of the Handicapped Child

In contrast with the sociofamilial factors previously dealt with, the individual attributes of the handicapped child, considered in this section, have more often been significantly related to the incidence of marital discord or disrupted family life. This would suggest that these physical defects and other child-related attributes are more crucial—at least as indicators or perhaps also as direct or indirect causal factors—to the quality of family life. The congenitally and chronically handicapped child is an extraordinary task for the parents and the family. The demands for the care of the handicapped child often cannot be met without serious sacrifice on the part of parents, siblings, and extended family members. Not only are there the ordinary demands of child care and training but the parents are faced with a search for a "cure" that will assuage their guilt or reduce their fears for the child's future. Most often this is a futile, frustrating search. The parents must also adjust to the world of the handicapped—the special schools, the frequent isolation from parents of normal children, and the embarrassment and anger that are common sequelae. Parents are torn between the needs of the handicapped child and their own personal and marital needs. They must find a way not to ignore their other children and to keep the household warm and harmonious. This is often the portrait of the family of the chronically handicapped child.

Following the model developed earlier, we have formulated a Family Distress Index-HC based on variables directly related to the handicapped child. The factors included in this index are as follows:

1. Age: under 60 months
2. Ordinal position: firstborn
3. Size of family: two children
4. Visual defect: vision not normal even with aids
5. Hearing defect: not able to hear at all; hears only gross sounds; hearing unable to be estimated
6. Neurologic defect: hard sign present
7. Cardiac defect: any cardiac defect

TABLE 11.2

Family Distress Index-HC: Demographic and Physical Attributes of the Handicapped Child and the Incidence of Family Distress

Family Distress Index-HC	Group			Proportion with family distress (in Percent)
	No Distress	Distress	Total	
0	8	0	8	0
1	8	3	11	27
2	12	7	19	37
3	8	9	17	53
4	3	9	12	75
5	1	6	7	86
6	0	4	4	100
7	0	2	2	100
	40	40	80	

Each child was assigned an index score based on the number of such factors present; the possible range is 0–7. The summary of our findings that relate Family Distress Index-HC to the incidence of distress versus no distress is presented in Table 11.2. The proportion of families of the Distress Group among the 8 children with an index of 0 is 0%. As the index rises to 6–7, the proportion increases to 100% (6 of 6 cases). The proportion of families in the Distress Group among those with an index at or below 3 is 35% (19 of 55), and for those with an index of 4 or higher, it is 84% (21 of 25). The 2×2 χ^2 of this comparison (0–3 versus 4–7) is significant ($p < .05$).

IX. Psychological–Behavioral Attributes of the Child

The impact of the handicapped child on family patterns is not only a function of characteristics of the family or the nature of the physical handicaps involved. The behavioral attributes of the child—mental retardation, behavioral disturbance, and patterns of temperament—also play a significant role. This has been a major concern of ours throughout the course of our work with rubella children (Chess, Korn & Fernandez, 1971). These characteristics often set the children apart even from other handicapped children and are reacted to by all who come into contact with the child—parents, family, neighbors, and teachers, among others.

A. Mental Retardation

Based on intelligence testing and clinical evaluation, 29 of the children were diagnosed as mentally retarded—from mild to profound retardation. Among these children, 76% (22 of 29) were from families in the Distress Group. For the remaining children who were not mentally retarded, the proportion was 35% (18 of 51). The 2×2 χ^2 for this set of relationships was significant ($p < .05$).

B. Behavior Disorder

Psychiatric evaluation of the children yielded 56 children with no behavior disorder and 24 with behavior disorders. The diagnoses included autism, partial syndrome of autism, and reactive behavior disorders—mild to severe. The proportion of families in the Distress Group from among those with no behavior disorder was 41% (23 of 56), and the figure for those with some psychiatric disorder, regardless of diagnosis or severity, was 71% (17 of 24). The $2 \times 2\chi^2$ was significant ($p < .05$).

C. Temperament

Following the pattern of the New York Longitudinal Study (NYLS) the children's temperament was also assessed (Thomas *et al.* 1963; Thomas, Chess, & Birch, 1968). Temperament refers to the behavioral style of the individual child. It is a term used to describe reactivity patterns independently of their contents and refers to the "how" rather than the "what" (capacities and abilities) or the "why" (motives and goals) of behavior. In our study of rubella children, temperament scores for each child were based on descriptions of the children's behavior and followed the methods and criteria established in the NYLS.

Our concern here is with the Difficult-Child Syndrome, because parents find such children hard to care for. The difficult child is "not easy to feed, put to sleep, bathe, or dress. New places, unaccustomed activities, and strange faces may produce initial responses of loud protest or crying. Frustrations generally produce a violent tantrum [Chess *et al.* 1971, p. 127]." The Difficult-Child Syndrome is a cluster of five of the nine temperament categories developed in the NYLS. The behavior patterns most likely to be encountered in this constellation include the following categories and response types:

1. *Rhythmicity:* Irregularity or nonpredictability of repetitive functions such as sleep-wake cycles, hunger and feeding patterns, and bowel and bladder functions. "He gets hungry at any time of day. He falls asleep at different times even though he's put to sleep at the same time every day." [Vulnerable polar extreme—irregular.]
2. *Approach–withdrawal:* Withdrawal or negative responses to new situations, foods, people, and procedures. "She resists going to new places. She is withdrawn with strangers." [Vulnerable polar extreme—withdrawal.]
3. *Adaptability:* Difficulty and slowness in changing an initial pattern of reaction to a socially desirable response. "He screams and fusses every time he gets his hair cut." [Vulnerable polar extreme—nonadaptive.]
4. *Mood:* Unpleasant, unfriendly behavior, and crying. "She cries and whines whenever I go out. She doesn't play when children visit." [Vulnerable polar extreme—negative mood.]

5. *Intensity*: High energy level of response regardless of its quality. "He laughs and jumps up and down to music. He screams when the least bit hurt." [Vulnerable polar extreme—intense.]

We used the median scores of the NYLS children on each of these five temperament traits as criteria for scoring. Any child whose score for one of these traits fell between this criterion point and the vulnerable polar extreme was considered to have a sign of the difficult child.

Given these five attributes, each child was assigned a score from 0 to 5 based on the number of signs of the difficult child. A high score would indicate a child that is temperamentally "difficult," a low score would indicate an "easy child" (Thomas *et al.*, 1968). Among the families of rubella children with 3–5 signs of the difficult child, the proportion in the Distress Group is 62% (24 of 38). For those with 0–2 signs, the figure is 34% (13 of 38). The 2×2 χ^2 is significant ($p < .05$).

D. Summary of Psychological–Behavioral Attributes

We can again follow our general model and construct a Family Distress Index-PB. This would be based on the following three psychological–behavioral characteristics:

1. Mental retardation: any level.
2. Psychiatric disorder: any diagnosed behavior disorder.
3. Temperamentally difficult child: at least three signs of the difficult child.

The maximum possible score on this index is 3. The result of the relationship between this index and the presence or absence of family dis-

TABLE 11.3
Family Distress Index-PB: Psychological–Behavioral Attributes of the Handicapped Child and the Incidence of Family Distress

	Group			Proportion with family distress (in Percent)
Family Distress Index-PB	No Distress	Distress	Total	
0	17	5	22	23
1	18	13	31	42
2	5	16	21	76
3	0	6	6	100
	40	40	80	

tress are presented in Table 11.3. As the index score increases, so does the proportion of families in the Distress Group—from a low of 23% among the children with a score of 0 to a high of 100% for the 6 children with a score of 3. Among the children whose Family Distress Index-PB is 0–1, the proportion in the Distress Group is 34% (18 of 53), and for those with an index of 2–3, it is 82% (22 of 27). The 2×2 χ^2 is significant (p < .05).

X. Conclusions

Our findings indicate that the impact of the preschool handicapped child on marital quality and family life is related to a broad range of variables. Marital discord specifically due or related to the handicapped child is relatively infrequent among the parents in our rubella sample. A more common effect is the disruption of family routines and the impairment of the parents' social lives due to the demanding care and social developmental problems of the congentially handicapped child. Our data are consistent with the view that this effect on the parents, and its distressing implications, also has a reverberating impact on the child. The presence of this interaction is of particular concern for both the theoretical and the practical reasons outlined in the preceding discussion. Future data we are planning to collect will be better able to establish the impact of such child–family reciprocities, since they will be longitudinal in nature.

However, even given the limits of our currently available data, we may conclude that the impact of the child on the family appears to be more related to the characteristics of the rubella children, with their wide variety and number of handicaps, than to the attributes of the parents. Where we have examined specific factors as possible indicators of the likelihood of family disruption, those variables that were found to be statistically significantly related were not the sociofamilial variables, such as race, religion, parents' education, or the presence of prior distress in the marriage or family. The factors related to the incidence of family disruption were specific characteristics of the child, such as the type and number of physical handicaps, mental retardation, behavior disorder, or whether the child was temperamentally a "difficult child." This suggests that the handicapped child presents an extraordinary stress—a chronic, long-term, and changing stress—to which the family must respond and continuously readjust.

Since no variable appears in isolation, there is obviously a compounding or interaction of contributing factors. Each isolated variable that is identified as being related to family distress may only be viewed as an *indicator*, not as a *causal* factor. The causes of family disruption and marital discord lie in the complex interaction among contributing factors—the parents, the child, and the environmental conditions—each of which affects the others. The actual dynamics of personal and family reactions to the stresses involved in caring for the handicapped child are the key issues in any analysis of causality. The variables must be viewed as an interacting complex: Some factors may compensate for one another, whereas some factors in combination may exacerbate the impact of either one alone. However, many of the specific variables enumerated in this study, as well as the factors clustered in each Family Distress Index, prove to be effective means of identifying families that are more likely to experience marital discord or family disruption. These indicators are very useful in planning for family services, and they may also facilitate a better understanding of family development when used as indices in developmental research.

References

Chess, S., Korn, S. J., & Fernandez, P. B. *Psychiatric disorders of children with congenital rubella.* New York: Bruner/Mazel, 1971.

Cooper, L. Z., Ziring, P. R., Ockerse, A. B., Fedun, B. A., Kiely, B., & Krugman, S. Rubella: Clinical manifestations and management. *American Journal of Diseases of Children*, 1969, *118*, 18–29.

D'Arcy, E. Congenital defects: Mother's reaction to first information. *British Medical Journal*, 1968, *3*, 796–798.

Farber, B., & Jenne, W. Family organization and parent–child communication: Parents and siblings of a retarded child. *Monographs of the Society for Research in Child Development*, 1963, *28*:7.

Fraiberg, S. Blind infants and their mothers: An examination of the sign system. In M. Lewis & L. A. Rosenblum (Eds.), *The effect of the infant on its caregiver*. New York: Wiley, 1974.

Gath, A. The mental health of siblings of congenitally abnormal children. *Journal of Child Psychology and Psychiatry*, 1972, *13*, 211–218.

Illingworth, R. Counselling the parents of the mentally handicapped child. *Clinical Pediatrics*, 1967, *6*, 340–347.

Jacobs, J. F., & Pierce, M. L. The social position of retardates with brain damage association characteristics. *Exceptional Children*, 1968, *34*, 677–681.

Klaus, M., & Kennell, J. *Maternal-infant bonding.* 1976, St. Louis, Missouri: C. V. Mosby, 1976.

Kogan, K., & Tyler, N. Mother-child interaction in young physically handicapped children. *American Journal of Mental Deficiency*, 1973, *77*, 492–497.

Mowatt, M. Emotional conflicts of handicapped young adults and their mothers. *The Cerebral Palsy Journal*, 1965, July–August, 6–8.

Ogden, T. Psychoanalytic psychotherapy of a patient with cerebral palsy: The relation of aggression to self and body representations. *International Journal of Psychanalytic Psychotherapy*, 1974, *3*, 419–433.

Richardson, S. People with cerebral palsy speak for themselves. *Developmental Medicine and Child Neurology*, 1972, *14*, 524–535.

Thomas, A., Chess, S., Birch, H. G., Hertzig, M. E., & Korn, S. J. *Behavioral individuality in early childhood*. New York: New York University Press, 1963.

Thomas, A., Chess, S., & Birch, H. G. *Temperament and behavior disorders in children*. New York: New York University Press, 1968.

The Study of Child–Family Interactions: A Perspective for the Future

12

Graham B. Spanier, Richard M. Lerner,
and William Aquilino

I. Introduction

There has been much appreciation of interdisciplinary theory and research in the history of American social science but only a limited number of instances of such endeavors. There have been both conceptual and methodological barriers to such attempts. The lack of an appropriate, interdisciplinary unit of analysis, the absence of a unifying conceptual scheme, and the unavailability of necessary empirical tools have limited true interdisciplinary projects.

Yet, both historical and conceptual transitions in social science seem to be signaling a change (Hartup, Chapter 2, this volume; Lerner & Spanier, Chapter 1, this volume). Hartup has argued that the disciplinary isolation that has characterized both the child development and the family sociology fields is waning. The unidirectional, "social mold" notions of socialization and the static, cross-sectional conceptions of family changes that have been involved, respectively, in these two disciplines, are giving way. As the influences of these orientations diminish, a concept of individual and family interaction is being elaborated. This interaction notion stresses the continual reciprocities between individual ontogeny and family change and, as such, promotes life-span and multidisciplinary orientations.

Accordingly, Lerner and Spanier (Chapter 1, this volume) see the current transition in social science as leading to a dynamic interactional conception of individual and family development. The interdisciplinary scheme they advance has as its unit of analysis the child–family interface—a bridging, integrative unit. Because of the reciprocal influ-

327

Child Influences on Marital and Family Interaction:
A Life-Span Perspective

ences of individual and social change, the child–family unit has method-ological import for social science not found in analyses of traditional units associated with only one discipline.

Specifically, Lerner and Spanier propose a transition in social sci-ence, from unidisciplinary, noninteractive, static views of individuals, social units, and contexts to an interdisciplinary, dynamic interactional conception of individual and social changes across the life-span, social contexts, and history. This proposal is as much a prospectus for future endeavors as it is a summary of changes in perspectives among social scientists (Hartup, Chapter 2, this volume).

II. A Synthesis of Perspectives

There is a major empirical implication of the dynamic interactional model proposed by Lerner and Spanier (Chapter 1, this volume). If behavioral and social change phenomena are studied through use of a reciprocal child–family unit of analysis, then the variance in behavioral and social change processes may be more adequately explained. The reciprocal, or dialectical, paradigm from which Lerner and Spanier de-rive their views of human development and family change specifies that individuals, their family, and their social world are inextricably united. Analyses that consider only one of the components of this unit will avoid assessing a ubiquitous part of the whole. As such, this omission will result in treating considerable amounts of true variance as error variance.

Thus, whether assessing personological aspects of individual functioning within the discipline of developmental psychology or changes in marital quality over the course of the family life cycle within family sociology, researchers have continually noted the small propor-tion of variance accounted for by measures of their target phenomena (Hartup, Chapter 2, this volume; Rollins & Galligan, Chapter 4, this volume). It is our view that such results are not only based on errors of measurement. Rather, they are based primarily on "omissions of mea-surement." Researchers have failed to examine empirically the recip-rocal impact of the variables and processes considered in other disci-plines on those suggested by their own discipline.

In our view, these omissions have derived from three interrelated sources. First, there has been an absence of a model linking the recip-rocal change processes studied within each discipline and all individual points in development. The multidisciplinary, life-span trend in social science and the resulting integrative theories, which stress reciprocal interchanges, have provided a basis for ameliorating this first reason for omission (Hartup, Chapter 2, this volume; Lerner & Spanier, Chapter 1, this volume). As already noted, the model presented by Lerner and Spanier represents just one instance of several converging attempts to provide a reciprocal, multidisciplinary, life-span model of change. Riegel (1975, 1976a, 1976b), Lewis and his colleagues (Lewis & Lee-Painter, 1974; Weinraub, Brooks, & Lewis, 1977), Sameroff (1975), and Looft (1973) have offered other similar arguments.

A second reason there has been little consideration of reciprocal child–family interactions is that data collection and data analytic strategies capable of dealing with the circular relations involved have not been adequate (cf. Lewis & Lee-Painter, 1974). This problem remains, to date, the major obstacle in exploring child–family reciprocities. Lerner and Spanier (Chapter 1, this volume) note that no existing method of data collection or technique of analysis is totally adequate. Both they and Klein, Jorgensen, and Miller (Chapter 5, this volume) suggest methods and techniques that may be used until others are developed. But the theories that will nurture the empirical inventions once they are born have not been present long enough to advance our thinking greatly. As a consequence, we can now do no more than suggest the dimensions of future methods and analysis techniques that will have to be devised.

In regard to method, procedures will have to be established to record reciprocal interchanges among all possible levels of analysis. Thus, observational techniques capable of recording molecular, moment-by-moment reciprocities, as involved in infant–mother interactions, will have to be devised. Additionally, procedures capable of providing an index of the molar reciprocities involved, for instance, in intergenera-. tional transmission of influence will be needed (Bengtson & Troll, Chapter 8, this volume). Moreover, still more elusive interchanges, as between sociocultural change and individual ontogeny, will need to be observed.

The need to understand simultaneously the reciprocal aspects of several, if not all, levels in one research effort may arise. The prototypic sequential design (Baltes, Reese, & Nesselroade, 1977) capable of ascertaining the relative contributions of age, birth cohort, and time of measurement to change functions might thus have to be expanded. Further differentiations within the cohort and time dimensions might be necessary.

Complicating these methodological issues are data analytic issues. As pointed out by Lerner and Spanier (Chapter 1, this volume), current statistical techniques, based on linear mathematical models and buttressed by Aristotelian logic, are not fully appropriate to analyze continual reciprocites. Circular statistical models, based on dialectical logic, and, as such, attentive to the unique measurement issues raised by this logic (for example, see Labouvie, 1975), will have to be devised.

These methodological and data analytic issues might seemingly preclude the exploration of reciprocal child–family interaction. However, we believe that because of the demonstrated theoretical and empirical need to study these interfaces, research consistent with a reciprocal model must indeed proceed. We must, however, keep the limitations of such research in mind. Rather than ask only those questions we can adequately answer, let us address issues at the "cutting edge" of conceptual advancements; thus, we will stimulate methodological development. Such research has not yet been initiated on any major scale. This absence leads us to specify the third reason why there has not been greater consideration of reciprocal child–family interaction.

Despite interest in reciprocal theoretical models and awareness that research can proceed with acknowledged methodological limitations, reciprocities between child and family have not been adequately explored because there have been an absence of specific conceptual and empirical illustrations. Advocates of reciprocal theoretical models have not offered sufficient, concrete indications of just how and where studies of child and family reciprocities can enrich specific research programs.

The chapters in this volume go a long way toward providing such an illustrative base. Yet, the need remains to draw a concrete example from the sociological research literature and show how a consideration of the life-span influence of the child will enhance knowledge. In turn, a specific illustration of how understanding of the life-span development of the person can be furthered through integration with family and network notions is also necessary. Accordingly, in the next section, we will offer examples of how one might expand and enrich knowledge in two specific research areas.

III. Child–Family Interactions and Life-Span Research

A. Sexual Interaction in Marriage

Dyadic interaction in marriage involves numerous dimensions of behavior. Sexual interaction in marriage is one such dimension that has attracted the interest of family sociologists. Limited data exist pertaining to changes in sexual behavior over the course of a marriage (Westoff & Westoff, 1971). Yet, the data are far from unequivocal in the trends they suggest, and the total variance in sexual behavior accounted for by the variables traditionally studied is probably small.

Understanding of changes in sexual function over the course of marriage could be furthered, and potentially more variance could be accounted for, if research questions were introduced that pertained to the effect of the child on the parents' sexual interactions. First, the mere introduction of the child into a dyadic family will probably alter the opportunities for, spontaneity of, and locations of sexual interaction. For instance, the introduction of the first child into the marriage should place caretaking demands on either or both spouses that would require alterations in their typical daily schedule. Feeding and toileting, for example, would occur at various times throughout the day, and such requirements will alter the availability of each partner for sexual interaction. Energy levels of each partner would be affected in relation to the infant's demands for care giving. Additionally, the demands of the infant would alter the possibility of sponteneity; and the infant's mere presence, as well as his or her state (e.g., asleep or awake), would affect the location in which sexual exchange could occur.

Moreover, given the active behavioral characteristics of the infant (Korn, Chess, & Fernandez, Chapter 11, this volume; Lamb, Chapter 6, this volume), these effects on parents' sexual behavior could be further altered. Children with difficult temperamental repertoires, for example, arhythmicity, negative mood, and intense reactions, would place greater energy expenditure requirements on parents and would not only make their care giving more trying but also make it difficult to predict when sexual interaction would be possible.

Together, these effects of the infant on their care givers might provide a basis of behaviors toward the infant that might be more unfavorable than favorable and consequently eventuate in even more "problem" behaviors of the infant. Thus, as this circular relation involving the child-family unit evolves over time, it might lead to (a) decreased frequencies of sexual interaction in the marriage; (b) lower marital quality; (c) negative child–care giver interactions (abuse is an extreme possibility); and/or (d) behavioral and/or emotional problems in any of the family members.

Moreover, as a child develops, the contexts of child–family interactions relating to parental sexual behavior may change, and the outcomes of interactions may vary. When children are older and more capable of independent locomotion, parents may have less control over their privacy and, as such, may resort to rules of interaction (e.g., "Don't bother mom and dad on Saturday mornings" or "Don't try to enter a room when the door is locked"), which will provide feedback to the child. Feelings of exclusion and of conditional love by the parents might emerge within the child, and as one consequence, particular meanings may be attached to sexuality by the child. These meanings may affect his or her own sexual functioning later, during adolescence and adulthood.

In turn, the meanings attached to sexuality by the child can affect the parent too. Adult children may look askance at sexuality in their aged parents (Hess & Waring, Chapter 9, this volume), and this discrepancy in generational orientation to parental sexuality might provide a basis of disengagement from the children by the aged. Of course, with sexuality among the aged gaining more attention in the public media and the professional literature (Schaie & Gribbin, 1975), the impact of the sexuality of aged parents on adult children, and the feedback the parents thus receive, will be altered as a consequence of social change across history.

Thus, a molar issue involving reciprocal intergenerational effects may be studied by focusing both on the child–parent dyad, and the nature of the development of molecular infant–care giver exchanges may be studied as well. In other words, clarification of the changing patterns of sexual behavior exchanged in a marriage may be furthered by focusing research on the evolving child–family unit, which provides a context for these parental interactions. Moreover, the role of social and historical change, as well as more molecular individual-psychological ones (e.g., temperamental style), can be as readily approached and enriched by use of this unit. Similar conclusions will be reached with our second illustration.

B. Attachment

Developmental psychologists have traditionally considered attachment to be a phenomenon involving a "bond" between infant and mother and thus a behavior having salience primarily in the early years of life. However, the convergence of data and arguments pertaining to the meaning of attachment has broadened the concept considerably. Data have shown that, despite some vagueness and thus variation in the operationalization of the term (Weinraub et al., 1977) infants show attachments to many people other than their mothers (Lamb, 1976, 1977; Weinraub et al., 1977). Whether or not indices involve emotional reactions in the infant (e.g., showing distress on a care giver's leaving) and/or motor (e.g., proximity maintaining) behavior, infants attach to a network of people (Weinraub et al., 1977). Infants attach to fathers (Lamb, 1976) and other relatives, friends, and "social objects" (e.g., the security blanket of Peanuts's Linus) in their network about as readily as they do to their mothers (Lewis & Feiring, Chapter 3, this volume).

Additionally, not only is attachment in infancy a more plastic social phenomenon than was previously thought but recent reviews (Antonucci, 1976; Lerner & Ryff, 1978) have shown that attachment is a life-span phenomenon. Consideration of the social world of the infant (Lewis & Feiring, Chapter 3, this volume) demonstrated a broader meaning of attachment within infancy, and this emphasis on the social embeddedness of attachment has stimulated others to consider what, if any, plastic components of attachment may be recognized as the person's social world changes through life.

Thus, ontogenetic linkages in attachment behavior have been seen as possible (Lerner & Ryff, 1978), whereas at the same time, alterations in attachment objects and behaviors across life seem probable. Children may become attached to pets, their best friend, or a school teacher; adolescents to their "gang" or peer group; and adults to their children, friends, spouse, and professional groups. In turn, the behaviors used to express attachment may vary across contexts and the life-span. Spouses may express their attachment by frequent, proximate interaction episodes, whereas an aged person might remain attached to his or her children through letter writing or telephone calls.

The point of the foregoing illustrations is to show that the study of a behavior heretofore considered an emotional or behavioral characteristic of the individual child can be enhanced within a particular portion of ontogeny, and enriched by giving it life-span meaning, by considering its social embeddedness. Recognizing that attachment is a plastic, social network, life-span phenomenon enables the researcher to ask questions about the role of the social context in the evolution of the behavior. Such questions pertain directly to the reciprocal child–family unit.

Within any period of individual development, questions may be asked about the impact of family structure and marital roles on modes of attachment behavior shown by a child. Simultaneously, the impact of such behavior on family structure and roles may be considered. In turn, the impact of such reciprocities for attachments in later life may be evaluated. For instance, researchers may ask questions about variations in attachment behavior accruing in relation to the child being embedded in a nuclear as opposed to an extended family system within a particular household. Or researchers may consider variation in attachment as a consequence of rearing in a father–absent as compared with a mother–absent family. In turn, the impact of having a child who is highly as opposed to only slightly attached to his or her parents and families could be considered. Additionally, the relevance of such variation in attachment behavior in one ontogenetic period for attachments in later ones can be evaluated. For example, a researcher may ask whether a child who forms familial attachments in a nuclear, as opposed to an extended, family household setting is more or less likely in later (e.g., adult) life to enter into and rear his or her children in such a context.

This last illustration shows the relevance of attachment behavior to intergenerational transmission of attitudes, values, and behavior. The nature and direction of such transmissions of attachment would be expected to vary depending on the societal prevalence of particular types of family structure. Consequently, one may explore the role of sociocultural and historical changes on intergenerational transmission of attachment behaviors and orientations and on intrafamilial exchange of attachment behaviors. In particular sociocultural settings at particular times in history, specific behaviors (e.g., kissing) may be differentially likely to be used to express attachments among certain network members (e.g., men).

In sum, through focus on the child–family relation we may expand and enrich the meaning and applicability of the attachment concept. Additionally, we may obtain such benefits whether our concern is molecular events (e.g., infant–care giver interactions involving proximity behaviors) or molar ones (e.g., intergenerational consistency in family structures generated to provide a context for attachment).

C. Implications

The foregoing discussion represents, of course, only a sample of the concrete research issues that may be addressed. The study of sexual interaction in marriage and the assessment of attachment are convenient examples, but they are not unique to our argument. Any of an infinite array of research topics within family sociology and developmental psychology can benefit from the approach presented. Moreover, although the preceding illustrations were selected because of their traditional consideration within a particular discipline, our analysis indicates convergence in the broad issues ultimately addressed.

Through focus on the child–family unit, both illustrations showed the utility of posing multidisciplinary, life-span-oriented questions. Moreover, these questions about the impact of reciprocity between child and family always led to a consideration of the additional impact of sociocultural and historical change. Furthermore, these characteristics emerged for reciprocities considered at either a molar or a molecular level.

In sum, despite differing disciplinary points of origin, researchers adopting the child–family interface as their unit of analysis will converge in their research efforts. They will move toward multidisciplinary, life-span research, and they will be able to integrate their endeavors through reference to circular, pluralistic models. To substantiate this point further, it is useful to move from a discussion of research issues for the future to an attempt to integrate existing data. By design, much of the data presented in this volume has dealt with marital quality and family interaction. It is thus appropriate to consider these data and see the extent to which pluralistic models, stressing circular influences across the life-span, are ultimately seen as useful.

IV. Issues in Marital Quality and Family Interaction

A. The Concept of Marital Quality

Research on marriage and the family has been hampered by the fact that variables such as marital quality, marital adjustment, and marital satisfaction are interpreted and measured differently by many researchers who use them (Spanier & Cole, 1976). On the whole, the contributions to this book have displayed this definitional confusion.

Rollins and Galligan (Chapter 4, this volume), who carefully evaluated the choice of available concepts and the implications of their uses, decided to use the concept "marital satisfaction" instead of "marital adjustment" in their presentation, because they feel that satisfaction is a subjective evaluation of marital quality by the marital partners themselves. This approach has the advantage of lifting from the researcher the responsibility for defining good and bad marriages. It has a major disadvantage, however, in that it ignores the possibility that more or less equal amounts of satisfaction (or dissatisfaction) can arise from qualitatively different types of marriages, with different patterns of interaction (Cuber & Harroff, 1965).

Other chapters in this volume have used terms such as *marital quality* very loosely. In most instances, the term is used to convey a generalized notion of "how well the marriage is going." To family sociologists in particular, who have conducted hundreds of studies with some variant of marital quality as the dependent variable, the use of this term and its etymological kin has become a focus of discussion (Lewis & Spanier, 1978; Spanier & Cole, 1976; Spanier, 1976).

We have a preference for using the term *marital quality* as the most general term indicating an overall evaluation of the functioning of the marriage. *Marital stability* refers to the "intactness" of a marriage. Stated differently, stability is an outcome variable describing whether the couple is still together (hence, a "stable" marriage is intact) or whether the marriage has dissolved by separation or divorce (hence, "unstable"). *Marital adjustment, happiness,* and *satisfaction* are terms that have narrower interpretations and usages, and such use varies from one researcher to the next.

A recently developed measure of marital quality, which tested the adequacy of a proposed definition of marital adjustment through factor analysis, confirmed the existence of four components of adjustment. From this analysis, we would propose that one viable working definition of marital adjustment, an indicator of overall marital quality, would thus be "a process, the outcome of which is determined by dyadic satisfaction, dyadic cohesion, affectional expression, and consensus of matters of importance to dyadic functioning [Spanier, 1976, p. 17]."

B. Methodological Issues in the Study of Marital Quality and Family Interaction

Family researchers need to develop techniques for assessing relatively stable patterns of marital interaction independently of the judgments of the marital partners themselves. In specifying the reciprocal influences in parent-child and parent-parent relationships, merely identifying a change in satisfaction or adjustment level reveals little about the process of change or the type of interaction pattern that can result from change.

What other concepts might be useful in elaborating the concept of marital quality? Hoffman and Manis (Chapter 7, this volume) looked at changes in marital power, division of labor, and the husband–wife affectional relationship at different stages of parenthood. Hoffman and Manis had husbands and wives respond to self-report questionnaires with items such as "Who does the dishes most often?" and "Who makes most of the important decisions in the household?" But instruments such as these are especially vulnerable to response sets, since couples may try to present their relationship in the best possible light. Because of the increasing sensitization to sex role stereotypes and the women's movement, it may be increasingly difficult to obtain an unbiased description of roles within the marital relationship from the marital partners themselves.

An alternative strategy is to use data from direct observation of family interaction, both in the laboratory and in the home. Such observation can be supplemented with interview and questionnaire data. Although it is apparent that a researcher can never obtain a completely unbiased account of family interaction, as just the awareness of being observed can alter behavior, the use of multiple techniques can provide insights into the kinds of bias that are likely to occur and the magnitude of errors that are likely to be made with a reliance on a single measurement device. There are, of course, important ethical issues involved in the collection of some observational data.

Lamb (Chapter 6, this volume) indicated a lack of confidence in the marital satisfaction variable and suggested alternatives for measuring change in the marital relationship. These include measuring changes in (a) the structure of the marital relationship in terms of traditional versus equalitarian sex roles; (b) the emotional distance between husband and wife; and (c) the marital partners' relationships with parents and in-laws, recognizing that family structure can extend well beyond the nuclear family. It's entirely possible that change in these areas could occur independently of change in marital satisfaction, since both highly traditional and highly equalitarian partners could be highly satisfied (or dissatisfied) with their marriages. It would be best to think of adjustment or satisfaction as a construct that has little meaning without reference to specific characteristics of marital interaction, such as proposed by Lamb, and Hoffman and Manis.

C. Marital Quality and Role Strain Across the Life-Span

The relationship between the development of children and changing marital roles is a theme that links together several chapters in this book. Rollins and Galligan (Chapter 4) introduced the term *role strain*, defined as the degree of felt difficulty experienced by the occupant of a social position and the stress experienced by a person perceiving that he or she cannot measure up to role expectations.

Role overload and role accumulation lead to increases in role strain, where the role accumulation of adult family members is influenced by family career transitions, such as adjustments to marriage itself, birth of a child, the child's entrance into school, the child's departure from the home, and the parents' retirement. Rollins and Galligan suggest a curvilinear (U-shaped) pattern of role strain across the life-span of the family. In other words, role strain is lowest before the birth of the first child and again after all children have left the home. Role accumulation would be greatest during the school-age and teenage stages of family development. The more dependent children in the home, the more role accumulation for the parents, according to Rollins and Galligan.

According to this theory, role strain would follow the same U-shaped pattern over family career transitions as role accumulation, and since role strain is the mediator between the presence of children and marital quality, marital quality should also adhere to the U-shaped pattern. There are legitimate questions, however, concerning the accuracy of findings suggesting a U-shaped pattern for marital quality across the family's life-span (Spanier, Lewis, & Cole, 1975).

Family career transitions are usually defined by the presence of children and the age of the oldest child. However, as Rollins and Galligan point out, this classification confounds age of oldest child with age of parents, length of marriage, and number of children in the home. Furthermore, there are important methodological limitations with the use of "stage of the family life cycle" as a stratification scheme for studying family development (Spanier, Sauer, & Larzelere, 1977). Nevertheless, Rollins and Galligan cite results from 12 cross-sectional and longitudinal studies showing a decrease in marital adjustment or satisfaction in the early family stages, with the largest decrease between the newlywed and infancy stages and an increase in satisfaction during the latter stages, when the children have left the home.

The U-shaped curve's implication that children are a detriment to marital satisfaction could be misleading, however. This research has been based, for the most part, on cross-sectional samples of married persons at different family life cycle stages. With each successive family stage, of course, more and more separated and divorced couples have dropped out of the married population. This cumulative, selective dropout of dissatisfied couples would have its most severe effect at later stages of the family career, causing a misleading upward trend in the level of adjustment or satisfaction reported (in a cross-sectional study) at about the time the children are leaving the home (Spanier, Lewis, & Cole, 1975).

Other methodological limitations in the use of cross-sectional data for assessing trends in marital quality across the life cycle have been pointed out. Persons who have been married many years may indicate greater marital quality, in part because they need to justify having remained together for so long. Cognitive consistency theory would suggest this interpretation. Furthermore, there may be age-related response sets, resulting in more favorable evaluations of marriage by older age or marriage cohorts.

Rollins and Galligan conclude that satisfaction and companionship decrease during stages where dependent children are in the home, though only a small percentage of couples, accounting for about 4–8% of the variance in marital satisfaction, actually follow this pattern. Support for the U-shaped curve is weak without the use of sequential designs allowing for the follow-up of couples through several stages of the life cycle.

The suggestion of the curvilinearity of marital quality is partly a function of the large drop occurring between the newlywed and infancy family career stages. The use of the newlywed stage as a reference point from which to measure subsequent change in satisfaction may be additionally troublesome. It can be argued that there is an induced notion that the newlywed period should be one of the happiest times in the participant's lives. The institutionalized customs of marriage, such as the ceremony, reception, gifts, and honeymoon, may lead to an artificially high self-evaluation of adjustment or satisfaction. The "drop" in satisfaction between newlywed and infancy stages may have more to do with the passing of the honeymoon stage and any correlated response sets than with the arrival of the first child. In short, the curvilinearity of marital quality over the family life cycle may be an artifact produced by artificially high evaluations of adjustment or satisfaction at the beginning of the marriage and the selective dropout of unhappy couples, age-correlated response sets, or the influence of dissonance reduction in the later stages of marriage.

D. Role Strain and Family Interaction

Although there is cause to reject the explanation of a U-shaped pattern of marital quality, the concepts of role strain, role accumulation, and role overload do have utility for studying structural changes in the marital relationship, and similar concepts can be found in the Lamb (Chapter 6), Hoffman and Manis (Chapter 7), Howard (Chapter 10), and Korn, Chess, and Fernandez (Chapter 11) presentations. The Rollins and Galligan theory (Chapter 4) linking the presence of children in the home, role strain, and marital quality has merit and deserves to be more fully tested.

More often than not, however, role concepts have not been used to develop fully reciprocal models of the interplay between child development and family interaction. The child is most often viewed as a stimulus for change in the marital relationship, with little attention given to the import of marital change for the child's further development. There is still a lack of attention to the child's role in his or her own socialization. One exception to this observation is Lamb's discussion of child abuse, but it stands alone as a fruitful attempt at depicting child and family reciprocity.

Lamb's (Chapter 6) discussion of the effects of pregnancy on family relations is consistent with a role strain interpretation. Lamb feels that research should describe *how* pregnancy changes the structure of marital relationships. For example, anticipating the parental role can have a traditionalizing effect on a childless couple's marriage. The wife may need to withdraw from work to concentrate on infant care, so that the family becomes more like a "traditional" nuclear family. The amount of role stress pregnancy induces in a couple may be a function of how "liberated" their sex role attitudes were before the pregnancy. In other words, more liberated couples will experience more change in role demands than traditional couples, and therefore more stress. Hoffman and Manis's (Chapter 7) data supported Lamb's contention; they found that traditionalism in marital roles increased with the age of the children, especially when the presence of young children was a detriment to the mother's employment.

A concern with reciprocal child–family interaction would lead one to ask what is the significance of this traditionalizing effect for the child's development, for the child's relationships with his or her parents, and for the parents' satisfaction with parenthood and marriage? Unfortunately, Lamb does not address these questions directly, but he does elaborate a theory of child abuse that captures the meaning of parent–child reciprocity by examining the relationship between child characteristics and parental role strain. The theory maintains that children can contribute to their own abuse. The infant's crying can be an arousing and aversive stimulus that increases the likelihood of aggressive behavior by parents. With a difficult infant, there may be extensive crying and unpredictability, and less positive parent–child interaction. Through a conditioning process, the baby may become an aversive stimulus. The more difficult the baby, the greater likelihood of role stress. In cases where the parents have had little opportunity to practice parental roles or where the pregnancy was unwanted, some form of child abuse may be more likely to result. Lamb's theory is reciprocal in that it recognizes the interaction of readiness for parenthood, role stress, and the infant's behavior in predicting child abuse.

The change in role demands brought about by the birth of a child need not always have negative effects on the parents. Hoffman and Manis found three examples of role satisfactions: (*a*) parenthood is a gateway to adulthood for many people; (*b*) it increases feelings of responsibility; and (*c*) it produces feelings of fulfillment. The feeling that children are fun to have also increased with length of parenthood and was greatest for parents of preschoolers. The Hoffman and Manis data indicate that if children are planned and desired, they can strengthen a marriage instead of weakening it.

The notions of role strain and role stress are applicable to the study of physically handicapped children's impact on family functioning and marital interaction. Korn, Chess, and Fernandez (Chapter 11) found that 26% of families with a child having congenital rubella showed significant stress, as measured by social work interviews. In 15% of these families, marital troubles existed before the birth of the handicapped child and were intensified after the birth. The best predictor of whether or not families would experience distress was the number of defects the child exhibited (e.g., visual, hearing, or neurological handicaps), and child characteristics as a whole were more predictive of the degree of distress than the demographic characteristics of the family.

Howard (Chapter 10) eloquently described the reactions of parents when a child's handicap is first recognized. The initial shock gives way to depression, a withdrawal from social relationships, guilt (where the baby is seen as punishment), denial, and finally, when the reality of the handicap is accepted, sadness and anxiety. Early attachment of the parents to the handicapped child is important, but distress with the child's abnormalties may interfere with this process. This is a clear example of the child contributing to his or her own socialization, since child characteristics, in part, form the basis for building the parent–child relationship. Previous family roles and routines are frustrated, and when the full extent of the handicap is recognized, reorganization must take place within the family.

Howard presents evidence of the debilitating effect of role strain. Parents with a history of problems (emotional, family, money, or marital) are most likely to reject the handicapped child. Marital problems, physical symptoms, anxiety, and depression all increase dramatically after the birth of the handicapped child. These phenomena can be explained with a role strain paradigm. Parents feel that they lack either the emotional or the physical resources to adopt the role of care giver to a handicapped child, or else the new role so conflicts with previous roles that the tension and stress generalize to all facets of their family lives.

Role strain has received a large share of the responsibility for explaining the contribution of the child to family life, for it represents a process mediating between the arrival and development of children and the change in the structural properties of the marital relationship. Before this concept can be used to its fullest extent, several problems need to be realized and solved. First, explanations of role strain have not led to a complete description of the reciprocities involved in the evolving child–family network of relationships. For the most part, causal inferences have been unidirectional. The influence of children on the marital relationship is considered with little attention to the circularity of influence within the family and the ontogenetic development of individual family members in relation to a changing family context. This state of affairs reflects the difficulty researchers are likely to experience in a transition to an interactional, reciprocal model of development, especially when theoretical language and methodological techniques are inadequate.

A second problem concerns the independent assessment of role strain as a mediating construct. Since change in role strain as a function of family transitions is the major concern, research efforts must begin to rely on sequential designs, allowing for data collection over a time span sufficient to cover several family life transitions. Between-cohort comparisons of families at the same family life transition would provide information about historical change in the sociocultural milieu in which the family is embedded.

The independent assessment of role strain would also require a pluralistic approach to data collection. To assess the degree of felt difficulty in assuming parental roles, marital partners could be asked, through a combination of interview, open-ended questionnaire, or structured questionnaire techniques, to describe in detail their experience in acquiring new roles. In order to avoid basing theoretical formulations on a single methodological strategy, experiential data could be collected.

For example, since tension and stress may be produced by role strain, physiological indicators such as blood pressure, heart rate, and muscle tension might profitably be obtained. Complete medical records could become important data sources. Self-report or direct observation of behavioral manifestations of stress (e.g., increases in smoking, drinking, eating, insomnia) could provide another independent assessment of the construct.

In summary, role strain could be a useful concept for models of reciprocal child–family interaction. It will be necessary, however, to go beyond unidirectional statements of causality and investigate the circularity of influence through pluralistic constructs and models.

V. Conclusions

This book has presented arguments for, and evidence of, a multidisciplinary synthesis. The interests of life-span oriented human developmentalists and of family sociologists are merging. Scholars of each discipline are considering how the changes considered by scholars of the other can enrich and expand understanding of their respective target populations and social or behavioral phenomena.

In this chapter we have attempted to provide a bridge between current thinking and practice and the future development of this synthesis. Although there have been at least three major reasons limiting the development of this synthesis, we believe that none of these reasons—alone or in combination—is sufficient to halt future endeavors. Although considerable work in all three areas of concern is necessary, the theoretical issues seem well articulated, the methodological problems are understood if not very well resolved, and concrete illustrations of the empirical utility of multidisciplinary effort are well drawn.

In fact, in this chapter we have shown that a life-span oriented, multidisciplinary synthesis is quite feasible when cast in terms of a model of reciprocal influence that uses the dynamic-interactional child–family interface as its unit of analysis. Indeed, focusing on this unit will result in enrichment and expansion of future endeavors in life-span human development and family sociology. Additionally, the dynamic-interactional model from which it is derived enhances the integration of existing data on marital quality and family interaction.

In sum, the heuristic value of a multidisciplinary approach to individual and social change that involves such reciprocal notions seems certain. The individual, his or her family, and the larger social context are dynamically linked over the entire history of changes within which each is involved. Social scientists who strive to do exemplary work can no longer ignore the continual, circular independencies between ontogeny and social and family change. This book has provided a justification of why such reciprocities must become the focus of social scientific work. To the extent that this book is a successful presage of the future, a future historian of science will see this volume as only one initial attempt.

References

Antonucci, T. Attachment: A life-span concept. *Human Development*, 1976, *19*, 135–142.
Baltes, P. B., Reese, H. W., & Nesselroade, J. R. *Life-span developmental psychology: Introduction to research methods*. Monterey: Brooks/Cole, 1977.

Cuber, J. F., & Harroff, P. B. *The Significant Americans*. New York: Appleton-Century-Crofts, 1965.

Labouvie, E. W. The dialectical nature of measurement activities in the behavioral sciences. *Human Development*, 1975, *18*, 396–403.

Lamb, M. E. (Ed.), *The role of the father in child development*. New York: Wiley, 1976.

Lamb, M. E. A reexamination of the infant social world. *Human Development*, 1977, *20*, 65–85.

Lerner, R. M., & Ryff, C. D. Implementation of the life-span view of human development: The sample case of attachment. In P. B. Baltes (Ed.), *Life-span development and behavior*. *Volume 1*. New York: Academic Press, 1978.

Lewis, M., & Lee-Painter, S. An interactional approach to the mother–infant dyad. In M. Lewis & L. A. Rosenblum (Eds.), *The effect of the infant on its caregiver*. New York: Wiley, 1974.

Lewis, R. A. & Spanier, G. B. Theorizing about the quality and stability of marriage. In W. Burr, R. Hill, I. Nye, & I. Reiss (Eds.), *Contemporary Theories about the Family*. Glencoe, Illinois: The Free Press, 1978.

Looft, W. R. Socialization and personality throughout the life-span: An examination of contemporary psychological approaches. In P. B. Baltes & K. W. Schaie (Eds.), *Life-span developmental psychology: Personality and socialization*. New York: Academic Press, 1973.

Riegel, K. F. Toward a dialectical theory of development. *Human Development*, 1975, *18*, 50–64.

Riegel, K. F. The dialectics of human development. *American Psychologist*, 1976, *31*, 689–700. (a)

Riegel, K. F. From traits and equilibrium toward developmental dialectics. In W. Arnold (Ed.), *Nebraska symposium on motivation*. Lincoln, Nebraska: University of Nebraska Press, 1976. (b)

Sameroff, A. Transactional models in early social relations. *Human Development*, 1975, *18*, 65–79.

Schaie, K. W., & Gribbin, K. Adult development and aging. In M. R. Rosenzweig & L. W. Porter (Eds.), *Annual Review of Psychology*. *Volume 26*, Palo Alto, California: Annual Reviews, 1975.

Spanier, G. B. Measuring dyadic adjustment: New scales for assessing the quality of marriage and other dyads. *Journal of Marriage and the Family*, 1976, *38*, 15–28.

Spanier, G. B., & Cole, C. L. Toward clarification and investigation of marital adjustment. *International Journal of Sociology of the Family*, 1976, *6*, 121–146.

Spanier, G. B., Lewis, R. A., & Cole, C. L. Marital adjustment over the family life cycle: The issue of curvilinearity. *Journal of Marriage and the Family*, 1975, *37*, 263–275.

Spanier, G. B., Sauer, W., & Larzelere, R. Family development and the family life cycle: an empirical evaluation. Paper presented at the annual meeting of the National Council on Family Relations, October, 1977.

Weinraub, M., Brooks, J., & Lewis, M. The social network: A reconsideration of the concept of attachment. *Human Development*, 1977, *20*, 31–47.

Westoff, L. A. & Westoff, C. F. *From now to zero*. Boston: Little, Brown and Company, 1971.

Index

A 8
B 9
C 0
D 1
E 2
F 3
G 4
H 5
I 6
J 7